RÜCKZUG

FOREIGN MILITARY STUDIES

History is replete with examples of notable military campaigns and exceptional military leaders and theorists. Military professionals and students of the art and science of war cannot afford to ignore these sources of knowledge or limit their studies to the history of the U.S. armed forces. This series features original works, translations, and reprints of classics outside the American canon that promote a deeper understanding of international military theory and practice.

Series editor: Roger Cirillo

An AUSA Book

RÜCKZUG

The German Retreat from France, 1944

Joachim Ludewig

Edited by
Major General David T. Zabecki, AUS (Ret.)

 UNIVERSITY PRESS OF KENTUCKY

Published by special arrangement with Militärgeschichtliches Forschungsamt [Military History Research Institute, MGFA], Potsdam, Germany

Copyright © 2012 by Militärgeschichtliches Forschungsamt (MGFA)

The original edition was published under the title Joachim Ludewig, Der deutsche Rückzug aus Frankreich 1944. Freiburg im Breisgau: Rombach GmbH + Co Verlagshaus KG [Limited Partnership] 1944.

All photos appear courtesy of the German Federal Archives

The University Press of Kentucky

Scholarly publisher for the Commonwealth,
serving Bellarmine University, Berea College, Centre College of Kentucky, Eastern Kentucky University, The Filson Historical Society, Georgetown College, Kentucky Historical Society, Kentucky State University, Morehead State University, Murray State University, Northern Kentucky University, Transylvania University, University of Kentucky, University of Louisville, and Western Kentucky University.

Editorial and Sales Offices: The University Press of Kentucky
663 South Limestone Street, Lexington, Kentucky 40508–4008
www.kentuckypress.com

16 15 14 13 12   5 4 3 2 1

Library of Congress Cataloging-in-Publication Data

Ludewig, Joachim, 1958-
 [Deutsche Rückzug aus Frankreich 1944. English]
 Ruckzüg : the German retreat from France, 1944 / Joachim Ludewig ; edited by David T. Zabecki.
   p. cm. -- (Foreign military studies)
 Translation of: Der deutsche Rückzug aus Frankreich 1944.
 Includes bibliographical references and index.
 ISBN 978-0-8131-4079-7 (hardcover : alk. paper) —
 ISBN 978-0-8131-4081-0 (pdf) — ISBN 978-0-8131-4080-3 (epub)
  1. World War, 1939-1945—Campaigns—France. 2. World War, 1939-1945—Germany.
 I. Title.
 D761.L8313 2012
 940.54'214—dc23   2012019147

This book is printed on acid-free paper meeting the requirements of the American National Standard for Permanence in Paper for Printed Library Materials.

Manufactured in the United States of America.

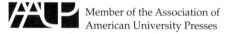

Member of the Association of
American University Presses

Contents

Photographs follow page 84
Maps follow page 196

World War II German Military Ranks

German Rank Title	Translated As	U.S. Army Equivalent
Generalfeldmarschall	Field Marshal	General of the Army
Generaloberst	Colonel General	General
General der Infanterie	General of Infantry	Lieutenant General
- der Artillerie	- of Artillery	
- der Kavallerie	- of Cavalry	
- der Panzertruppen	- of Panzer Troops	
- der Pioniere	- of Engineers	
- der Gebirgstruppen	- of Mountain Troops	
Generalleutnant	Lieutenant General	Major General
Generalmajor	Major General	Brigadier General
Oberst	Colonel	Colonel
Oberstleutnant	Lieutenant Colonel	Lieutenant Colonel
Major	Major	Major
Hauptmann	Captain	Captain
Oberleutnant	First Lieutenant	First Lieutenant
Leutnant	Lieutenant	Second Lieutenant

Note: German officer rank titles during World War II differed slightly from the rank titles used by the German Bundeswehr today. In all cases the German rank titles in this text have been translated directly into English, without trying to correlate a given rank with its U.S. Army equivalent of the period. This table shows how the various rank titles lined up.

Foreword

The Allied invasion of Normandy on June 6, 1944, marked a dramatic turning point in the history of World War II. There was a fundamental change in the political and military situation, similar to the "Turn before Moscow" in the winter of 1941. The landing on France's Atlantic coast had been carefully prepared for more than three years and had indeed been anticipated by the German High Command. Adolf Hitler, a World War I combat soldier, now faced the realization of his worst nightmare. This second front in the rear of the desperately struggling German army on the Eastern Front altered the political and military strategic calculations of the wartime coalition and those of the German Reich leadership in various ways and in varying degrees of significance. Operations OVERLORD and NEPTUNE resulted in the largest amphibious landing in the history of warfare. The success was based on total superiority of air and naval forces as well as a unique and gigantic logistics capability. The landings immediately relieved the pressure on the Red Army, tying down in the west fifty-nine German divisions under Field Marshal Gerd von Rundstedt, which included Army Group B with the Seventh and Fifteenth Armies under Field Marshal Erwin Rommel.

The German Army in the East lacked Panzer divisions for mounting large-scale, defensive, mobile operations—especially those units that had been beefed up with fresh manpower and with the modern Panther and Tiger tanks. Instead of being able to launch an operational-level counter-stroke, Hitler's war-fighting option was now limited to just holding on. This situation decisively enhanced the Soviet Union's political and military leverage in dealing both with its wartime allies and with the German Reich. The German Army in the East no longer had the initiative and was forced into a reactive mode.

The German leadership found itself facing the dilemma of which theater of war would be the focal point of the military main effort, in an attempt to set the political and military conditions necessary to achieve an acceptable end to the war that did not resemble unconditional capitulation. The possibilities of a separate peace between the two dictators, Hitler and Stalin, or of a "Western solution" that might result in the Western Allies advancing quickly into the territory of the Reich, dominated the thinking of the key political and historical actors in the war—Churchill, Roosevelt, Stalin, and Hitler and their general staffs.

With the final battle for the Reich, a race now began to determine who would be the victor and the first to hoist his flag over the Reichstag building in Berlin, the capital of the Reich. That race developed against the background of this conflicting combination of factors based on differing motivations.

This study was first published in Germany in 1994 by the German Military History Research Institute. The idea originated with a doctoral dissertation by Andreas Hillgruber and was further developed by Jose Dülffer at the University of Cologne. It describes in a detailed manner the operations that followed D-Day: The formation of the Falaise Gap in Northern France, the Battle of France as it developed from the additional landings of Allied invasion forces in southern France, and the climax of the fall of Paris on August 25, 1944.

Dr. Joachim Ludewig is the first historian to analyze the German military situation along the Western Front during the months of August and September 1944 that actually decided the outcome of the war. The result is a detailed assessment based on German and Allied official records. He presents a well-balanced picture of operational events, specific military situation estimates, opportunities, and the decision errors of both the German and Allied sides. The German retreat in the west between August 20 and September, the surrender of Paris (which contrary to Hitler's orders had not been destroyed), the fall of Antwerp, and the final establishment of the German rear defensive position at Dijon are the central elements of this story. The author examines how, despite considerable Allied military superiority, especially air superiority, the German Army in the West was able once again to stabilize the Western Front by September and thereby establish the conditions necessary to prepare for the subsequent Ardennes Offensive in December 1944.

Ludewig's study covers a period of time that is not dealt with in the previous studies by Dieter Ose and Hermann Jung. It is an essential contribution to understanding the conditions behind the final struggle for the Reich.

> Brigadier General Günther Roth, Ph.D.
> Chief, Military History Research Institute,
>   1984–1995
> Federal Republic of Germany

Author's Acknowledgments

This book is the revised version of a dissertation that was accepted by the Department of Philosophy of the University of Cologne during the 1989–1990 winter semester.

Prof. Dr. Jost Dülffer was the first examiner, and Prof. Dr. Günter Kahle was the second examiner. The oral portion of the doctoral examination took place on February 3, 1990.

The author is indebted to the Hans Seidel Foundation of Munich, which provided financial support for his doctoral endeavor between 1987 and 1990.

With full gratitude the author remembers Prof. Dr. Andreas Hillgruber, who, until his death, patiently and with great interest supported his work. Even in difficult situations, he often helped the author with guidance and encouragement.

This work could not have been published in its present form without the spontaneous support of Prof. Dr. Jost Dülffer, who mentored the author and guided him through the doctoral procedure. He deserves special appreciation for that.

The author would like to thank the staff members of the Military History Research Institute and the Federal Archives–Military Archives in Freiburg for generously allowing him to examine important documents, providing many items of detailed information, offering practical suggestions, and constantly being ready for discussion and advice. At this point, he also would like to mention Senior Government Counselor Dr. Dieter Ose and Archive Counselor Brün Meyer, as well as Brigadier General Hansgeorg Model (Ret.) and Ministerial Counselor Dr. Hubertus Dessloch, who gave generously of their time to the author in his work.

The latter is, above all, true of Lieutenant Colonel Klaus-Jürgen Thies (Ret.), to whom the author is indebted for his swift and most accurate preparation of the maps.

Last but not least, I want to express my heartiest thanks to my wife, Birgit, for typing the clean copy of the manuscript and for her patience and sacrifices; my father, Ehrhard, and my sister, Kirsten, for doing the corrections; Mrs. Marianne Göhre, for inserting the corrections; and my friend Heinrich Riggert for his advice and effective help in the field of electronic data processing.

Joachim Ludewig
Cologne, November 1991

A Note on the English Edition

The German federal government's translation service, Bundes-sprachenamt, initially translated this book into English. I edited the entire work, ensuring that the English translations flowed smoothly and that specialized military terms and concepts were properly translated. Dr. Ludewig then reviewed and approved the edited version. One example of technical military terminology is the difference between what the Germans called a *Heeresgruppe* and an *Armeegruppe*. The former is what the Allies designated an "army group." The latter was something short of a full army group, for which the Allies had no equivalent. In this volume *Armeegruppe* is translated as "army task group." Military rank titles have been translated directly from the German, without any attempt to correlate the differences between German and Allied ranks. Hence *Generalleutnant* is translated as "lieutenant general," although a German lieutenant general of World War II was really the equivalent of an American or British major general. A table on page ix provides a complete comparison between German and American army officer ranks. I have made every effort to ensure that the citations in the endnotes are as full and accurate as possible; however, the bibliography remains in the original German.

D. T. Z.

Abbreviations

Ia	German General Staff Officer Ia, the operations officer at divisional level and above.
CCS	Combined Chiefs of Staff, the joint British and American chiefs of the respective military staffs.
COSSAC	Chief of Staff to the Supreme Allied Commander.
ETO	Allied European Theater of Operations.
FFI	French Forces of the Interior.
G-2	American general staff officer in charge of the intelligence section at divisional level and above. Also the intelligence section itself.
G-3	American general staff officer in charge of the operations section at divisional level and above. Also the operations section itself.
G-4	American general staff officer in charge of the logistics section at divisional level and above. Also the logistics section itself.
MTO	Allied Mediterranean Theater of Operations.
OB Südwest	Oberbefehlshaber Südwest. The headquarters of the senior German military commander in southwestern Europe (Italy). Also the commander himself.
OB West	Oberbefehlshaber West. The headquarters of the senior German military commander in western Europe. Also the commander himself.
OKH	Oberkommando des Heeres. The High Command of the German Army.
OKW	Oberkommando der Wehrmacht. The Supreme Command of the German Armed Forces.

PzKpfw V	Panzerkampfwagen (armored fighting vehicle) Mark V. The Panther tank.
SHAEF	Supreme Headquarters Allied Expeditionary Forces.
SS	Schutzstaffel (security echelon). The primary paramilitary organization of the Nazi Party.
Waffen-SS	The Armed SS. Selected SS units formally organized and equipped along army lines, although technically independent from the German Army.

Introduction

Traditionally, German military history research has concentrated on two groups of topics in analyzing the ground warfare operations in the west in 1944. The Allied invasion in June and the defensive fighting in Normandy,[1] followed by the preparations for and execution of the Ardennes Offensive in the autumn and winter of 1944,[2] were the primary subjects of scholarly investigation. Nonetheless, there so far has been no corresponding study of the breathtaking interim campaign of maneuver and the rapid sequence of combat actions that shifted into a situation of positional warfare conducted along fixed lines.

Within this period, encompassing the months of August and September 1944, the focal points of military events shifted over distances of up to one thousand kilometers in a matter of just a few days: from Normandy and from the French Atlantic and Mediterranean coasts into the region of the Netherlands, Germany's western borders, and the Vosges Mountains of Alsace.

The retreat of the German military forces from the sectors of Western Europe that had been occupied since 1940 constitutes an important facet of the final phase of World War II that is quite worth studying in terms of its course and consequences.[3] The military events in France meant that Germany lost the advantageous strategic position it had held when its continental back door was still secure—something that Hitler considered essential in any successful move to the east. The nature of the German retreat, especially the rapid progress of operations following the Allied breakout from the Normandy beachhead in early August, caused the Allied military commanders to nurture the hope of finishing the war in Europe in 1944. That estimate of the situation was also shared by many of the German senior commanders.[4] The fall of Paris on August 25 was perceived by world opinion as a symbolic indicator that the end of the Third Reich was near. Instead, following the disastrous defeats and the heavy losses during the fighting withdrawal, the German army within a matter of days was able to reestablish a contiguous front line and achieve a relative consolidation of its situation in the west.

The object of this study is a detailed investigation of this phenomenon, which even at the time caused surprise and produced assumptions that remain controversial to this day. The sudden change in the situation produced an operational pause, and not only in the immediate combat actions. The stabilization of the front line, which happened even without the German commanders in the west realizing it initially, made it possible for Hitler to consolidate his plans for the Ardennes Offensive. That last German large-scale offensive of World War II, whose indirect effects were fatal for the German Army in the East and the population of eastern Germany, also made the British and American political negotiating positions at Yalta more difficult.

Modern German military historiography increasingly has made an effort to achieve a broad perspective and take a pluralistic approach to the in-depth study of World War II. This has resulted in a shift of emphasis toward an approach that is oriented in social-history terms.[5]

The author of this study, however, feels the obligation to pursue a more traditional approach in his analysis. In so doing, he cites the words of Wolfgang von Groote, who stressed that the military historian continues to have the fundamental task of closing "gaps in our knowledge as to the *course of military events* . . . by carefully, critically, and expertly analyzing the sources."[6] Proceeding accordingly, the objective of this study is to describe and analyze the planning and the combat actions of the time within their geographic context, and above all from the German perspective—from the level of the German Supreme Commander West (Oberbefehlshabers West—OB West).

A complete and balanced study, however, is impossible solely on the basis of the German military records. To prevent the study from becoming too one-sided and thus producing distorted judgments, we will consider the operational objectives of the Allies, and especially their attendant problems of coalition warfare. As a consequence, however, we must forego the investigation of some of the interesting questions that arise in the context of the wartime events in general. The reciprocal interdependencies of the Western Front and the Eastern Front, the situation within the Reich, and the operations conducted by the German navy and the Luftwaffe are not covered, or they are merely touched on in this study.

General interest in World War II continues unabated, and down through the years there have been more than one hundred thousand publications on this topic.[7] Nevertheless, the general state of existing research for the period from 1943 to 1945 still offers some areas that are wide open to investigation. Compared to events on the Eastern Front during those years, the scholarly work on the ground operations against the Western Allies—at least from the German perspective—has so far remained an "intellectual side show," as Professor Dennis E. Showalter so aptly put it.[8] For the period of time to be investigated in this work, we initially have the book by Werner Haupt, which does not lay claim to being a scholarly study because Haupt in his introduction readily admits the lack of official documents in his effort.[9] The book by Rainer Mennel, *The Final Phase of World War II in the West: 1944 and 1945* (Osnabrück, 1981), is based on official records, but its narrow focus is indicated by its subtitle: *A Study of Political Geography.* Several other works address topically relevant individual problems and individual events, but they also work from a differing point of view. Along with the numerous divisional unit histories, these works include: Alan F. Wilt's *The French Riviera Campaign of August 1944* (Carbondale, Ill., 1981) and Jörg Staiger's *Rückzug durchs Rhônetal: Abwehr- und Verzögerungskampf der 19. Armee im Herbst 1944 unter besonderer Berücksichtigung des Einsatzes der 11. Panzerdivision [Retreat Through the Rhône Valley: Defensive Fighting and Delaying Action by the Nineteenth Army in the Autumn of 1944, with Special Emphasis on the Operations of the 11th Panzer Division]* (Neckargemünd, 1965).

Some studies published in the 1980s and 1990s address the course of wartime events in the western territories of the Reich from the limited perspective of regional history.[10]

The unpublished records available in the German Federal Military Archives in the city of Freiburg im Breisgau constitute the most important foundation of this investigation.[11] The analysis is based primarily on the files of the Supreme Command West, which are almost completely preserved. Rounding out the picture, the author has used the available material of the subordinate commands, including Army Group B, Army Task Group G, the field armies, and some of the corps. The author also referenced selected relevant records from the Armed Forces High Command (Oberkommando der Wehrmacht—OKW), the Army High Command (Oberkommando des Heeres—OKH), the Military Administration in the West (Militärverwaltung im Westen), and the Luftwaffe and navy headquarters in the theater of operations. In addition to these sources, I used personal notes by Colonel General Alfred Jodl[12] and Colonel General Otto Dessloch (intermittently the commanding general of the Third Air Fleet). Documents on the biography of Colonel General Johannes Blaskowitz that are available in Freiburg and at the Institute of Contemporary History in Munich offered valuable supplementary data as well.

Interviews with Brigadier General Hansgeorg Model and the use of his private files (hereafter cited as: Model's Private Archives) helped round out the image of the personality of his father, Field Marshal Walter Model, beyond the few of his posthumous papers that are on file in the German Military Archives.[13] The *Foreign Military Studies* series, compiled by former German officers after the war by order of the U.S. Army, and copies of which are maintained by the Military History Research Institute, were very helpful in clearing up individual questions.[14] The same reservations, however, apply to them as to the comprehensive bibliography of memoirs. I essentially relied on the American and British official histories of World War II for the entire complex of questions relating to Allied operational command.[15] I also attempted to include in my investigation the role played by Allied signals intelligence, specifically ULTRA,[16] in the coverage of combat operations in the published literature.[17]

Before proceeding, I should identify one fundamental but unavoidable danger that affects studies based on the file material of higher command authorities. That is the danger of not grasping the war in its full dimension, of not being able to describe it on the basis of the selected level of observation as "what it really was, that is, miserable suffering."[18]

Part 1

The Initial Situation Facing OB West in the Middle of August 1944

The Situation in Northern France and the Allied Landings along the Mediterranean Coast

Chapter 1

The German Reich's Military-Political Situation

Development of the General Conditions up to the Summer of 1944

Operation BARBAROSSA had failed. Its operational timing was thrown off when the German offensive ground to a halt in front of Moscow at the end of 1941. But it also was a failure in terms of Hitler's vision of worldwide *Blitzkrieg*. When it still looked like the Soviet Union would be defeated, it was hard to foresee that the war could not be continued on Hitler's terms, with Germany in a consolidated European world power position. But the end of 1942 and the start of 1943 brought the final turning point in the war, both against the German Reich (with the landings of the Allies in French northwest Africa, the British offensive against German Army Group Africa, and the German failure at Stalingrad) and against Japan in the Pacific (at the battles at Midway and Guadalcanal). The military initiative had shifted to the side of the anti-Hitler coalition, and the German war-fighting machine was increasingly forced on the defensive. By the time Grand Admiral Karl Dönitz was forced to recall his submarines from the mission of attacking Allied convoys in the North Atlantic in the spring of 1943, the Allies had secured the lifelines between the Old and New Worlds. Their certain victory in the Battle of the Atlantic also set one of the key conditions for large-scale operations against German-occupied Europe. Hitler was forced to drop the overseas phase of his program, a phase that had envisioned colonies and systems of bases to support an international policy reaching beyond Europe. All efforts on the German side now concentrated on holding onto what was called Fortress Europe. Germany's central geographic position had always exposed it to the danger of a two-front war, but now in July 1943 that threat had a direct effect on military operations for the first time. The Germans were forced to break off their limited offensive against the Kursk salient in reaction to the Allied landings on Sicily. The Allied penetration into the southern periphery of Fortress Europe allowed them to establish strategic air bases, which further contributed to the increasing of Allied air superiority starting in the summer of 1943. Fortress Europe had no overhead cover, no roof, which meant that the traditional advantage of interior lines was of much less value to the defender. Through naval and air superiority the Allies had established decisive prerequisites for the success of their planned invasion of France in 1944. The German shift to the defensive resulted in the implementation of a rigid hold-the-line strategy that was diametrically opposed to Clausewitz's teachings. By November 1943 Hitler concluded that the point of main effort now had to be shifted once again to the west to defeat the anticipated landings. A successful invasion in the west would threaten the vital core of the German armament capacities faster than any Soviet offensive from the east, because of the short distance between the point of the invasion and the center of Germany's heavy industry. Additionally, Germany with its remaining resources was capable of achieving a decisive military victory only in the west. In Hitler's view, such a military success could still offer possibilities for overall strategic exploitation. In contrast to what would happen in the east, any developing western invasion front would cover at least initially a geographically relatively limited combat area, and the Germans would not immediately have to face an overwhelming enemy force-ratio superiority. According to *Führer Directive 51* of November 3, 1943,[1] the Allied invasion was to be repelled through "decisive battle on the landing beaches." Failing that, and after any initial enemy successes, the objective then would be "to throw the enemy back into the sea by means of a counterattack." The success of either course of action would support Hitler's ever-growing hopeful conviction that he could trigger the collapse of the Allied coalition and then implement his basic alliance-policy idea of an accommodation with Great Britain, or at least the British withdrawal from the war. The "long-range struggle against England," emphasized in *Directive 51*, and the means with which the British were to be worn down by the vengeance weapons—the V-1 Buzz Bomb and V-2 Missile—to the point where they would at last be bombed into pacification, was a rather absurd notion, considering that the Allied bombing raids on Germany's large cities had so far produced little success.

Hitler believed that a military success in the west was the last chance to bring about a turning point in the war. If nothing else, he hoped to gain some maneuver room for the Reich, which since early 1943 had been faced with the Allied demand for unconditional surrender that was now the only basis for any negotiations. The underlying intent of *Führer Directive 51* can be seen in the continuity of its systematic and racial-ideological concepts. The idea was to maintain or restore the situation of a secure continental back door that had been achieved in 1940, and therefore lay the foundation for a renewed offensive toward the east. Thus, this final major phase of Hitler's military thinking was characterized by a strategic concept that merely echoed the period before the earlier victory over France. But the decisive factor in this case was the fact that this concept retained its validity even as the Reich's overall situation deteriorated so rapidly throughout the year 1944 that, compared to 1940, there was an almost immeasurable gap between idea and reality.[2] Apart from the events in France, the overall situation in the summer of 1944 looked just about hopeless. It was marked by the constant retreat of the German front lines and the gradual defection of the allies of the Third Reich, starting with Italy in September 1943. The situation in the Italian theater of war, of course, had essentially stabilized. The units of OB Südwest (Supreme Command Southwest) gradually withdrew to the Apennines position until September 1944. But on the Eastern Front the Wehrmacht suffered its most serious setbacks to date in the fight against the Soviet Union.

Because a center of gravity was forming in the west, the Eastern Front was weakened correspondingly and it no longer received the forces it might have expected otherwise.[3] Just as the center of gravity was being shifted, the German Eastern Front was severely disrupted by the large-scale offensives mounted by the Soviets during the summer months. The Soviet pincer offensive launched on June 22, 1944, triggered the collapse of German Army Group Center and resulted in the decisive defeat of the German army during the war in the east. Along with the tremendous manpower losses of twenty-eight divisions and 350,000 men, the Soviet offensive also meant that by the end of July Germany's eastern boundaries were now directly threatened. During the next several weeks this disastrous situation spread to the frontline sectors of German Army Groups

North, North Ukraine, and South Ukraine. The resulting German defeats and retreats also made the positions of Germany's allies untenable. Between August and September, Romania, Bulgaria, and Finland broke with the Reich, leaving Germany completely isolated in the foreign policy arena. Hungary, which only barely hung on to the German side, and Japan, with which there had never been any meaningful coordination of military operations, remained the last major allies of the Reich. Raw material shortages kept spreading throughout Germany's armament industries, along with the progressive shrinkage of the German-controlled "defensive regions" that supplied the Reich's war-fighting capabilities with material resources and labor. More than anyone else, it was Albert Speer[4] who in 1942 reorganized Germany's defense industry along the basic lines of decentralized economic management to the maximum extent possible. Because of his efforts, Germany's war industry did not collapse during this period of attritional warfare. In the summer of 1944, many branches of the armament industry were still able to achieve peak production, but the bottlenecks in the petroleum sector alone indicated clearly that the end of all modern military mobility was coming sooner than later. The end seemed to be just around the corner following the Allied bombing raids on the synthetic fuel processing plants starting on May 12, 1944, and certainly with the capture of the Romanian oil fields around Ploesti on August 30, which for the armaments industry meant the loss of the war.

As long as Hitler clung to his fixed idea that the enemy coalition was bound to fall apart, he did not come to terms with the real situation in the summer of 1944. But the conclusions that could be drawn from the disastrous development of the situation in the west and the establishment of the second front in France were only too clear. In his book, *Mein Kampf,* Hitler had written: "Germany will either be a world power or it will not exist at all."[5] In his mind the war had to be fought to the complete exhaustion of all available potential. Fully following his maxim of all or nothing, Hitler therefore never considered capitulation, especially since he desperately clung to the conviction that he could turn the situation around in the end with a powerful thrust in the west. Considering this course of action, any potential maneuver room for seeking a political solution was extremely restricted at best. But any maneuver room had already ceased to exist in practice because of the Allies' announced demand of unconditional surrender,[6] which amounted to a total governmental and political capitulation based on the standards of international law.[7] This Allied policy made it quite clear that either discontinuation of the war or defeat would result in not only the downfall of Hitler's empire but also the end of Germany's status as a major power. The result was a confirmation of at least a partial intersection of the vital interests between Hitler's regime and Germany's old leadership groups in the government bureaucracy, in industry, in the military establishment, and in diplomacy.[8] These circumstances certainly contributed to the steadfastness of German defensive fighting on all fronts, even after the final outcome had largely been decided.

The German propaganda effort was made easier not only by the unconditional surrender policy, but also by the subsequently publicized Allied plans for postwar Germany. Those plans, announced at the Teheran Conference at the end of 1943, included dismemberment of Germany, occupation zones—designated in the spring of 1944—and finally the Morgenthau Plan of September 1944. German propaganda, of course, was directed by Dr. Josef Goebbels, who on July 25, 1944, was also appointed Reich Plenipotentiary for the Total War Effort.

The majority of the German population found itself chained to a regime whose propaganda skillfully stirred up anxiety about an uncertain future, fear of the Red Army in the east, and the militarily senseless bombing raids against Germany's large cities. German propaganda thus exploited the impotent rage of the population for its own purposes and fed the flames of resistance based on the hopes for a final, ultimate victory that, in retrospect, appears completely irrational.

Like propaganda, governmental power springing from Nazi terror directed against the population and which had been increasing since 1943 prolonged the war to an extent that should not be underestimated.[9] Once the war had clearly turned, ideology pervaded almost all aspects of German life. Visible symbols of the effect of this process on the Wehrmacht can be seen in the December 22, 1943, introduction of the National Socialist Guidance Officer and the so-called German salute on July 23, 1944. The spreading influence of the Nazi Party and the SS also resulted in the party's provincial gauleiters (regional leaders) being appointed to the office of Reich defense commissar, effective November 16, 1942. Reichsführer-SS Heinrich Himmler, who already had been the Reich interior minister since 1943, also became the commanding general of the Replacement Army after the attempt on Hitler's life on July 20, 1944.

The German population, which during the second half of 1944 was more firmly than ever before under the control of the National Socialist leadership, nonetheless remained largely uninformed of the racial policy crimes of the regime.[10] Consequently, the majority of the Germans at the time were unable to see clearly that which we know for a fact today—that the state of injustice that destroyed all legal standards could no longer lay any legitimate claim to obedience and that resistance had long since become a moral imperative.[11]

Chapter 2

The Initial Situation on the Allied Side

1. The Global Strategic Context

The strategic blueprint drafted by the Allies to defeat the German Reich had solidified for the most part following the EUREKA meeting of the Big Three—Roosevelt, Churchill, and Stalin—in Teheran from November 28 to December 1, 1943, followed immediately by the Second Cairo Conference, code-named SEXTANT, held December 3 to 6, 1943. The most significant decision reached was the final scheduling of the date for the invasion of northwestern France, Operation OVERLORD. The Allied leaders also decided that the main operation would be supported by landings along the coast of southern France, Operation ANVIL. Following the statement released by the British-American Combined Chiefs of Staff[1] designating Operation OVERLORD and Operation ANVIL as "the supreme operations for 1944," the war in the Pacific became a secondary priority to the European Theater of Operations (ETO).[2] The program for 1944 promised to achieve the basic Germany First objective that the Allies had agreed to much earlier, and it also indicated that the main effort would be mounted in France, while the Mediterranean and Far Eastern Theaters of Operations were designated by the Western Allies as "holding theaters," which would remain relatively static.[3] The outcome of the Teheran Conference reflected clearly the shift that had taken place within the anti-Hitler coalition. Until the middle of 1943 British concepts had decisively influenced Allied strategy, but now the United States increasingly assumed the leadership role because Great Britain's military and economic resources were stretched to the limit. After Teheran, Stalin emphatically urged setting a firm date for Operation OVERLORD. He also definitely advocated supporting that operation by a landing in southern France. He particularly endorsed the American concept of "Decisive War" by rejecting as a sideshow the alternatives proposed by the British in the Mediterranean area. Stalin unambiguously advocated Operation ANVIL and considered it valuable, even if it was to be staged only *after* the main invasion in the north.[4] His position reflected two Soviet mid- or long-range objectives that were closely intertwined. First, because of his own military experience with pincer operations, Stalin believed that the ANVIL supporting operation was the best insurance for the successful establishment of the long-delayed second front. Second, with the Western Allies heavily committed in France, there would be no further danger of their involvement in southeastern Europe, including the Balkans, which was something Stalin considered undesirable for his power-politics game.

The fact that the Soviets were able to make a decisive contribution to solidifying the military strategy decisions made at Teheran also indicates a significant shift in the perception of the role of the Soviet Union in the eyes of the Western Allies. The evolution of American strategy must be seen against this background.

By the end of 1942 and the beginning of 1943, roughly coinciding with the fall of Stalingrad, the Americans began to realize that they had been underestimating the Soviet force potential all along. In 1941–1942 the prevailing assumption had been that the Soviet Union would collapse under the weight of the Wehrmacht's offensive. But now there was the conviction that the Soviets would be able to continue to sustain the main burden of ground warfare against the Reich. Thus, a fundamental reorientation of the American war economy as well as of the American strategic concept now seemed necessary. There was no longer any need for expanding the U.S. Army to 215 divisions, as the original plan in 1941 had required.[5] Instead, the expansion emphasis now shifted to naval and air forces, with the Army limited to a strength of ninety divisions.[6] On the one hand the American leadership believed that with the ninety-division program it had found a realistic balance between military and economic requirements, something of a "guns-and-butter policy" that did not inhibit economic production while still continuing to support the American high standard of living.[7] On the other hand, this self-imposed restriction meant a limit on future strategic options. On the basis of the rather limited American ground forces alone, the concept of the Decisive War—the basic idea of attacking Germany by the most direct route possible and inflicting the decisive defeat on Hitler's war machine by concentrating all available military resources with a minimum of losses, cost, and time[8]—was bound to gain momentum against a peripheral strategy that was not directly aimed at the very center of Fortress Europe. That would have been a continuation of the British approach, which placed priority on efforts in the Mediterranean area and had special significance considering Britain's view of its imperial position and long-standing traditions. Britain, therefore, advocated conducting a large-scale war of attrition before the Reich was finally given the coup de grace through the invasion of the Continent.[9] Considering the still unresolved problem of Japan, it would have been difficult from the U.S. perspective to justify a continuation of the peripheral approach, especially because of its long-term consequences.[10]

At Teheran, American president Franklin Roosevelt resisted delaying the invasion, as had been proposed by British prime minister Winston Churchill, who wanted to increase combat operations in Italy or in the eastern Mediterranean. Roosevelt pushed for the establishment of the second front in Western Europe that Stalin had been demanding since 1941. Part of Roosevelt's position was based on the fact that the American side was now tremendously overestimating the Soviet Union as a factor in the war.

Considering the predominance of the Soviet Union in postwar Europe as inevitable, the U.S. Joint Chiefs of Staff recommended to the president in August 1943 that he pursue a course of definite cooperation with the Soviets. According to this blueprint, which Roosevelt followed until 1945, the development and strengthening of friendly relations with the Soviet Union were in the vital interests of the United States.[11] This assumption was the foundation of the American position in the Operation ANVIL discussions, which continued into August 1944 and which in the end turned into one of the sharpest wartime disagreements between the Western Allies.[12]

The results of the Teheran Conference set the stage for linking Operation OVERLORD with the Mediterranean area to form an overall strategy. Yet, the differing strategic and political priorities of the United States and Great Britain remained a source of friction. Churchill continued to uphold the old empire tradition and wanted increased combat operations in the Mediterranean Theater of Operations (MTO), which were under the supreme command of British general Sir Henry Maitland Wilson. Instead of OVERLORD, Churchill wanted to establish the decisive front in the MTO, particularly in Italy. If that were achieved, ANVIL then would have been utterly superfluous. Churchill's line of argument thus followed an ever-clearer line of power politics. This also can been seen in Churchill's negotiations with the Soviet leadership, which started in May 1944 and which focused on drawing the dividing lines for operational zones in southeastern Europe, through which he hoped to limit by treaty provisions Soviet expansion into the British sphere of interest.[13] Operation ANVIL ran counter to Churchill's concept of integrating the political reservations about Soviet ambitions into the military strategy directed against Germany. ANVIL would result in limiting his own options in the Mediterranean. On July 1, 1944, Churchill tried to convince Roosevelt that the landings in southern France would result in the first major strategic and political mistake that they both would have to answer for. But Roosevelt held firm and was not even swayed by Churchill's argument that ANVIL and the extensive concentration of the Western Allies in France would in the long run help the Soviets gain "control over eastern, central and southern Europe."[14]

Churchill's proposed alternatives would cause complications with the third power in the "Strange Alliance,"[15] and simply could not be reconciled with Roosevelt's policy of cooperation with the Soviet Union. The American position was to leave the settlement of territorial questions in Europe for the end of the war. The decisive factor for Roosevelt, who had taken the Americans into war, was his intent to finish the war as quickly as possible and without the risk of any further military or political entanglements. That objective was driven by his frail health as well as domestic policy considerations.[16] The "Quick and Decisive War" concept, combined with Stalin's promise at Teheran to join the war against Japan after the defeat of the German Reich, only reinforced the decision of the American leadership to stick undeterred to the joint conference resolutions. Operation ANVIL, therefore, would proceed. That the Americans prevailed in the end is yet another indicator of the leadership role they had assumed in relation to their British ally. Commenting to U.S. general Dwight Eisenhower on August 9, 1944, Churchill bitterly noted that the United States was the "big, strong and dominating partner."[17] In contrast to the prime minister, Roosevelt was not interested in a restoration of the balance of power system, something which seemed hardly attainable anyway considering the limited strength of the U.S. Army. Instead, Roosevelt was concerned primarily with finishing the war militarily as soon as possible. In order not to jeopardize that goal, and following the American tradition of becoming involved as little as possible in internal European affairs, any political problems that might cause conflicts were to be glossed over by following a "Policy of Postponement," which meant they were to be left for settlement after the war. Roosevelt's strategic goal,[18] which seems to have been based on a mixture of idealism and pragmatism, of optimism and realism, was limited to guaranteeing American security through the establishment of a bridgehead for the United States as a naval and air power on the western part of the Continent, as well as along the East Asian coast of the Pacific.[19] Such a bridgehead would be accepted by the Soviet Union. With all of the cautious planning characterized by an excessive reluctance to accept risks and the Allies' overestimation of Germany's resistance,[20] U.S. Army Chief of Staff General George C. Marshall[21] remained convinced that this goal could be attained with the ninety-division program, later described as one of the war's boldest calculations.[22] Responding to objections raised by U.S. secretary of war Henry Stimson that the lack of experience of American units demanded for tactical and psychological reasons an overwhelming numerical superiority in the fight against the German Wehrmacht, Marshall reiterated the reasons for his own expectations of success. Those included America's superiority in the air, the numerical preponderance of the Soviets on land, and the quality of the U.S. Army divisions that were armed with superior equipment and had the advantage over their opponents of having the strongest possible artillery and close air support.[23]

2. Military Planning for the Invasion of Northern France

The military planning for the invasion of northwestern France unfolded against this background. The staff that had been charged with this task operated under the direction of British lieutenant general Sir Fredrick Morgan,[24] who was designated Chief of Staff to the Supreme Allied Commander (COSSAC). Morgan's staff had submitted initial planning drafts to the delegations of the Western Allies during the August 1943 QUADRANT Conference in Quebec, but it was only after the decisions that were made at Teheran and Cairo that Morgan was even sure that OVERLORD would actually be executed.[25] The plans, revised in detail multiple times right up until the start of the invasion, designated several phases that were to follow Operation NEPTUNE, the actual landing operation in Normandy.

The objective of Operation OVERLORD, which was scheduled for a duration of ninety days of combat, was to establish for the Allied forces a sufficiently large lodgment area on the Continent, from which the follow-on offensives could be launched toward the Reich, ending in the final victory.[26]

The fact that the U.S. Army operated with far higher supply and equipment requirements and a higher level of demand than European armies, combined with its very pronounced security-oriented thinking, explains the tremendous significance of logistics in its military planning. An American division, for example, had a daily requirement of about six hundred to seven hundred tons of supplies,[27] whereas a German unit of comparable strength got along with about two hundred tons.[28]

The Supreme Commander of all Allied invasion forces,[29] General Dwight D. Eisenhower,[30] was appointed in 1943 during the Cairo Conference. When he issued his commander's intent he stressed that the essential task was to establish a wide entrance corridor in

Comparison of Required Strength Figures			
	Personnel	Combat Motor Vehicles	Nonmotorized Vehicles
U.S. Infantry Division	ca. 14,300	ca. 2,100	
British Infantry Division	ca. 18,400	ca. 3,300	
German Army Infantry Division	ca. 12,800	615	1,450 horse-drawn
U.S. Armored Division	ca. 11,000–14,000	ca. 3,700, including 270 tanks	
British Armoured Division	ca. 15,000	ca. 3,400, including 290 tanks	
German Army Panzer and Panzer Grenadier Divisions	ca. 11,000–16,000	ca. 3,000, including 170 tanks/assault guns	
SS Panzer and Panzer Grenadier Divisions	up to 21,000	Roughly the same equipment as the Army Panzer and Panzer Grenadier Divisions	

Note: Data for the Allied side according to: Ellis, Victory in the West, I, pp. 535–541; Leighton, Coakley, Global Logistics and Strategy, p. 724. Data for the German side according to: Mueller-Hillebrand, "Heer," III, p. 138; Ose, Entscheidung im Westen, pp. 67 ff; Ellis, Victory in the West, I, pp. 553 ff; RH 10/141, RH 10/148, RH 10/149, RH 10/163, RH 10/172, RH 10/178 (Strength reports of the Panzer and Panzer Grenadier Divisions).

order to move every possible man to the Continent and to supply him there.[31] According to the agreements made in 1943, British general Sir Bernard L. Montgomery was designated the commander of the ground forces for the landing. By the start of the invasion, thirty-seven divisions had been assembled on the British Isles.[32] Another forty divisions on standby in the United States were to be brought in after the success of the landings. The Allied planners believed that the most important objective after the assault phase was the seizure and subsequent operation of the larger ports. Cherbourg, first of all, was to be taken as quickly as possible, which the planners figured could be accomplished in about two weeks (D+14).[33] The follow-on plans called for widening the bridgehead to the east, toward the Seine River, and to the south toward the Loire River. Simultaneously, two to four U.S. corps operating behind this shield were to clear Brittany.[34] The Breton harbors, down to the mouth of the Loire River (Nantes and St. Nazaire), were very important for the supply of all the American units arriving directly from the United States. The British, on the other hand, would operate their logistics via the Channel. The basic scheme of deployment put the Americans attacking on the right (western) wing and the British and Canadians on the left (eastern) wing.

Eisenhower's statement to Montgomery, "We must not only have the Brittany Peninsula—we must have it quickly," underscored the importance of Brittany in the Allied planning.[35] The planners expected that at least the Germans would defend the more important ports, and destroy the facilities before capture. The Americans, therefore, planned to establish a brand-new harbor complex in the Bay of Quiberon.[36] Just one to two months after the landing, the Allies expected the first supply shipments via St. Malo (as of D+27), Brest (as of D+53), the Bay of Quiberon (as of D+54), and Lorient (as of D+57).[37]

During the initial stages of the invasion almost all logistics operations had to be conducted across the open beaches in the bridgehead area. This was the primary method of supply until Cherbourg was operational. The Allies constructed two artificial harbors, codenamed "Mulberries," to provide some off-shore protection against storms.[38] According to Allied calculations they were the key element in the logistics system until D+90. In addition to unloading platforms, the artificial harbors also prolonged the usability of the beaches, if necessary, into the autumn period of bad weather. The Allies assumed that the Germans would not try to fight a decisive battle in northwestern France; rather, after the fall of Cherbourg they would concentrate initially on defending the Seine–Paris–Loire line.[39] Therefore, during the ninety-day OVERLORD phase the Allies had to establish additional logistics facilities to support an offensive against and across that line. In addition to the issue of harbor capacities, the time required for the development of the supply lines played a decisive role in Allied planning.

The complex logistics problem included the operation of airfields, the restoration of the highway and railroad networks, and the establishment of intermediate supply depots between the coast and the front lines. The Allies also constructed a pipeline system that fed from smaller harbors in the beachhead and even from Great Britain[40] to facilitate the transportation of fuels and lubricants, which alone accounted for one-quarter of the total required tonnage.[41] The underlying assumption behind all the logistics planning was a uniform Allied rate of advance that would not reach before September 4 (D+90) the line from the mouth of the Seine River to Rouen and then along the course of the Eure River all the way to Dreux, Chartres, Orléans, and the Loire River. The logisticians assumed that after reaching that line the Allies would need an operational pause lasting one month to consolidate the lodgment area and to maintain an orderly buildup of personnel and materiel before a large-scale offensive could be launched across the Seine River.[42] According to a study by the SHAEF G-4 section (the logistics section of the General Staff of the Supreme Headquarters Allied Expeditionary Force), even the three months planned for Operation OVERLORD seemed logistically feasible only under certain conditions. Among other things, this meant that the Allied advance would at first not be pushed beyond the Seine–Loire line, in order to prevent the supply lines from being stretched too thin. Besides, the buildup had to be tightly limited to bringing up those units that were absolutely necessary for the planned follow-on operations.[43]

The basic features of the post-OVERLORD operations that were planned to start about one month after the consolidation and deployment phases were already largely determined by the start of the landings.[44] The primary objective was Germany's industrial Ruhr region. The Western Allies certainly recognized Berlin as the ultimate Allied goal, but the planning staffs thought the capital of the Reich was too far to the east to be a realistic objective for the invasion forces.[45]

Berlin was in the Soviet Occupation Zone anyway—if only as an enclave—and the issue of the subsequent demarcation line between East and West had already been decided by that point. The arguments advanced by the British, and especially by the COSSAC, General Morgan, as early as July 1943 finally were resolved in the January 15, 1944, proposal for the Western Allies to reach the Lübeck–Helmstedt–Eisenach–Hof line.[46] Although the protocol assigning the exact occupation zones was yet to be signed, the Soviets on February 18, 1944, and then Roosevelt on April 3, 1944, agreed to the proposal. This result, which was a pleasant surprise to the Soviets, also looked like a favorable solution for the British.[47] The proposal was based on the war situation around the turn of 1943–1944 and was influenced heavily by the previously noted overestimation of the Soviet Union. On top of that, the success of the Allied landing was hardly a sure thing, and even Eisenhower considered failure a possibility as late as the spring of 1944.[48] Thus the Lübeck–Helmstedt–Eisenach–Hof line decision was bound to look good to the Anglo-Americans against the background of the then-current situation estimates. A military penetration by the Soviets deep into the west, possibly all the way to the Rhine River, seemed at the time more probable than a thrust by the western invasion forces into the eastern part of Germany. All the initial staff studies concluded that any such advance would be very time-consuming.

Logistical factors were major elements in the concept of Operation OVERLORD.[49] But from the very beginning of the planning activities in the summer of 1943 the establishment and maintenance of air superiority was considered an overriding factor, a prerequisite for success.[50]

3. Allied Supporting Forces

(a) The Air Forces

Without going into the details of the war in the air, and especially the hopeless inferiority of the German Luftwaffe, we nonetheless must sketch out the basic outlines of Allied air employment. During the Casablanca Conference in January 1943 the Allied leaders made the decision to mount Operation POINTBLANK, the Combined Bomber Offensive against the vital centers of the German nation.[51] The general objectives of this operation, which was prosecuted with shifting centers of gravity, were the progressive destruction or disruption of the German military and economic system, the severance of vital infrastructure communications lines, and the most extensive neutralization of the Luftwaffe possible.[52] Following lengthy staff deliberations, the targeting priorities were redefined in March 1944 to better support the invasion preparations.

The strategic bombers based in Great Britain had the mission of neutralizing the Luftwaffe and striking at the fighter aircraft industry in the Reich. Another key target was the transportation network in northwestern Europe. The key objective was to paralyze the northern French and Belgian railroad systems so as to prevent the Germans from rapidly moving up reserves toward the lodgment area. The Transportation Plan raids were concentrated in the area between the French and Belgian coasts, along a line via Reims–Paris–Tours and the Loire River. Priority targets were the main railroad junctions, the marshaling yards, and the technical rail facilities, such as depots and production and repair plants for rolling stock.[53]

Eisenhower had two tactical air forces to support the OVERLORD preparations, both operating under the command of British air chief marshal Sir Trafford Leigh-Mallory. The U.S. Ninth Air Force, under Lieutenant General Lewis Brereton, and the British Second Tactical Air Force, under Air Marshal Sir Arthur Coningham, operated a total of about eight thousand aircraft.[54] In France they faced only nine hundred German aircraft of the Third Air Fleet under Field Marshal Hugo Sperrle. As of early June only some five hundred of the German aircraft were operational, including about one hundred fighters.

The general numerical superiority of the Allies over the Germans was from 16:1 to 20:1.[55] That lopsided ratio would not change for the rest of the war.

Despite the stubborn resistance of the Allied air commanders, Eisenhower was able to obtain operational control of the strategic bombers of the U.S. Eighth Air Force, commanded by Lieutenant General James Doolittle, and the British Bomber Command, commanded by Air Chief Marshal Sir Arthur Harris.[56] Other forces were committed to the direct support of the preparations for the invasion, and would remain so committed until the lodgment area was secured and OVERLORD was clearly a success. Starting in April, the around-the-clock raids against the Reich by the four-engine bombers became the secondary priority after the targets designated to support the invasion.

By the start of the invasion most of the air objectives had been achieved. Aircraft of the four air forces had dropped seventy-one thousand tons of bombs on transportation installations alone. Of the eighty key targets selected by Allied railroad experts, only four remained undamaged. Key bridges across the Seine and the Loire rivers and about 475 locomotives in France had been destroyed. The railroad belt around Paris had been knocked out, and the frequency of traffic movements throughout France had dropped by 70 percent.[57] According to German estimates, the air missions directed against the Luftwaffe had by the first few days of the invasion resulted not only in Allied air superiority but in absolute command of the air. The approximately one hundred airfields within a radius of five hundred kilometers around the invasion beaches had been repeatedly and thoroughly destroyed.[58] As a result, German supply movements had become enormously difficult and Allied bombing raids and strafing attacks were an ever-present threat to marching columns. Even individual vehicles were fired on from the air, and major German troop movements could be carried out during the day only under extreme risk.[59] Raids against the coastal fortifications of the Atlantic Wall and the identified launch sites of the V-weapons were less effective, although such missions were flown as part of the invasion preparations.

The roughly twenty-three thousand tons of bombs dropped on the concrete pillboxes along the Atlantic and the Channel coasts did not yield results commensurate with the actual effort.[60] Most of the fortifications survived intact and personnel losses were minor. Quite mistakenly, the Allies feared the V-weapons would constitute a threat to the invasion preparations, which is why Eisenhower in April 1944 assigned special priority to bombing them.[61]

During Operation CROSSBOW all ninety-three of the identified V-weapon launch sites were wiped out through a tremendous effort that dropped some thirty-two thousand tons of bombs by the middle of June. Nonetheless, the effort was largely a failure because the V-1 "ski jump" launch sites—named because of their shape—that were attacked were decoys constructed by the Germans.[62] The very first bombing raids on the ski jump sites caused the Germans early in 1944 to introduce a completely new launch ramp system that was easier to install and was better camouflaged against observation from the air.[63] In the end, the Allied air raids merely forced a time delay in the employment of the V-1s. But that delay was as much the result of technical bugs in the development of the weapon system.

Considering the huge resources available to the Allies, the commitment of their air forces was not guided by a completely uniform operations plan in support of the OVERLORD preparations, which left much room for the "bomber generals" to pursue their own agendas.[64] Without compromising in any way the invasion preparations, Air Chief Marshal Harris especially managed to continue his carpet bombing raids against the German cities, albeit on a smaller scale than during the preceding months.[65]

Of greater significance militarily was the fact that Lieutenant General Carl Spaatz, the commanding general of the U.S. Strategic Air Forces in Europe, was not able to prevail with his plan to support the invasion preparations by assigning the top targeting priority to the German fuel industry. The systematic raids against the German hydration plants started only on May 12, 1944.[66] In contrast to other industrial sectors, these plants could not be decentralized and were particularly vulnerable from the air. Thus, the Germans were rather amazed that the Allied bombing raids on these targets had not started earlier.[67] Even these air attacks,[68] which were rather limited considering Allied capabilities, initially dropped only about fifty-two hundred tons of bombs, but very quickly produced lasting results.[69] By the end of May the Wehrmacht operations staff was already reporting a drop in the fuel output in Romania of roughly 50 percent, and in Germany the figure was about 33 percent.[70]

Albert Speer described the potentially catastrophic impact of the raids against the fuel production facilities on Germany's war-fighting potential in a series of memos he wrote to Hitler, known as the Hydration Memoranda of the summer of 1944. Speer noted that by September there would be an unbridgeable gap in the Wehrmacht's fuel supplies and that "no further operational movements of the forces would be possible in October or November."[71] Allied intelligence analysts arrived at similar conclusions at roughly the same time. On July 20 the British Joint Intelligence Committee reported: "Germany's shortage of oil has become the major factor limiting German strategy and operational efficiency." Just a month later the situation estimate even noted the possibility of a German collapse because of fuel shortages.[72] The Allied air forces had accomplished the mission assigned to them for the OVERLORD preparations, and they would continue to do their job in supporting the ground forces. Nevertheless, it remained to be seen whether additional and generally more significant targeting opportunities could be exploited properly. There would be a possibility of knocking out the German fuel industry and thus decisively paralyzing Germany's resistance by about the same time the OVERLORD lodgment area was secured, thereby making the strategic bombers available for new priority targets. Whether it would be possible to achieve successes commensurate with the magnitude of the Allied air potential depended on the materialization of an operations plan that established new priorities, that would be acceptable to the bomber generals, and that could be carried out with precision. In any event, a less precise plan was drafted only at the end of September 1944, at a point in time when the great operational opportunities of the campaign of maneuver had already passed.[73]

(b) The French Resistance

The French Resistance movement and its operations, which receive wide coverage especially in French literature, deserve some discussion as an element of the Allied supporting forces.[74] Although the supporting role of the partisans is rather debatable, there is little doubt about the degree and the significance of their irregular brand of warfare on a larger scale. Although as Ose observed in the case of Normandy, "they were not decisive to the outcome of the battle,"[75] nor in the progress of the fighting in German-occupied Western Europe, they nevertheless did play the role of a useful ally of the regular forces. But there was no cooperation on a larger tactical scale with that useful ally, because the required equipment and command and control systems simply were absent.[76] Or was the Resistance, as Eisenhower said in May 1944, a "strategic weapon"?[77] He did, after all, maintain that the Resistance had been the equivalent of fifteen combat divisions.[78]

In the following chapters we will examine on a case-by-case basis just what effect partisan warfare really had on the actual combat operations through the autumn of 1944. But first we must clearly establish some of the basic understanding in approaching this complex question.

Successful partisan warfare always depends on a stronger sponsoring power.[79] The French Resistance was cradled in the hope of the superior Anglo-American potential.[80] Great Britain and the United States became the mentoring and nurturing powers that supplied weapons, money, and communications to the Resistance. France's liberation could be foreseen clearly following the turning point in the war in 1943, and as a result key basic ideas began to take shape within the Resistance movement. By the spring of 1944 paramilitary units started to form in the interior of France.[81] The *Armée Secrète* that emerged reflected the organization, goals, and personality of the diverse *mouvements*.[82] The purely militarily organized Army Resistance Organization (ORA)[83] that sprang from the former French Armistice Army and the Communist Francs-Tireurs and French Partisans constituted the *Forces Francaises de l'Interieur*—French Forces of the Interior (FFI). According to Allied estimates, the numerical strength of the FFI just before the start of the invasion totaled around 250,000 men, of whom only 100,000 had weapons.[84] That, however, is not necessarily a measure of their military significance. In the first place, this resistance army was characterized by a rather haphazard level of organization. Its members had different levels of military training and a variety of weapons.[85] More importantly, the questions of overall command and the basic forms and objectives of their combat operations had been resolved only superficially. General Charles de Gaulle, headquartered in Algiers, insisted on maintaining tight military control over the FFI's role in France's liberation. With his leadership position undisputed by Frenchmen outside France, he was considered the leading symbol of the Resistance in the interior of France.[86] In the final analysis he wanted to ensure that France collected its share of bargaining chips for its role in the defeat of the Reich in order to restore national prestige and return France to the family of major powers.[87] But up until at least July 1944, Roosevelt firmly resisted de Gaulle's efforts to use French military support of the invasion to consolidate his own political legitimacy within the Allied camp. The American president, who in November 1943 had commented that France would not again be a major power "for at least 25 years,"[88] was not prepared to recognize the French National Liberation Committee as the provisional government, led by the general who loudly stated the undisguised French claims and demands.[89] Doubting de Gaulle's democratic legitimacy to begin with, any such recognition would have run counter to Roosevelt's intent to keep European problems on the back burner as long as possible. For the time being de Gaulle was accepted only as a military leader, and that was the way the instructions to Eisenhower were worded.

The Communist-dominated *Résistance Intérieure* (Domestic Resistance) opposed de Gaulle's efforts to consolidate his claims to French political-military leadership. By appointing General Pierre Koenig in London as commander-in-chief of the FFI and sending "military delegates" to France under the direction of General of Brigade Jacques Chaban-Delmas, de Gaulle intended to bring the Resistance movement under his control. For tactical reasons the Communists avoided any appearances of a break with the symbolic figure of de Gaulle, but they still kept their options open.[90] The Communists were interested in something far more than facilitating Allied operations through a national uprising. They were pursuing a different kind of partisan warfare above and beyond military events. If not a revolutionary transition to a "new France," they nonetheless wanted to ensure a favorable political starting position in the postwar period. The FFI was to play a trail-blazing role in establishing the groundwork for spontaneous mass uprisings, especially in the large cities, thereby triggering a "people's war."[91] This spirit of autonomous action and the independence of the directives emanating from London or Algiers resonated deeply in French noncommunist circles, which stressed the special legitimacy of the Resistance forces that had remained in France after 1940.

The question as to how and by whose orders the rank and file would actually go into action was resolved once and for all by including General Koenig in the command structure of the invasion forces[92] and by the proclamation of the provisional government on June 9, 1944,[93] designating the FFI as a component of the regular French Army.

At first the Wehrmacht did not recognize the unilaterally declared combatant status, and the members of the FFI continued to be considered guerrillas on the basis of the provisions of Section X of the World War I armistice agreement. Their operations were labeled as "gang or terrorist activities."[94]

The Allied invasion planners nonetheless did not attach any major significance to the Resistance because of the imponderable factors associated with any guerrilla army. As drafted out by General Morgan's COSSAC staff in June 1943, the Resistance was considered a bonus factor rather than as an essential component of OVERLORD. Nor was there any essential change in that estimate prior to the invasion.[95] The Western Allies hesitated until the very last moment to include the French in the details of Allied operational planning.[96] That, plus the fact that the French Resistance was never given top priority among the European Resistance movements for support, limited any role that could be assigned to it for combat operations.[97]

But as noted above, Eisenhower's comments in the spring of 1944 grant a somewhat greater significance to the Resistance. In a letter to Koenig's predecessor, General Francois d'Astier, Eisenhower emphasized the Resistance's "great value" in the OVERLORD preparations.[98] But it is most likely here that Eisenhower was trying to defuse political complications and mitigate French umbrage with the Americans that might possibly have a negative impact on the military operations. Furthermore, considering the difficulties inherent in his task as well as the general overestimation of the enemy,[99] it is quite understandable that the supreme commander of the invasion forces—who was very security-oriented in his thinking—valued greatly any form of potential support, and he therefore assigned special significance to the role of the FFI.

According to the Allied plans, the actions of the Resistance were by no means considered necessary prerequisites for the success of OVERLORD. Nevertheless, the Resistance was able to execute genuinely important missions within specific limits.[100] SHAEF initially believed that the primary mission of the FFI would be to delay the movement of enemy reinforcements toward the landing area.[101] The movements of German reserves were to be harassed, and communications and supply lines were to be cut. Beyond that, the objective was to tie down major German forces in the rear areas.[102]

Both the OVERLORD planning staff and French military leaders agreed that the proper way to employ these forces was through subversion and sabotage missions rather than major, independent operations.[103] The geographic requirements for partisan warfare had to be taken into consideration. Minor, isolated attacks were possible in the combat zone itself, but the center of gravity of FFI operations would be in the hinterland.[104] The conditions were particularly favorable in those areas where the occupying power could not make full use of the weapons and equipment superiority of the regular army.[105] These inaccessible regions included forests, mountains, and big cities. The sabotage operations would be aimed at paralyzing the German transportation system, jamming the communications network, and collecting information. In the event, the results by far exceeded the expectations of the invasion planners.[106] But that assessment made at the end of June 1944 must be seen against the background of their initially skeptical opinion of the FFI's effectiveness. The situation looked somewhat different from the German perspective. The operations of the Resistance did cause considerable time delays for units marching toward the front, but they did not decisively influence the outcome of the Battle of Normandy.[107] The situation estimate issued by OB West on June 13 noted that sabotage in the interior was on the rise, but not to the extent anticipated.[108] And according to a German report issued on June 20, there had been "no serious disturbances" in the areas of long-occupied France.[109] Seen against the background of the primary battlefront, the effect of FFI operations amounted to little more than pinpricks.[110]

Chapter 3

Development of the Situation through the Middle of August 1944

1. The Situation through the End of July

At the time of the Allied landings there were forty-eight infantry and ten Panzer divisions based in France in the area of responsibility of OB West.

The OB West himself, Field Marshal Gerd von Rundstedt, did not report to the Oberkommando des Heeres (Army High Command, or OKH) but rather to the operations staff of the Oberkommando der Wehrmacht (Armed Forces High Command, or OKW). France and the occupied areas in the west were designated OKW theaters of operations. That arrangement, however, did not have any important practical effect on the command channels, because all military command authority converged on Hitler, who in 1938 personally assumed the position of Supreme Commander of the German Wehrmacht and in 1941 further assumed the position of Supreme Commander of the German Army.

The primary subordinate headquarters of OB West were Army Group B (Heeresgruppe B), commanding all German forces north of the Loire River, and Army Task Group G (Armeegruppe G), commanding the southern sector. (See Map 1.)

In addition, Rundstedt was able to draw on security units under the Military Commander in France, the supreme chief for German military administration in the country. As OB West, Rundstedt was the latter's superior in all matters relating to the country's security.[1]

At the start of the campaign the Military Commander in France was General of Infantry Carl-Heinrich von Stülpnagel. On July 23, 1944, he was replaced by General of Aviation Karl Kitzinger. Except in the areas of the German army's direct combat operations, the Military Commander in France was responsible for law and order in the occupied territories. He was supported by a general staff for military matters and an administrative staff for civil concerns. In his four (later five) districts,[2] he had nineteen security regiments with about one hundred battalions.[3] Their combat effectiveness, however, was limited at best because they consisted mostly of older and previously wounded soldiers. The security units also were armed only with light infantry equipment. Quite often the soldiers carried captured weapons.

In addition to the army units, OB West had operational control of the Luftwaffe field and parachute divisions stationed in France, plus the units of the Waffen-SS.[4] Beyond army command channels, OB West coordinated with the Third Air Fleet under Sperrle and with Navy Group West under Vice Admiral Theodor Krancke.

On June 6 only seven German divisions were deployed in Normandy in the sector of Army Group B under Field Marshal Erwin Rommel.[5] On that day the first wave of Allied forces totaling some eight divisions managed to establish beachheads along the Calvados coast by conducting an air-land-sea three-dimensional operation.[6] The impressive efficacy of this combined-arms effort was one of the key factors in the Allies' favor in the western theater throughout the war.

The success of the landing operation was clear by June 11, when all the separate beachheads were finally linked up. With the loss of the battle for the beaches, which earlier had been touted as the decisive battle, the long-dreaded second front had at last become a reality. The war was now a multifront fight. Nevertheless, Hitler resisted accepting the necessary conclusions of the situation. Quite the contrary, the order was to carry on.

To accomplish that, the Germans throughout the month of June tried to conduct an "offensive defensive fight." In the process, Rundstedt came back to the view he had advocated before the landings, in agreement with General of Panzer Troops Leo Geyr von Schweppenburg, during the "Panzer Argument" with Rommel. Rundstedt believed that the invasion had to be defeated by a major tank battle that would be fought against the Allies in the country's interior. Prior to the Allied landings, when the controversy revolved around the deployment of the Panzer units, Hitler had decided on a compromise that was probably the worst solution possible from a military operational perspective. Now Hitler once again failed to make a comprehensive decision on the Panzer divisions, thereby depriving Rundstedt of one important resource in his attempt to solve the problem.

The Germans could not establish the necessary basic conditions to successfully execute Rundstedt's plan. That fatal handicap would continue to haunt the German Army in the West. Since it was impossible to reduce the Allies' command of the air, German offensive operations could be mounted only during periods of bad weather or at night. Another problem was that because of the prevailing command structure chaos,[7] German units either arrived too late or were not available because Allied deception operations through the beginning of August kept the German High Command convinced that the Allied main attack would still be coming in the Pas de Calais, in the command sector of the Fifteenth Army. As a result, considerable troop concentrations were held back from the fighting front.[8] The Allies, therefore, were able to conduct successful attacks that cut off the Cotentin Peninsula on June 18, and by the end of the month they captured Cherbourg, the first major port. Meanwhile, the Germans kept postponing their planned counteroffensive until its original objective was overcome by events on the ground.

Field Marshal Günther von Kluge took over as OB West on July 3, after the two advocates of the tank battle plan, Rundstedt and Schweppenburg, had been relieved of their commands. The former had demanded an immediate free hand to conduct operations, while the latter had called for flexible combat operations.[9] Von Kluge's name is most associated with the transition to the "defensive defense." His job was to fight a battle of attrition against the Allies. By that point, however, the "improvised German front line, running straight across Normandy," already resembled a "wire that would break if it were hit forcefully at a single point."[10]

The Allies had the advantage of sufficient forces to conduct a two-pronged operation. The British attacked at Caen, while the Americans attacked in the area around St. Lô. Although the Wehrmacht lost Caen on July 9 and St. Lô on July 18, the German forces still managed for about another two weeks to maintain a contiguous defensive line and to keep the Allies contained on the peninsula. But the duration of the German staying power was only a matter of time, weakened by the command structure problems and the retention of seventeen divisions in the Fifteenth Army sector through the end of July. The phase of the battle of attrition conducted along firmly held lines relentlessly drew to a close, primarily because there was no longer any hope of getting any reinforcements from the Eastern Front, where the Wehrmacht had been shredded by the Soviet summer offensive.

2. The German Leadership and the Military Situation of July–August 1944: Hitler and the Crisis in the West

During the conference held on the night of July 31–August 1 in his headquarters at the Wolfsschanze (Wolf's Lair), Hitler, urged on by Colonel General Alfred Jodl, took a close look for the first time at the preparations for an operation that since the middle of June had been recognized as necessary by both Rundstedt and Rommel.[11] Hitler, however, avoided considering the withdrawal of the German Army in the West to a new major defensive line.

Hitler finally agreed that such a withdrawal might become necessary, but *only if he* considered the continuation of the battle of attrition utterly impossible because of the disintegration of the Normandy Front, or in the case of another Allied landing. But at the same time, Hitler's comments hinted that even if the conditions for a successful defense in Normandy should fade completely—and he was still not convinced that would happen—he nevertheless would not deviate from the overall strategic concept he had specified in *Führer Directive 51*. At the start of that nighttime conference it looked as if Hitler would not even consider Jodl's recommendations. Delivering one of his typically rambling monologues, the German führer confused realities with vain hopes in his projections of the developments that might materialize in the respective theaters of war.

According to his "most sacred conviction,"[12] the situation in Russia could be stabilized by the commitment of the fifteen new grenadier divisions.[13] In doing so, Hitler thought that the main threat of a reversal of the German alliances in the southeast, the Balkans, could be eliminated.[14] He also insisted that the Apennines Front in Italy had to be held at all costs to tie down a large number of Allied forces "that otherwise might launch operational actions somewhere else."[15] On the other hand, he assigned a much more fundamental importance to the events in the west. This was where "Germany's fate will be decided," as he put it.[16] To Jodl's great surprise, however, Hitler believed that for the time being the outcome of that decision could be shaped favorably by continuing the current strategy of holding rigidly. Above all else, a withdrawal from France would mean that Germany would lose its base of operations for submarine warfare, plus an important source of raw materials, including tungsten and bauxite. Besides, the divisions of the German Army in the West were utterly incapable of conducting ambitious operations.

Hitler arrived at that conclusion through an astonishingly realistic analysis of the grim general conditions in Normandy. As he stated: ". . . in terms of their armament and other equipment, the major units are not at all capable of any kind of mobile warfare . . . and the sum total of forces . . . cannot be measured by the number of divisions that we . . . have here. This can only be estimated instead by the small number of major units that are actually capable of maneuvering. And that is only a very small fraction."[17]

In Hitler's opinion neither the Wehrmacht's degree of mobility nor the strength of its units at that point would permit a withdrawal from northern France. The available units were only just barely able to hold the Normandy Front. It therefore appeared to him "utterly hopeless" to order a movement into what would necessarily be a longer rear line, "regardless of where I [Hitler] might put it."[18] The result, he emphasized, would be an absolute collapse. Jodl's hope for an immediate withdrawal order was dashed once and for all by Hitler's demand that it would "have to be made clear to Army Group [B], that it must in this very place [its current positions], under all circumstances, conduct the fight with utmost fanaticism."[19] While Hitler's negative arguments in favor of the holding strategy did not fully hold water, he nevertheless underestimated the potential effects resulting from fixing Army Group B firmly in place. He obviously had not yet realized the full scope of the threatening situation. Within a matter of days, the alternative between holding and withdrawing would only leave limited options. The result would either be the destruction in place of the German Army in the West, which was fighting fanatically for every yard of ground, or the initiation of the delayed and therefore very costly retreat. Despite these options, and the fact that he could hardly get a word in edgewise, Jodl, while not able to get a decision on establishing operational guidelines, still managed to work out with Hitler certain general measures in the event a disengagement from the Normandy Front might become necessary.

The way ahead seemed clear when Hitler began to speculate on the effects of an Allied breakthrough on the invasion front or another landing, situations he downplayed as "development of a crisis."[20] But as a consequence of everything that had happened, Jodl, the chief of the Wehrmacht operations staff, was now able to cut into Hitler's monologue more frequently and he found the führer more willing to make far-reaching decisions. Thus, if the crisis did develop the major units of Army Task Group G were to be pulled out immediately. In other words, southern and southwestern France were to be evacuated. Hitler also decided that in the event of a crisis, "the center of gravity of the entire operation would be again shifted to the west—the way it used to be."[21] This resulted in two significant consequences. First, the position of OB West, at least so long as Kluge held the job, was downgraded to little more than a mere recipient of orders. In Hitler's view the vast number of new problems expected to arise meant that he could not leave the decision-making responsibility with OB West, because "everything depended on the campaign in the West."[22] Hitler also planned to move his Führer Headquarters west to the Black Forest or the Vosges Mountains—possibly to a compound near Diedenhofen (Thionville)—from where a specially established element to be called the "Subordinate Operations Staff" would issue clear directives to Kluge continually.[23] That would mean taking Kluge out of the loop when it came to major command issues. As Hitler summarized his intent: "OB West no longer needs to know anything other than what he must know." Most importantly, ". . . he has to fight there no matter what happens." And finally, ". . . any notion of free-wheeling operations is pure bunk."[24]

That statement reflected Hitler's distrust of the army staff in France, which he slandered as a "pigsty."[25] He also stated: "We have no idea what kind of operational information leaks out of there will tip off the English."[26] As Hitler repeated over and over again during the conference, all necessary directives and orders must conform to a plan, *but the military staffs in the west had no need to know what that plan was.* Thus, Hitler's determination to shift the command center of gravity "to the West again" indicates exactly how he understood the next phase of the war. His comment, "the way it used to be," was a reminiscence of the "glorious six-week victory" of 1940, which had no relation to the completely different situation of the present.[27] In the final analysis all Hitler wanted was to play for time, the time needed to seize the initiative again and to bring about "a turning point."[28] His plan to accomplish that was based, of course, on the fundamental realization that the Wehrmacht "could not operate on its own, but it could make it tremendously difficult for the enemy to operate throughout the depth of the sector."[29]

Hitler thus bluntly stated exactly what was to be the desperate mission of the German Army in the West, at least into September. The forces of OB West somehow had to attempt to slow down the Allies' advance and thereby gain valuable time. Hitler thought that the best and perhaps even the only way to put the brakes on the otherwise boundless potential of the Allies[30] was a defense at all costs, or possibly the destruction of the major maritime ports,[31] which had been his first idea. Otherwise, he insisted, the Germans would have to "discard the idea that we could withdraw only with essential forces." But if it proved possible to deny the Allies the use of the major supply transloading facilities until the period of bad weather set in, which Hitler estimated for six to ten weeks, that would mean a great deal in the struggle to gain time. The führer believed Germany must be prepared "simply to sacrifice certain units" as fortress garrisons in the major ports.[32] For the moment he wanted to designate those ports that had to be held at all costs. As early as January 19, 1944, IJmuiden, Hoek, Dunkirk, Boulogne, Le Havre, Cherbourg, St. Malo, Brest, Lorient, St. Nazaire, and the northern and southern mouths of the Gironde River had been designated as fortresses. Later the Channel Islands, La Rochelle, Marseille, and Toulon were added to the list.[33] The fortress commandants were to be selected carefully to avoid another recurrence of the "disgrace at Cherbourg."[34] Moreover, Hitler hoped that a comprehensive destruction program would create scorched earth conditions in France that would restrict the superior operational capabilities of the Allied units.[35]

Hitler previously had dismissed the idea of withdrawing into a rear defensive line as a hopeless effort, and by the middle of July Jodl had predicted "all France is lost following the rupture of the German front containing the invasion." The thinking at the time was that the Maginot Line or the old German West Wall might provide the best positions to establish a defensive line.[36] Nonetheless, the question of establishing a line running straight across France was the central point of the July 31–August 1 situation conference, and Jodl was visibly relieved that he could convince Hitler to move closer to addressing the problem of the withdrawal. But now the people in the Führer Headquarters began to cling to delusional possibilities that long before upon sober consideration had been discarded as hopeless. Even if, according to Hitler's calculations, it should prove possible to restrict the Allies' options by blocking the harbors and with a comprehensive scorched earth program, it nevertheless remained highly questionable whether the major units of Army Group B that provisionally had been designated as mobile and the divisions of Army Task Group G could be pulled up from the south only *after* the "crisis" occurred, and that they would be able to get into position in time to reestablish a new front line that still ran through France. Jodl, at least, was able to convince the führer that the so-called Seine line was out of the question for any lasting defense.[37] But people at the Führer Headquarters entertained exaggerated expectations about the possibilities of the so-called Seine–Marne–Saône–Jura line, which had been reconnoitered in 1943.[38] (See Map 8.) Completely miscalculating the available time, Hitler ordered that this line, which only existed as a line on a map, should now be developed with all possible resources. The position was to be constructed specifically "with concrete pillboxes" because Hitler assigned the highest importance to it for the more distant future.[39] Thus, in his pessimistic but as it later turned out realistic analysis, the new position would only serve as a very short delaying line. Any serious resistance would only be possible anchored along the West Wall and the Vosges Mountains.

The West Wall then once again moved to the front of Hitler's field of vision, although as early as June Jodl had already evaluated its defensive quality rather pessimistically and as being very dependent on the number of troops that could be pulled back.[40] For the time being, however, much of Hitler's thinking was dominated by verbal reminiscences of olden days. He quite mistakenly assumed that "not much needed to be done for the West Wall,"[41] which explains why his defensive concepts focused so heavily on the Somme–Marne–Saône–Jura line.

At the end of the conference Hitler admitted that if a crisis did come in the west, followed by withdrawal—a sequence of events Hitler was still not convinced would come to pass—then the success of that withdrawal and its measured progress would depend less on prior planning than it would on improvised execution. Hitler anticipated that events would play out with unit commanders down to the tactical echelons left to their own devices, often under chaotic conditions. He realized that in such a situation units would have to be "commanded in a very informal and mobile manner," otherwise "the cause was lost."[42] In the same breath he said: "I must . . . push the Luftwaffe to make 12 or 15 groups[43] ready."[44] Thus it was during that nighttime conference that Hitler's determination to mount an offensive emerged, despite the rather somber prospects of a withdrawal. This remark made at the beginning of the conference reinforced his comment that bringing about a turning point in the west would only be possible "if we somehow, halfway, get our Luftwaffe back in shape." He intended to commit the Luftwaffe units that were then being organized to the point "where the final die would be cast."[45]

Hitler's about-face implicitly assumed a counteroffensive in the west. Although not mentioned expressly during the conference, such a counteroffensive was necessary in order to close the continental back door. It was also necessary to establish the conditions for the objective Hitler restated precisely one month later—a peace "that would also secure the life of the coming generations."[46] But for Hitler such a peace was only conceivable in conjunction with the ideological crutch of *"Lebensraum im Osten"*—living space in the east. Following this basic guideline of his strategic blueprint, the initial objective was to gain time until the new aircraft models could be deployed in the west in sufficient numbers or until the weather favored German operations—bad weather that would limit severely Allied air operations. Hitler also counted on the Allies running into logistical problems because they lacked efficient harbors.[47]

The measures just being launched by Goebbels, the Reich Plenipotentiary for Total War, were supposed to result in the release of a "maximum of manpower for the Wehrmacht and the arms industry."[48] Hitler's hopes were only reinforced by his unrealistic expectations for the "war of the vengeance weapons" and the so-called "armament boom."[49] Hitler's determination to correct the situation in the west "by offensive means" became such an overpowering obsession that he later tried to exploit even the very slimmest possibilities of technological miracles, totally misreading in the process the military realities.

The Crisis in the West materialized on July 31 with the American breakthrough at Avranches. According to the concept Hitler had laid out at the conference, that should have triggered the withdrawal operation *immediately,* especially from southern and southwestern France. Nonetheless, any such considerations and preparatory orders were simply discounted, because Hitler gambled everything on issuing an order to launch an immediate counterattack to close the breakthrough gap.[50] Once again, the general withdrawal that had become necessary long ago was delayed by at least two more weeks, costing even more valuable time.

3. Deterioration of the Situation in Northern France and the Significance of August 15 for the German Army in the West

As the Allies fought the worn-out forces of OB West, they continued to reinforce their beachhead. By the end of the month Army Group B, which Kluge had assumed direct command of after Rommel was wounded on July 17, had about twenty-five divisions in the combat zone. That did not include the divisions of the Fifteenth Army under Colonel General Hans von Salmuth. As per orders, those units continued to sit inactive along the Channel coast. At least eleven of Kluge's available divisions were no longer fully combat-capable. They were organized under eight army corps, which in turn operated under the command of the Seventh Army, under Oberstgruppenführer and Colonel General of the Waffen-SS Paul Hausser, and Panzer Group West (renamed the Fifth Panzer Army on August 5), under General of Panzer Troops Heinrich Eberbach. All these divisions registered as only remnants or battle groups on the situation maps for the west.[51]

On August 1 the Allies had some thirty-one operational divisions on their side of the line. According to the command structure that took effect that day, the headquarters of an American army group was activated to command the American units.[52] The 12th Army Group of Lieutenant General Omar N. Bradley, with a total of seven corps, consisted of the U.S. First Army under Lieutenant General Courtney H. Hodges, and the newly inserted U.S. Third Army under Lieutenant General George S. Patton.[53] General Montgomery's 21st Army Group, with five corps, consisted of the Canadian First Army under Lieutenant General Henry D. G. Crerar and the British Second Army under Lieutenant General Sir Miles Dempsey.

During the first days of August, Patton's U.S. Third Army managed to exploit the Avranches breakthrough of Army Group B's front line along the southwestern tip of Cotentin and thrust out with the U.S. VIII Corps into the interior of France. (See Map 2.)

The breakout ushered in a new phase in combat operations, a campaign of maneuver. The Allies now held the initiative completely. During the first half of August the German leadership, including Kluge, focused their attention on the effort to close the breakthrough gap without paying proper attention to the deployment of enemy forces between the Seine and Loire rivers. After Rennes was evacuated and following the pullout from Nantes on August 11, the

Americans had Brittany completely cut off. The six divisions of the German XXV Army Corps deployed on the peninsula had no option other than to withdraw to the last fortresses of St. Malo, Brest, Lorient, and St. Nazaire. As those units prepared to defend their positions and awaited their fate, they were no longer of any use to the fighting along the main front. Nor were the approximately thirty-one thousand German soldiers based on the Channel Islands, who remained there until the end of the war.[54] The breakthrough had totally smashed the left wing of the German Seventh Army, which now hung in the air.[55] The German counterattack against Avranches on August 8 failed, primarily because of Allied air superiority. Hitler nevertheless continued to insist on closing the breakthrough gap through a counterattack using all German resources. That was the order even after Le Mans fell and when American troops were not only probing into the Orléans area along the Loire River, but also when elements of the U.S. XV Corps were beginning to wheel north toward Falaise and Caen.

The failure of the German counterattack against Avranches definitely demonstrated the doubtful value of Panzer attacks in the face of enemy air supremacy. Nevertheless, OB West still did not abandon the basic concept, and he therefore maintained his major units in their exposed positions. Kluge gave up hope only shortly before the Canadians launched a major offensive from the Caen area against the Fifth Panzer Army and moved toward a link-up with the American units that were approaching from the south. On August 13 Kluge asked for further guidance for the conduct of combat operations.[56] The next day he urged in vain that the "Big Decision" had to be made to prevent all of Army Group B from being lost.[57]

The campaign of maneuver resulted in the grave threat of the encirclement of the German forces by the Allies, but it did not trigger the eastward withdrawal movement that had become necessary far earlier. The formation of the Falaise Pocket, the first major catastrophe to strike Army Group B, had begun.

The war of maneuver also created an increasingly precarious situation for Colonel General Johannes Blaskowitz's Army Task Group G, which was operating south of the Loire River. The danger came from the north, in the area of the boundary with Army Group B, where American troops advanced unopposed toward Chartres and Orléans. It was an area completely devoid of German forces. As the enemy raced through this area, creating all sorts of operational opportunities, the Germans attempted to establish some sort of improvised security line between Paris and the Loire River. In an effort to accomplish this, the headquarters of the German First Army, under General of Infantry Kurt von der Chevallerie, was withdrawn on August 12 from its current area of operations blocking the Loire River crossings and screening the Atlantic coast in the sector of Army Task Group G and put back under the command of Army Group B.[58]

Field Marshal von Kluge was seriously worried about the fighting in the Normandy area and the continued advance of American units between the Seine and Loire rivers. Making matters worse, another decisive Allied thrust had been looming for some time in the Mediterranean area along the coast of Provence. It finally started on August 15 with the early morning landings of Lieutenant General Alexander Patch's U.S. Seventh Army.

The opportunity of withdrawing the forces of Army Task Group G while still not under enemy pressure and using those units to establish a new front line behind the beleaguered Army Group B had been frittered away.[59] In fact, just the day before, on August 14, the headquarters of OB West received a Führer Order that repeated the existing mission: "Defense of the coast in sector of Nineteenth Army against impending landings."[60]

Thus, by August 15 the German Army in the West was facing a double threat resulting from the landings in the south combined with the operational developments in the north against Army Group B, where the spearheads of the Allied pincers attempting to encircle the German forces had approached to within eighteen kilometers of each other.[61] (See Map 3.)

A third event that day gave the whole situation the appearance of the climax of a drama. Around 0930 hours all communications were lost with OB West. Kluge had left his headquarters the day before to inspect the front in the vicinity of the Falaise Pocket.[62] For several hours Kluge could not be reached by his headquarters, by OKW, or by Hitler. His whereabouts were unknown.[63]

Although Kluge had not been actively involved in the attempt on Hitler's life, he nevertheless assumed that he himself might become a victim of the wave of persecutions that followed immediately. He had been in contact several times with the men of the July 20 plot via his former operations officer in Russia, Major General Henning von Tresckow.

As General of Infantry Günther Blumentritt later commented; "One cannot commit oneself to fight for one's people under the most difficult situations and struggle in the front lines if at the same time there is a threat hovering in the rear of courts-martial and other trials."[64] That psychological stress combined with the fact that Hitler blamed Kluge for the mess in Army Group B may partly explain why the OB West now made frequent trips to the front lines to expose himself personally to the same dangers that his men were facing, and thus tried to tie his own destiny to the catastrophe threatening Army Group B. That was the tragedy of Field Marshal von Kluge, who had taken over command in the west full of confidence early in July. The mission given to him, to reconcile the discrepancy between Hitler's orders and that which was militarily achievable and necessary, was obviously too much for him.

The events of August 15 clearly indicated another factor that worked against military effectiveness: the faulty command structure in the west that resulted when Kluge, in addition to his job as theater supreme commander, also was forced to assume direct command of Rommel's Army Group B.

As the Allied landings progressed along the coast of Provence, the Wehrmacht now had to fight on two fronts in France. But the German commander responsible for coordinating the entire fight, OB West, had disappeared somewhere in the area of the Falaise Pocket and simply could not be found for several hours. He was so deeply involved in the crisis facing Army Group B that his entire thinking and actions were dominated by the immediate threat at this decisive point.[65] He started out on his trip to the front despite having already received messages indicating August 15 as the day of the invasion in the south.[66] He was, in fact, unable to cope with both missions. Clear evidence of this can be seen in the phone conversation the following day when Kluge finally checked in with Blumentritt, his chief of staff.[67] Kluge was obviously still shaken by his unnerving experience during the trip to the front when his radio command car had been attacked by Allied fighter-bombers, killing four of his men. Facing the developing situation in southern France, Kluge appeared all but helpless.

On August 15 the situation became increasingly difficult for Blumentritt, who in Kluge's absence was exercising the command authority at OB West headquarters. The situation in the rear of the Normandy Front was deteriorating. When the field marshal did not check in for more than nine hours, Blumentritt phoned Jodl at the Wehrmacht operations staff and informed him of Kluge's disappearance. Blumentritt requested that an acting supreme commander be designated and also demanded that the "Big Decision" finally be made—the order to retreat, to withdraw, and above all to evacuate the Falaise Pocket, which was still possible at that point.[68]

Hitler believed his suspicions about Kluge were confirmed by the field marshal's apparently inexplicable disappearance. There was only one decision Hitler could make, and that was to replace the OB West.

The combination of the command crisis and the critical operational situation on August 15 caused Hitler two weeks later to call that day the worst of his life.[69] Anxiety reigned, not only in the various headquarters in the west, but also in the Führer Headquarters.[70] After he decided to relieve Kluge of his command, Hitler had to resolve the problem of a successor. Initially, as Blumentritt had demanded, an officer was put in command temporarily of the elements of Army Group B. Hausser, until then the commanding general of the Seventh Army, also assumed command of the Fifth Panzer Army and Panzer Group Eberbach.[71] Although Blumentritt kept pushing for a comprehensive decision, including the abandonment of any ideas about launching offensives, Hausser was still bound by Hitler's order to advance and attack and to launch a thrust southeastward against the U.S. XV Corps.[72] But Hitler considered Hausser's command appointment as only an interim solution.[73]

To prevent the looming catastrophe in the west, Hitler wanted a commander who had extensive experience in mastering such situations. Hitler's short list included two field marshals, Albert Kesselring and Walter Model, both of whom were summoned to Führer Headquarters on that same day.[74]

Kesselring had been OB Southwest in Italy since 1943, and up through that August he had been able to halt the Allied offensives in Italy south of the so-called Green Line—also known as the Gothic Line, which ran from La Spezia to the Apennines, and then to Pesaro. Kesselring in the process had forced the Allies into a long, drawn-out, and costly fight.

Model was not promoted to the rank of field marshal until the end of March.[75] In 1939 he had served as the chief of staff of the IV Army Corps in Poland. During the 1940 campaign in the west he had the same assignment with the Sixteenth Army. From there his wartime service had been exclusively on the Eastern Front in various assignments as a commander. Kesselring's selection as OB West appeared obvious because of his experience as a supreme commander in the adjacent theater of war in Italy. He was already familiar with the warfighting style of the Western Allies and the problems that developed along the boundary between the two theaters resulting from the Allied landings in southern France. Model, on the other hand, had earned Hitler's high esteem as a field army commander on almost all sectors of the Eastern Front. Late in the evening of August 15 it appeared initially in the Führer Headquarters that Kesselring was certain to be the new OB West, because Model had returned to his Army Group Center headquarters on the Eastern Front, which was no longer all that far from Hitler's headquarters at Rastenburg in East Prussia.

But Hitler selected Model during the night between August 15 and 16. At 2300 hours OB Southwest headquarters was informed that Kesselring was no longer being summoned to a conference at the Wolf's Lair because he was needed elsewhere.[76] The commanding general of Army Group Center was again ordered to report to the Führer Headquarters on the following day. Earlier, Rastenburg had received a message reporting that Kluge's whereabouts had been resolved, but that message was no longer relevant. Meanwhile, the events in southern France were rushing headlong toward an initial climax before the change of command took effect at OB West headquarters.

Chapter 4

The Initial Situation in Southern France

1. Plans and Assessments

(a) The German Command and the Problem of a Landing in the South

As early as June 1943 an intelligence assessment prepared by the Wehrmacht operations staff had identified the organization of a French expeditionary corps as an indicator of an enemy offensive directed at southern France.[1] Concrete fears about an Allied landing along the French Riviera, however, did not solidify among the German leadership until August 1943, when units of OB West relieved the Italian Fourth Army in the sector to the east of the mouth of the Rhône River.[2]

The Germans took over coastal defenses with little difficulty, but following the forced evacuation of Sardinia and Corsica serious concerns soon arose based on the still rather vague indicators of an enemy landing. OB West touched on that problem in his October 1943 situation estimate. As Rundstedt noted: "I believe that the attack options open to the Anglo-Americans exist primarily along the Channel, probably in conjunction with an attack . . . against the French Mediterranean coast."[3] But Rundstedt also pointed to the hitherto largely ignored Bay of Biscay sector held by the First Army as the possible target of a large-scale landing, combined with attacks in the area of the mouth of the Rhône River. The scope of such a threat was far out of proportion to the available defensive resources. Rundstedt concluded that all the Germans could do along the Atlantic was to increase observation efforts. Thus, there was a blatant shortfall between the resources available and the potentially worthwhile invasion targets on either coast. Rundstedt considered a landing along the Mediterranean very possible because of the significance of Toulon and Marseille. The Rhône Valley, which was a natural gateway to the north, would then be a "decisive and important direction of the enemy thrust."[4] According to the OB West situation estimate, however, the southern coast would only be the scene of a secondary operation to support the main offensive in northern France. With *Führer Directive 51*, the southern sector assumed a greater significance, essentially accepting Rundstedt's ideas and reinforcing the Western Front.

In early 1944, Jodl and Hitler anticipated Allied landing operations along the periphery of Fortress Europe that would dissipate German forces and support the Allied main effort, which would fall along the Channel. Since the turn of the year there had been an increasing flow of intelligence about the buildup of a strong Allied reserve in North Africa. All the indicators seemed to confirm that this reserve would not be fed in to support the landings at Anzio-Nettuno, but rather would be committed to develop Corsica into an Allied "unsinkable aircraft carrier." The potential participation of French troops forced the German leadership to conclude that the coasts of southern France and of Liguria were particularly vulnerable. On February 17, 1944, Jodl offered the assessment that "the next major enemy operation was planned in the western Mediterranean, specifically against the French Mediterranean coast."[5] Hitler thereupon approved the reinforcement of that sector. Because it supposedly was impossible to organize a full army group (*Heeresgruppe*) with its corresponding wartime strength, as Rundstedt had wanted,[6] only an army task group (*Armeegruppe*) was activated.[7]

On June 6, Army Task Group G consisted of two field armies of seven corps and sixteen divisions, including eight based in the threatened Mediterranean sector. Blaskowitz, the commanding general, thought at that point that it should be possible to commit the Nineteenth Army along the Riviera "for the purpose of beating off landings, or if they are successful, to drive the enemy back into the water with a counterattack."[8]

But the heavy losses from the fighting along the invasion front in the north did not leave the forces of Army Task Group G unscathed. Although a major enemy operation in the Mediterranean area was considered certain,[9] and landing exercises had already been observed, several major units were withdrawn from Army Task Group G, despite the potential threat of a second invasion.[10] That fact alone shows the seriousness of the German personnel shortages in France. Thus, with Army Task Group G so weakened, it proved impossible to do the very thing that Field Marshals Rundstedt and Rommel had advocated as early as June—the evacuation of German forces from southern and southwestern France while not yet under enemy pressure and the redeployment of those forces to reestablish in adequate time a new front line straight across France.[11] But now the obvious advantages of such a redeployment and the resulting considerably shortened supply lines were no longer available for exploitation.

Hitler insisted on holding the south. All Blaskowitz could do was report that "the defensive strength of [the Nineteenth] Army has been so weakened from the reassignment of men and weapons that a successful defense of the [southern] coast can no longer be guaranteed."[12]

But now the German leadership was no longer even certain that the Allied landings would take place in Blaskowitz's Mediterranean sector. According to a short situation estimate issued by the Wehrmacht operations staff on July 27, they now anticipated an operation against the Ligurian coast.[13] About a week later Field Marshal Kluge learned that according to the latest assessment, a "direct threat to the French south coast was currently no longer considered realistic," and Kluge therefore should consider withdrawing more forces from the south. Kluge thereupon demanded that he be assigned for immediate transfer to Normandy one corps headquarters, three infantry divisions, and most importantly the 11th Panzer Division, the last mobile reserve of Army Task Group G.[14] Knowing full well that transferring those forces would be tantamount to the end of any serious defensive efforts in the south, Kluge added: "This campaign will be decided in northern France."[15] But once again Hitler's decision was only an unsatisfactory compromise. On the one hand, he left Army Task Group G with its Panzer division as the only major formation capable of mobile combat operations, and again he rejected the requests the field army commanders in the west had submitted repeatedly since June for the transfer of that division to Army Group B.[16] On the other hand, Hitler approved the withdrawal from the already seriously weakened Nineteenth Army and the redeployment to the north of the 338th Infantry Division. He also approved the withdrawal of the antitank companies[17] of the 242nd, 244th, and 198th Infantry Divisions, thus seriously reducing the firepower of those units.[18]

In the meantime, the various German headquarters continued their guessing game about the objective of the Allied Mediterranean operation, which multiple indicators suggested was imminent. According to an intelligence report from Madrid on August 10, ten troop transports had been observed putting to sea from North Africa.[19] Just the next day OB West reported to the Wehrmacht operations staff systematic air raids against German radar installations along the coast of southern France.[20] Finally, on August 12, reconnaissance aircraft from the German 2nd Air Division reported spotting "south of Ajaccio two big convoys with between 50 and 100 merchant vessels and warships, plus two aircraft carriers."[21] But the Wehrmacht operations staff was still not sure whether the operation was directed against Liguria or against southern France. According to the entry in the OKW war diary: "Grounds could be cited for both conclusions, but they balanced each other out until the last moment."[22] The war diary entry also noted that following the Allied breakout in Normandy there were "strategic considerations indicating that the landing would take place in southern France rather than Italy . . . which at the moment was only a secondary theater of war." But, "so long as there was no certainty, an effort was made to reinforce *both coasts simultaneously* to the extent possible."[23] General of Artillery Walter Warlimont, the deputy chief of the Wehrmacht operations staff, told the war diary officer on August 12 that in his opinion an offensive along the French Riviera was unlikely and that "the indicators instead pointed to a thrust against Liguria."[24]

In the past the commanders on the spot had agreed essentially with this situation estimate. According to later comments by Blaskowitz as well as his chief of staff, Major General Heinz von Gyldenfeldt, they expected an invasion in the Gulf of Genoa, especially after the Allied successes in northern France.[25] As Gyldenfeldt saw it, the Allies were bound to know about the low combat effectiveness and the immobility of Army Task Group G units, which posed no real threat to landings in that sector. An offensive in the Genoa area, on the other hand, could cause the German front in Italy to collapse and therefore would appear to be the more effective alternative.[26]

But the events of the preceding days, the destruction of the bridges across the Rhône and Var rivers, the repeated air raids against the radars and battery positions east of the Rhône, and the rumors circulating among the population that the Allied landings would take place on "Napoleon Day," shifted the focus.[27] On August 12 the situation estimate issued by Army Task Group G reported to OB West headquarters the completion of the first phase of preparations for an impending landing between the Rhône and Var rivers. Simultaneously, Blaskowitz immediately ordered the Nineteenth Army to go to Alert Level Two, while urgently requesting the halt of the transfer of the 338th Infantry Division to Army Group B.[28] But the Wehrmacht operations staff simply could not make that decision, even though Hitler on August 13 had once again ordered that the front held by the Nineteenth Army be defended against landing operations.[29] The delay in stopping the bleeding off of the Nineteenth Army, despite the looming threat, was also partially the result of a lack of clear understanding of Allied intentions. Although the volume of Allied air raids in the Nineteenth Army's sector had tripled over the week before, it was still not possible to identify the direction of the enemy operation until the very last moment. The Allies bombed targets both in Liguria and in southern France, including the Rhône River bridges, railroad installations, and airfields.[30]

The situation deteriorated further on August 14, as Army Task Group G reported the thorough destruction of the transportation network between the Rhône and Var rivers.[31] The message to OB West headquarters reported that "there are numerous indicators pointing to a landing along the French Mediterranean coast."[32] The Wehrmacht High Command then finally approved halting the northward transfer of the 338th Infantry Division and leaving the division's units that had not yet departed with the Nineteenth Army. Thus, the German leadership was uncertain until the very last moment about the exact time and place of the expected Allied Mediterranean operation, which in turn frustrated their ability to establish a defensive center of gravity.

There were other problems that deserve close examination. Why did Hitler, even through the middle of August, still resist the course of action proposed by Rundstedt and Rommel to withdraw from southern and southwestern France while the German forces were still not under enemy direct pressure? As Hitler probably saw the situation:

1. A voluntary withdrawal would be tantamount to an admission of military weakness;
2. A withdrawal to a rear-area line ran the risk of triggering an uncontrollable, panic-like flight;[33]
3. Access to important raw material deposits would be abandoned earlier than necessary;[34]

4. An unopposed landing would give the Allies greater opportunities for attacking lucrative objectives, including La Rochelle, the mouth of the Gironde River, Bordeaux, Marseille, Toulon, or a thrust into the rear of the Italian Front.[35]

The decisive factor, however, was undoubtedly Hitler's assumption that he could resolve the situation in Normandy by launching a counteroffensive. If successful—and Hitler did not seem to doubt that it would be—then it was unnecessary or even premature to abandon southern France. Might not a withdrawal of Army Task Group G attract the expected Mediterranean operations to the coast of the Riviera, which would then be undefended? Hitler might well have entertained these or similar considerations.[36] Typically overestimating his own situation, Hitler's optimism that was not based on facts led him to assume the success of a counterattack in Normandy merely as a result of his issuing the order.[37] But that unrealistic optimism was the decisive obstacle that prevented any early evacuation of the south.

(b) Operation DRAGOON from the Perspective of the Allied Military Leaders

Almost eight months of severe controversy raged around Operation ANVIL, later redesignated DRAGOON.[38] Although the decision had already been made at the political level, the controversy was not settled until just a few days prior to the start of the landings. The American military leadership, which throughout the debate strongly advocated DRAGOON as a supporting offensive, now found itself faced with a dual problem. On the one hand, DRAGOON had to be coordinated with the Normandy landings in terms of time and forces, and in such a way that the success of neither the primary nor the secondary operation would be endangered. On the other hand, the requirements of the on-going fighting in Italy had to be reconciled with the planning for DRAGOON. Conflict was inherent in this dilemma because the Italian Theater of Operations was under a British commander, who, acting as an agent of his nation's political and military leadership, questioned the efficacy of DRAGOON.

Initially proposed by American military planners in August 1943, the original objective of what was then called Operation ANVIL was the establishment of a bridgehead in the Marseille area to facilitate the Normandy landings by tying German forces down in that part of the country.[39] When the controversy erupted in January 1944, Eisenhower stressed in a letter to General Marshall the tremendous significance of that advantage.[40] Moreover, he saw two additional arguments that mitigated in favor of the execution of ANVIL:

1. It would deliver on time the promises made to the Soviets at Teheran, and
2. It was the best possible use of the French divisions that had been equipped by the Americans and that, according to de Gaulle's insistence, were to be committed primarily in the southern part of France.[41]

Nonetheless, the Allies were forced to make an essential change to the ANVIL plan because all available landing craft were needed for OVERLORD, and simultaneously the deteriorating situation in Italy made it impossible to withdraw Allied units from the front line there. On March 21, 1944, the Allied Combined Chiefs of Staff agreed to a compromise that gave priority to the operations in Italy until such time as the Allies were able to resume the offensive there. As a result, the landings in southern France were postponed indefinitely.[42] That meant that ANVIL-DRAGOON did not disappear entirely, as the British hoped, but rather it had been scrubbed as an operation to be conducted simultaneously with OVERLORD. Thus, one key argument advanced by the ANVIL-DRAGOON advocates, that of tying German forces down to relieve pressure on OVERLORD, had now lost its usefulness.

From the American perspective there was a danger that the strategic combination of OVERLORD and ANVIL-DRAGOON would be lost—but that was one factor that Churchill did not believe in anyway.[43]

After the front in Italy broke loose again in May 1944, following the fall of Monte Cassino and as soon as the Anzio bridgehead had been integrated into the Allied lines, the discussions about the landings in southern France were back on the table. The Americans again advanced their long-standing and often repeated line of argument. The main disadvantages of dropping ANVIL-DRAGOON were the potential political difficulties with the French, the loss of ten combat divisions for support of OVERLORD. The retention of those forces in Italy would add more weight to any proposal to advance into southeastern Europe via Italy.[44] The Normandy invasion was already set, but the date for the landings in the south had not yet been established. It was not until the middle of June that another line of argument entered the debate, one that the Americans considered vitally significant.

During a June 17 meeting with Mediterranean Theater of Operations supreme commander Henry Maitland Wilson, General George Marshall argued that ANVIL-DRAGOON should take place as soon as possible to seize the ports along the Riviera, Marseille, and Toulon. That was the only way for the thirty to forty divisions currently standing by in the United States to move to France quickly.[45] Wilson appeared impressed. Two days later he offered his support for ANVIL-DRAGOON with the proviso that the Combined Chiefs of Staff would also assign priority to the seizure of the major ports. Although the climax of the controversy was yet to come in the form of an exchange of telegrams between Churchill and Roosevelt lasting several days, the first breach had been made in the wall of Great Britain's previously solid military opposition. A few days later Eisenhower added more support to Marshall's arguments. In his letter to the Combined Chiefs of Staff, Eisenhower stressed the fact that ANVIL-DRAGOON would not only tie down German units but would also result in the seizure of some vitally needed harbors.[46]

The logistics problem was becoming increasingly troublesome for Eisenhower because Cherbourg had not yet been taken by that time and the Allied troops in Normandy had no major supply handling facilities. That situation was made worse when the OVERLORD forces had a close call on June 21. The two artificial harbors (Mulberries), which had been handling all of the supplies, were seriously damaged by storms along the coast of Normandy and were temporarily put out of commission.

Operable maritime ports and unrestricted access were a problem that gained increasing significance during the course of the debate, contributing to the July 2 decision to schedule the start of Operation ANVIL-DRAGOON for August 15.[47] Just nine days before the operation was to be launched, Churchill made one last attempt to cancel DRAGOON by addressing the problem of harbors in his own way. He suggested that the landing be shifted from the Mediterranean to the Breton coast, because of the greater significance of the Atlantic ports of Brest, Lorient, and St. Nazaire.[48] Despite offering some advantages, Churchill's alternate plan was hardly feasible at that point because of the advanced state of the preparations for DRAGOON. But it did highlight a rather crucial point in the complicated logistics system, and logistical constraints continued to restrict the way the Western Allies fought the war at least until the end of 1944.

Early on, the German leadership had accurately analyzed the factors that critically influenced the outcome of the debate on Operation ANVIL-DRAGOON at the very highest political level, as well as on the military level. In *Führer Directive 40*, issued on March 23, 1942, Hitler emphasized that the exact time and place of the landing operations might be estimated not only from operational factors, but also by "failures in the other theaters of war and the Allies' political obligations."[49]

By the end of 1943, Field Marshal von Rundstedt, as OB West, had assessed the most likely Allied course of action as a landing along the Channel combined with an attack against the French Mediterranean coast. As he explained the interrelationship of the two in logistical terms, "Getting Toulon and Marseille is important to the enemy quite apart from any political considerations."[50]

But the German leadership failed to take the decisive countermeasures at the right moment. The required conditions for such actions no longer existed by the summer of 1944 because of the severe attrition of German units during the fighting in Normandy and the uncertainty over Allied intentions in the Mediterranean area.

2. Prerequisites on the German Side

(a) The Situation along the Atlantic Coast

By the middle of August 1944, Blaskowitz had the following forces available in his area of command. In the western sector, along the Atlantic coast between the mouth of the Loire River and the Pyrenees, he had only a "system of mere [sic] security," in accordance with the directive issued by OB West. But that specifically did not include the fortresses along the Gironde River and the La Rochelle defensive perimeter.[51] General of Engineers Karl Sachs, whose LXIV Army Corps consisted of two infantry divisions, could not establish more than a thin security screen along the coastal front that ran 857 kilometers in length. Besides, the structure of the headquarters Sachs assumed command of on August 11 was still being reorganized from that of a reserve corps to that of an army corps subordinate to a field army. The technical requirements of that process overwhelmed the headquarters staff. The staff earlier had been provided with the personnel and equipment necessary to make the transition, but effective exercise of command was still difficult because the communications facilities were inadequate.[52] The state of readiness of the two major subordinate units was also rather worrisome.

The 16th Infantry Division, commanded by Lieutenant General Ernst Haeckel, was deployed north of the Gironde River. It had been formed only a short time earlier from remnants of the 158th Reserve Division and the Luftwaffe 16th Field Division, both of which had been smashed in Normandy. When first organized it had been primarily a training unit, with poor mobility and rated as having only limited defensive capability.[53] A comparable situation existed south of the Gironde. The 159th Reserve Division, commanded by Lieutenant General Albin Nake, was rated as having only limited defensive capability. Like the 16th Infantry Division, it had three regiments totaling seven infantry battalions. The increased numbers of foreign volunteers along the Atlantic coast indicated the growing shortage of well-trained German soldiers in the German Army of the West's entire area of operations. The 950th Indian Grenadier Regiment with its three battalions, for example, took over a part of the coastal defenses and Italian volunteer soldiers were assigned to defend the island of Noirmoutier.[54]

The approximately twenty-four thousand German army soldiers in the sector of the LXIV Army Corps included some eighty-five hundred men of other nationalities. They included fifteen hundred Italians, four thousand troops of the 360th Cossack Regiment, and three thousand in the Indian Regiment.[55] The critical question was whether or not they would be prepared to continue risking their lives for a foreign power that was now definitely on the losing side. But this mixture of nationalities in the coastal defense units was unavoidable, as Rundstedt put it in 1943, in order "to have any men at all along the thin front lines."[56] Headquarters OB West recognized that coastal security was little more than a map exercise with no real practical value.[57] Moreover, as of early August it was no longer even the primary mission of the LXIV Army Corps. Following the American push to the south that resulted from the breakthrough in the Army Group B sector, Blaskowitz recognized the threat to the corps' main supply line, which ran from Paris via Orléans to Tours. But he also had a reason to fear something far worse. If the Americans got across the Loire River line to the south, they would be able to thrust into the rear of his Army Task Group G almost unhindered.[58] At that very moment the Americans in the area north of the Loire River were already less than half as far away from the Vosges Mountains as the German units deployed in southern France. For that reason alone, as Blaskowitz's chief of staff, General von Gyldenfeldt, put it, the holding of the Loire River line was vital to Army Task Group G.[59] OB West also realized that it was necessary to shift the LXIV Army Corps' center of gravity.[60] By August 14, and without the express permission of the Wehrmacht High Command, elements of the 16th Infantry Division had already been pulled out of their coastal sector and had been moved to the Loire River. Nevertheless, German commanders realized clearly that the ad hoc–formed Blocking Force Haeckel could hardly prevent a serious attempt by the Allies to cross the Loire River.[61] Although initial enemy contact along the Loire had involved only American reconnaissance probes, the immediate German reaction was the abandonment of the positions along the northern bank of the river and the demolition of bridges, including those at Angers and Nantes.[62]

(b) The Situation along the Mediterranean Coast

General of Infantry Friedrich Wiese commanded the threatened southern sector of Army Task Group G's area of operations. To defend the 650-kilometer-long Mediterranean front from the French-Italian border to the French-Spanish border, his Nineteenth Army initially had three army corps with seven divisions deployed directly along the coast.

That force included the headquarters of the Luftwaffe IV Field Corps, under the command of General of Aviation Erich Petersen. It was deployed to the west of the Rhône River and was rated as having limited capability.[63] In the area between Montpellier and the Spanish border the IV Field Corps had three divisions with a total fighting strength of nineteen thousand men.[64] After the transfers to Normandy the corps' personnel strength was significantly reduced. Only the 198th Infantry Division, under the command of Major General Otto Richter, was rated as conditionally capable of offensive operations.[65] The other two divisions were considerably weaker. The 716th Infantry Division, under Major General

Wilhelm Richter, was deployed on the right wing of the corps. That unit had been mauled in Normandy. It was in the process of being reconstituted, but it was completely immobile and its personnel strength had been augmented by two battalions of eastern volunteers.[66] Deployed on the left wing, the 189th Reserve Division, under Lieutenant General Richard von Schwerin, had only the strength of about a regiment. Because of the state of its training and its assigned area security mission, it was rated as having a low mobility capability.[67]

The sector of the LXXXV Army Corps (Special Purpose),[68] under General of Infantry Baptist Kniess, was held by some nineteen thousand troops of the 338th Infantry Division, commanded by Lieutenant General René de l'Homme de Courbière, and the 244th Infantry Division, under Lieutenant General Hans Schaefer. These two units were designated as stationary divisions and were likewise capable only of defense. The combat effectiveness of the troops stationed in this coastal sector was the biggest concern for Nineteenth Army commander Wiese. Although the order to transfer the 338th Infantry Division was later cancelled, initially some one-third of the effective strength of that division was en route to Normandy, including one infantry regiment, one artillery battalion, and one antitank company. The 244th Infantry Division was on the left of the 338th. The 244th originally had been assigned only to defend the Marseille defensive perimeter, but now it had to extend to take over part of the sector along the mouth of the Rhône River.[69] The soldiers of the four eastern volunteer battalions, who ironically were called "Russians in France Fighting for Germany against America," were another major concern for General Kniess. Their fighting spirit, quite understandably, was a big question mark. Nevertheless, they constituted one-quarter of the infantry units committed to the coastal defense sector of the LXXXV Army Corps.[70]

The sector between Toulon and the Italian border was held by the twenty-one thousand troops of General of Infantry Ferdinand Neuling's LXII Army Corps. The subordinate divisions were the 148th Reserve Division, under Major General Otto Fretter-Pico, and the 242nd Infantry Division, under Lieutenant General Johannes Baessler. The 242nd Infantry Division was responsible for the defense of Toulon. Both divisions, however, were capable of only limited mobile combat operations. Several foreign volunteer units were in this sector as well. Of the twelve infantry battalions of the 242nd

Infantry Division, three were manned by Armenian and Azerbaijani soldiers.[71]

Although the southern sector of Army Task Group G might have been designated as a coastal defense zone along the Atlantic, that fact did nothing to cover over the critical shortcomings that caused Blaskowitz to develop his pessimistic estimate of the situation:

1. The pitiful status of equipment resulted first and foremost in the lack of motor transport; but other equipment problems included:
   - Some sectors had no antitank weapons at all.[72]
   - The inadequacies in artillery were a function of the many different types of artillery pieces used by the coastal artillery regiments and the resultant ammunition problems. For example, fifty-three out of the sixty coastal batteries were equipped with captured weapons of Russian, French, or Italian origin. Moreover, some batteries were manned by gun crews of which only about 30 percent were German soldiers. Italian volunteers filled out those crews.[73] An even more critical shortcoming was the impossibility of covering the coastline with overlapping arcs of fire. An artillery exercise conducted in July revealed that this shortcoming was particularly obvious in the sector between Toulon and the Italian border.[74]
   - The communications system was a crucial weakness throughout the entire command sector.[75] The Nineteenth Army's telephone network was based almost exclusively on the infrastructure of the French Post Office. The trunk lines of the telecommunications cables ran through so-called "terrorist regions" in the Rhône River Valley. Those lines were cut so repeatedly by sabotage that by the middle of August teletype and telephone communications had all but faded out.[76] The radio communications network could provide only limited expedients. Radio equipment capable of long-distance transmission was simply not available, and radio messages were always vulnerable to degradation from heavy atmospheric disturbances. Army Task Group G had only one radio teletype unit.
2. The difficult manpower situation in Army Task Group G was further aggravated by the fact that many of the billets were

filled by semi-disabled enlisted men and officers who were no longer fit for frontline duty or for assignment to the Eastern Front.[77] Thus, Blaskowitz's main problem continued to be his utterly inadequate combat strength. For example, the sectors of the divisions deployed for coastal defense in the Nineteenth Army area of operations ran for widths of between 60 and 130 kilometers.

As ordered by Hitler, the coastline was to be the main line of resistance. But that, compounded by the personnel and equipment limitations, meant that it was possible only to establish a weak linear defense with inadequate tactical reserves to respond to emergencies. These were much the same handicaps that German forces had been under two months earlier in Normandy. The wide defensive sectors made it impossible to deploy in any depth. The Nineteenth Army's divisions were only able to pull back individual companies as reserves.[78]

Beyond the coastal defenses, Blaskowitz had an additional three army units under his command. Only the 11th Panzer Division, however, was capable of functioning as a mobile, hard-hitting reserve. But Blaskowitz also needed the other two units badly. The 157th Infantry Division, commanded by Lieutenant General Karl Pflaum, was under Blaskowitz's operational control. It had been deployed behind the Nineteenth Army's left flank in the French-Italian border area around Grenoble, a major center of Resistance activities. Even the Volunteer Depot Division, which trained the replacements for all of the Eastern and Turkish ethnic units, was integrated into the defensive plans. On August 10, Gyldenfeldt reported to OB West headquarters that the constant withdrawal of personnel made it necessary to transfer some of the volunteer units to exposed positions that urgently needed to be secured, but even that measure would not guarantee their defense. But as he noted, that was still better "than leaving entire stretches of the countryside completely without any occupying units."[79] Finally, after many months of tug-of-war between OB West and Army Task Group G, Hitler decided that the only unit capable of offensive operations, the 11th Panzer Division, would remain in the south. Nevertheless, even this decision of the führer's was not a clean one. The 11th had to give up one of its Panzer battalions, probably in consideration of the German counteroffensive Hitler still wanted in the sector of Army Group B.[80]

On August 11 that battalion, with its sixty-one PzKpfw IV tanks, arrived in the Army Group B sector. That left the 11th Panzer Division with 101 tanks and assault guns, which was only about 60 percent of its authorized wartime strength of seventy-eight PzKpfw IVs, seventy-three PzKpfw Vs, and twenty-one assault guns.[81] The serious consequences of reducing the 11th Panzer Division's strength were only compounded by the flood of indecisive and partly contradictory orders about the commitment of the division coming from the German leadership. On August 9, Hitler had once again rejected OB West's request to move the entire division north.[82] Instead, the 11th Panzer Division was to be moved from the Toulouse area eastward, over a distance of three hundred kilometers, and then committed to reinforce the front line of the Nineteenth Army. Kluge, however, took the precaution of halting that movement just two days later, because he was still hoping that he might after all be able to pull the Panzers north. The division could be transported to the Army Group B sector faster via the Bordeaux–Tours railroad line than via the stretch of rail in the Rhône River Valley, which had been destroyed completely in the area around Lyon.[83]

After Kluge's request was turned down once again, he was forced finally to release the division. But that did not end the confusion. At first the unit's march objective was to be the area of Nîmes–Alès–Millau, west of the Rhône River. Kluge amended that order, too, probably taking into consideration Blaskowitz's estimate of the situation, which projected the enemy landing to be made east of the river.[84] As a result, the point of the defensive main effort was to be placed east of the Rhône River, specifically, near the coast, in order to ensure the fastest possible response to an enemy landing.[85] But because of the time lost by the countermanding orders, the 11th Panzer Division was still en route at the moment the Allies started landing in the south.

In the meantime, Blaskowitz and Wiese ordered what limited measures they could to reinforce the Mediterranean Front:

- The last reserves of Army Task Group G, the 668th and 669th Engineer Battalions, were placed under the Nineteenth Army.
- To the west of the Rhône River, all available vehicles were requisitioned and the three divisions of the Luftwaffe's IV Field Corps were alerted in a rather improvised fashion to make it possible to shift units quickly to the threatened area. The

first elements of the 198th Infantry Division, the only effective division of the corps, were pulled out of the coastal defense positions and set in motion toward the mouth of the Rhône River.[86]

- During the night leading up to August 15, the Wehrmacht operations staff finally approved halting the transfer of the elements of the 338th Infantry Division and those antitank companies that had not yet departed.[87]
- Wiese had tried to prepare his corps commanders for the invasion by conducting map exercises during the preceding weeks. As a result of the last exercise on August 8, General Neuling was advised to reorganize the defensive sector of his LXII Army Corps between Toulon and the Italian border. Wiese was thinking in particular about the sector of the 242nd Infantry Division. Neuling was told to make sure that German companies were inserted between the foreign volunteer units to serve as "corset stays." Further reinforcement plans called for one regiment to be transferred from the 148th Infantry Division in the Nice area behind that sector as the corps reserve.[88]

But, by August 15 all these measures had been executed only partially. Most critically, the corps reserve had not yet been assembled in the Le Muy area.[89] (See Map 4.)

3. The Situation on the Allied Side

(a) Military Preparations and Objectives

The Allies' military preparations had been completed while the ANVIL-DRAGOON debate was still in full swing. The final DRAGOON plan of July 29 called for the invasion forces—initially under Wilson as the Allied Supreme Commander in the Mediterranean Theater of Operations—to commence landings east of Toulon at 0800 hours on August 15. The Allied planning group under the direction of U.S. Lieutenant General Patch considered the approximately seventy-kilometer-wide coastal sector between Cavalaire sur Mer and Agay on the Gulf of Fréjus to be especially suitable for the landings.

1. From there it would be possible to attack the ports of Toulon and Marseille in the rear from the landward side. That was es-

pecially important because the heavy concentrations of German coastal artillery made a frontal assault landing in both areas virtually impossible.[90]

2. The road network made it possible to cross the Maures Massif into the interior of the country and also offered good connections to the Rhône River Valley to the west.

3. The geography favored landing operations between Cavalaire and Agay, with good, flat, and sandy beaches mostly in small bays in various areas. Until the seizure of a harbor, however, they were not adequate for bringing in additional troops and supplies.

In addition to other issues, including the technical naval factors of the landings—such as the depth of the landing bays and egress routes from the beach for tracked vehicles—a key advantage of the designated sector was the ability of the French Resistance to provide accurate intelligence on the German coastal defenses, much as the Resistance had done in June in Normandy.[91]

Major General Lucian K. Truscott, a veteran of various amphibious operations, spearheaded the landings of Patch's U.S. Seventh Army with his U.S. VI Corps.[92] The U.S. 3rd, 36th, and 45th Infantry Divisions landed during the assault phase. To the west, the 3rd Infantry Division under Major General John E. O'Daniel landed at Alpha Sector, in the area of Cavalaire and St. Tropez. In the center the 45th Infantry Division under Major General William E. Eagles landed at Delta Sector, around St. Maxime. On the right flank, the 36th Infantry Division under Major General John E. Dahlquist landed at Camel Sector, in the area of St. Raphael–Fréjus. The Allied intent was to link the beachheads on the first day and then to push inland up to thirty kilometers to an objective designated as the Blue Line.

As at Normandy, the main landings were screened by special operations units. Romeo Force, consisting of some one thousand French commandos, had the mission of blocking the coastal road to the west of the landing sector in the area of Cape Nègre. Sitka Force, with some two thousand Americans and Canadians of the 1st Special Services Force, was sent against the Hyères Islands, also located to the west of the invasion zone. Sitka Force's most important mission was to knock out the 164mm coastal battery there to prevent it from firing against the landing in Alpha Sector. Since the threat to the landing force was relatively minor from the east, only a small detachment of French naval commandos, designated Rosie Force, with sixty-seven men, landed in the area around Théoule.

The strongest special operations unit was the 1st Airborne Task Force, commanded by Major General Robert T. Frederick. It was designated Rugby Force, with nine thousand men, which included the only small element of British troops to land in southern France. Its mission was to land by parachute and take the highway and railroad junction at Le Muy, about fifteen kilometers upstream along the Argens River, and to hold it until the main landing forces arrived. The supporting special operations missions were launched during the night of August 14 or during the early morning hours of August 15. By the evening of the first day of the landings the Allied command hoped to have fifty thousand to sixty thousand troops and sixty-five hundred vehicles ashore.[93] The three American infantry divisions in the first wave were in no way comparable in personnel strength and equipment to the German units deployed along the south coast. Each American division had a strength of sixteen thousand troops. Each division also had attached to it one tank battalion with sixty tanks and one tank destroyer battalion with sixty antitank guns.[94]

After the American units landed, the insertion of two French corps, with a total of seven divisions under General Jean de Lattre de Tassigny, was to start on August 16. The French units had the mission of capturing Toulon between D+15 and D+20 (August 30–September 4, 1944), and then according to the plan taking Marseille about three weeks later, between D+35 and D+40 (September 19–24, 1944).

The final preparations for Operation DRAGOON began with the embarkation of the American divisions in Naples, starting on August 9, and the loading of the French units in Taranto, Brindisi, and Oran. With an original course set toward Genoa to deceive the German leadership, the landing fleet only changed course for its final objective at 2218 hours on August 14.[95] The Allies took other deceptive measures during that night. Five hundred paratrooper dummies, for example, were dropped between Marseille and Toulon.

Once the landing phase was secured, Operation DRAGOON would continue with its primary missions of securing adequate harbor capacity and building up Allied supply lines from the south coast to the north, and most importantly, neutralizing all possible major German forces and then thrusting up the Rhône River Valley via Lyon to link up with the OVERLORD units.[96] After the successful link-up the DRAGOON forces, now designated Lieutenant General Jacob L. Devers's 6th Army Group, would be detached from the Mediterranean Theater of Operations command and come under Eisenhower's European Theater of Operations.

(b) Allied Regular Supporting Forces

As in the case of the Normandy landings, the Allies had far superior naval and air support than did their German opponents. The Western Task Force, under Vice Admiral H. Kent Hewitt, consisted of some 880 ships, including five battleships, 24 cruisers, 111 destroyers, and about 100 mine-clearing ships, plus 1,370 smaller vessels, mostly landing craft.[97] That mighty landing fleet was reinforced on August 12 by a carrier task group out of Malta with nine aircraft carriers.[98] In addition to its transport function, Hewitt's task force had the mission of providing naval gunfire shore support for the landing troops.

The bombardment of the German positions began with the heaviest guns early in the morning on August 15. After about an hour and a half of shelling, at around 0730 hours the naval guns fell silent. The coastal area had been hit by about sixteen thousand shells. The access routes for the landing craft were then cleared of mines.

The Allied air preparations for DRAGOON began considerably earlier. Lieutenant General Ira C. Eaker[99] mustered a force of 4,056 aircraft, roughly half the number that had supported OVERLORD.[100] The first phase of the three-phase air offensive started as early as April with a strike against Toulon. During the first phase, which lasted until August 10, the Allied raids targeted highway and railroad junctions, bridges, and German airfields. The successful bombings of the Rhône River bridges isolated the landing sector. By August 9 five out of the six major bridges between Lyon and the Mediterranean were unusable. The first phase, totaling 6,000 sorties and 12,500 tons of bombs dropped, finished with raids against the German forward airfields. During the second phase, between August 10 and 15, some 7,500 tons of bombs were dropped on the coastal batteries and radar stations along the Mediterranean coast. But to keep the German leadership guessing about the exact site of the invasion, the Allied air missions did not concentrate on the designated landing sector alone. The final phase of the air preparations started on the morning of August 15 by carpet-bombing the landing sectors to attrite the German units manning the coastal defenses. Another eight hundred tons of bombs were dropped by 0730 hours. The Luftwaffe was unable to prevent the Allied air operations. Although the Allies conducted more than one thousand sorties between August 10 and 15, only fifty aircraft did not return to their bases, thereby dramatically confirming Air Marshal Sir John Slessor's observation that the Luftwaffe could "basically be ignored."[101]

(c) The Role of the French Resistance

The invasion was an opportunity for the Resistance in southern France to enhance its relevance, and it therefore stepped up its activities before the start of the landings. The advantage of being able to operate over vast stretches of land with favorable geographic conditions and the continually reduced levels of German troops resulting from the fighting in Normandy gave the Resistance the chance to mount a sudden surge in its guerrilla actions.[102] In the German military sectors in the south, the French population, as in northern France,[103] was largely passive well into August, and even showed a somewhat lethargic willingness to help their occupiers.[104] Even so, certain centers of active resistance started to form in the huge hinterland of the Army Task Group G sector that extended up to the Loire River. These areas included the Massif Central, the area from the Rhône River Valley to the Alps, and the region around Nevers–Auxerre–Troyes between the Seine and the Loire rivers.

According to Allied estimates, the Resistance by July 1944 consisted of seventy thousand armed individuals in southern France.[105] With some of its operations conducted by units of up to battalion strength,[106] the Resistance now made German travel in the rear areas possible only with heavily armed escorts.[107] In the end, even the main roads and rail lines were no longer considered secure because of the increasing sabotage activities,[108] which led to the continual interruption of almost all telecommunications cable links in the Army Task Group G sector.[109]

The hinterland was no longer under German control. Things were quiet only where the German troops were still physically present. This disquieting situation, which worried the German leadership in the south, did present operational-sized threats, although the situation was by no means untenable at that point. Because of its manpower shortage, the Wehrmacht necessarily concentrated on protecting the few main communications lines.[110] Some of the more unimportant regions in which guerrilla forces had been reported were left mostly to themselves, or they were turned over to the overworked German security units; but the French Forces of the Interior was not capable of tying down German divisions in the rear areas for any length of time.[111] The Germans themselves knew that the worst was yet to come. The total mobilization of the Resistance was expected for August 15.[112] The most likely opportunities for the FFI to exert any decisive influence on military operations existed in southern and southwestern France, and especially in the event of a German retreat from the coast, which would have to be conducted through hundreds of kilometers of territory that was no longer under German control. Above all, it remained to be seen in southwestern France, where the commitment of regular Allied troops was not planned, whether the FFI's levels of organization and military training would allow it to create a military effect beyond what they had achieved so far with guerrilla operations. In other words, how valid was the claim made as early as June that the FFI was an organic component of the French Army?

4. From the Start of the Invasion to the Retreat Release Order

(a) August 15 in the South

As the Germans observed the Allied landing preparations with growing concern, they remained largely uncertain as to the precise landing sites. On the afternoon of August 14 some general staff officers at the Nineteenth Army headquarters tried to develop a more specific assessment from the position and course of the convoy observed by German aircraft near Ajaccio. Assuming its objective was actually the coast in the sector of the Nineteenth Army, the analysis showed that the Allied fleet might well be off the Riviera by the early morning hours or off Marseille by daybreak. Based on this analysis, an operation to the west of the Rhône River was rather unlikely, because the landing would have to start there during the morning in full daylight.[113]

The picture began to clarify during the night leading up to August 15. After the deception raid on Marseille, the Nineteenth Army requested permission to start demolishing the harbor facilities in anticipation of a rapid Allied success there. After some haggling back and forth, with Admiral Krancke primarily resisting the request, OB West decided that the harbor demolition would be initiated only if it became clear that the Allied objective was Marseille. Even then, demolitions would be restricted to only those facilities that could not be defended.

On the other hand, the Germans could do nothing to prevent either the Allied flanking operation landing on the Hyères Islands, first identified at 0325 hours, or the landings of the French commandos to the west of Cape Nègre.[114] That latter effort had already been reported erroneously as having been beaten off.[115] The first event that forced the Nineteenth Army commander, General Wiese, to make an immediate decision was the dropping of the Allied paratroopers in the Le Muy–Draguignan area, reported at 0520 hours.

The drop zone at Le Muy centered on a major highway and railroad junction along National Highway No. 7 that ran into the hinterland in an east-west direction and that connected Fréjus and Aix-en-Provence to the Rhône River Valley near Avignon. The Allied airborne landings there had to be counterattacked, immediately if possible, because the position they were occupying was key terrain, as well as threatening to the transportation network.[116] Le Muy is located in the Argens Valley, which runs between the Maures Massif and the Estérel Mountains and which opens toward the sea in the direction toward Fréjus. It offered a path for an outflanking thrust against the coastal defenses. The Nineteenth Army headquarters recognized the potential threat to the area in adequate time, but no action was taken on the recommendation that the area be secured by the commitment of a reinforced regiment.[117]

Thus, the more than five thousand Allied paratroopers in the first wave were faced by only three German companies and elements of the 242nd Infantry Division's supply train.[118] With these few troops it was impossible to exploit the typical period of weakness immediately after every airborne landing, the time between the jump and the assembly of the units on the ground. Consequently, the airborne landing proceeded relatively unobstructed. The second wave came in with the cargo gliders at 0920 hours, while the Nineteenth Army was desperately looking for the reserves to engage this "puss boil" behind their front.[119]

At 0700 hours Wiese issued orders to release and commit infantry forces of roughly divisional strength. Those forces included troops that were originally earmarked for the defense of Marseille. But all Wiese could do was accept "a weakening of the coastal defenses . . . for the sake of establishing a point of main effort along the frontline sector that was under attack."[120] That meant he temporarily had to disregard the order to keep Marseille and Toulouse occupied with one division each.[121] The 932nd Grenadier Regiment, under Colonel Carl Bründel, and an artillery battalion from the 244th Infantry Division were sent to Brignoles. Lieutenant General von Schwerin, commanding the 189th Reserve Division, was ordered to take command of the units that had been scraped together there and mount a counterattack. Along with the troops of the 244th from the Marseille defensive perimeter, Schwerin had one battalion each from the 338th Infantry Division and the 189th Reserve Division, plus two antitank companies expected in Brignoles. He therefore would have an ad hoc force patched together from four divisions. The 11th Panzer Division also was ordered to advance immediately. Simultaneously, the 148th Reserve Division, following Wiese's plan, was to push with strong forces against the American paratroopers from the opposite direction, from the east.[122]

Even before the first units had departed for Brignoles, the Allied main landings started in a sector that essentially was defended only by the lone 765th Grenadier Regiment, part of the 242nd Infantry Division whose rear was being threatened by the paratroopers.

The U.S. 3rd Infantry Division was committed on the left, in the Alpha Sector near Cavalaire, and the U.S. 45th Infantry Division in the Delta Sector, near St. Maxime. Starting at 0800 hours both divisions landed without major problems. Just about one hour after they first stepped on French soil, the combat teams of the first wave reported that German resistance had been knocked out along the beaches and that the advance into the interior could begin immediately.

The rapid Allied successes were made possible largely by the preparatory missions flown by the air forces and the heavy naval gunfire.[123] The non-German units, such as the Armenians and Azerbaijanis deployed at Cape Nègre and near St. Tropez, had proved especially vulnerable to the tremendous psychological pressure generated by the heavy artillery barrage.[124] Those units offered hardly any resistance, and some even defected to the Allies.[125] But the fact that the coastal sectors had been defended only by a series of strongpoints was an even more decisive factor. The American troops advanced between the individual centers of resistance and then mopped them up with tank support from the landward side.[126] The fact that the antitank guns had been removed from those positions shortly before the landings caused a huge disadvantage for the defending troops, who were fighting bravely.[127]

Events in the Camel Sector on the right developed somewhat differently, resulting in heavier losses for the American troops. German antitank guns sank three out of fourteen landing craft of the lead regiment of the 36th Infantry Division as it was landing near St. Raphael.[128] But the rest of the landing in that sector went according to plan and the German coastal defenses were knocked out quickly. The 36th Infantry Division did fail to secure its objective in the Gulf of Fréjus. Starting at 1400 hours one of its regiments attempted to land there near the mouth of the Argens River. But German artillery fire thwarted the efforts to clear the mines from the landing craft channels. A renewed air strike and an even more powerful naval gunfire barrage silenced the German guns, but then the Allied leadership scrubbed the landings in that sector. That was the only success for the defenders that day, made possible by properly operating artillery.[129]

Because telecommunications had broken down for the most part, neither Army Task Group G nor OB West headquarters were adequately informed on the development of events and therefore were unable to develop a situation analysis until that afternoon.[130]

Blaskowitz's headquarters was finally able to forward a message from the Nineteenth Army to OB West at 1150 hours. The message reported the airborne drop at Le Muy and the landings on the Hyères Islands. "We do not have as yet a clear picture about the beach landings between Toulon and Cannes," the report emphasized.[131]

There was no way of telling at that time whether the observed landings constituted the *main* operation or whether additional attacks from the sea might be coming. The telephone report received by the intelligence section at OB West headquarters only reinforced the uncertainties. Accordingly, the assessment as late as 1250 hours still considered it possible that the Allied landing might merely be intended to split the boundary between the French and Italian theaters of operations and that the real invasion would still come in the Genoa area. At 1355 hours Army Task Group G reported to the OB West intelligence section that it had no further details to provide.

The reaction was an immediate order to send out all available reconnaissance elements, including motorcycle messengers and military police. As the order put it, "We must know absolutely whether this is a major landing or just a commando raid."[132]

The German leadership at that point still remained uncertain as to which way the Allies intended to go, whether their main thrust would be against southern France or against Liguria. Compounding the problem, OB West headquarters still had to worry about the area around Marseille, which was considered to be under direct threat.[133] Since Kluge was still missing somewhere around Falaise, Blumentritt therefore made the only command decision about the situation in the south that he would make on August 15. The units that had been withdrawn from Marseille to launch an attack against the airborne landings had to be replaced immediately.[134]

Similar reservations also prevented the Nineteenth Army headquarters from stripping the defensive sectors that were already thinly manned and immediately committing those forces to the fighting along the landing front.[135]

Under such conditions, especially the information vacuum and the resulting uncertainty within the German leadership, the situation Blaskowitz had projected as early as August 4 was bound to come to pass. He had expressed the fear that because of the weakness of the Nineteenth Army by that point, "a successful defense of the coast . . . could hardly be guaranteed any longer."[136] It is highly doubtful, therefore, that a rapid "offensive-defense" against the Allied invasion could have been successful, even assuming that the reserves were available.

The German leadership in the south was not even concerned with that at this point. Direct attacks against the beachheads along the coast were a secondary matter to the commanding general of the Nineteenth Army. At 1325 hours he ordered the headquarters of the LXII Army Corps to attack immediately to wipe out the paratroopers at Le Muy. In so doing he committed elements of the 242nd and 148th Infantry Divisions, as well as Battle Group Schwerin.

Only after the airborne landing had been mopped up would the Allied forces landing along the coast be attacked, with the ultimate objective of restoring the old main line of resistance.[137] If reserves were brought up quickly, Wiese figured he had at least a chance against the paratroopers, especially since their strength was estimated initially at only one battalion and because the Germans did not realize at first how quickly those paratroopers were being reinforced. (By the evening of August 15 almost nine thousand Allied airborne troops had landed.[138]) The defenders' hopes of achieving at least a partial victory depended on assembling as quickly as possible in the Brignoles area the divisional-sized Battle Group Schwerin. In the event, only one battalion from the 932nd Grenadier Regiment of the 244th Infantry Division had arrived in the area. The rest were expected during the night at the earliest.[139] The movement delays were partly the result of the destruction of the remaining, mostly smaller Rhône River bridges between the mouth of the Rhône and confluence with the Drôme River, some 120 kilometers to the north.[140] The Allied air forces had knocked out those bridges during the day, and the efforts to isolate the battle zone produced the first major success. The five German battalions that were to be assembled from the Luftwaffe IV Field Corps and the lead elements of the 11th Panzer Division were stuck along the Rhône River.[141] The commander of that force, Lieutenant General Wend von Wietersheim, estimated a delay of six to seven days before the 11th Panzer Division would be able to join the fighting on the other bank of the Rhône. It thus became clear that no really combat-effective force was available at that critical moment.[142]

Wiese abandoned the hope of quickly being able to mop up the airborne landings in the rear with the support of the units that had been summoned. The Nineteenth Army headquarters, taking the longer view of the fighting ahead, refrained from risking its sole remaining pontoon bridging equipment, which would suffice for only a single bridge.[143] Instead, ferrying operations commenced over the Rhône River, but that was a rather long and drawn-out process.[144]

In order to develop a first-hand appreciation of the unfolding situation, Blaskowitz and his chief of staff, Gyldenfeldt, started out from Rouffiac (near Toulouse) at around 1700 hours and headed toward Avignon, the headquarters of the Nineteenth Army. En route, Blaskowitz met with General of Aviation Petersen at the headquarters of the Luftwaffe IV Field Corps in Capendu (near Carcassonne), but he was unable to get any current intelligence there. During the conference, at around 2100 hours, a staff officer arrived from the Nineteenth Army headquarters who was able to brief on the course of the fighting.[145] Blaskowitz learned of the intent to press the ordered attack to contain the airborne landing first and then to "throw the enemy back into the sea."[146] That, of course, sounded a bit utopian at this point. Although the intent behind the order might have been to restrict at a minimum the enemy's freedom of movement in the important Argens River Valley and to relieve the headquarters of the LXII Army Corps encircled in Draguignan, the reality of the situation made it simply impossible.[147] Baessler, the commanding general of the 242nd Infantry Division, had been given the assignment of coordinating the operation in place of General Neuling. Baessler subsequently learned that the Allied paratroopers had been reinforced to a strength of three regiments.[148] That was another reason why the ordered attack was not feasible on August 15. Only two battalions had been able to assemble near Brignoles just before midnight, which meant there could be no hope of the attack accomplishing its assigned objectives of annihilating the enemy airborne forces and then following through with a breakthrough to St. Raphael.[149]

The first day of Operation DRAGOON thus ended as a complete success for the Allies. A total of 60,150 troops and 6,737 vehicles were put ashore in the three beach sectors. The spearheads of the American divisions had been able to thrust as far as sixteen kilometers into the interior, pushing past isolated strongpoints, some of which, like those at Fréjus and St. Raphael, were still resisting stubbornly. There had been no full-fledged battles for the beachheads, as there had been at Normandy. The lead elements of the U.S. 3rd and 45th Infantry Divisions had linked up by 2100 hours.

The Nineteenth Army headquarters assumed that the Americans' initial objectives would be to link up with the paratroopers by thrusting north and northwest and to seize the approaches to the Maures Massif.[150] (See Map 5.)

At OB West headquarters Blumentritt was briefed in the afternoon by the Nineteenth Army about the unfavorable developments along the Mediterranean Front.[151] He realized clearly that the situation was bound to become critical very soon if the Germans could not win the defensive fight there. Along with Marseille and Toulon, the Rhône River Valley offered the Allies the best operational-level opportunities. If they managed to interdict the valley, then the Nineteenth Army's supply lines and the only possible route of retreat would be cut off. Under such circumstances Blumentritt concluded that the overall cohesion of the Western Front would be threatened.[152] But because of the simultaneously critical situation facing Army Group B, OB West, or, rather Blumentritt, was unable to offer Blaskowitz any kind of tangible support. The catastrophic telecommunications outages also made it impossible to provide command and control support. The only viable course of action was to rely on "the independence of Army Task Group G."[153]

Although Blumentritt's attention that day was concentrated mostly in the north, the sporadic and rather somber news from the southern coast led him at 1830 hours to ask Jodl to finally "make the big decision."[154] But making that decision was impossible because of Hitler. The führer did, however, consider the potentially disastrous situation facing the Nineteenth Army, and that day he issued guidelines that contained the essential outline of a withdrawal from southern and southwestern France.[155] But these contingencies could not yet be translated into orders. Hitler believed that the right moment had not yet come for any withdrawals in the west because he still hoped that the situation in Army Group B could be stabilized.

(b) Development of the Fighting in the Coastal Area until the Receipt of Hitler's First Withdrawal Order

The situation in the coastal area deteriorated further by the time Blaskowitz arrived early on the morning of August 16 at the Nineteenth Army headquarters in Avignon to meet with Generals Wiese and Botsch.[156] Signal communications with the LXII Army Corps had been cut during the night. According to the last messages, General Neuling and his staff had established a defensive perimeter around his command post after destroying their classified materials.[157] If the German relief attack did not succeed, then it was only a question of time before the Allied paratroopers would overrun Neuling's headquarters.[158] In the meantime, Schwerin's prospects for mounting a successful attack had not improved. Most of the units that had been ordered to move up, six battalions minus the 11th Panzer Division, were still stuck along the Rhône River.[159] Despite feverish efforts, ferrying operations had not yet been established. In the opinion of Wiese's chief of staff, Botsch, the reinforcements could not reach their designated assembly areas before noon.[160]

Looking at the overall situation, Blaskowitz and Wiese agreed that the most important thing was to gain the time necessary to move up German forces, especially the 11th Panzer Division.[161] But at best the available resources were only tactical expedients. The immediate task was now for Schwerin to try without further delay to fight his way through to Draguignan and extract the headquarters of the LXII Army Corps. German units also had to seal off the key roads leading from the coastal areas to the north and northwest. The two German commanders hoped that with those measures they could at least temporarily limit the Allied advance.

Blaskowitz and the Nineteenth Army headquarters had been thinking along similar tactical lines for some time. Early in 1944, when the strength situation of Army Task Group G was roughly comparable to what it was in August, the chiefs of staff of the First and Nineteenth Armies—Lieutenant General Walter Feyerabend and Lieutenant General Walter Botsch—realized that any major enemy landing attempt on either coast was bound to be successful, and they worked out a set of basic principles for the conduct of defensive operations.[162] The key assumption was that the engaged commanders and units would have the nerve to wait for the motorized units to assemble before launching the deliberate counterattack. The necessary time would be gained first by fighting along the coast, following up with a hasty counterattack using local reserves, and finally fixing the enemy ashore along a line advantageous to the defenders, thereby facilitating the complete deployment of the OB West reserves behind that line. The actual course of events had not produced any surprises to that point, but in the final analysis the OB West reserves on which the defensive plans were based were not available. Blaskowitz and Wiese were faced with the immediate question of whether or not a blocking position could be established at all, and then whether it could hold long enough for the 11th Panzer Division to arrive. Then at that point they had to decide whether or not it was still worth risking a frontal attack, especially since the Allies were continuing to build in strength. The 11th Panzer Division was the only unit in the Nineteenth Army capable of putting up any kind of a good fight, but the efforts to establish the blocking positions had already run into serious difficulties. Schwerin's attack jumped off at 0630 hours with only two battalions supported by a single artillery battalion.[163] It made good progress initially, but then it ran into stronger resistance at Le Luc and was finally defeated after additional airborne troops dropped squarely into the middle of the attacking German units.[164] The Allies' total command of the air contributed to the counterattack's failure, as unopposed Allied fighter-bombers dove with full force into the German formations.[165] As a consequence of the counterattack's failure, General Neuling and his headquarters were unable to extract themselves from their dangerous position and German forces were unable to close up the front by linking up with the 148th Infantry Division at Draguignan. With no more German forces available for counterattacks in the area, Fretter-Pico was ordered to try to get to Draguignan with his 148th Infantry Division alone, and especially to block the road leading from there to Digne to prevent the Allies from having a clear route to the north.[166] In the meantime, the relatively weak alerted units of the 242nd Infantry Division had already been pushed from the crossing points over the Maures Massif. Wiese now hoped to be able to establish a blocking line located farther to the northwest, between the positions at Toulon and the Draguignan area. But as of noon the forces earmarked for that effort were still not available because of the time-consuming crossing operations over the Rhône River.[167] Wiese then decided out of necessity to weaken further the defensive perimeter around Marseille and to commit another regiment of the 244th Infantry Division—the 933rd Grenadier Regiment. Wiese's decision was made easier for him by an estimate of the enemy situation issued by the Nineteenth Army headquarters, which concluded that there was no longer any probability of another Allied landing, especially in the Marseille area.[168]

Meanwhile, the situation along the Rhône River deteriorated drastically. Units waiting to cross were caught in major traffic jams that developed during the day at the three ferry sites at Arles, Vallbregues (north of Tarascon), and Avignon. The bridge at Roquemaure (north of Avignon) also was back in operation for light equipment. As soon as the ferry operations started during the early morning hours they came under constant air attack, as the Allied air forces concentrated their efforts over the Rhône River delta on August 16.[169] The attacks from the fighter-bombers launched from aircraft carriers offshore were so devastating that the Germans were forced to suspend completely the river crossing operations.[170] As that was happening, the follow-on units assembled along the fifty-kilometer section of the Rhône between Arles and Roquemaure. Those units included the 11th Panzer Division, one regiment of the 198th Infantry Division, one regiment of the 338th Infantry Division, the 669th Army Engineer Battalion, and a battalion each from the 189th and the 338th Infantry Divisions.[171] Once assembled, that force made up the strongest concentration in a long time of German troops in southern France, the equivalent of almost three divisions. But a force of that size was entirely too much for the capacities of the ferries. Army Task Group G headquarters itself was caught in one of the developing traffic jams that morning.[172] The headquarters had to suspend its move to Pierrelatte because the ferry for Avignon was completely busy putting units of the 11th Panzer Division across.[173] The crossing operations, however, were too slow, and as a result the reserves that were being moved up could only be fed into the battle in driblets. Blaskowitz reported to OB West: "[My] command is doing everything possible[174] to get forces . . . across the Rhône River. At this point in time this is the *decisive factor* for the entire course of combat operations."[175]

By the evening of August 16 only the one regiment of the 338th Infantry Division had reached the east bank. Most of the other units were scheduled to cross that night. In the meantime the Allies continued to build up their bridgehead relatively unopposed and tackle the job of eliminating some of the isolated German defensive points that were still holding out. The Nineteenth Army headquarters assumed that the enemy beachhead between Cape Nègre and St. Raphael had been consolidated. Based on the follow-on landing waves the Germans had observed, they estimated the strength of the invasion forces to be already four divisions, including armored units and one airborne unit.[176] Indeed, the first combat teams of the French II Corps under General de Lattre de Tassigny had landed on that day.[177] The French II Corps had the mission of liberating Marseille and Toulon.

Blaskowitz, in a situation estimate prepared for OB West, clearly identified this initial operational objective of the Allies. But he could not project whether or not the Allies intended to continue the operation in the direction toward the Rhône River Valley after cutting off the major ports. The other course of action he considered possible, and which was now considered for the first time, was an advance via Digne directly to the north toward Grenoble. Presumably Blaskowitz had been alerted to this possibility by the airborne landings at Draguignan, combined with the fact that the establishment of a blocking position was still completely up in the air in that area along the boundary between the 242nd and 148th Infantry Divisions.[178] Blaskowitz believed that the Digne–Grenoble option would give the Allies the advantage of establishing contact with the strong guerrilla forces in the region of the Western Alps. Even more important would be the opportunity for the Allies to enter the middle Rhône Valley unopposed by quickly pushing to the west. Without exactly saying so, Blaskowitz had already postulated a "bypassing pursuit" that could turn into a lethal threat to the Nineteenth Army.

On August 16, decisions were made in Rastenburg that were most likely inconceivable to the German leadership in southern France. Apparently at Blumentritt's urging, Jodl once again approached Hitler with the request for a "new directive for combat operations."[179] But even now the führer did not make a conclusive decision. If at all, he would only consider authorizing a retreat by Army Task Group G in two distinctly separated phases.[180] The immediate result of this half-measure approach was an order issued on the same day by the chief of staff of the Wehrmacht High Command, Field Marshal Wilhelm Keitel, directing all German soldiers and members of other organizations in the sector of Army Task Group G west of the Orléans–Clermont-Ferrand–Montpellier line to move immediately behind the Seine–Yonne–Bourgogne line. As might be expected, the units holding down the fortresses and the defensive perimeters along the Atlantic were expressly excluded from that order. The Nineteenth Army was to commit the forces thus released west of Montpellier "to clear up the situation in the Toulon area."[181] In addition to the evacuation of southwestern France, the obvious objective of this order was to set the conditions to continue the fight for the Mediterranean coast, which simultaneously would continue to provide cover for the rear of the Italian Front, which the Wehrmacht High Command continued to believe to be particularly vulnerable.[182] The new order was full of inconsistencies and Blaskowitz did not even receive it until the evening of August 17, about twenty-four hours after it was issued.[183] Stripping the southwestern French coast to commit those forces in the battle zone was a basically correct action, of course, but it only made sense if there was any possibility of improving the situation. But that was impossible under the existing circumstances.[184] Another inconsistency was the selection of the Orléans–Clermont-Ferrand–Montpellier line, which had almost none of the features necessary to establish a stable front line and seemed to have been drawn rather arbitrarily on the map.[185] The line had not been prepared or developed on the ground in any way, and it ran straight through one of the regional partisan centers, the Massif Central.

Major General Karl Zimmermann, the General Staff Officer Ia (operations officer) at OB West, later noted that the order was further evidence that "the supreme command was not at all calculating in terms of time, strength, and space."[186]

Blaskowitz and his staff, however, tried to make the best of it. With the words, "We cannot wait for any further measures from OB West—we have to act," Blumentritt gave them free rein to do so.[187] But Blaskowitz didn't realize that the LXIV Army Corps withdrawal plan that was drafted based on that guidance and then developed into specific orders was already overcome by events. A day and a half earlier Hitler had made another decision, a more comprehensive one this time. But that word had not yet reached Army Task Group G.

(c) The Final Retreat Order for Army Task Group G and Its Problems

The crucial reason for the führer's sudden change of mind was the dramatic way in which the situation had deteriorated in northern France. According to the latest reports from the Mediterranean coast, the Allied main effort was aimed at the major ports and the Rhône Valley, which meant that the rear of the Italian Front did not seem now to be a primary objective.[188] Therefore, the contingencies that Hitler himself had formulated more than two weeks earlier could now be put into action.

On August 16, just a few hours after Keitel approved the evacuation of southwestern France, Hitler signed the withdrawal order for the Nineteenth Army, which was then heavily committed to combat operations.[189] Army Task Group G headquarters received that order with a sense of relief.[190] The essential elements of the order stated: "Because the development of the situation in Army Group B makes it appear possible that the Nineteenth Army . . . might be cut off, I hereby order . . . Army Task Group G to disengage . . . from the enemy and to link up with the southern wing of Army Group B."[191]

Approval of the withdrawal even caused astonishment at the Nineteenth Army headquarters in Avignon, because any talk of pulling back had until then been forbidden.[192] The Nineteenth Army staff had already come to terms with the concept that their field army would be sacrificed in southern France, because of the repeated and stereotypical directives from the High Command insisting that the coast had to be defended.[193] There was still a possibility, however, that Hitler had tied his withdrawal approval in with a series of specific provisos that extended down into the tactical area, but which were no longer realistic because of the actual situation on the ground.

The basic question was whether or not Army Task Group G would be able to reach the Sens–Dijon–Swiss border covering position by the designated time and then whether it could link up with Army Group B. All of that depended to a major extent on the speed with which this large withdrawal operation could be carried out. The course of the combat operations on the weak southern wing of Army Group B would probably play the decisive role, primarily depending on the objectives and the combat capabilities of the U.S. Third Army. Blaskowitz, however, had no real way of influencing that operation. If there was any possibility of reestablishing a cohesive new line on the Western Front, then Army Task Group G had to move with utmost haste. But Hitler also insisted that it could not just simply pull back, it also had to leave a broad swath of destruction behind. "No locomotive, no bridge, no power plant, no repair shop must fall undestroyed into enemy hands," he ordered.[194] That unrealistic order, which completely misread the situation of Army Task Group G's available time and strength, was later made even more impractical with the addition of a requirement from Jodl that all the local inhabitants of military age were to be taken along during the withdrawal movement.[195]

No less problematic for the German leadership in southern France, but hardly surprising considering the source, was Hitler's additional requirement that fortresses and defensive perimeters along the western and southern coasts were to be defended to the last man, specifically, "Marseille and Toulon by one division each."[196] The already weak Nineteenth Army, for better or worse, had to supply the forces necessary for that task. The chances of success looked slim at best even at the very point when Hitler signed the order. There was every indication that the landward defenses around the ports would be the main objectives of the Allies. But the Germans had not yet finished developing the defenses in those sectors. The shortage of mines and explosives made it impossible to establish either the planned fifteen-kilometer-wide destruction zone along the approaches to the defense perimeters or the mine belts and other barriers necessary for the "airtight" Panzer screen that Hitler ordered.[197]

Hitler's withdrawal order repeated down to the very last detail the basic principles that had been established during the July 31 conference. Even at the time, Hitler conceded that a decision would have to be made "simply to sacrifice certain troops" in order to deny the enemy the use of the harbors, thereby buying the time for the German maneuvers. The supporting scorched-earth action especially was to be conducted ruthlessly.[198] Gaining time to be able to continue the fighting in the west was certainly necessary. But most of the necessary actions had been initiated too late, and it therefore was doubtful whether it was still possible to achieve the objective. The measures set in motion, in fact, might somehow turn out to be counterproductive. The risk was that two divisions would be pinned down in Marseille and Toulon and would thus be sacrificed, even though they could hardly accomplish their assigned missions because of the deficient fortifications protecting the harbors.

The general conditions for a withdrawal from southern France that were laid down for Jodl at the end of July also required the continued occupation of the French-Italian border. Consequently, and probably as a result of the intervention of Field Marshal Kesselring in Italy, the withdrawal order included the stipulation that the LXII Army Corps with the 148th and 157th Infantry Divisions would be placed under the command of OB Südwest and would then withdraw into the Alpine passes under enemy pressure.[199] It was precisely that proviso which clearly revealed that the order was not based on an analysis of the current situation, but rather was founded on ideas that were two weeks old and outdated. The order considered neither the fact that the airborne landings had severed all contact with the LXII Army Corps headquarters near Draguignan, nor that there might be an enemy offensive aiming directly north from that area, as Blaskowitz earlier had projected.

If OB Südwest were to withdraw both divisions into the Alpine passes too soon, then the Allies would have a clear path to Grenoble via Digne.[200] In other words, Army Task Group G lost not only two divisions, but that loss also opened up an operational-level threat to the German withdrawal from the Rhône Valley.

The worries of the German High Command about the Italian Front were by no means unjustified, but those concerns did have a negative effect on the German units in southern France. Zimmermann, the operations officer at OB West, described Hitler's order as ". . . illogical because it primarily weakened the fighting field army."[201]

Every hour counted in a withdrawal operation of that scope, but valuable time was lost during the transmission of the order. Signed by Hitler on August 16, its contents were known to OB West headquarters and Army Group B headquarters the next morning.[202] But Blaskowitz in Avignon did not get the order until the morning of August 18, after approximately another twenty-four hours.[203] And even then the Nineteenth Army did not receive permission to start withdrawing until that afternoon—forty-eight hours after Hitler signed the order.[204]

Army Task Group G tried but utterly failed to inform the headquarters of the LXIV Army Corps along the Atlantic coast of the order.[205] With all radio and telephone contact out, the attempt finally was made to transmit the order by motor messenger.[206]

Blaskowitz's terse observation that "the modern command style was impossible" hit the nail on the head.[207] The tremendous delays, combined with the order's vital importance, were bound to result in grave consequences at the operational level. This was especially true considering that the Allies' ULTRA intelligence gave them an accurate picture of the German intentions. The critical retreat order was decoded by the afternoon of August 18 and transmitted with top priority to the various Allied field headquarters.[208] That made it possible for the Allies to launch encircling maneuvers in pursuit before the German leadership on the ground was in any kind of position to react.

Now even Hitler realized that all the signs since August 16 indicated a rout in the west. Kluge, who had surfaced again, demanded with ever greater urgency the necessity of withdrawing Army Group B.[209] Kluge finally shouted in exasperation, "There can no longer be any talk of an attack by Panzer Group Eberbach." The High Command could order whatever they wanted to, but the available forces "simply could no longer do the job."[210]

Only now did Hitler start to back off from his original notion that the situation in Army Group B could be stabilized by launching offensive thrusts. In the afternoon he finally gave the permission for the start of the withdrawal in the north.[211]

Hitler now could no longer ignore the other requirements tied to the withdrawal. The start of Army Group B's retrograde motion had to be coordinated in time and space with the withdrawal movement from the south. That was an absolute requirement. Synchronizing the two withdrawals offered the only hope of ever reestablishing a contiguous front line in the west.

The shift to a new phase of combat operations in the west, long overdue and now finally accepted by the High Command, also resulted in a command personnel change, as the Eastern Front defensive expert Model was appointed as Kluge's successor.

From left to right, Colonel General Johannes Blaskowitz, Field Marshal Erwin Rommel, and Field Marshal Gerd von Rundstedt during a conference in Paris in May 1944. (Bild 101I-719-0247-17A/Jesse)

General of Infantry Günther Blumentritt, September 1944. (Bild
101I-717-0010-03/Wörner)

From left to right, SS-Obergruppenführer and General of the Waffen-SS Sepp
Dietrich, Major General Hans von Obstfelder, and General of Panzer Troops
Heinrich Eberbach during a conference following the Allied landings in June
1944. (Bild 101I-721-0370-15A/Jesse)

Colonel Rudolf Christoph Freiherr von Gersdorff, August 26, 1944. (Bild 146-1976-130-51)

General of Artillery Alfred Jodl, Chief of the Wehrmacht Operations Staff. (Bild 146-1971-033-01)

Field Marshal Hans-Günther von Kluge speaking to a group of officers at La Roche-Guyon, June 1944. (09-Bild 101I-721-0352-33A/Grimm)

Lieutenant General Hans Krebs, March 1944. (Bild 146-1978-111-10A)

Field Marshal Walter Model with members of the Hitler Youth in Monschau, September 1944. (Bild 183-J28036/Jäger)

From left to right, Lieutenant General Hans Speidel, Captain Lang, and Field Marshal Erwin Rommel during an inspection of the Atlantic Wall in the Pas de Calais, April 18, 1944. (14-Bild 101I-719-0240-22/Jesse)

General of Infantry Dietrich von Choltitz, Wehrmacht commander of Greater Paris. (Bild 183-E1210-0201-018)

French civilian forced labor digging an antitank ditch in September 1944. (Bild 101I-590-2332-26/Arppe)

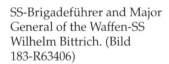

SS-Brigadeführer and Major General of the Waffen-SS Wilhelm Bittrich. (Bild 183-R63406)

General of Panzer Troops Heinrich Eberbach, commander of the Fifth Panzer Army, following his capture by British troops on August 31, 1944. (Bild 146-1987-120-20A)

Field Marshal Wilhelm Keitel (front left) and Adolf Hitler with a group of National Socialist political officers at Hitler's *"Wolfsschanze"* headquarters, August 1944. (Bild 183-R98380/Hoffmann)

Field Marshal Hugo Sperrle (center), commander of the Luftwaffe Third Air Fleet, during a situation briefing in France, summer 1944. (24-Bild 101I-493-3368-01A/Güntzel)

Lieutenant General Hasso von Manteuffel in his command tank, August 1944. (Bild 146-1979-035-19/Broenner)

Left to right, Major General Hermann Ramcke and General of Parachute Troops Kurt Student. (Bild 146-1979-128-26)

A Horsa glider of the British 1st Airborne Division burning on the ground after the landings near Arnhem in September 1944. (Bild 183-J27850)

Following the liberation of Paris, French women who collaborated with the German occupiers were shaved and paraded through the streets of the city. (Bild 146-1971-041-10)

A heavy infantry support gun in the Hürtgen Forest, November 22, 1944. (Bild 183-J28303/Jäger)

German civilians working on the West Wall defenses in the autumn of 1944.
(Bild 101I-497-3519-30/Röder)

Chapter 5

The Initial Situation in Northern France

1. Change of Command: Model in the West—August 17

Model initially resisted his reassignment to France. On the evening of August 16 he received briefings at Rastenburg on the situation and the possible future developments in the West.[1]

In the meantime, Kluge, who had reestablished communications from the command post of the Fifth Panzer Army, was working with his two operations staffs—OB West and Army Group B—and with Jodl to deal with the problems of the withdrawal from the encirclement at Falaise.[2] Even before Hitler's written withdrawal approval arrived, Kluge had Lieutenant General Hans Speidel, the chief of staff of Army Group B, draft orders for the retrograde movements of the Seventh Army and Fifth Panzer Army.[3] Kluge put those orders into effect.[4] Apart from that, Kluge's last actions as OB West dealt with the situation in Paris, as the area of combat operations was now in the immediate vicinity of the French metropolis.[5]

The various German headquarters based in and around Paris were now under heavy threat. General Blumentritt had already issued a threat alert on August 15, a day that was full of crisis situations and frantic message traffic. In his request for the authorization to transfer the various command posts, he stressed that if the situation deteriorated rapidly, the entire command and control structure in the OB West area of operations might be lost.[6] Unfortunately, OB West himself deferred to Hitler's decision on that problem, which in turn hobbled the leadership of the German Army in the West. It was not the last time that would happen. After receiving approval from the Wehrmacht High Command, Kluge ordered the displacement during the night of August 16 to 17 of the OB West command post from St. Germain to Verzy, with the forward command post at Metz.[7] Army Group B was supposed to move its headquarters from Margival, near Soissons, into the "Wolf's Gorge II" command post, which had been built as a headquarters for Hitler but was never used except once, on June 17, 1944.[8] The Wehrmacht High Command, however, held back on releasing the installation, preventing Army Group B headquarters from moving.[9]

These facts show that apart from Kluge's noticeable feelings of resignation, he was no longer functioning as the independently acting commanding general in the west during the last few days prior to his relief. The personality of his designated successor would be the main factor in determining whether the loss of the significance of OB West's position in the military command structure could be reversed after the command change.

On August 17, Model arrived at Army Group B headquarters in La Roche-Guyon to assume supreme command in the west.[10] Up to that point, Kluge had not even been informed that his relief decision had been made almost two days earlier. Model gave Kluge a handwritten letter from Hitler notifying Kluge that ". . . as a result of his state of health [he] was no longer able to meet the requirements arising from the heavy burden of command in recent weeks," and he therefore was transferred to the Führer Reserve.[11]

Kluge's replacement by Model did have some parallels to Rundstedt's dismissal a month and a half earlier. But after his relief Rundstedt remained in Hitler's good graces, and in September 1944 he was once again recalled to serve as OB West. The events leading up to Kluge's dismissal, combined with the ominous final sentence in Hitler's handwritten letter, directing that "Field Marshal von Kluge must indicate to which part of Germany he intends to go," led Kluge to realize that the degree of suspicion against him had solidified.[12] There seemed to be a definite linkage between the new phase in operational command which began as Model took over, the organization of the withdrawal movement in the west, and Kluge's personal catastrophe. Fully aware that the crisis of the German Army in the West would be blamed on his failure, and only guessing what was in store for him,[13] Kluge committed suicide on the way back to Germany on August 19.[14]

Model came to France with preconceived notions, much as his predecessor had.[15] Even before he was able to assess the situation personally by visiting the front, Model told his two chiefs of staff, Blumentritt and Speidel,[16] that in his opinion too little had been done in the west. His intention was "to clean up the mess and to keep a tight rein."[17] The commanding general of the Panzer-Lehr Division, Lieutenant General Fritz Bayerlein, got a taste of that when he went to Army Group B headquarters to coordinate pulling his division out of the line for reconstitution, which had been approved already. Bayerlein ran into Model, who curtly remarked; "In the east the divisions are refitted at the front, and that's the way it's going to be here in the future also. You stay where you are."[18]

Model's initial actions during his first few hours as OB West can probably be explained by a combination of three factors. Like his predecessor, Model had most recently commanded on the Eastern Front and had earned his military reputation there by turning around apparently hopeless situations. Presumably he had not yet gotten a firsthand look at the combat conditions in the west, which were entirely different than in the east. He therefore did not initially assess correctly the seriousness of the situation. Like Kluge before him, Model was still caught in a kind of east-west prejudice frame of mind that resulted in a reciprocal underestimation of Eastern Front or Western Front commanders and their opponents. His initial statements show that the rather fleeting situation briefing he had received at the Führer Headquarters did little to change his attitude.[19]

On the evening of August 16 the command personnel situation resulting from Kluge's pending dismissal probably overshadowed any questions of substance in Rastenburg, and Model therefore was insufficiently briefed on what was actually awaiting him.[20]

The third factor was a characteristic in Model's leadership style, which has been reported by various sources. The new commander-in-chief had the rather odd habit of frequently assuming a sarcastic and sometimes even offensive tone, especially in talking to generals and staff officers.[21] He typically demanded the impossible as a means of attaining the maximum effort.[22]

2. OB West's Mission and Army Group B's Situation

The mission assigned to Model at the Führer Headquarters was to establish in conjunction with Army Task Group G a new front line "as far as possible away from the Seine–Yonne line."[23] Although Hitler considered Model the potential savior of the Western Front, the führer must have known that even Model could hardly accomplish that mission.

On July 31 the führer, in an effort to deflect Jodl's constant urging for a voluntary withdrawal, dismissed as "completely hopeless" the option of establishing a defense along a rearward line, no matter which way it ran. But if it did become absolutely necessary to withdraw, then Hitler thought at that time that the Seine line might possibly serve as an intermediate expedient.[24] Hitler believed that a stable defensive line could only be established along the Somme–Marne–Saône line.

In fact, the conditions that Hitler himself had considered necessary for an unpressured withdrawal simply did not exist. The measures that were supposed to facilitate such a move for the German command, such as blocking the harbors, had not yet been carried out. In any event, the Allies did not seem to be held up in any way. Quite the contrary, their advance had picked up speed.

The most critical factor, however, was the fact that despite the comments he had made on July 31, Hitler immediately after the start of the crisis neglected or perhaps even deliberately refused to withdraw Army Task Group G to central France to establish a new front line. The crisis began with the Allied breakthrough at Avranches. Based on the all-or-nothing principle, to which OB West had acquiesced for far too long, the führer insisted on bringing the situation of Army Group B under control by launching offensive thrusts, and he therefore kept Army Task Group G in position in the south. But two weeks had gone by in the meantime. Now it was no longer possible to move Army Task Group G quickly because the main body of Blaskowitz's units, the Nineteenth Army, had become engaged in battle.

Despite these facts, Model was fixed on holding an initially untenable line, a problem he would be confronted with continually. Hitler continued to stick to his basic principle that "OB West need not know any more than he needs to know."[25] Above all, he expected Model to buck up the morale and cohesion of the German Army in the West. That was something the field marshal was known for, with his tireless personal commitment. He therefore was supposed to gain the time so urgently needed for the "subsequent reorganization in the west."[26]

What then was the situation Model found in Army Group B? Only the Channel coast sector had been spared combat operations up until that point. Deployed in that sector were the units of the Fifteenth Army, under Colonel General Hans von Salmuth, as well as units under the Wehrmacht Commander of the Netherlands, General of Aviation Friedrich Christiansen. The Fifteenth Army headquarters controlled the area between the Seine and the mouth of the

Scheldt River. Along with the Pas de Calais, that sector comprised the part of the coast that originally had been considered the most vulnerable prior to the Allied landings.

Well prior to the June 6 landings the Allies had launched FORTITUDE, a large-scale and sustained deception operation designed to lead the Germans to believe that a 1st U.S. Army Group (FUSAG) under the command of Patton was preparing to attack in the direction of Pas de Calais.[27] Those deception measures only reinforced the convictions held by the German leadership prior to the invasion. OB West, therefore, was afraid of a second but decisive main thrust at the Pas de Calais. Only after several of the units that were supposed to be assigned to Patton's fictitious army group were identified in Normandy did Kluge conclude that a large-scale landing on the Channel coast was no longer as likely.[28] Starting in early August, units withdrawn from the Fifteenth Army were redeployed to the front.[29] By the time Model took command, Salmuth still had eight infantry divisions.[30] The rest of his previous units were already either in the combat zone or en route to the front.[31]

Although the assessment of the Allied intentions had changed, the Fifteenth Army's primary mission of securing the Channel coast remained in effect until the end of August 1944.[32] In support of that mission it even received the remaining two new divisions that recently had been raised in the Reich. Earmarked for the Western Front, those units were part of the Wehrmacht's twenty-seventh unit activation cycle.[33]

The reason for the continuing focus on the Channel coast was the Wehrmacht operations staff's belief that the security of the deep northern flank and the launching sites of the long-range V-weapons systems remained a priority mission.[34] Because Allied airborne units had not been seen in action for quite some time, the Germans figured that while a second major landing might not be coming, there was still the risk of a limited objective operation along the Channel, possibly to knock out the V-1 launch bases.[35]

Thus the basic assessment expressed in *Führer Directive 51* anticipating an Allied invasion in the area of the V-1 launch bases remained in effect through the middle of August, although in a somewhat modified form. The focus, however, had changed somewhat. The original assumption was that the long-range rocket bases would serve as bait and that the anticipated landings could then be pulled into the sector of the Fifteenth Army. By the middle of

August the vengeance weapons launch campaign had been in progress for two months, which in turn tied down the German divisions along the Channel coast to protect those weapons systems. That, of course, meant those forces were not available for the main fight on the Western Front.

But up through mid-August the V-1 firings had produced no positive effect whatsoever for the German military situation. The primary objective of the V-1 campaign, initially limited only to the London area, was to "bomb the population to the point where it would be ready for peace." But that unrealistic objective remained an illusion, even with daily launchings of one hundred rockets.[36] In retrospect, there was no longer any justification to keep the Fifteenth Army committed to its mission.[37]

From Hitler's perspective, however, the major units of the Fifteenth Army had to stay in place along the Channel coast for another reason. Dunkirk, Boulogne, and Le Havre were three ports with capacities comparable only with Cherbourg and Brest in the north, and with Bordeaux and Marseille in southern France. Those three ports were in Salmuth's command area of responsibility. The Allies had already taken Cherbourg, and the Germans therefore were now all the more focused on denying the enemy the other key logistical nodes.[38] Salmuth was forced to tie a portion of his units down to occupy those three major ports, which meant of course that those units were not available for commitment elsewhere.[39]

When Field Marshal Model assumed supreme command in the west he had ten divisions under four corps headquarters available in the northern sector of Army Group B.[40]

In the sector of Wehrmacht Commander, Netherlands: the LXXXVIII Army Corps, with the 347th and 719th Infantry Divisions.

In the sector of the Fifteenth Army: the LXVII, LXXXII, and LXXXIX Army Corps, with the 47th, 70th, 136th (Special Missions), 182nd, 226th, 245th, 348th, and 712th Infantry Divisions. The 59th and 64th Infantry Divisions were still moving up.

By the end of August the Fifteenth Army's supplemental mission had become one of serving as a troop pool for the Battle of Normandy. But it also was becoming obvious that the Fifteenth Army in the future would be able to accomplish that mission only to a limited degree. Along the actual battlefront of Army Group B, three field army headquarters were deployed—Fifth Panzer and the Seventh and First Armies—which nominally commanded forty-four divisions under a total of ten corps. Upon his arrival Model found the following order of battle:

The First, Fifth Panzer, and Seventh Armies commanded the XXV, LXXIV, LXXXI, LXXXIV, and LXXXVI Army Corps, and the I SS, II SS, XLVII, LVIII Panzer Corps, and the II Parachute Corps. The LXVI and LXXX Army Corps came under the German Military Commander in France for the purpose of establishing the Kitzinger Line.

Model's ten corps controlled the 48th, 49th, 77th, 84th, 85th, 89th, 243rd, 265th, 266th, 271st, 272nd, 275th, 276th, 277th, 319th, 326th, 331st, 338th (main body with Army Task Group G), 343rd, 344th, 346th, 352nd, 353rd, 363rd, 708th, and 711th Infantry Divisions; 91st Air Landing Division; Luftwaffe 17th and 18th Field Divisions; 2nd, 3rd, 5th, and 6th Parachute Divisions; 1st, 2nd, 9th, 10th, and 12th SS Panzer Divisions; 2nd, 9th, 21st, 116th Panzer Divisions, the Panzer-Lehr Division; and the 17th SS Panzer Grenadier Division.

The divisions moving up included the 26th and 27th SS Panzer Divisions, both of which were only brigade strength and were later on put under the operational control of the 17th SS Panzer Grenadier Division. Also moving up were the 3rd and 15th Panzer Grenadier Divisions from Italy. The 29th and 30th Waffen-SS Grenadier Divisions (Russian Divisions Nos. 1 and 2) were also en route but were not committed because of their unreliability.

Many of those major formations, however, had already been heavily battered and then had only been inadequately reconstituted for personnel and equipment, giving Model units far below authorized combat strength to begin with.

A look at the front situation map illustrates the precariousness of the German position.[41] Adjacent to the Fifteenth Army along the boundary of the Seine River in a southwesterly direction was the sector of the Fifth Panzer Army, under SS-Oberstgruppenführer and Colonel General of the Waffen-SS Joseph "Sepp" Dietrich. The frontline trace of the Fifth Panzer Army ran from the Channel coast near Cabourg along the course of the Dives River, roughly south for a distance of forty-five kilometers. Adjacent to that sector, which was held by the LXXXVI Army Corps under General of Infantry Hans von Obstfelder, and along the boundary with the I SS Panzer Corps, a bulge in the front line extended far to the west across the Orne River. That salient, which was being squeezed concentrically by Allied forces, held the bulk of Dietrich's major forces in the north, and in the south the entire Seventh Army, under SS-Oberstgruppenführer and Colonel General of the Waffen-SS Paul Hausser.[42] That was the dangerous situation in the center of the Army Group B that Hitler and even Kluge had for entirely too long assumed could be stabilized, with the front line restored all the way to the coast by launching a Panzer thrust from the left wing of the Seventh Army. That was the main reason Panzer Group Eberbach had been formed on August 10. Such a Panzer thrust would at the same time cut off from their rear communications those American units that had already penetrated into the interior of France. But to secure the staging areas necessary for such an operation, the major units of the Seventh Army and Panzer Group Eberbach had to be kept in what amounted to a rather exposed position to the west. In the meantime, however, the left [southern] wing of the Seventh Army had been pushed back to the east and was finally pressed so far to the north that an encirclement seemed to be developing from what at that point was still a wide-open arc of Allied forces. The situation deteriorated further by August 17. The major offensive by the Canadian First Army, which had been under way for several days now, punched through the northern front of the arc, while at the same time major U.S. forces achieved individual penetrations of the German line at Domfront and Argentan. The points of the Allied spearheads were now only a few kilometers apart, and the withdrawal of the German forces that had been approved just a short time before was now hardly feasible.

Model was no longer able to do much for his major units that were being squeezed into a pocket only twenty to thirty kilometers in diameter. The critical task at that point was to execute in the shortest possible time the retreat movements that had been ordered by his predecessor. The new line that Kluge had been trying to establish ran Channel coast–Dives sector–Morteaux–Couliboeuf–Trun–Gacé–L'Aigle, under the command of the Seventh Army, and from there L'Aigle–Paris west under the Fifth Panzer Army.[43] But by the evening of August 17 that line had already been crossed by the Canadians. They also broke through several places along the front line of the LXXXVI Army Corps, which was holding the front from the coast to the pocket, in the process pushing the German units across the Dives sector to the east.[44]

Model was now facing a catastrophe. Elements of fourteen divisions, totaling around one hundred thousand troops and including the headquarters of four army corps and two field armies, were trapped in the center of Army Group B, making them unavailable for commitment elsewhere.[45] (See Map 6.)

Army Group B's situation was dire, and not only because of the Falaise Pocket. At the same time a new and serious Allied main effort was forming in the south in the vast area between the Pocket and the Loire River. The Americans had committed nine divisions between the Dreux–L'Aigle line and the Loire River.[46] Lieutenant General Alfred Gause, the chief of staff of the Fifth Panzer Army, identified the Allied offensive intentions in that area during a telephone report to Speidel. Based on information from captured maps, one American armored division was supposed to reach the area of Dreux–Evreux, which was fifty to seventy kilometers northwest of Paris.[47] At that time, the German units in the Pocket were still about 180 kilometers from Paris.

Accordingly, the Allied attack objective would be the southern wing of Army Group B, where Model had only weak forces. General of Panzer Troops Adolf Kuntzen's LXXXI Army Corps was screening the threatened area between the rear of the Falaise Pocket and Paris. But Kuntzen had only three divisions available to defend this ninety-kilometer line.[48] On August 8, OB West headquarters alerted the Wehrmacht High Command of the threat to that sector. In response, Chevallerie's First Army was ordered to move up.[49]

The mission assigned to the First Army was to establish a security line between Kuntzen's units and the boundary with Army Task Group G in the Chartres–Orléans area. Hitler thought it should be possible "to cover Paris and the rear of Army Group B" by moving up three infantry divisions.[50]

Up to that point, however, Chevallerie only had been able to establish a rather loose chain of strongpoints that had a low level of combat effectiveness, because the major units promised to him had not yet arrived. For the time being he remained the commanding general of a "field army" responsible for a sector whose only combat-ready units included one assault battalion, two headquarters companies, ten military police patrols, and units of the 1st, 6th, and 1010th Security Regiments, which belonged to the German Military Commander in France.[51] It was hardly possible for Chevallerie to accomplish his mission with the assortment of forces scraped together from the most varied sources.[52] Those units also had widely differing equipment.[53] At best there was a possibility of delaying the

American advance with roadblocks and similar means to bridge the time gap until the arrival of reinforcements.

All of these improvisations were typical of OB West's instructions to Colonel Hermann Oehmichen, whom Hitler had given the mission of establishing a tank obstacle zone in front of Paris. The colonel was to see to it that "all German armed personnel . . . , regardless of rank, duty assignment, and branch . . . , would immediately become tough, resolute close-combat tank fighters," even though they had nothing but single-shot Panzerfausts with which to fight.[54] But the developments on the southern wing of the Army Group B could not be influenced decisively, either by the commitment of the units of the Military Commander in France—which betrayed the extent of the personnel shortages—or by hollow slogans hyping "Morale versus Materiel."

Between August 10 and 14 the Americans remained relatively quiet in that sector. On August 15 they began a more aggressive advance at various points along the security line manned by the LXXXI Army Corps.

Even as Model was being briefed on the situation, the front of the LXXXI Army Corps had already been pushed back or penetrated in a northeasterly direction between Dreux and Chartres. The U.S. spearheads were northwest of Paris, only about fifteen kilometers from the Seine River.

American units also had already rolled over or simply bypassed the chain of strongpoints established by the First Army. The Germans abandoned Chateaudun and Orléans, and their defenders withdrew to the east.[55] Fighting, however, was still going on in Chartres. The First Army's assault battalion and the lead elements of the 48th Infantry Division that had arrived from the Channel coast made a vain attempt to extract the 6th Security Regiment, which was trapped in the city.[56] Simultaneously American reconnaissance squadrons continued to roll to the east and approached the Seine River from south of Paris in the Fontainebleau area.[57]

General von der Chevallerie knew about the Allied attack plans in his area of operations based on captured documents. But since only one battalion of the fresh units he expected had reached his army's sector, Chevallerie shifted the security line farther to the east.

That forced withdrawal resulted in a loss of contact with the LXXXI Army Corps. The security line that was supposed to have been established on August 17 was now located in the area south of

Paris. Nevertheless, the Americans did not, as Blumentritt had projected in a conversation with Speidel, head directly for the French metropolis, which was wide open before them.[58] Instead, the Americans maintained the direction of their advance.

As a result, the Germans were left unopposed for the time being to continue their defensive preparations in front of Paris. The anti-aircraft artillery ring that already existed around the city was to be reinforced and converted into a ground barrier belt.[59] But because the time was too short and the available forces were insufficient, the Germans were able to establish only a provisional defensive system that covered the avenues of approach.

Under the worst-case scenario Model was anticipating losing fourteen divisions at Falaise. But then the push by the U.S. Third Army against the southern wing of Army Group B developed into the second-most significant crisis for the Germans in northern France. The immediate operational threat came from the U.S. XV Corps attacking in a northerly direction from the area around Dreux. The OB West staff immediately assessed that the Americans intended to push down toward the Seine, to the northwest of Paris, to block any withdrawal by the Fifth and Seventh Armies.[60] By so doing they could immediately form the next pocket right behind Falaise.

The situation in Brittany, on the other hand, no longer required any special attention from Model. The general conditions for future combat operations in that area had already been set. The U.S. VIII Corps, with effective support from the FFI, had cut off Brittany by August 11.[61] The remaining German troops on the peninsula withdrew to the four designated fortresses of St. Malo, Brest, Lorient, and St. Nazaire, as well as to numerous smaller strongpoints along the coast.[62] Those positions were to be defended to the very last man. Ever since then, those units of Army Group B had been isolated. General of Artillery Wilhelm Fahrmbacher, the commanding general of the XXV Army Corps remaining in Brittany, commanded all German personnel deployed on the peninsula from his "Kéroman" bunker in Lorient.[63] Only the commandant of Fortress Brest, General of Parachute Troops Hermann Ramcke, had managed to be put directly under Army Group B.[64] The fighting for St. Malo, which fell on August 18, was nearing its end as Model arrived in the west.[65] The Americans then stood fast in front of the other three fortresses. Except for a few hasty but abortive raids, they limited their operations to selected reconnaissance-in-force probes against the defensive systems.

Model's main concern was with those losses he had to write off as he calculated his available strength. At St. Malo, OB West lost two divisions.[66] In the other three fortresses he lost some ninety-two thousand soldiers organized into four field divisions and the headquarters of one army corps.[67] The units holding the fortresses, of course, were able to accomplish one of their primary missions by denying the Allies the use of the harbors. (St. Malo was still blocked by the unit holding Ile de Cézembre). On the other hand, it was impossible for the trapped German units to tie down larger enemy forces. General Eisenhower, the Allied Supreme Commander, had other priorities, although he did need the additional harbors.

The bottom line for Model was that along with the 319th Infantry Division based in the Channel Islands, eight semi-well-trained and fully equipped major units had to be scratched. The resulting Army Group B order of battle on August 17 looked as follows: Of the fifty-four assigned major units, fourteen were threatened with encirclement at Falaise.[68] Seven had to be considered as lost in Brittany or on the Channel Islands. Another eleven had been attrited so badly that they only could be committed as battle groups.[69] Ten of the remaining twenty-two divisions were still along the Channel coast, leaving Model with only twelve combat-effective divisions in the front lines. Considering this situation, combined with the fact that the elimination of the Falaise Pocket would release additional Allied major units to support the follow-on operations already in progress, Kluge's original doubts seemed only too justified. In his farewell letter to Hitler he had stated: "I do not know whether the highly capable Field Marshal Model will gain control of the situation, but I wish him that with all my heart."[70]

What made it all the more doubtful that Model could manage to pull it off was the opposing forty-five to forty-nine Allied divisions that Army Group B's intelligence section estimated were in all of France.[71] That meant Model's weakened forces in northern France alone were facing thirty-seven Allied divisions.[72]

Combat losses were comparably equal on both sides up through the middle of August, with the Germans losing some 160,000 soldiers and the Allies 180,000. But the decisive factor was the Allies' ability to replace their losses quickly, while the major units of OB West were gradually bleeding to death. The replacements received by the German divisions during that period amounted to only about 40,000 men.[73] The equipment replacement shortfall also was becoming increasingly noticeable. At the beginning of the invasion the Germans had some 1,700 tanks and assault guns in the field. By the end of July that number had shrunk to 750. Tank strength had dropped by more than 50 percent. The far heavier tank losses on the Allied side did not alter the fact that the overall ratio was shifting increasingly against the Germans.[74]

3. Allied Operational Command

(a) Deviations from the OVERLORD Plans

The development of combat operations so far deviated from the original Allied plans. The advance of the invasion forces had been extremely restricted during the first seven weeks until after the breakout at Avranches. By the end of July the advance was almost thirty days behind the planned schedule.[75] That meant that some of the logistical requirements originally considered essential had not been met to support follow-on operations. Cherbourg was supposed to be delivering five thousand tons per day by the end of June, but the port only started operating on July 16. The Breton harbors, especially Brest and the Bay of Quiberon, were still not available. At the end of July about 90 percent of the total supply volume was still coming across the open beaches.[76] But the harbor capacity shortfall had not yet produced a negative overall effect on the Allies. Although supply throughput did fall below requirements, the Allied troops were nonetheless receiving adequate logistical support. The cargo handling capacities of the smaller harbors and especially the flow across the beaches exceeded expectations by far.[77] The relatively static warfare of the first seven weeks also meant that fuel consumption was far below the initial calculations and the lines of communications distances from the coast to the forward areas remained short.

Nonetheless, the devastating storm in June that destroyed the American artificial harbor showed that such improvised solutions would only work for a short time. The Allies needed to gain control of foul-weather-capable harbors by the start of the autumn. Brittany continued to have top priority, but it was clear in July 1944 that things were still not going according to plan and adjustments were necessary. The Allies now were planning on having control of the Breton harbors early in September (D+85 to D+90), not early in August as originally planned.[78]

Brittany continued to be a high priority for the U.S. troops as a logistics base. It also was considered a secure position because of its geographic location on the peninsula. The G-4 division (logistics) of the SHAEF staff thought there were no other alternatives to the advantages offered by Brittany.[79] The importance of logistics and especially the security requirements of the logistics system, which had dominated the invasion planning, remained unaltered assumptions for just about as long as those assumptions that overestimated the combat power of the German Wehrmacht held sway.

That assessment, however, started to change following the Avranches breakthrough and the onset of maneuver warfare. Early in August, Eisenhower, in agreement with Montgomery and Bradley, made decisions that resulted in a considerable deviation from the original OVERLORD concept.[80] The main focus of the operations was no longer directed toward the capture of additional harbors. Instead, the Allies now would attempt to inflict the decisive blow and defeat the Germans west of the Seine.[81] That new concept, which replaced the logistics-driven original plan, also included the effort to establish bridgeheads on the east bank of the Seine before the Germans could establish defensive positions there.

Eisenhower's operational concept was basically set by August 7.[82] Although his directives were typically rather vague and subject to varying interpretations, the liberation of Brittany was now a secondary objective—although it remained an important mission that had to be executed *simultaneously* with delivering the decisive blow.[83]

Based on the changing enemy situation estimates prepared by SHAEF headquarters, which now resulted in an underestimation of the German resistance in Brittany, only the U.S. VIII Corps under Major General Troy H. Middleton was committed to take the peninsula instead of the four corps in the original plans. Nevertheless, the Allies proceeded on the assumption that they could capture the harbors within a month.[84] Patton, whose Third Army was the higher headquarters of VIII Corps, even made a bet with Montgomery that Brest would be in American hands within a week.[85]

Middleton's four divisions fanned out, expecting a swift and easy victory. The American units reached St. Malo, Brest, and Lorient almost at the same time, but the result wasn't what they expected. As one American division commander put it, they expected that the Germans would surrender merely as the result of a show of force, a demonstration of military power.[86] The demands for capitulation sent to the commandants of St. Malo on August 4 and 5 and Brest on August 8 were just as meaningless as the messages sent to Patton on August 6 predicting the capture of Lorient and Brest in only a matter of hours.[87] The opportunities that had existed during the first days of August slipped by unexploited because of the poorly coordinated and piecemeal commitment of the American major units.

The Americans underestimated the fighting spirit and resolution of the fortress commandants and the strength of their available forces.[88] They were surprised, therefore, by the stiff German response. After the initial skirmishes, the Americans, as they had done earlier at Lorient, began to form an encirclement ring and pushed forward reconnaissance-in-force probes. The attackers failed to detect the initial weaknesses in the defenses of the various fortresses, including frontline sectors that were still only partially occupied. Before the Americans started any major operations, the combat strength of the fortresses had been reinforced by elements from the various German divisions that had been able to fight their way into those positions.[89]

The operations in Brittany did not develop as smoothly as anticipated. St. Malo did not fall until August 18, and instead of a mere show of force, it took tough fighting and the use of napalm to finally capture it. Nonetheless, Eisenhower stuck to his basic concept. Neither he nor Montgomery were prepared to commit additional forces only to capture the ports.[90] Such a measure did not seem necessary because the Allies in the middle of August were still convinced that a concentric attack on Brest would succeed in short order.[91]

Bolstered by ULTRA intelligence on August 9 and 10, the Allied leadership finally understood what they might be able to achieve by launching a consistently exploited strike in Normandy.[92] The chance of encircling a large part of the German Army in the West by conducting a deep envelopment with the American right wing was now the top priority.[93] Simultaneous with a much deeper encirclement along the Seine, Montgomery planned a "short hook," which resulted in the Falaise Pocket.[94] The battle at Falaise ended with what was up until then the worst defeat suffered by the Germans in the west. The losses were catastrophic, totaling some forty-five thousand to sixty thousand soldiers.[95] Tank losses were at least four hundred Panzers, more than 50 percent of the available tanks.[96] For the first time German tank losses were higher than those of the Allies.[97]

The victory, however, was not as overwhelming as the Allies had expected.[98] Some 40 to 50 percent of the encircled German soldiers, which according to Allied estimates were no more than forty thousand,[99] plus the headquarters of the two armies, three of the four corps headquarters, and almost all of the fourteen encircled division headquarters, were able to escape from the trap.[100] (See Map 7.)

The disappointing outcome at Failase was the result of the fighting skills and desperate courage of the German troops, combined with faulty Allied decisions during the battle. The Pocket itself was not completely closed until August 19. To avoid the danger of a collision between the spearheads of the two pincers, Bradley six days earlier had ordered Major General Wade Haislip's U.S. XV Corps attacking from the south to halt along the boundary between the two Allied army groups that had been established by Montgomery. If the advance had continued, the encirclement almost certainly would have been closed earlier.[101] Bradley did not yield to Patton, who wanted to continue pushing the advance and, as he stated with his typical bombast, "chase the British back to the sea in a second Dunkirk."[102] Eisenhower supported Bradley's decision.

At the very highest levels, the decisions were basically inconsistent with the magnitude of the opportunity that the Allied leadership had recognized earlier on. Instead of a certain measure of boldness, priority was still given to a cautious style of operating. As a result, problems arose at the tactical level. At that moment the encirclement was closing. The exact command structure along the southern arm of the pincer remained confused. Since August 15, Haislip had been focusing on his follow-on mission, the deeper encirclement along the Seine.[103]

Nonetheless, the victory at Falaise reinforced an overall increasingly confident situation assessment on the Allied side, which in turn provided further impetus to modify the OVERLORD plan. The expectations that the Allies would be able to gain control of the complex logistics problems involved with Brest seemed to be working out. On the other hand, they had not been able to pull off successfully the hoped-for battle of annihilation. But the Allies thought that objective was still within immediate reach. According to Allied estimates, the U.S. Third Army's "long hook" along the Seine should make it possible to encircle some seventy-five thousand Germans with around 250 Panzers. A sentence from one of Montgomery's directives, "Let us finish off the business in record time," describes the mood among the Allied leadership at that point.[104]

These high-flying expectations were boosted by the impressions of a collapsing German front line. Along the Seine near La Roche-Guyon the U.S. 79th Infantry Division ran headlong into the headquarters of Army Group B. The staff was barely able to escape under enemy fire.[105] On that same day, August 19, Eisenhower decided to continue the pursuit of the battered enemy across the Seine.[106]

It was thus clear that the transition to the post-OVERLORD phase would take place without the originally planned one-month operational pause. Initial indications of supply problems, however, were already emerging. Thirty-seven divisions had to be supplied with about twenty thousand tons daily.[107] The fuel requirements of the U.S. Third Army could be met only with the help of transport aircraft. On the day of Eisenhower's decision, August 19, the daily emergency airlift to the Third Army began.[108]

(b) The Resistance in Northern France

Considering the events in northern France through the middle of August 1944, one might well agree with Henri Michel's thesis—with some modification: "Without the Allied invasion, the Resistance would have failed in the end. Without the materiel delivered by the Allies, it would have remained powerless. But without support from the Resistance, the task of the Allies would have been incomparably more difficult and their success would not have materialized as quickly."[109]

It appears difficult to document exactly the idea that the events in northern France were accelerated as a result of the actions of the French Forces of the Interior. Despite the successes they have been credited with, along with their undoubtedly important intelligence information collection effort, their contribution was nonetheless secondary.

Of course, Eisenhower writing after the war did credit "special significance" to the actions of the FFI in Brittany.[110] The occupation of the areas evacuated by German units (with the exception of the fortresses) and the engagement of scattered German units and the administrative agencies that remained behind played a subordinate role, albeit on a large scale. The FFI was twenty thousand strong in Brittany.[111] They did quickly mop up the peninsula in close coordination with American forces, but they did not contribute to the accomplishment of the Allies' operational objective. The ports remained in German hands and regular forces were needed to take those ports.

In the area of the Loire River the FFI did provide a flank screen toward the south for the U.S. Third Army while it was pushing toward the Seine.[112] But in the final analysis it was protection against a threat that did not exist at all. Early in August at Avranches several German Panzer units had failed to hit successfully the Americans in the flank in an attempt to plug the breakthrough gap. A similar type of action could hardly be expected from the two underequipped motorized infantry divisions of the LXIV Army Corps, which were simply lost in the vast region between the mouth of the Loire River and the French-Spanish border. This screening function provided by the FFI nevertheless was emphasized as having been important. This was probably more the result of a subjectively felt screen against a theoretically possible but not very real threat.

Part 2

From the Retreat of the German Army in the West to the Climax of the Crisis

Combat Operations from August 20 to September 4, 1944

Chapter 6

The Start of the Retreat in the West

1. Model's Initial Measures and the August 20 Führer Directive

Early in the morning of August 18 Model started out from La Roche-Guyon for the command post of the Fifth Panzer Army to get a firsthand picture of the situation along the front. His impressions developed during this first trip to the front, the threat of the ever-present Allied air forces, and his firsthand look at the scope of destruction did away with his initial convictions that the battlefield problems could be solved and brought quickly under control by executing a "short cross-country gallop."[1]

Based on discussions with Dietrich, the commanding general of the Fifth Panzer Army, and other leading officers, the field marshal began to doubt the very feasibility of his mission. As Model now summarized the situation and the immediate and most important task: "First of all, the important thing is once again to form a continuous front line." Whether that would be accomplished in front of the Seine, as he had been ordered, or behind the river would depend entirely on how the situation developed.[2]

That same evening Model reported that his burned-out units could no longer be expected to do a credible job of fighting if the following conditions were not met:

1. Limitation of the enemy's absolute mastery of the air ". . . *within the next few days."*
2. Replacements amounting to 25 battalions ". . . *without loss of time."*
3. Immediate supply of at least 270 Panzers and 288 artillery pieces.
4. At least nine thousand metric tons of bulk transportation capacity.[3]

These minimum requirements addressed to the Wehrmacht High

Command for immediate submission to the führer, combined with Model's lack of reluctance to demand—but without success—the immediate support of all available Me-262 jet fighters characterized the self-confident approach of the new OB West.[4] He realized quite clearly that all of his demands could not be met by the established deadlines.[5] But unless he received large-scale support, there was good reason to fear the very worst: Apart from the consequences of the disaster at Falaise, the southern wing of Army Group B was facing operational-level threats.[6]

To head off the Allies' already-in-progress efforts to effect a second encirclement along the Seine, Model intended to deploy his available Panzer units on the left wing into the Evreux–Mantes sector, along the boundary of Chevallerie's First Army. But it was doubtful that maneuver could fend off the American thrust from the southeast. The Panzer divisions already had suffered heavily, with eight of the eleven divisions in Army Group B's sector reporting a provisional combat strength totaling no more than seventy Panzers.[7]

The First Army's situation between Paris and the Loire River was the most problematic. That area was the link for Model's follow-on primary mission, to combine his Army Group B with Army Task Group G. The First Army, therefore, was of tremendous importance, but in reality its strength existed mostly on paper. The First Army just didn't have the capability to counter any Allied offensive aimed at a deep encirclement of Army Group B, an attack into the rear of the Fifteenth Army, or a thrust to the southeast to cut off Blasko-witz's Army Task Group G.

Model ordered the reinforcement of the First Army with the transfer of two divisions from the Fifteenth Army and two brigade-strength SS units, plus the subordination of the remnants of other divisions. Those measures, however, were little more than a ban-dage.[8] The effectiveness of those reinforcements would depend on the reaction of the Allied command.

On August 20 Model received Hitler's *Directive for Further Combat Operations*. That document established the primary mission as "holding bridgehead west of Paris and . . . preventing an enemy breakthrough south of Paris . . . in the direction of Dijon." The order for the First Army to cover on both sides of Montargis the retreat of the German forces from the south was symptomatic of the totally unrealistic thinking prevailing at the Führer Headquarters.

If the primary mission proved impossible, then the major units of the German Army in the West were to be reorganized behind the defensive line that ran Seine–Yonne–Canal de Bourgogne–Dijon–Dôle–Swiss border.

Thus, there was a withdrawal option, starting with the remnants of the Seventh Army across the Seine. The exception would be the retention of the bridgehead west of Paris, because Hitler placed a high value on the French capital.[9] Aside from that, however, Model had no other indicators of the follow-on intentions at the Führer Headquarters.

The day Model received the directive, Hitler also signed the *Order for the Improvement of the German Western Position*.[10] Model, however, did not know about that second order, nor did he know that Hitler for the first time spelled out his intention to regain the initiative in the west. On August 19 Hitler stated that Jodl should: "... get used to the idea that we will go to the offensive in November, when the enemy cannot fly." Hitler also gave Jodl the warning order to be prepared to transfer some twenty-five divisions to the west within one or two months.[11] Model, meanwhile, took what he knew of the führer's intentions and focused straight ahead, devoting all his efforts to dealing with the situation at the front.

Any quick and fundamental improvement in the German strength situation was virtually impossible. Aside from the 3rd and 15th Panzer Grenadier Divisions coming from Italy, Model could not expect to receive further major units before the end of the month, two weeks away. Three infantry divisions and two Panzer brigades were projected to arrive by then. The ninety field howitzers and eighty-eight Panzers that were already in the pipeline would replace only a small portion of the battle losses sustained during the fighting in recent days.[12] Thus, Model was left to his own devices for the time being. He ordered twenty thousand combat troops to be procured as replacements for the front by combing out the rear echelon units and by committing special headquarters elements along the Somme–Marne–Saône line to organize the scattered elements.[13] His intention, at least temporarily, was to plug the gaps as they developed. The crucial question for OB West continued to be whether such measures and the expected reinforcements would be too little, too late.

Model at that point was fully engrossed in dealing with the problems of his Army Group B. In his capacity as OB West, he left the organization of the retreat from southern France to his trusty "Blasko," who earlier in peacetime had been Model's superior.[14]

2. The Withdrawal from the South of France

(a) Headquarters Retreat Preparations

According to Blaskowitz's directive of August 18, General of Engineers Karl Sachs and his LXIV Army Corps were to evacuate the Atlantic coast, with the exception of the Gironde fortresses and the La Rochelle defensive perimeter. Sachs was then to lead his units via Bourges into the region of Sens–Venarey les Laumes, northwest of Dijon.[15]

For the units of the Nineteenth Army, the Rhône River Valley was the only route of retreat, and the area between Dijon and the Swiss border was the objective. Early on Blaskowitz developed concerns about the rear security of the territory his troops had to cross. He wanted to make sure that at least the most important march routes were secured.[16] But he had no units available for that mission. His only recourse was to draw from the units under the control of the territorial military commanders. On August 18 the headquarters and security units of the Army Territorial Commandant, Southern France, General of Infantry Ernst Dehner, and the Commander, Northeastern France, Lieutenant General Wilhelm Hederich, were placed under the operational control of Army Task Group G.[17]

The tremendous and sudden increase in Resistance activities entirely justified Blaskowitz's concerns. Organized Resistance units controlled and coordinated by their own higher headquarters were identified operating in the Rhône River Valley around Cevennes in the west and the Grenoble area in the east. That put the Resistance on both sides of the Nineteenth Army's retreat route.[18]

Blaskowitz was already working on the coordination of the troop movements on a broad scale when General Sachs in Poitiers received the retreat order.[19] But Sachs only received it in the evening of August 18 via the navy radio station in Royan, and even then the order came in garbled.

Sachs faced considerable difficulties. Some two-thirds of the eighty-seven thousand Germans in his area of command were soldiers unaccustomed to fighting and marching, or they were Wehrmacht administrative troops.[20] They included fifteen thousand navy personnel; twelve thousand Luftwaffe troops; five thousand headquarters administrative personnel; three thousand railroad operations troops; two thousand customs officers; two thousand members of the Reich Labor Service; and two thousand female auxiliaries.[21] The first task was to organize this heterogeneous mix into coherent march units, assigning each to the control of a combat unit. Because the partisan threat was so serious, an attempt had to be made to avoid sending smaller detachments of Luftwaffe or navy personnel through southwestern France on their own. Despite requisitioning all the last available French motor vehicles, the transportation capacity of the LXIV Army Corps was woefully insufficient.[22] That resulted in unavoidable delays in the forming of the march units. Most of the administrative and support troops were forced to evacuate via horse-drawn vehicles, bicycles, or simply by foot march.[23] The railroads likewise were almost completely unusable because of demolitions and air raids.

On the morning of August 19, General Sachs in Poitiers specified the next steps to be taken. In order to sidestep the partisan threat in the entire territory beyond the demarcation line (i.e., that part of the southwest that had belonged to what was unoccupied Vichy France), Sachs planned to have his march units avoid direct routes.[24] Rather, he intended to send them at first north through the French Departments located along the Atlantic. Then the march units would detour via Poitiers before turning east toward the Sens–Dijon objective area. In that way Sachs hoped to bring the eighty-seven thousand people who were entrusted to him back safely.[25] Meanwhile, the units manning the Gironde fortresses[26] and the La Rochelle defensive perimeter, totaling twenty thousand men,[27] had to remain in position along the Atlantic coast and await their fate there.

Since communications had broken down completely, Blaskowitz initially was unaware of the problems of the LXIV Army Corps. But he was able to coordinate directly with General Wiese in Avignon on the preparations along the Mediterranean coast. The geographic features along the Rhône River Valley made it very hazardous as a retreat route. The foothills of the mountains extended almost to the river from both the west and the east sides. On the east bank the mountain ranges, rising to elevations of three hundred to eight hundred meters, were segmented and compartmentalized by multiple tributaries running down from the Alps. The larger of these tributaries, the Durance, the Drôme, and the Isère, were followed by good highways that formed lateral connections between the Rhône River Valley and the national highway that ran farther east from the Riviera to Grenoble.

The Allies seemed to be in a position to exploit this situation. Blaskowitz contemplated with great concern the center of gravity of the enemy pressure in the Draguignan area, where there was a gap in the front between the 242nd and 148th Infantry Divisions.[28] If the Americans succeeded in advancing quickly along the road leading to Grenoble, they would have several excellent opportunities for pushing west along the lateral connections and cutting off the German withdrawal in the Rhône River Valley.

The development of this encircling pursuit maneuver, which Blaskowitz feared early on, became clearly recognizable on August 18.[29] Blaskowitz submitted an urgent request for aircraft to monitor the Allies' actions along the eastern flank of his force.[30] It was, as he put it, impossible to get along without aerial reconnaissance in the area of Draguignan–Digne–Valence.[31] His request, of course, was not answered.

Most immediately, the question of the withdrawal march tempo was most important both for Blaskowitz and Wiese. Both commanders agreed to execute the retreat as quickly as possible because of the uncertainty of the situation in Army Group B. Blaskowitz first set August 23 as the jump-off date in the Avignon region.[32] That would give the units of the Luftwaffe IV Field Corps and the 564th Main Liaison Staff (Toulouse) near the Spanish border a chance to reach the Rhône River Valley in time. By that point a blocking position would be in place around the city.

But even by that deadline it seemed hardly possible to get all the soldiers into the Rhône River Valley over distances of as much as three hundred kilometers. General Wiese, commanding the Nineteenth Army, wanted to use ships for transportation along the coast to the Rhône River delta.[33] But the tremendous time pressure of the situation forced the hasty evacuation to the west of the river to start on August 19.[34] (See Map 8.)

The poor mobility of the German troops was another restricting factor. The first indicators of crumbling discipline, resulting from the precipitously implemented measures, materialized all too quickly. Frequent disputes erupted between army and navy commanders over the requisitioning of motor vehicles.[35]

Nonessential supply trains and all noncombatants[36] were routed north into the Rhône Valley before the combat units withdrew. That phase of the operation was completed relatively smoothly by August 21. A few hours after receiving the retreat order, Wiese submitted a detailed withdrawal plan to Blaskowitz, who approved it immediately.[37]

1. General of Aviation Petersen, commander of the Luftwaffe IV Field Corps, was to coordinate movements on the west bank of the Rhône River, while General of Infantry Baptist Kniess, commander of the LXXXV Army Corps, was to do the same thing on the east bank. Both were given Wehrmacht authority—in other words, they had full command authority over the military personnel of all three components of the German armed forces.
2. The 11th Panzer Division was assigned to support the LXXXV Army Corps against enemy forces that were pushing up from the south. Simultaneously, it was to reconnoiter in the direction of the threatened eastern flank. According to Wiese's plan, the 11th Panzer Division was to function as a fire brigade. The risk was that the division might become too fragmented by responding to its many different missions and in the end might not be able to accomplish any of them.
3. After all units converged in the Rhône River Valley by August 23, it would become necessary to defend the established lines of resistance. Because of Allied air supremacy and the clear summer weather, the march movements were scheduled for only at night, moving from blocking line to blocking line, some twenty-five to thirty kilometers in each jump.
4. Wiese focused special attention on the missions assigned to the commander of his combat engineer forces, Major General Johannes Kaliebe, who was responsible for executing the crossings of the numerous rivers and the maintenance of steady ferry traffic on the Rhône River. To accomplish those missions he was given control of all the suitable forces available, including units from the navy and the construction units of Organization Todt.

Wiese's plan was issued as *Order for Redeployment to the Rear.*[38] Of the approximately 196,000 troops in the Nineteenth Army area of responsibility, 138,000 started working their way through the Rhône valley.[39] That left thirteen thousand German troops behind to man the Marseille defensive perimeter, and another eighteen thousand at Toulon.[40] Additionally, some twenty-seven thousand troops, including the 148th Infantry Division and several thousand volunteer auxiliary troops, were not covered by Wiese's plan.[41]

Once the plans and preparations were complete, almost a quarter of a million people started the march back from southern and southwestern France, covering distances up to one thousand kilometers.[42] But some fifty-one thousand men in the Army Task Group G sector had to abandon all hope of ever returning to their homeland on their own. They remained in the fortresses and defensive perimeters along the coasts of the Mediterranean and the Atlantic.

(b) The Nineteenth Army Retreat Starts

During the first few days the withdrawal from the beachhead front to the east of the Rhône River went off according to plan. The LXXXV Army Corps moved into a blocking position between the coast and the Durance River on August 19, and with relatively few problems linked up with the German positions around Marseille. The next day the corps moved into a line around Aix-en-Provence.[43]

This was a significant accomplishment because General Kniess had only five combat-ready battalions. The units of the 244th Infantry Division, initially deployed in the beachhead sector, also moved back into the Marseille defensive perimeter to reinforce that position to divisional strength, as specified in the Führer Order.

The 198th Infantry Division and the 11th Panzer Division, however, still had not completely crossed the Rhône River. From time to time, the crossing tempo dropped because Allied air forces again targeted the Roquemaure bridge and knocked it out.[44] The crucial 11th Panzer Division was particularly hard hit by problems encountered during the approach march. Partisans in the Carcassonne area had cut the rail lines using demolitions. Consequently, forty PzKpfw V Panther tanks, half the division's main battle tanks, had to complete their movement by taking a long detour.[45]

The relatively smooth German withdrawal maneuver contributed to a somewhat hesitant Allied advance. The Allies had intended to seize three objectives simultaneously. The II French Corps under Lattre de Tassigny prepared to launch an offensive against the major ports. Task Force Butler and the U.S. 36th Infantry Division were to attack to the north. And the U.S. 3rd and 45th Infantry Divisions were to attack toward the mouth of the Rhône River.[46]

The movements of the German troops were now flowing

smoothly. On the west bank Petersen's Luftwaffe IV Field Corps was able to route the flow of retreat into an orderly pattern. Nevertheless, Wiese and Blaskowitz looked at the developing situation with some skepticism. Blaskowitz reported to OB West that there was a chance of executing the withdrawal movements according to plan only if the enemy did not conduct deep flanking operations, neither from the north heading toward Dijon, nor along the eastern flank of the withdrawal.[47] But that precisely was the threat, as the intelligence indicators showed clearly a developing Allied thrust by way of Digne toward Grenoble or Valence.[48] Somewhat bitterly, Wiese noted that the Grasse–Digne–Grenoble route had been abandoned because the 148th and 157th Infantry Divisions had been ordered to remain in place along the French-Italian Alpine border. Thus the enemy would be able "easily to thrust deep into the German flank."[49]

Blaskowitz now was no longer worrying about the utterly unrealistic order from the Wehrmacht High Command to move the 338th Infantry Division into the Paris area as soon as possible. In his situation estimate he noted rather tersely, "The withdrawal of more units from the front is intolerable."[50]

Blaskowitz was mostly worried about the situation along the eastern flank. The Luftwaffe was not anywhere to be seen, which of course had a negative psychological effect on the troops.[51] Blaskowitz, therefore, considered it necessary to immediately push strong reconnaissance-in-force elements to the north and east. On August 21 the lead units of the 11th Panzer Division advanced between the Durance and Drôme rivers to block the roads coming from the Alps.[52]

The German commanders had no way of knowing that in the evening of August 20 the Americans had initiated the very actions they feared most. At 2045 hours Lieutenant General Lucian K. Truscott, commander of the U.S. VI Corps, ordered one task force to advance eastward, heading toward the Rhône River Valley and the Montélimar area.[53]

For the moment, however, there was no noticeable deterioration in the German situation. The Luftwaffe IV Field Corps was moving briskly along the west bank, and in the east the LXXXV Army Corps occupied the blocking position around Avignon as planned.[54] On August 21, one battle group of the 11th Panzer Division made enemy contact for the first time at Aix-en-Provence. After that the American advance toward the Rhône River delta became more hesitant.[55] Gyldenfeldt, the Army Task Group G chief of staff, believed that the hesitation was the result of an American "reluctance to fight or march at night."[56]

Blaskowitz suspected that the Allies would attempt to force the situation, not by launching a thrust from the south through the German blocking position, but rather through an encircling pursuit maneuver. By the afternoon of August 22 he thought that his suspicions had been confirmed. While the Army Task Group G command post had been displacing to Lyon the day before, the headquarters column with both Blaskowitz and Gyldenfeldt had been caught by heavy machine gun and mortar fire at Montélimar. At first they mistakenly assumed the French Forces of the Interior had caused the trouble.[57] But 11th Panzer Division reconnaissance patrols between the Durance and Drôme rivers ran into tough Allied resistance in the area northeast of Montélimar, making it clear who the Germans were immediately up against.

The Montélimar region was very important because from its steeply rising ridges observers had a clear view far and wide of the surrounding terrain. Regular troops supported by artillery could easily dominate any movement along the valley highway.

A message from the 11th Panzer Division at 1700 hours reported the capture at Montélimar of personnel from the U.S. 36th Infantry Division. The Rhône River highway was already blocked by artillery fire. Wiese immediately took action, ordering the units of the 11th Panzer Division to concentrate on attacking the enemy in the bottleneck to clear the march route again—the route that was the "lifeline of Nineteenth Army."[58]

Simultaneously, the prospects for Army Task Group G to effect a linkup with the German Western Front were deteriorating considerably. Blaskowitz, meanwhile, learned about the push by the U.S. Third Army all the way into the Troyes area along the southern wing of Army Group B. If that attack were to continue toward Dijon, then Army Task Group G's route of withdrawal would be cut off there once and for all.[59] Time was now the decisive factor. Blaskowitz sent a message to the Nineteenth Army ordering that the "situation southeast of Paris . . . requires extreme acceleration. . . . The maximum effort, therefore, must be expected of the troops because everything is at stake."[60]

The key requirement for speeding up the retreat march tempo was the reopening of the valley roads on the east bank of the Rhône

River. The 11th Panzer Division launched an attack on the morning of August 23. But the hastily assembled battle group, consisting of only two battalions and ten Panzers, was too weak to push the enemy off the high ground at La Coucourde. A renewed effort launched during the night also failed. Wiese ordered the LXXXV Army Corps convoys that were jamming up on the roads to continue the march to the north despite the artillery and mortar fire. On August 24, however, the movement, which had resumed during the night, bogged down again under American fire along the mouth of the Drôme River. After daybreak the Americans were able to call in accurately adjusted fire from the dominating high ground.[61]

Wiese, meanwhile, was shown captured documents indicating that the Americans intended to continue blocking the Montélimar–Valence area.[62] The 11th Panzer Division again was ordered to attack on the following morning, August 25.[63] Their mission would become extremely difficult to accomplish if the Americans stuck to the basic principle of establishing a main effort and if they actually occupied the critical highway sectors, rather than just bringing them under artillery fire. The Nineteenth Army's fate now hung on the ability of Lieutenant General Wend von Weitersheim's units to clear the route of retreat. (See Map 9.)

(c) The Significance of the French Forces of the Interior for the German Command

Blaskowitz was sure that the Nineteenth Army was in good hands under Wiese. Following the long-standing German General Staff tradition, he therefore did not interfere with his subordinate commander but instead went to Dijon on August 24. From there, Blaskowitz would be in a better position to manage things on a large scale than he would have been from the frequently changing command posts of recent days.[64] Blaskowitz, above all, was worried by the increasing activities of the French Forces of the Interior.

The resistance centers were located in the rear of the front that had mostly been stripped of German troops. Again and again, reports came in of combat actions and "terrorist troubles" in the Massif Central and the Alps. There already had been fighting in the area of Lake Geneva since August 17.[65] Cities such as Thonon, Evian, and Annecy were occupied by the FFI, and the German security units stationed there were either crushed or driven away.[66] In the Alpine region, the Grenoble area was another focal point of heavy guerrilla activity.[67] The attacks in the Massif Central were aimed at the garrisons of Tulle, Brive, Egletons, and Limoges.[68]

The Germans were afraid that the FFI would also turn directly on the march columns of Army Task Group G. Serious trouble had already occurred during the fighting in the invasion zone. Telecommunications cables had been cut and the arrival of 11th Panzer Division had been delayed. In his August 21 situation estimate Blaskowitz had emphasized that the Resistance bands sometimes "involved well-organized, strong enemy units."[69] Botsch, the Nineteenth Army chief of staff, believed that the Luftwaffe IV Field Corps was in real danger.[70] That unit had to cross the mountainous terrain to the west of the Rhône River.

The German generals, however, overestimated the direct influence that the FFI exerted on the course of operations. So far, the withdrawal movements had not been stopped by any French actions. The crisis to the east of the Rhône River was precipitated by American units, especially by their artillery fire. Nonetheless, Petersen's Luftwaffe IV Field Corps was able to continue its march according to plan on the opposite bank, despite the concerns. Petersen's last units crossed the Gard River on August 24 heading north.[71]

To the surprise of the German command, it turned out, as Botsch noted later, that the FFI to the west of the Rhône River "immediately withdrew the moment the German combat troops showed up."[72]

Not only did the FFI not delay in the least the retreat of the German units, the French operations in the rear areas were for the most part meaningless. But whenever they were able to control completely terrain sectors that were vitally important for the withdrawal movements, then they went from being mere secondary forces to those that potentially could influence decisively the outcome of combat operations. Such opportunities continued to exist. The German command had detected guerrilla concentrations in the area of Châteauroux[73] and "along the Rhône River roads south of Lyon"[74]—areas that the German forces still had to cross.

There was little Blaskowitz could do to counter that threat. General Hederich, the Commanding General, Northeastern France, was ordered to secure the covering line in the area between Sens and the Swiss border and to establish assembly areas there.[75] Simultaneously, General Dehner, the commandant of Army Region Southern France, was ordered to hold Lyon open for the Nineteenth

Army. Both commanders, however, had very few security units and those had rather insignificant levels of combat readiness. Success, therefore, was doubtful considering the gap between the missions and the available forces. There had already been firefights in Lyon, which, according to the plan, the Nineteenth Army was not scheduled to pass through until early September. The German commanders also anticipated a general uprising of the French population at any time.[76]

(d) Developments in Southwestern France (LXIV Army Corps)

On August 24 Blaskowitz failed to establish communications with General Sachs from Dijon. One week after the retreat orders had been issued, Army Task Group G headquarters still had no information whatsoever about what supporting measures had been initiated there. According to Sachs's order issued on August 19, three major march movement groups were to be formed:

1. The Northern Group (in the Loire–Poiters area) under the command of Lieutenant General Ernst Haeckel. His 16th Infantry Division would be the nucleus of the group that in the end numbered twenty thousand to twenty-five thousand men.[77]
2. The Central March Movement Group (southwest of Poitiers) under the command of Major General Hans Täglichsbeck with twelve thousand to thirteen thousand men.[78] To accomplish his combat missions, he only had available the 360th Cossack Regiment and the 950th Indian Infantry Regiment.[79]
3. The Southern Group (Bordeaux area) under the command of Lieutenant General Albin Nake. His 159th Infantry Division was the backbone of this march formation. Nake had the most difficult task. All of the German positions all the way down to the Pyrenees had to be assembled into a group that in the end numbered some fifty thousand to sixty thousand men.[80] (See Map 8.)

Considering the time-consuming assembly phase resulting from the tremendous organizational problems, Sachs ordered the actual retreat to start on August 27.[81] But he also estimated that everything would not actually be moving until around August 30.[82] This estimate proved to be entirely justified because unexpected difficulties cropped up. On top of everything else, Sachs had to protect the harbor of Bordeaux longer than planned because of two submarines that were in need of repair. The navy had persuaded the Wehrmacht High Command to issue that order.[83]

Another hardly surprising problem cropped up during the night of August 19–20, as the assembly phase began. The soldiers and noncombatants had become accustomed to peacetime conditions because they had been stationed there for many years. They, therefore, could not be expected to keep up with the standard march movement pace. As Sachs later commented rather tersely, the "situation looked just about shattering."[84]

Panic and an every-man-for-himself mentality had all the makings of a catastrophe, considering the heterogeneous makeup of the various march units. Sachs tried to apply psychology by issuing individual march orders designating only the objective of the next phase, thereby concealing the actual scope of the retreat and the attendant hardships.[85] Liaison officers distributed propaganda leaflets and news bulletins that were intended to produce a calming effect.

Sachs, much more so than Wiese in southern France, had to concentrate his attentions on the problems of maintenance of internal cohesion. The movements started rather sluggishly, probably so as not to tax the morale of the troops with immediate forced marches. Thus, the troops of the 541st Local Administrative Headquarters of Major General Botho Elster, who had the longest way ahead of them, did not depart from the little towns of Mont de Marsan and Dax in the southern tip of the corps sector until August 22–23.[86]

In Sachs's opinion, the main threat to the retreat of his corps would come from the U.S. Third Army in the north.[87] The weak units[88] that were used to secure the Loire River bridges were supported by a regimental-strength blocking unit of the 16th Infantry Division, but that did not constitute an effective flank screen.[89]

Initially the march element leaders had more trouble with internal coordination issues than with external events. During this period, which was vulnerable to all kinds of trouble, the FFI units that had penetrated into the German assembly areas achieved relatively little. There were firefights and minor obstacles encountered here and there, such as the guerrillas turning the road signs the wrong way. The French population remained mostly quiet.[90] The two bridges across the Garonne River in Bordeaux and the few crossings of the Dordogne River were worthwhile targets for guerrilla attacks because the retreat of the Southern Group could have been obstructed considerably if those bridges had been blown. No attempts, however, were made on the bridges.

Lieutenant General Otto Ottenbacher found himself facing a different initial situation. He had to lead the units that were still in the Massif Central northward to the covering line, independently of the other two major withdrawal movements of the Nineteenth Army and the LXIV Army Corps.[91] With an aggregate of some twelve thousand men,[92] Ottenbacher's initial objective was to assemble these forces into a march group[93] in the area of Montluçon–Clermont-Ferrand.[94] In contrast to what happened along the Atlantic, there were clashes with the FFI units in that sector during the assembly phase, resulting in a delay of the departure. Ottenbacher first had to extricate through combat action the isolated regional defense battalions from places like Egletons and Gueret. The extractions, however, were not successfully accomplished in all locations.[95]

The individual events documented in the records show a clear pattern in what was happening in southwestern France. Despite their considerable numerical strength, the march units actually had an extremely low combat effectiveness that was in no way comparable to that of standard army units. These groupings were improvisations born of necessity, often without any modern command systems and without internal cohesion. This was typical of Ottenbacher's group, which at twelve thousand men was numerically equivalent to an infantry division. And that group consisted almost entirely of soldiers. The inadequately equipped security units, with leaders who were unfit for frontline service but who until then had been capable of performing occupation duties, could be expected to accomplish their military missions only to a limited degree. Major General Walter Gleininger, the 586th Local Administrative Commandant in Limoges, was in rather poor health. He quickly abandoned all hope after the city was surrounded and he was ready to capitulate to the FFI. To his misfortune, his decision was premature, because the German occupation unit did manage to break out of Limoges. Gleininger was then arrested by his own men, but he shot himself to avoid the inevitable court-martial.[96]

Ottenbacher was able to assemble his march unit formation by August 24, despite all difficulties. The retreat in the direction of Moulins began on the next day.[97] But the general situation was critical for Army Task Group G. Blaskowitz, its commanding general, did not have a full grasp of the big picture of the problems confronting him.

Headquarters, OB West, in Verzy, on the other hand, had a more complete picture. A large part of the Nineteenth Army was threatened with encirclement in the Rhône River Valley. Simultaneously, the retreat of some one hundred thousand Germans from southwestern and central France had not even started. The march units had not even finished assembling along the Atlantic. Field Marshal Model, who returned from the front to Army Group B headquarters at Margival around 2000 hours, now finally realized how unrealistic it had been of Hitler to order the Seine–Yonne–Dijon line. One essential requirement for the defense of that line, the rapid movement of Army Task Group G units into the southern sector, simply could not be accomplished. Model received devastating answers in response to his impatient questioning.[98] If everything went according to plan, the Nineteenth Army was calculated to reach its assigned sector toward the end of the first ten-day period in September, while the march units of the LXIV Army Corps would reach their sectors only around September 15.[99]

On August 24, Army Task Group G received a flood of orders directing it to speed up the withdrawal movements despite the circumstances. But the OB West headquarters did not entertain any illusions about the situation.[100] Blumentritt was quite aware that the march tempo, with all sorts of requisitioned motor vehicles and horse-drawn carts, was way out of proportion to the speed of the fully mechanized enemy.[101]

Considering the German situation at that point, a letter written by Eisenhower to Churchill on August 24 was not at all exaggerated. Eisenhower described the course of Operation DRAGOON so far as a "wonderful show" and he was optimistic about the future progress: "I am sure that he [DRAGOON] will grow fat and prosperous. . . ."[102]

3. Combat Operations in the Sector of Army Group B Up to the Fall of Paris

(a) The Retreat of the Seventh Army across the Seine

All things were quiet on August 20 along the security line of the weak First Army between Paris and the Loire River. It seemed that the Allies were planning to launch a deep operation there only later. The main effort of their attacks was assessed for the first time as having the objective of cutting off the retreat of the German army in Normandy across the Seine River. Headquarters OB West recognized the acute danger.[103]

On August 20, Model gave Dietrich, the commanding general of the Fifth Panzer Army, command over the entire sector between the coast and Paris.[104] Seventh Army headquarters was taken out of the front line. (General of Panzer Troops Heinrich Eberbach had replaced Hausser as commanding general of the Seventh Army after the latter had been wounded during the breakout from the Falaise Pocket.) The units of the Seventh Army were completely exhausted. The surviving formations were thoroughly mixed up and had escaped from the pocket minus their heavy weapons.[105] Those units had to be moved to the far bank of the Seine River for reconstitution. The most immediate problem was that there were no longer any bridges standing across the Seine River in the vicinity of Paris. The troops could cross only by using ferries and other improvisations.[106] Besides, there was no telling how long Dietrich's screening units would be able to withstand the concentric attack of the Allies, which would start on August 21. Dietrich had only fourteen divisions to the west of the river.[107] (See Map 10.)

The Fifth Panzer Army's main line of resistance was roughly organized into two sectors. The Canadians and British attacked along the western sector, which ran from Villers sur Mer to the south via Vimoutiers and up to about Gacé. The Americans, with a total of about twenty-five major units, attacked the southern sector from Gacé to the east, all the way into the Dreux area.[108] The left wing of the southern sector had been bent back considerably by a push from the U.S. XV Corps. It ran roughly from Dreux along the Eure River in a northerly direction into the area of Vernon, and then to the Seine River. The wedge, pushed by the Americans, caused the line defended by General of Panzer Troops Adolf Kuntzen's LXXXI Corps to be subdivided into a Eure River sector and a Seine River sector— up to the point where it linked up with the barrier belt around Paris.

Model worried especially about developments along that southern sector. The LXXXI Army Corps, with its three infantry divisions—the 331st and 344th Infantry Divisions and the Luftwaffe 17th Field Division—and the remnants of 116th Panzer Division, was too weak to withstand a determined push. The bridgeheads that the Americans had established in the area of the Seine River between Vernon and Mantes looked particularly dangerous.[109] It was possible to seal off this crucial point only by redirecting the 49th Infantry Division and the Luftwaffe 18th Field Division, originally earmarked for the First Army, to that point "with all means of improvisation."

If the Americans followed up on the opportunity by crossing en masse at these sites and if they then were to push along the north or east banks toward the mouth of the Seine River, then the fate of the two German field armies would be sealed.

Lieutenant General Alfred Gause, Dietrich's chief of staff, thought that any further fighting west of the river could only involve a "planned withdrawal in the face of the superior enemy."[110] To gain time for the crossing operation, Model intended to economize his forces along the western sector of the Fifth Panzer Army by means of a delaying action. That would then allow him to feed Panzers to the southern sector.[111]

The 1st SS Panzer Division, 12th SS Panzer Division, and 2nd Panzer Division were ordered to the southern sector immediately after the end of the fighting in the Falaise Pocket. Those three units, however, were not sufficient to stabilize the confused situation in the LXXXI Army Corps area, where in the meantime two American armored divisions had penetrated. By the afternoon of August 21 the three Panzer divisions together could not muster more than ten Panzers.[112]

Model now only saw the possibility of pulling out the 2nd and 9th SS Panzer Divisions. Nonetheless, it seemed to him possible to prevent the development of major gaps in the western wing that was heavily attacked near Lisieux by withdrawing during the night to the Toucques sector (Deauville–Lisieux–Orbec–L'Aigle).[113]

The events of the next several days confirmed something that Army Group B headquarters had suspected.[114] There was no sound foundation whatsoever to Hitler's order to fight in front of the Seine so as to maintain "contact between Fifth Panzer Army and Paris by means of a concentric attack."[115]

After the front had remained mostly quiet during the morning of August 22, the major American offensive against the southern sector began that afternoon. Eight carpet bombing missions were flown in the Conches area alone.[116] Then 130 Sherman tanks attacked the LXXXI Army Corps. The twenty-five Panzers of the two

SS divisions that Model had ordered forward were still tied down at Lisieux. Gause's orders to "hold under all circumstances, because otherwise nobody gets across the Seine River anymore," simply did not change the lopsided strength ratios.[117] The regiments of the Luftwaffe 17th Field Division on the left wing of Kuntzen's corps simply "flew apart" under the assault.[118]

The Americans broke through the front line and pushed all the way into the area south of Louviers. That meant the crossing sites were directly threatened. At that time some twenty major ferries that could carry heavy equipment and several smaller ones were operational in the Rouen area.[119] Since August 20 the remnants of the Seventh Army and the supply trains of the Fifth Panzer Army had been crossing the river with relatively little trouble, but too slowly.[120] Nonetheless, Colonel Rudolf von Gersdorff, the Seventh Army chief of staff, still hoped to get his units to the east bank of the Seine within two days.[121]

But the crossings were bound to come to a halt within a few hours if the American attack continued unopposed. Faced with the threat of a second pocket, Model was now determined "rigorously to strip" the western wing.[122]

That meant that infantry elements were simply ground up in order to pull the available Panzers toward the breakthrough point. General of Infantry Hans von Obstfelder, commanding the LXXXVI Army Corps, and SS-Gruppenführer and Lieutenant General of the Waffen-SS Wilhelm Bittrich, commanding the II SS Panzer Corps, both felt that the western sector was already so thin that the British "could walk through wherever they wanted."[123] Lisieux, for example, was held by only about one hundred men of the 272nd Infantry Division.[124]

Model's risky but only feasible options were not foiled by the Allies. The British and Canadians were generally inactive on August 23, and the American main effort was only on the west bank, rather than astride the Seine as the Germans had feared.[125]

With the battle groups of the 49th Infantry Division and the Luftwaffe 18th Field Division and a few Tiger tanks, Lieutenant General Gerhard Graf von Schwerin was able to reduce the American bridgeheads somewhat and even recapture La Roche-Guyon. Schwerin, commanding general of the 116th Panzer Division, had assumed temporary command of the Seine sector in the absence of a corps headquarters to control the operation.[126]

OB West believed that the measures taken by Dietrich along the southern front were inadequate. Dietrich did not execute Model's intention quickly enough to hit immediately the flank of the American wedge pointing toward Rouen. Such an attack with the combat-ready elements of five Panzer divisions—the 1st and 2nd SS Panzer Divisions and the 2nd, 21st, and 116th Panzer Divisions, was supposed to have shifted the front south to the Conches–Evreux–Vernon line.[127] Model reprimanded Dietrich in his typically brusque manner, whereupon Dietrich requested his immediate relief from command, saying that he was "not some little schoolboy you could pull up by his ears."[128] Earlier in the day Dietrich had seen for himself on the battlefield that such an attack had hardly any chance of success. In the event, it failed quickly. Fuel shortages prevented the 21st Panzer Division from even reaching its assembly area at Le Neubourg. The attacking force itself comprised only worn-out remnants with a few battalions and at most thirty Panzers.[129] Model finally realized that Dietrich was facing an impossible task. Via the chief of the Wehrmacht operations staff, Model reported to Hitler that even the toughest orders could not alter the unfavorable situation, because the "Panzer divisions are nothing but *torsos* [*sic*]."[130]

Meanwhile, the Americans had pushed beyond Louviers toward Elbeuf, some ten kilometers south of Rouen. The only way to prevent the impending formation of a pocket was to attack the enemy, regardless of his superiority. For that mission the ad hoc Panzer Group Schwerin[131] was given the 2nd SS Panzer Division and the 21st Panzer Division.[132]

The withdrawal of the western wing, therefore, had to be sped up, first to the Bernay line during the night between August 23 and 24, and twenty-four hours later to the Risle sector. Those movements went off according to plan, although only twelve Panzers of the 9th Panzer Division were available as an immediate reaction force.

Nonetheless, the strength of Panzer Group Schwerin was insufficient to push the front line forward to the south. Despite the bitter defensive fight put up by the Germans, the Americans reached the Elbeuf and were now advancing to the Seine.[133]

Once again, there developed the danger that the Allies might cross the river and overrun the ferry sites from the rear. Model had nothing with which to oppose such a maneuver. The last available armored force, the 9th SS Panzer Division, had already been sent to the Elbeuf area.[134] Model ordered the continuation of the crossing of the Seventh Army and all vehicles "ceaselessly and at maximum speed."[135]

Some four thousand men and fifteen hundred motor vehicles crossed the river during the night between August 24 and 25.[136] On the following day mobile combat operations prevented the Americans from achieving any decisive successes in the southern sector. Schwerin's Panzers even pushed the Americans out of Elbeuf temporarily. The dreaded Allied thrust from the bridgeheads north of the Seine did not materialize.[137]

The Allies, of course, were able to destroy several ferries and a pontoon bridge by ceaselessly committing fighter-bombers and artillery of all calibers.[138] Nonetheless, the remnants of the Seventh Army had escaped. Out of nine infantry divisions, Eberbach's staff was able to assemble around fifteen hundred to twenty-five hundred soldiers per unit on the north bank of the Seine.[139] According to German records, some twenty-five thousand vehicles of all kinds had made it back across the Seine River.[140]

The south bank was held only by those elements of Dietrich's Fifth Panzer Army that were combat capable. They had a combined combat strength of around 18,000 men, supported by 314 artillery pieces and 42 Panzers. But they faced an Allied force of tremendous superiority. According to German calculations, the enemy force totaled 110,500 infantrymen, 1,320 artillery pieces, and about 1,900 tanks.[141]

Thus, the prospects for getting the Fifth Panzer Army across the Seine were poor at best. On August 25, Lieutenant General Gause said that if it were to be successful at all, "the withdrawal movement would have to be carried out in a single phase."[142] (See Map 11.)

(b) The First Army's Situation South of Paris

The acute threat of the formation of a pocket at Rouen had passed, at least for the Seventh Army. On the other hand, the deep operation of the Allies that the Germans feared would come from the south of Paris was definitely starting to assume a clearer shape.

That sector had remained relatively quiet on August 19–20. The American attack, which began the next day, very quickly exposed the gap between Hitler's orders and reality. Chevallerie, the commanding general of the First Army, was not able to hold to the west of the Seine with his forces.[143] Nor was he able to accomplish his screening mission at Montargis or prevent an American push toward Dijon.[144] He had nothing with which to mount the concentric attack he had been ordered to execute.

The crises in the Rouen–Paris area and in southern France tied down divisions that Model originally had wanted to use to reinforce the conglomeration of units of the First Army. When the American attack jumped off in the forenoon of August 21, Chevallerie only had one complete division, the 48th Infantry Division.[145] His Army sector did have the divisional headquarters of three Panzer or Panzer Grenadier divisions, but with their units smashed they could only wait for fresh personnel and equipment.[146]

The situation developed swiftly. With very little difficulty the American XX Corps and XII Corps advanced with six divisions, pushing the German security line back to the east along a broad front between Paris and the Loire River.[147]

Model could do little else but stand by and watch. He did not have any powerful forces with which he could have stabilized the situation. In his response to the Führer Directive he expressly noted that Chevallerie's army was too weak to accomplish the missions assigned to it.[148]

The situation on the left wing of Army Group B also threatened to turn critical quickly because the Allies were preparing for a broad operation along the lower Seine River. That was contrary to the initial German assessment that such an operation would be launched only after the encirclement attempt. Model, therefore, on August 21 ordered the 3rd and 15th Panzer Grenadier Divisions, which were expected to arrive from Italy, farther north to the Tonnerre–Troyes–Chalôns sur Marne area, rather than to Dijon.[149]

Considering the pace of the American advance, that order quickly appeared to have been overcome by events. The 48th Infantry Division had been able to withdraw behind the Seine River section between Corbeil and Montereau, linking up in the process with the Paris barrier ring, but the situation was not at all clear south of there. All contact had been lost with the elements of the 338th Infantry Division that were deployed at Montargis on the Loing River. By that evening they had been cut off. American troops had crossed the Loing River and the Yonne River at Sens and were just a few kilometers away from Troyes.[150]

The Americans had struck the vulnerable nerve of the German

front, along the weak southern wing of Army Group B. For the time being, the Germans had nothing with which to counter a continued Allied offensive from the Sens–Troyes area toward Germany or toward Dijon. All Chevallerie could do was to try to maintain contact with Paris and try to forestall an attack heading north into the rear of Army Group B. He intended to swing his army's left wing, whose outpost line ran from Paris south, back in a west-east direction at Montereau. The left wing would be reconstituted in a somewhat patchwork manner behind the Seine River between Montereau and Troyes. The forces available for that effort were the two arriving SS brigades plus the combat-capable elements of the three divisions that were forced to finish their reconstitution prematurely.[151, 152] The front line of the First Army ended with the 27th SS Panzer Division, which was defending Troyes after just having been detrained. To the south a huge gaping hole ran all the way to the units of Army Task Group G.

Facing that situation OB West urged the maximum speed in the development of the Somme–Marne–Saône defensive position. Little work had been done to that point because General of Aviation Karl Kitzinger had only about twenty thousand men available to reinforce a distance of some 650 kilometers.[153]

Model thus ordered that all available Wehrmacht units plus the civilian population—if necessary, by force—be committed to the entrenching work.[154] Unless a maximum effort started immediately, the Americans could be expected to arrive there before "the first spade had been turned."[155]

The success of those measures was doubtful from the very start. Kitzinger had estimated that at least three months would be required even to erect a skeleton of field positions.[156] And, of course, all such efforts would do little good if there were no troops to defend the line. At Model's direction, Colonel Bodo Zimmermann, the OB West operations officer, estimated that the job would require at least thirty-six infantry and eight Panzer divisions.[157] But that was the theory. Model, therefore, demanded that the Wehrmacht High Command *"instantaneously"* make available at least one outpost force in the strength of eight divisions as a nucleus around which the defense could be established.[158]

Even if that demand could be met, everything depended primarily on the way the Allies conducted their operations in the First Army sector. OB West headquarters believed that it was unlikely that Model's demand could be met, but they wanted to give the Wehrmacht High Command a clear and unvarnished picture of the seriousness of the situation.[159]

As Colonel Zimmermann observed, if the Americans seized the opportunity either by wheeling southeast toward Dijon to cut off Army Task Group G or by breaking through the weak outpost lines along the upper Seine River to push via Chalôns to Metz, then the value of Kitzinger's defensive position would be nullified.[160]

But the intentions of the Americans remained a mystery for the time being. Air reconnaissance sorties were impossible because all available aircraft were needed in the area over Rouen.[161] Based on past experience, however, Chevallerie thought there was a possibility that the enemy would start a major offensive only after regrouping and deploying according to plan.[162]

Model had also figured that the Allies might take an operational pause after reaching the Seine River. General of Panzer Troops Walter Krüger and his LVIII Panzer Corps headquarters were assigned the mission of organizing the reconstitution of Army Group B's Panzer divisions. The first fifty battle tanks were scheduled to arrive in the Beauvais–Senlis area, only fifty kilometers northeast of the river.[163] Army Group B headquarters informed Krüger that his mission would probably take about three weeks.[164]

But the Americans, at least for the time being, remained completely quiet at the Germans' weakest point, the extreme left wing of the First Army. The Americans now shifted their attacks to the Paris–Montereau sector of the Seine River and to the French metropolis itself. On August 23, American troops were able to push back the 48th Infantry Division, which was defending a fifty-kilometer-wide sector. The Americans also were able to put strong units across the Seine River at Melun.[165] The next night they achieved the same thing at Fontainebleau. The FFI had seized the bridge there just in time, preventing the Germans from blowing it.[166] The 48th Infantry Division withdrew after hard fighting that cost both sides heavy casualties, with the Americans losing twelve tanks in just a few hours.[167]

After additional attacks on August 25, the Germans lost the section of the Seine River south of Paris. In the meantime, the Americans established bridgeheads in four locations. Those attacks forced the First Army to withdraw during the following night to a new line running about twenty-five kilometers to the east.[168]

Those events, however, paled against the background of events that were coming to a head in Paris at about the same time. Military necessity made it absolutely essential for the First Army to maintain contact with Dietrich's forces in the north. Both German headquarters expected the French capital to fall soon. Paris, therefore, was to be blockaded east of the Seine River to deny the Allies the use of the main traffic arteries that expanded from the city in a radial pattern.[169] The commanding general of the First Army now faced the problem that the forces earmarked for that purpose, the 47th Infantry Division and about forty-five tanks from the Panzer-Lehr and 9th Panzer Divisions, now could not be withdrawn from the First Army's increasingly shaky left flank.[170] Speidel was aware of this, but could not see any possibility other than "simply to accept the maximum possible risk" there.[171]

Model intervened personally and redirected the Panzers. Instead of sending them toward the Seine River bridgeheads to the south, their objective now was the area to the east of Paris.[172] In the afternoon of August 25 Chevallerie once again alerted OB West to the danger by phone. He reported that "all available Panzers . . . have been committed to the fight for Paris." He added, "no forces were available . . . to beat off the enemy thrusts [along the southern wing] . . . , not to mention throwing the enemy back across the Seine River."[173]

Chevallerie's words were confirmed almost simultaneously as the Americans again began to move in the Troyes area, initially pushing southeast from there with reconnaissance vehicles. The leading infantry units of the 15th Panzer Grenadier Division, which were just detraining along the Canal de Bourgogne fifty kilometers south of Troyes, were thrown immediately into action.[174]

Blumentritt reported to Jodl that there was reason to fear that the enemy would reach the Dijon area sooner than Army Task Group G.[175] But before that happened, Model had to try to hold together the cohesion of his Army Group B. The operational threat developing from the Allied maneuvers south or southeast of Paris was now very clear, but the German strength situation limited Model to plugging gaps only at the acute crisis points at the expense of other frontline sectors. On top of that, Hitler's Paris Orders severely restricted Model's freedom of action.

Chapter 7

The Situation around Paris

Within the total scope of the military operations in the west in 1944, the fall of Paris might appear to have been of secondary significance. The French metropolis did not become the scene of decisive combat operations, nor was Hitler's threat of utter destruction carried out. Paris happily was spared the fate of so many major European and non-European cities.

Taking a synoptic approach to the events of August 1944, however, the significance of Paris can be seen in clearer context. Many elements of the operational problems were tied together in time and space, issues that had to be resolved by the local commanders on both sides. Political-ideological and subjective factors either influenced or prevented the execution of many decisions that otherwise might have been made on the principle of military efficiency.

1. The City's Significance for German and Allied Planning

A glance at the map shows the highly centralized position of Paris within metropolitan France. It is a country subdivided into many sectors, all of which look to the metropolis. In 1944 the Paris urban area had about 5 million inhabitants.[1] It was bound to have military significance, especially as a traffic and transportation junction. No fewer than seventeen lines of the national rail network converged on Paris, and the well-built *Routes Nationales* highway system radiated out from Paris in all compass directions. The more than sixty bridges in the Paris area—including thirty-two in the municipal area itself—that were spared during the Allied pre-invasion bombing raids were almost the only intact crossings between the metropolis and the mouth of the Seine River at Le Havre.

Consequently, Paris had a decisive role in supplying the German army in Normandy and for troop movements from and to the front. The very highest command nodes of the Wehrmacht in the West had established their headquarters in or near the city to take advantage of its technical and communications advantages. The Germans especially were dependent on the French telephone system, which was centered in Paris.

As the Allied invasion campaign unfolded and the front line drew nearer, however, the great operational significance of Paris for the Germans declined increasingly. Despite Allied air raids on marshaling yards and French sabotage, the Germans managed to maintain the supply movements from Paris across the Seine, but those movements came to a dead stop by August 19.[2] The main body of the units of Army Group B that were still fighting to the west of the river at that time found itself cut off from direct contact with Paris by the American thrust.[3] The position of Paris as a command and control center was now entirely too exposed: The headquarters of OB West, Navy Group West, the Third Air Fleet, and of the Military Commander, France, had evacuated to the east immediately after Hitler gave his approval. The Seine River bridges now were no longer significant for German troop movements, because the stream of the remnants from the divisions that had been smashed in Normandy and other scattered elements gradually ran dry.[4] Fresh units crossing to move toward the front could no longer be expected. From that point on, Paris no longer offered any direct advantages for Germany's conduct of combat operations.

But the city still held vital significance for Hitler. He assumed that the liberation of the French metropolis would be a central concern of the Allied operations plan, and therefore a main-effort offensive toward Paris was a logical assessment.[5] If the Germans were to concentrate their defensive effort there, and in the process force the Allies into costly and time-consuming house-to-house fighting, it then might be possible to absorb the punch of the enemy offensive. At the least, the tempo of the enemy advance could be slowed considerably.[6] Therefore, it was one of Model's most important missions, as Hitler had ordered on August 20, "to hold a bridgehead west of Paris" and "if necessary . . . to fight around and in Paris, regardless of the city's destruction."[7]

Hitler's hope for a significant defensive victory and his ensuing orders could be justified militarily only so long as the Allied advance conformed to his expectations. But by August 22 it was quite obvious that the Americans had other intentions. By that point they had crossed the Seine River or the Seine River and the Yonne River, both north and south of Paris.[8] Control of the city's bridges, therefore, was no longer an attractive objective for a main-effort attack. Instead, there was every indication that the Americans would simply bypass Paris. That put an end to Hitler's intention to turn the metropolis into an embattled bastion in the Seine–Yonne line. Nevertheless, Hitler continued to insist that Paris had to be defended at any price. He continued to maintain his presumptions of the military requirements and his belief that the city was "of decisive . . . political significance." As he noted somewhat prophetically in his August 23 order: "In history, the loss of Paris . . . always signified the loss of all of France."[9] This might have been true. Certainly the loss of Paris would be considered throughout the world as a sign of German defeat in the west. Above all, the French would see it that way and would increase their resistance actions accordingly. Thus, Hitler had now discarded the military factors in his line of reasoning. The more his thinking wandered away from real-life combat events, the more radical and even more irrational his orders became. The last sentence of his August 23 order shows this quite clearly: "Paris must not fall into enemy hands or, if it does, only as a field of rubble."[10]

Initially the Allies had no intentions of attacking Paris. According to studies prepared by the planning staffs prior to the start of the invasion, Paris was to be bypassed during the advance and then encircled from the rear because of the anticipated heavy German resistance. Once encircled, the inevitable capitulation of the trapped German forces would only be a question of time.[11] By the middle of August the various Allied headquarters were still not thinking any differently. And at that point another serious factor combined with the prospect of a strong German defensive position in the French capital to mitigate against a major operation aimed at Paris.

The Allied leadership was already seeing the first indicators of an impending logistics crisis. Nevertheless, Eisenhower on August 19 decided to continue the offensive after defeating the enemy forces that were still west of the Seine and then push immediately across the river and beyond. That day, despite its general atmosphere of rising optimism, also marked the first climax in the strategic controversy among the Allied commanding generals. The subject of long-drawn-out discussions, especially between Eisenhower and Montgomery, revolved around the precise procedure for bringing about the final German collapse, which presumably was near at hand. Impressed by the extent of their successes in Normandy, the Allied commanders were already looking all the way to the Rhine

River.[12] In the broader operational scope of things, the liberation of Paris might have second-ranking significance at best; but it was still undesirable based on purely military factors. Since early August, the SHAEF G-4 section, which was responsible for logistics in Eisenhower's staff, had been warning about the implications of the capture of the city and the subsequent demands on the supply system that would seriously compromise the ability to continue the advance across the Seine River.[13] The city's daily supply requirements were estimated at about four thousand tons.[14] It therefore made sense to bypass Paris until such time as the rail lines from Brittany—even though there were no operational harbors available there as yet—as well as Normandy had been repaired and put back in operation, and until the Allies held the ports of Rouen and Le Havre.[15] The planners estimated that the capture of Paris would no longer restrict the flow of Allied operations only after the end of October 1944.[16]

By taking Paris too soon, then, the Allies would run the risk of overloading the already straining American transportation system, which in turn would result in serious supply and movement restrictions for the frontline units. With this complex problem in mind, Montgomery on August 20, in agreement with Eisenhower, ordered that the French metropolis would be liberated only if such a maneuver became justifiable based on the military situation.[17] For U.S. president Franklin D. Roosevelt the military logistical argument only reinforced the political reservations that were connected with the person of General de Gaulle. In accomplishing France's liberation, Eisenhower's mission was merely to leave behind favorable prerequisites for the formation of a freely elected, representative French government.[18] The long-held American view at that point was that the liberation of Paris might actually work against the development of those prerequisites.[19]

The Americans doubted de Gaulle's democratic legitimacy. They did recognize his provisional government, but they did not want to give him an opportunity to establish that government in the center of France and thus to create a fait accompli. The Americans were not especially inclined to contribute to the stabilization of such a government, which in their opinion did not represent the will of the majority of the French people and therefore might possibly provoke a civil war. During the planning phases for the invasion, therefore, the "Paris Problem" was treated in a rather cursory fashion. The deep-seated reservations against de Gaulle gradually decreased only upon a reevaluation of France's internal situation, although much mutual distrust remained. Finally, on August 17, the British-American Combined Chiefs of Staff expressed no objections to having the French march into a liberated Paris. At the same time they advised Eisenhower to receive de Gaulle as the commanding general of the French forces, but not as the head of government.[20]

In the end, however, all objections and arguments against the early liberation of Paris fell by the wayside because of pressure from the French side and the developing dynamics of the situation. The inherent political disagreements made it almost impossible to develop accepted objectives and procedures or even consistent plans among the various French factions that were fighting against the occupation. There was at least enough of a basic consensus, however, to make the French accept a wider approach to the coalition warfare necessary to defeat the German Reich.[21] That common denominator made it possible to combine various driving forces, despite the more emotionally driven objectives of restoring French prestige and national pride, the maneuvering for key positions in postwar domestic politics, and the restoration of France as a major power. During the process of liberating French territory, the capital and the country's various resources were bound to emerge as factors that would take on lives of their own independent of Allied military planning.[22] There was no disagreement within the French camp that the Resistance movement in Paris would take up arms before the arrival of regular Allied forces.[23] But in the end there were two elements of uncertainty that helped determine the course of events. The Allies had no way to predict the timing of any uprising in Paris, nor was it possible to assess with certainty what the German reaction would be.[24] Hopes and anxieties competed with each other in driving events. The range of possibilities fluctuated between the extremes of a bloodless liberation of Paris, such as had been experienced in Rome that June, or a replay of the insurrection in isolated Warsaw, during which the Polish *Armija Krajowa* (Home Army) was fighting a desperate losing battle in that same month of August 1944. For de Gaulle's ambitions, it was essential that the liberation should take place "under the auspices of a military and national operation."[25] In other words, as a result of a popular uprising that was closely linked to military support from the outside.[26] For de Gaulle, the key significance of the uprising would be as a triggering event. It would be unleashed at the designated moment, be as short as possible, be disciplined, and facilitate a speedy return to normalcy under the aegis of a provisional government headed by de Gaulle.[27] His intent to keep the insurrection limited and controllable was a function of his own basic distrust of the Resistance, which for the time being was not under his direct control in the still occupied parts of France. Paris's special tradition as a city of revolution may have underscored this skeptical attitude on his part. Indeed, the Resistance movement there was decisively influenced by the Communists. They held key positions in the hierarchy of the local political resistance organizations and in the FFI.[28] The potential for autonomous action among the rank and file could not be ignored.[29] That was particularly true of the *Franc Tireurs et Partisans*, the powerful nucleus of Paris's armed resistance, and which consisted mostly of Communists and labor union members of the General Confederation of Labor. Its commander, Henri Rol-Tanguy, was a fighting man who had proved himself as a member of the International Brigades during the Spanish Civil War. He held the position of regional commander of the FFI. The plans of de Gaulle's provisional government were threatened by Rol-Tanguy's clearly stated intentions for a spontaneous revolutionary mass uprising that would seize the important positions of power.[30] His intentions were motivated more by domestic political factors than by military considerations. Hitler's statement about the "decisively political significance" of the city of Paris and its key function in the situation in France as a whole therefore became quite relevant, although for reasons other than those he originally envisioned. Dark memories of the 1871 Paris Commune Uprising caused de Gaulle to try to influence the local Resistance groups to follow his lead and thereby prevent the city from becoming the "captive of anarchy."[31] But de Gaulle failed to bring the Resistance movements into line through his personal agents, such as General of Brigade Jacques Chaban-Delmas, the National Military Delegate in Paris. The command hierarchy, imposed from the outside and directed from London or Algiers, turned out not to be strong enough to force the autonomously operating Resistance groups to accept its authority.

The Communist Party achieved an initial success with the call for a general insurrection that was publicly proclaimed on August 19.[32] But it soon turned out that while the FFI alone could stir up considerable trouble, it could not drive the Germans out of the city. Numerous emissaries from Paris, including a delegation from FFI commander Rol-Tanguy, now arrived at the nearby Allied head-quarters and strongly urged that regular forces be committed.[33] Considering their own weakness, the fear of German retaliation was probably the primary motive behind their actions.[34] In his August 21 letter to Eisenhower, however, de Gaulle was guided by other considerations. De Gaulle reinforced the French pressure with almost ultimatum-like demands addressed to Eisenhower, which contributed decisively to the modification of Allied operational plans. De Gaulle continued to fear the political implications connected with the uprising, much more so than any military problems that might result from a German reaction. De Gaulle at any rate estimated the threat to be so great that he was prepared to take unconventional measures and, if necessary, resort to insubordination. Eisenhower, he insisted, should issue the orders for the march on Paris, which de Gaulle believed was the only way to restore order in the city. Even the damage to the city that might result from the fighting was secondary in his eyes. If the Allied Supreme Commander did not concede to his demands, then de Gaulle assured him that he would order General of Division Philippe Leclerc's French 2nd Armored Division to attack.[35] Indeed, Leclerc at that point already had sent an advanced detachment toward Paris, quite contrary to orders from his American superiors.[36] On August 22, Eisenhower made his final decision with the words: "It seems we are forced to march into Paris."[37] In going along with French demands, Eisenhower's decision was also justified by the fact that it was necessary to avoid any further controversy and not to place any grave burden on American-French relations, especially within the framework of coalition warfare. Eisenhower's decision was alleviated somewhat in military terms because the various Allied headquarters no longer had to account for the possibility of any long and drawn-out street fighting in the city.[38] Based on the not always accurate information received from the Resistance, Eisenhower's staff also had reason to assume that the German commander, General of Infantry Dietrich von Choltitz, and his garrison would withdraw the moment Allied troops crossed the city boundaries.[39]

2. Von Choltitz, the German Command in the West, and the Development of the Situation in Paris to August 23

As a consequence of the July 20 assassination attempt against him, Hitler appointed a new city commandant for Paris. His choice fell on Choltitz, who assumed the imposing title of Commanding General and Wehrmacht Commander of Greater Paris—a title that carried very little in the way of actual military authority, as it would later turn out.

This short, energetic Saxon was now fifty years old.[40] He started the war as a battalion commander in the 16th Infantry Regiment. In May 1940 he distinguished himself at the head of his battalion during the airborne landings in Holland. Probably the greatest moment in his military career was his participation in the successful siege of Sevastopol in the summer of 1942. Later, as commander of the 260th Infantry Division, Choltitz was promoted to major general. After other assignments in the Russian Theater he was given command in June 1944 of the LXXXIV Army Corps on the Western Front, facing the potential Allied invasion. But luck deserted him on that assignment: At the end of July the Americans penetrated into his sector and then a few days later broke out at Avranches. Although Choltitz was personally blameless for the situation, then-OB West von Kluge immediately relieved him of command. Nonetheless, Choltitz still had the reputation for being a tough man—and that was a decisive criterion for Hitler.[41] The reassignment of Choltitz to a command was therefore only a matter of time.

Choltitz, however, had not yet come to terms psychologically with the harsh battlefield realities in Normandy.[42] On July 15 he talked about a "tremendous meat grinder," such as he "had not experienced in eleven years of war."[43] He also was psychologically depressed by the overwhelming superiority of the Anglo-Americans. His corps had been softened up for the American assault by the intense carpet bombing, without any chance of putting up a real defense. According to his own memoirs, Choltitz's visit to Führer Headquarters on August 7, 1944, did anything other than boost his morale. Rather, his confidence in the supreme leadership was severely shaken by Hitler's behavior.[44] Those factors, combined with his impaired state of health resulting from a heart ailment, must be considered when evaluating his subsequent behavior.

At first Hitler's assignment did not seem to be too much of a burden to the new Wehrmacht Paris Commander. Choltitz's main tasks in Paris were to maintain law and order, to eliminate any and all so-called rear echelon phenomena, and to comb out the various headquarters to find men who were still fit to fight.[45] But the swift Allied advance introduced the problem of how the city could be defended against external attack. Initial guidance came from Kluge, the OB West at that time, who analyzed the situation correctly and assessed as unlikely any major Allied push to Paris.[46] Kluge noted expressly that defensive efforts would have to be concentrated entirely on the barrier belt that ran to the west of the city.[47]

Here was at least a chance of beating off enemy reconnaissance probes with the help of field fortifications and tank barriers along the outgoing streets, as well as with the 88mm batteries of the Paris antiaircraft artillery belt.[48] Kluge wanted to avoid street fighting, and for that matter any fighting at all in the city. As for the initiation of the so-called "paralysis and demolition measures"—which were entirely customary during withdrawal operations to slow down the enemy's pursuit—Kluge stipulated that any such actions in Paris would be initiated only on his specific orders.[49]

To keep a handle on things at all times and to prevent any independent actions, Kluge had the Wehrmacht Paris Commander report to him directly. Even after Kluge was relieved, Choltitz continued to make every effort to conform to the intentions of the former OB West.[50] Model, the new OB West who had just arrived in France, did not have the time to address in detail the rather secondary problem of Paris.

Thus the priorities were established. The main body of the twenty thousand men available in the Paris area was employed to the west of the city.[51] Remnants of the decimated 352nd Infantry Division were also deployed to the front of the barrier ring.[52] Given their heterogeneous and provisional makeup, neither those units nor the two regimental battle groups committed there under the command of Lieutenant Colonel Hubertus von Aulock could possibly carry out a delaying defense along the approximately forty-five-kilometer-long barrier belt.

The higher-level staffs were entirely familiar with these problems. As early as August 16 higher headquarters estimated that the enemy would at any time be in a position to penetrate the only lightly manned defensive positions.[53] But the various headquarters in the west had no idea of what should be done in the case of an offensive. A telephone conversation between chiefs of staff Blumentritt and Speidel indicates clearly the existing doubt as to whether the city of Paris should be defended at all.[54]

Once the barrier belt had accomplished its mission of gaining time, there was nothing to prevent any evacuation of the metropolis without a fight. The notion that Paris, like Rome, could be declared an open city might have been a factor, although there was no indication at the time that the Allies would honor any such declaration.[55] Choltitz's original mission to preserve stable internal conditions grew increasingly more difficult as the unrest bubbling beneath the surface of the city rose to the point of near eruption. Despite the Allied successes in Normandy, the population of the city initially had adopted a wait-and-see attitude. That mood was now changing, driven, among other things, by inadequate food supplies. Paris was now cut off from its sources of supply, which had been located to the west. And with the rail lines destroyed, food shipments reached Paris only irregularly by highway.[56] The French *Ravitaillement General* (the general supply system), which until then had done the job of distributing the few arriving goods in coordination with the German military, collapsed or was put out of action by the Resistance.[57] Paris was on the brink of starvation. Compounding the tensions were rumors that the entire male population of the city capable of working would be deported.[58] Such a decision was actually under consideration in the Reich Chancellery, which estimated a labor force of some one hundred thousand to two hundred thousand men.[59] Those rumors increasingly drove Parisians into the arms of the militant Resistance. Especially after the point when the defensive main effort was placed in the outer barrier ring, Choltitz had forces within the city with which to oppose the more than twenty thousand (albeit poorly armed) members of the FFI.[60] The 325th Security Division, first organized in 1942, with the 1st, 5th, 6th, and 190th Security Regiments, was the force assigned to the Commandant of Greater Paris for maintaining internal control.[61] The 325th Security Division, however, no longer existed as such. All Choltitz had was the 2nd Battalion of the 190th Security Regiment, the 17th Technical Battalion, two companies of the 5th Security Regiment, and remnants of the 317th Reserve Antiaircraft Artillery Battalion.[62] That meager force was supported by a few Panzers and World War I–era French-built tanks.[63] That was the only tactical reserve Choltitz had available. The desolate situation of the defenders inside the city, totaling some five thousand men, was augmented by four so-called "Paris Alert Battalions," patched together partly from Military Administration civilian officials, who were quickly put into Wehrmacht uniforms and placed in various buildings that were designated as strongpoints.[64] In the event of any fighting, the decisive advantages would be with the FFI, which fought with guerrilla tactics. They had the ability to pop out from the population at any moment, execute their action, and then merge just as quickly back into the population. Thus restricted in his military options, all Choltitz could do was try somehow to defuse by other means the tense atmosphere. If he could do that, he could buy time until either the evacuation of Paris was authorized by the Führer Headquarters or adequate reinforcements arrived to put the resistance down. The possibility of reinforcements for Paris was something the various German headquarters in the west still considered a real possibility at that point. Such notions did not originate out of thin air. The First Army, in whose sector Paris was located, was supposed to receive control of not only the 48th Infantry Division but also the 47th and 49th Infantry Divisions from the Channel coast. Additionally, the remnants of three Panzer or Panzer Grenadier divisions were then refitting in the immediate vicinity of the city.

For the time being, however, Choltitz was entirely left to his own devices, both for his available resources and for his decisions. During those days, he could see the visible signs of at least the temporary collapse of Germany's position in France.[65] On August 17 the representatives of the Vichy government under Pierre Laval left Paris, followed by the personnel of the German embassy. The higher military headquarters also left Paris, including that of the Military Commander in France, General of Aviation Karl Kitzinger, which had considerable expertise in dealing with the French.[66] Increasingly isolated, Choltitz did everything he could to avert a threatening escalation. With little to work with, he could only do that by bluffing, by simulating a position of strength, and by simultaneously seeming to accommodate the FFI. Choltitz assembled all available military personnel for one last demonstration march through Paris.[67] Addressing Pierre Taittinger, the president of the Paris City Council, Choltitz threatened that any sign of an uprising would be nipped in the bud by SS regiments and Panzers.[68] Simultaneously, Choltitz displayed a readiness to negotiate on certain points. Swedish consul-general Raoul Nordling played a significant role in that process. Through him, Choltitz was able to establish otherwise unavailable contacts with the French political leaders and with the FFI, without immediately undermining his own credibility since all such contacts were indirect. Choltitz, therefore, was willing to use the informal channels while keeping within his interpretation of the limits placed on him by his official orders. He stuck to that basic idea when the first major fighting erupted on August 19. Choltitz did not turn a deaf ear to Nordling, who wanted to discuss the possibilities of a general armistice in Paris.[69] Choltitz already had approved the release of the political prisoners who were left in the city, and that action was followed by an agreement, the details of which are documented rather spottily in the German records.[70] The surviving documents do show that Choltitz entered into agreements through the Swiss and Swedish consulates with the "new rulers in Paris"—in other words, with the representatives of the FFI.[71] Accordingly, Choltitz stated that he was prepared to see to it that FFI prisoners would not be shot if they laid down their arms; that French policemen could go back on duty; and that the German occupation authorities would work to end the strikes.[72] The general was entirely aware of the explosive nature of even these seemingly sparse points. Significantly, he then added that his word would now apply in every situation—in other words, even if the Wehrmacht operations staff did not endorse the agreement.[73] The Intelligence Section of OB West also interpreted the agreement that way. Such an agreement was wholly unexpected because Choltitz seemed to be striving for a diplomatic solution, something that Army Group B immediately criticized with the comment that it looked "odd . . . that a Wehrmacht headquarters in a city occupied by the German military is conducting negotiations via foreign missions."[74] Choltitz clearly was in violation of Wehrmacht High Command orders, because he intended to consider FFI prisoners not as guerrillas but rather as prisoners of war according to international law.[75] Indeed, in adopting this position Choltitz only anticipated a policy that was to be adopted later in other German-held areas. Given the situation, it became especially clear that reprisal measures in the end would only endanger the fate of German troops and that outright punishment measures threatened to boomerang on their executors. The German strength figures made the situation even more obvious.[76] The times when one could afford simply to ignore the FFI militarily were long gone, at least in Paris. To be able to continue influencing future events, Choltitz was thus forced to play a double game, not only in dealing with the Resistance but also with his own superiors. In his highly visible duty position, he could be sure that Hitler would always be watching what he was doing.[77] Choltitz therefore could not overplay his hand. Keeping the fate of his wife and three children always in mind, he had to give the impression that he was doing everything to accomplish his assigned mission. On the other hand, he obviously was unwilling to obey orders that would further complicate the already difficult situation. The agreement of August 19 led the French authorities to believe that it would depend solely on the behavior of the FFI as to whether or not Choltitz would take extreme measures. The armistice, Choltitz speculated, would cause confusion within the FFI. It would aggravate the disputes between the advocates and opponents of the armistice, and it would thus deflect the pressure from the Germans.[78] From his earliest youth, Choltitz had been educated to think and act like a soldier. His family, after all, had pursued that career for eight centuries.[79] But he also felt that this situation, which called for conspiratorial talents rather than military decisions, was "obnoxious," as he put it later.[80] Nevertheless, he was successful—at least in the beginning. The armistice may not always have been respected, but it helped quiet things down in the city at least temporarily.[81] The time he therefore gained sustained his hope that some higher agency would somehow intervene to help him.

Since Hitler's directive of August 20, which stated that if necessary "the fight around and in Paris was to be conducted regardless of the city's destruction," any hope of assistance was limited to military reinforcements.[82] But at the same time it was becoming ever clearer what fate the Führer Headquarters had in mind for the French metropolis.

The gap between such orders and what was militarily justifiable at any given point can be documented impressively as events unfolded. In the initial reports, the commanders in charge in the west occasionally found themselves forced to adopt a rather odd rhetorical style to conceal this disparity. These commanders formally complied with the contents of such orders, but in the final analysis they executed only those elements that seemed absolutely necessary. Model, who believed that the defense of the barrier ring but not of the city itself made sense, reported accordingly to Hitler's directive: Paris remains "a big military problem because in the event of fighting all around combined with a simultaneous major uprising, the area could not be held militarily with the available 20,000 men." He also noted that he had already issued an order to reconnoiter an emergency reserve line north and east of Paris, just in case.[83] In other words, behind the city.

Such an action did not preclude an extreme, last-ditch defense of the city, but it did indicate what OB West was driving at. Model reacted similarly to the inquiry put to him by Colonel General Jodl, the chief of the Wehrmacht operations staff, as to whether the bridges across the Seine River in Paris had already been blown. The Wehrmacht operations staff held the opinion that the fight must be conducted ruthlessly and the bridges must be blown.[84] A short time later, Model concluded that such preparations were necessary, but at the same time included the caveat that the "vast number of bridges" made it impossible to do a complete job—which of course made the military senselessness of such an undertaking quite obvious.[85]

In his reactions to the orders coming from Rastenburg, Choltitz constantly had to keep in mind not only their effects on the tenuously stabilized situation in Paris, but also their potential consequences for the fate of his troops, his own person, and his family. It is no longer possible after the fact to determine with precision which of those motivations was the decisive factor in his decisions. At any rate, Choltitz intended to refrain from doing anything that could lead to a further escalation of tensions. As for blowing the bridges, Choltitz reported that he was unable to execute such measures.[86] Later he pointed out that such an impossible undertaking only would have driven a large part of the population into the enemy camp.[87] Thus, Choltitz also resisted Hitler's wishes to broadcast a warning threat to the population reminding them of the fate of Warsaw.[88]

Choltitz's disastrous military strength situation was the basis of his actions, which were cautious in dealing with the French at least. Choltitz released three of de Gaulle's captured representatives after they had assured him that they would urge compliance with the armistice.[89] In the final analysis, however, Choltitz's efforts to play the factions of the Resistance against each other were meaningless because the reinforcements he was hoping for never arrived.[90]

Choltitz's hopes did not last long. Instead of the divisional-sized units he was hoping for, Choltitz received only an engineer and an artillery unit of battalion strength,[91] plus the 11th Assault Gun Brigade with twenty combat vehicles.[92] That was all Model was able to spare, because of the threat facing Army Group B. The 47th and 49th Infantry Divisions from the Channel coast were immediately deployed against the Seine River bridgeheads above and below the city; the 47th Infantry Division was halted dead in its tracks as Allied fighter-bombers shot up the locomotives of the trains moving the unit.[93] In the meantime the food situation had taken a dramatic turn for the worse, compounding Choltitz's hopeless situation. He had ordered the release of more than four thousand tons of rations from Wehrmacht stocks for distribution to the population, primarily to the quiet boroughs of the city. But that was not enough by far.[94] In a resigned mood, Choltitz informed OB West on August 23 that supplies would be exhausted by the end of the month at the latest. Bread, the staple item, had not been available for one or two days. And even if it were possible to restore law and order in Paris, the food supplies were still not there.[95] Now the double game Choltitz had been playing with the Resistance lost all effectiveness. Things were still quiet along the outer barrier belt thanks to Allied passivity.[96] In the meantime, however, the "terrorist movement" in Paris had swept up the entire city.[97]

Various actions taken by Model indicate that the German command in the west had given Paris up as lost on August 23.[98]

The reactions to the "Rubble Field Order"—as it was now mockingly called—from the Führer Headquarters were crystal clear. Hitler's demands for resorting to "the severest measures upon the first indication of an uprising, such as demolition of residential housing blocks, public executions,"[99] were based on an utterly wrong estimate of the situation. Choltitz had seen that immediately, with no little indignation. As he reported to Model in a telephone conversation that day, one had to expect "that Paris would soon be wrested from the German armies, possibly by the internal enemy, because the enemy has now recognized our weakness."[100] That evening Model advanced the same opinion in a telephone conversation with the chief of the Wehrmacht operations staff, and he urged that the existing directive be amended. In response to Jodl's hesitant reply that "Paris would have to be held *for the moment*," the OB West thundered that he did not want "provisional orders" but a clear directive in case of the loss of Paris. A city of millions of people, Model insisted, could not be defended internally or externally with the weak forces available. Model further insisted that "these situation assessments be reported to the führer clearly."[101]

It was all in vain; Hitler's mind could not be changed. As a consequence, Choltitz lost the more promising and militarily significant opportunity of withdrawing from Paris and organizing the defenses along the eastern edge of the city without the permanent threat to his rear from the FFI. But now Choltitz's position was exceptionally precarious because he had gone out on a limb by his actions and his harsh criticism of Hitler's order. His only remaining chance of avoiding a rather somber fate while at the same time fulfilling his sense of duty as a soldier was to hold out at his post to the bitter end. To avoid exposing his men to the FFI with no protection and therefore leaving them to face the explosion of stored-up popular anger, Choltitz hoped that he would be able to continue fighting, at least until such time as he was facing regular Allied units.[102]

3. Comments on the Fall of Paris, August 25, 1944

The decision that Choltitz had sought was now not long in coming. On August 24 the U.S. 4th Infantry Division and the French 2nd Armored Division attacked the outer barrier belt under the operational control of the U.S. V Corps.[103] Spearheaded by Leclerc's French tank units, the attack turned out to be more difficult than expected. Disregarding the orders of the V Corps commander, Major General Leonard Gerow, Leclerc ran into stiff resistance from the German units manning the barrier belt along the axis of advance he had selected.[104] Skeptical comments of American commanders—such as Bradley's remark that he did not want to wait until the French had "danced their way" to Paris—indicate that the attackers were not anticipating a German defense, probably the result of faulty intelligence.[105] Nonetheless, the route was opened only after several hours of bloody fighting.[106]

Late in the afternoon Choltitz reported that the Allies had broken through with forty tanks and were heading for downtown Paris.[107] Shortly thereafter he phoned Blumentritt to alert him to the seriousness of the situation in Paris, which was getting worse by the hour.[108] Model hoped that Choltitz would be able to hold on for some time in the city and thus would be able to draw the full attention of the Allies to events in Paris, at least for the short run. That would have helped the primary mission, which was to get the two field armies across the river northwest of Paris and then organize the defenses along the eastern edge of the city along with Chevallerie's forces.

But the appearance of regular Allied units quickly put an end to the rather odd standoff that had developed between the Germans and the FFI. The former had entrenched themselves in their strongpoints and were relatively secure from attack; while the latter controlled the streets but were unable to drive out Choltitz's troops.[109] The German command in the west did not entertain any illusions about the situation. Shortly before midnight Choltitz took his leave of Army Group B with the somewhat premature words: "This will probably be my last phone call."[110] The fall of Paris was merely a question of hours. Leclerc's forces were already on Place de L'Etoile and in front of the Palais du Luxembourg.[111] But with the end near, Choltitz had to make every effort to give the impression that he always had followed the intentions of the Supreme Command as best he could. That is probably why he informed Speidel a short time after his presumed farewell phone call that the order to blow the Seine River bridges had been issued, at least for the eastern part of Paris.[112] The issuance of that order cannot be proved. Most probably it was a so-called War Diary Order, an order whose execution was not intended or even feasible under the situation, but which had to be documented in the files to dispel any charges of disobedience. By early in the afternoon of August 25 the saga of the German occupation of the French metropolis was at an end. After Leclerc's troops attacked Choltitz's headquarters at the Hotel Meurice and the guards were overpowered, Choltitz gave up the fight. Up to that point he had rejected three previous surrender ultimatums.[113] In return for Leclerc's assurance that the German soldiers would be protected against the furious civilians, Choltitz ordered his men who were still holding the strongpoints to immediately cease their resistance.[114]

The fate of his men was an important enough reason for Choltitz to defy Hitler's orders and Model's expectations. Roughly at the same time, the various German headquarters in France received a fresh order from the Wolf's Lair that triggered astonishment, because it was totally unrealistic in light of a situation that kept getting worse.

Among other elements the order stated:

"Furthermore, security units must be brought in from the outside and special weapons systems must be employed (assault howitzers and assault tanks) to reduce the center of the uprising in order then to wipe out with the support of the Luftwaffe (dropping high-explosive and incendiary bombs) those sections of the city that are involved in the uprising."[115]

Just a few hours before that, Hitler had ordered a similar action against Bucharest, Romania, which was indeed carried out.

The proposal of conducting a bombing raid against that city, which politically was an act of complete folly, had originated with a Luftwaffe commander, Lieutenant General Alfred Gerstenberg.[116] Nobody among the military command in the west, however, had such an absurd notion for Paris. The initiative came from Hitler alone. Although there were far more urgent problems, OB West had to react to that order. In the case of the German counterattack toward Paris, which was mounted by elements of the Panzer-Lehr Division prior to Choltitz's capitulation and which was repulsed with bloody losses, there had been at least a chance of strengthening the defensive efforts in the city and thus gaining time.[117] But now those opportunities no longer existed. In answer to a direct question from the commanding general of the First Army whether he was to fight the bridgeheads south of Paris and at the same time also recapture Paris, Model had but one answer, and that was to refer him to Hitler's attack order. The field marshal, however, inserted the proviso that "the mission continues to exist *in keeping with available forces.*"[118] That caveat made his attitude on the issue quite clear. In the event, no further attack preparations were made. Model's order can thus be considered merely a formal response to Hitler's intentions, much like Choltitz's order to blow the bridges. The irrationality with which orders kept coming out of the Führer Headquarters is typical of the last Führer Order for Paris that ordered "a larger number of bridges" be kept open.[119]

The deterioration in the way orders were issued, which practically were forced from the top down, can be documented in the events of the time, especially the court-martial proceedings Model initiated against Choltitz on August 28. Choltitz, in the meantime, had been captured.[120] There were several reasons that persuaded the OB West to take such an action. First of all, Choltitz had violated his orders by ordering a halt to direct defensive actions, and in so doing he prevented for several hours or even days the continuation of the fighting in Paris "to the last round." And, of course, the requested court proceedings might help the commanding general of a shaky front to deter his subordinate generals from yielding to any similar defeatist tendencies. Finally, Model, who knew that Choltitz's situation was untenable in the long run, probably felt that he should initiate the action in order to preempt any possible revenge efforts on Hitler's part. There was good reason to fear just that. Simultaneously, the OB West, with one eye on Rastenburg, documented the fact that there was no room in his command for disobedience. Any interference from topside, therefore, was superfluous. By taking the initiative himself, there was also a chance that he might be able to bring his influence to bear in Choltitz's case and, strange as it might sound, preserve the latter's reputation and above all save his family from an even worse fate.[121] Such an interpretation is supported by the explanatory comments that Model added to his petition for a court-martial. The OB West noted that the possibility had to be considered that Choltitz's failure was caused by the effects of war or that his willpower was weakened by the threat of such enemy actions as the use of chemical warfare agents.[122] If, as it certainly appears, Model really intended to generate some understanding for Choltitz's actions, he was indeed successful.[123] Witnesses who testified during the Reich court-martial, including Speidel, Lieutenant General Wilhelm von Boineburg-Lengsfeld, Ministerial Counsellor Dr. Hermann Eckelmann, Major Doertenbach, and Major Brink, presented an accurate picture of the difficult situation in which Choltitz had found himself, while simultaneously avoiding the more ticklish points, such as his efforts at negotiations.[124] And the above-cited expert report from the Wehrmacht operations staff agreed that "the city as such could no longer have been defended," even if individual strongpoints had continued to fight.[125] It was probably on the basis of these extenuating circumstances that the court-martial did not find Choltitz's violation of his orders sufficient for a finding of condemnation "with disgrace."[126]

Aside from the questions of whether Choltitz could have defended Paris more resolutely and whether he therefore could have relieved the pressure at least partially on the Army Group B front line, the fact remains that he did not comply with Hitler's "Rubble Field" order. But then, the entire German command in the west never seems to have seriously considered such an action. A good indicator of this is the actions of Colonel General Otto Dessloch, the new commanding general of the Third Air Fleet, who had just arrived in France.

Taking everything into consideration, however, Choltitz's argument in his postwar writings that he preserved Paris from destruction principally on moral-ethical grounds requires closer examination.[127] By the time Choltitz received specific orders he lacked both the materiel and personnel to carry them out fully. But Choltitz consciously decided against carrying out whatever degree of destruction that was within his capabilities. With somewhat better insight Choltitz followed the path laid out earlier by Field Marshal von Kluge.

General Dessloch, the new Third Air Fleet commander, also followed a similar course. Just a few days earlier Dessloch had reported to Model as the successor of Field Marshal Hugo Sperrle, who was rather corpulent and no longer considered dynamic enough to work with the new OB West. Dessloch found himself trapped in the contradictions of the August 25 Führer Order, while he was still busy reorganizing the headquarters of the Third Air Fleet in Reims.[128] What he found when he got there was what he considered to be a "completely disorganized club" and the "senile and incapable group of dining companions of the field marshal." But on top of that Dessloch was saddled immediately with the responsibility of carrying out Hitler's order for the Luftwaffe to support the operations to annihilate those sections of the city that were involved in the uprising.[129] The realization of this responsibility made him remember the ironic foreshadowing of the words he had spoken to his wife before leaving home: "Mönchlein, Mönchlein, you have a tough row to hoe."[130] The Franconian general decided not to comply with Hitler's order, or at least the objective of that order, with its contempt for human life and its military senselessness.[131] It is likely that Dessloch's convictions were confirmed by the images of his personal reconnaissance of the Western Front. The August 18 entry in his diary records how deeply moved he was by the ghostlike impressions that reminded him of the once-beautiful city of Munich that was now just so many bombed-out houses.[132]

Nonetheless, Hitler's order had to be complied with somehow. Thus, during the night between August 26 and 27 the Luftwaffe did conduct an air raid with 111 bombers of the IX Air Corps. But according to *Operations Order No. 125*, the mission was directed primarily against the main supply routes along the southern edge of Paris. That operations order expressly contained the sentence: "In all circumstances, avoid the city center."[133] The attack, which had been coordinated with Speidel at Army Group B, had nothing to do with Hitler's ideas of annihilation.[134] The objective of that raid was purely military, and there was no indication of any possible intent to wipe out entire sections of the city.

For the German military command—apart from subsequent V-weapon strikes[135]—the issue of Paris was essentially finished.[136] The city was now the Allies' problem, especially the logistics demands.

Supplying Paris, which had been a headache for the Germans since 1940,[137] now took a huge bite out of the American resources.[138] Especially painful was the fact that until the beginning of September more than 37 percent of the American airlift tonnage—which itself was an improvisation to keep the frontline units supplied—had to be diverted for the French metropolis.[139]

Some friction developed between the French and the Americans resulting from the political issues that arose over the liberation of Paris.[140] They resulted primarily from de Gaulle's efforts to consolidate the power base of "his" provisional government against his own fellow citizens. In the process, the political potential of the members of the Paris militia and the FFI units,[141] whose ranks reportedly had swelled to one hundred thousand, was neutralized by absorbing those forces.[142] This explains why de Gaulle essentially filed away the order issued by Major General Gerow for the 2nd Armored Division to pursue the retreating Germans.[143] Instead, de Gaulle made sure first and foremost that the French armored division paraded through Paris. The motive was the same behind de Gaulle's request to Eisenhower to leave two divisions near the capital for the time being. De Gaulle wanted to have the necessary force on hand to cope with any possible unrest.[144] The American generals, for the most part, were simply helpless in trying to cope with domestic French problems and events. Gerow, in whose sector Paris was located, was probably referring to the "cleansing" that had begun in the midst of joyful celebrations, featuring killings and mistreatment of collaborators or persons who were charged as having been collaborators, when he complained to Bradley's U.S. First Army staff: "Who the devil is actually the boss in Paris? The Frenchmen are shooting at each other, each party is at each other's throat. Is Koenig the boss . . . de Gaulle . . . or am I the senior commander of the troops in charge?"[145]

French efforts to assert emphatically that they were once again running things in their own country—after, of course, regaining their freedom under the protection of American arms—often led to tensions with the American commanders over seemingly minor formalities.[146] The Allied Supreme Commander described this behavior as "a little bit hysterical."[147] The very noticeable French tendency to discount the American contribution to their liberation[148] may have contributed to giving Eisenhower, as he later wrote, a "slightly bitter aftertaste" following the events in Paris.[149]

On the other hand, much of the French attitude is understandable, considering the terse relationship between Roosevelt and de Gaulle and the long hesitation of the Allied military leaders to start or give the go-ahead for the march on Paris. American historian Martin Blumenson's thesis, formulated for the Allied side, seems a bit overstated. He maintained that the wonderfully brilliant facade of the liberation of Paris concealed the intrigues and disputes of the American-French conflict more than it settled a fight between the Allies and the Germans.[150] From the German perspective, however, the responsible military leaders in the west had to cope with a higher command that had become completely unrealistic and that issued orders without any relation to the actual situation. During critical moments those demands absorbed far too much attention, which was diverted from the really crucial points along the front.

Chapter 8

Command Decisions and the Course of Operations Leading to the Climax of the Crisis

1. The Initial Major Situation Estimate of OB West

The recent events and orders clearly showed that Hitler and the Wehrmacht High Command were not able or willing to control combat operations in any meaningful manner.

During the night between August 24 and 25, Model prepared his first major situation estimate. The Führer Directive that had been issued just four days earlier was now outdated in all its essential points. OB West, therefore, only briefly touched on what Hitler had dictated to him as the "most important tasks." Model stubbornly stuck to the idea that the Seine–Yonne–Dijon line—which the Americans had already crossed—could be held or regained only if within two weeks fifteen fresh German divisions could be moved into the most operationally vulnerable sector. That was the area between Troyes and the Swiss border.[1]

Apart from such demands, which were unsupportable to begin with, Model in his sober analysis projected how events would actually play out. "Our troops," he stressed, were "burned out," and reinforcements could only be expected by September 1. By then the worst-case scenario would have the Allies reaching the Somme position and the area between Paris and Reims or Dijon.

Although Eisenhower had a superior number of infantry and armored divisions available, the actual Allied numbers were grossly overestimated by the Germans.[2] On the other hand, Model was not especially concerned about any commitment of the Allies' First Airborne Army.

Rastenburg seemed to be concentrating mostly on the Paris problem. Model, therefore, did not waste his time with requests or proposals for further combat operations in the west. Seizing the initiative, he took action. In his situation estimate he merely informed the Führer Headquarters of those actions he would take in the future, some of which he had initiated already.

For Model the most important thing was to bridge the time gap at least up to September 1 without losing the cohesiveness of his front line. It was therefore important to hold the bridgehead west of the Seine River to tie down enemy forces and to enable Dietrich's Fifth Panzer Army to get across. But Model, in direct violation of Hitler's orders, also ordered the withdrawal from the bridgehead as soon as the disadvantages of holding it outweighed the advantages.

Model intended to continue fighting in the area of the Seine River downstream from Paris with twelve infantry divisions, or whatever was left of them by then.[3] The remnants of six Panzer divisions were to be combined into a mobile reserve between the Seine and Somme rivers. The field marshal realized quite clearly that it would depend solely on the enemy's advance whether or not time could be gained there.

Model emphasized that if the enemy really conducted his operations aggressively, then all he could do was withdraw quickly behind the Somme–Marne line. Eberbach's Seventh Army, therefore, was ordered to move immediately the very weak remnants of the twelve divisions that were supposed to be reconstituted into that line as an outpost force.[4] But that move produced no major increase in combat effectiveness. Those divisions were urgently in need of a rest.[5] Their fighting spirit had suffered considerably from barely escaping annihilation twice in short succession.[6] Five of those divisions were so weak that Model a few days later had to order them to withdraw back to Germany.[7]

Since no reserves whatsoever were available, refitting rarely meant more than a few days of rest. That action had to be accomplished near the front and for the most part in those sectors where the next Allied attack concentration was expected. That was especially the case for the Panzer divisions. Krüger, who had started the job of reconstituting the Panzer units between the Seine and the Somme rivers, was ordered to move up to the front immediately. The refitting areas for the Panzer divisions were now established behind the Somme–Marne line, with the center at Laon–Reims–Châlons.[8]

Now Model's attention was necessarily concentrated on that position, which was not as yet defensible. Eberbach's divisions were ordered to cooperate in quickly reinforcing it. There could, of course, be no consideration of establishing any solid positions, including elements such as concrete pillboxes, which Hitler considered to be the very basis of a delaying defense.[9]

Nevertheless, Model obviously was hoping, and not without reason, considering the original OVERLORD plan, that the Allies would not quickly resume their offensive. If they didn't, there would be some chance of being able to fortify the Somme–Marne line, at least in an improvised manner.

But Model's intent, which influenced Hitler considerably, only had a chance of succeeding if the Allies did pause. The field marshal's concept was to meet the operational threat there by attacking with seven to eight Panzer divisions along the southern wing of the German First Army and thereby screen the withdrawal of Army Task Group G. Nonetheless, Model was pessimistic. The crisis in the Rhône River Valley and the much-too-slow withdrawal movement led him to estimate that many of Blaskowitz's seven march units would not make it back. At best, the 198th Infantry Division and the 11th Panzer Division might manage to break through to the north.[10] (See Map 12.)

Regardless of how events might develop in detail, the field marshal concluded his situation estimate by stressing the point that the Somme–Marne line was not a permanent solution. He was not reluctant to state openly something that hardly anybody among the military leadership dared mention: "Furthermore, as is being done on the East Front now . . . , additional rearward positions, up to and including the West Wall . . . must now be prepared."[11]

There was at least some kind of backing in the West Wall, which by that point in the war had become technologically obsolescent. Hitler generally accepted Model's analysis and demands.[12] Hitler then issued his *Order for the Improvement of the German Western Position*, which arrived at OB West headquarters a few hours later.[13]

The actions of the Allies would determine whether all of Model's fears and hopes would materialize. As he wrote to his son, he hoped "somehow to patch up this totally messed-up engine."[14]

But Eisenhower's August 19 directive soon made it clear that the Allied operational pause that the Germans were so hoping for would not be forthcoming immediately, at least not along the Seine River. The Allied supreme commander decided to have his forces continue their advance almost at the same time as OB West developed his situation analysis.

2. The Allied Situation Analysis

(a) The Strategy Debate and Eisenhower's August 24 Decision

As the Allied units closed to the Seine River, they reached the boundaries of the designated lodgment area. Operation OVERLORD was essentially complete, eleven days earlier than planned.

The Allies, however, did not see any problems arising from port capacities, although those problems had not yet been resolved. The American generals expected that the concentric attack launched by the VIII Corps against Brest on August 25 would succeed within a week.[15] And then the German forces holding the other coastal fortresses would be persuaded to surrender.[16]

But one key factor lingered in the background of the apparent resounding victory of the initial Allied campaign of maneuver.[17] The encirclement along the Seine River and the intended annihilation of the German army in Normandy had not up to that point been a complete success.[18] According to a British intelligence estimate on August 24, forty thousand of the seventy-five thousand German troops trying to cross the Seine were still west of the river. The rest had escaped.[19]

The decisive blow had not fallen upon the Germans as it might have. Nonetheless, the fact remained that the German front was becoming increasingly wobbly. The German weakness and the explosively swift Allied advance of recent days generated optimistic expectations. As the SHAEF G-2 Section noted: "The August battles have done it, and the enemy in the west has had it."[20] The Allied assumption was that the end of the war in Europe was in sight. Montgomery believed that the German forces were disorganized and were incapable of putting up any delaying resistance.[21]

The concept of the Broad Front advance, which in the spring of 1944 had been considered the best course of action for the post-OVERLORD phase of operations, now lost its general credibility because of the changed situation on the ground.[22] The Broad Front concept was characterized by a distinct lack of operational originality. It called for a cautious approach, avoiding risks, and was based on the estimate of the German combat capability, which the Allied planners at the time were still overestimating. By orientating along two offensive axes on both sides of the Ardennes, the Allies would keep open the option of shifting the point of the main effort, and thereby minimize the danger of a German flanking thrust. The Allied planners hoped that the defensive strength of the Wehrmacht could be fragmented by threatening simultaneously the opening of multiple gaps leading into the Reich.

Starting from the Seine River, the northern axis of advance ran via Amiens–Maubeuge–Lüttich to the industrial region along the Ruhr. The actual point of the main effort was located there because of the Ruhr's industrial importance and because of the nearby ports to the north of that route. The southern axis pointed toward the Saar region via Reims–Verdun–Metz.[23]

The planners originally had assumed that the tempo of the post-OVERLORD advance would be slow. The front line by December (D+180) was to follow roughly the Abbeville–Amiens–Laon–Reims–Sens line. The Belgian-French border and the upper course of the Aisne River would be reached at the turn of 1944–1945. The border of the Reich finally would be reached in the Aachen area early in May 1945 (D+330), by which time the area around Metz also would have been reached.[24]

But Montgomery now believed that final victory was still possible in 1944. He therefore pushed for a bolder course of action, an offensive focused in a single sector. With the combined might of two army groups, he proposed to push into Belgium and then eastward via the Ruhr region into Germany.[25] In his opinion, nothing could withstand this steamroller of some forty divisions attacking north of the Ardennes. He wanted to be in Berlin before the winter.[26]

Simultaneously, American generals were also developing a similar Narrow Front option. The point of main effort of the American plan, of course, was in the south, the American sector. Patton in particular argued that he could cross the German border within ten days via Metz–Nancy–Epinal with his U.S. Third Army.[27]

These plans were based on the idea that a point of main effort established clearly in operational and logistical terms would quickly bring about the German collapse. Eisenhower was more skeptical. The risk of long, exposed flanks that would result from a single thrust appeared too high, even apart from the question of its logistical sustainability. Factors other than operational also influenced his thinking.[28]

Eisenhower was not the typical frontline commander. Compared to Montgomery and Patton, he lacked practical experience commanding field armies. This lack of experience contributed to his hesitation in exploiting the opportunities that were suddenly within reach. He also was by nature a consensus builder. Compared to Montgomery, Eisenhower was a "committeeman."[29]

Eisenhower's extraordinary ability to consolidate the most widely differing concepts into a single solution probably justifies the judgment that he "was a military statesman rather than a warlord."[30] The search for consensus, for a decision that if possible all army group and field army commanders could at least support, naturally had certain drawbacks.[31] Such an approach may be necessary in the political sphere, but for military-operational problems compromise solutions are almost always ineffective. The constant search for consensus also exposed Eisenhower to political pressures from the governments of the Western democracies. With irritation, he discovered the fact that a resounding victory alone was not enough for the press and the public, and that the questions of how it was done and, above all, by whom it was done were just as important.[32] The single-thrust option, therefore, was an inherently thorny proposition, because it could be commanded only by either a Briton or an American.

Eisenhower could hardly afford to stop completely the advance of one or the other wing at the moment of great expectations of victory. An August 22 confidential communication from the British prime minister made it clear to him how sensitive that point was. On September 1, the day that Eisenhower was scheduled to assume from Montgomery the role of combined ground forces commander, the latter would be promoted to field marshal.[33]

Considering the various conflicting directions in which Eisenhower was pulled, it is little wonder that as he made his decision he stuck closely to the original, safe Broad Front concept.[34] Nonetheless, Eisenhower on August 24 decided to establish temporarily a definite point of main effort along the northern wing. The annihilation of the main body of Army Group B, the capture of the V-1 launching sites in the Pas de Calais, the seizure of airfields in western Belgium, and the establishment of a secure base at Antwerp were objectives of tremendous importance to the Allied supreme commander.[35] Consequently, Montgomery's offensive to the northeast also would be supported on the right flank by the U.S. First Army, which was allocated the lion's share of the American logistics flow.[36] Maximizing every possible resource, Eisenhower instructed Montgomery to plan for the commitment of the Allied First Airborne Army in the Pas de Calais.[37, 38]

The secondary offensive in the south was postponed only temporarily. Eisenhower made it clear that as soon as the designated objectives in the north were reached, Patton's Third Army would resume its offensive to the east.

After securing the Antwerp area, Eisenhower intended to realign the Allied forces. But Eisenhower's decision to shift north temporarily halted for the time being the strategy debate, the course of which was often driven by personal animosities.[39]

(b) The Perception of the Supply Situation in the Allied Command

All of the estimates initially developed by the planning staffs were quickly outdated by the unexpectedly fast pace of the Allied advance since the breakout. But the buildup of the logistical system proceeded based on the original scenario that the planners had charted, and therefore was unable to keep pace with actual developments on the ground.[40] The problem was not so much the fact that the Allied armies reached the Seine River eleven days earlier than projected, but rather the more serious fact that during the previous thirty days the Allies had covered distances that originally were supposed to have taken two months to cover.[41]

The first bottlenecks emerged as the lead elements reached the Seine River. Transportation was the primary problem. The Allied bombing campaign against the French railroad installations and rolling stock now contributed to the inability to put the rail system back into operation quickly enough.[42] Competing priorities in various categories of supplies prevented material for pipeline construction from being delivered forward on time. The direct airlift to the frontline units of the U.S. Third Army received a reduced priority because transport aircraft were diverted for the planned airborne operation to the north, as well as due to French concerns for supplying Paris.[43]

Motor transport, therefore, bore the main burden, but it was barely capable of meeting the daily supply requirements. Nor was it possible to establish enough intermediate depots between the coast and the front lines.[44] Additional improvisations became necessary to support the armies beyond the line of the Seine. In contrast to their opponents, of course, the Allies were able to initiate impressive material-intensive measures of expediency.

The Red Ball Express, initiated on August 25, was a round-the-clock, long-distance operation using all available trucks combined into convoys. It ran between the base depots in Cotentin and the Chartres–Dreux area.[45] By August 29, 132 truck companies with some six thousand vehicles were already operating on the Red Ball routes, which were off-limits to any other traffic.[46]

A more important issue, however, is the question of how the broader problems were perceived by the Allied side at that time—problems that were partly obscured by the successful improvisations. The gap between the planned and the actual advance, with all of its logistical implications, was bound to grow wider with the decision to continue the pursuit immediately, without the originally planned month-long operational pause along the Seine River.

The logistical problems were one argument Eisenhower used against the single-thrust proposals.[47] Indeed, neither Montgomery nor Patton had assigned any special significance to the logistics question. When it came to operations planning, Patton hardly ever paid any attention to the objections raised by the supply officers, because he mistrusted them.[48]

At the time he made his decision, Eisenhower merely knew that logistics problems did exist. But there apparently was no analysis of the causes and the potential remedies, or, if such studies were made, they were not included in his directive. The wording of that directive seems to indicate that Eisenhower himself did not have the complete picture. The "fastest possible mop-up of Brittany," which of course meant the capture of Brest, would make additional harbor capacity available, but that would not solve the forward transportation problem, which was the decisive issue at the moment. Brest was even farther away from the front line than Cherbourg and the invasion beaches, and that front line continued to move east.

The term "harbor" does not appear once among the objectives Eisenhower established for Montgomery's main offensive in the north. Eisenhower noted the intention of gaining a "secure base in Antwerp" only at the very end of the directive and in a rather vague manner.[49] At that point in time the capture and operation of a harbor such as Antwerp obviously did not have top priority; but being far closer than the Normandy ports to the Allied front lines, Antwerp offered considerable capacity and transportation advantages.

Nor was Antwerp mentioned in Montgomery's briefing to the British General Staff on Eisenhower's decisions.[50] Because the British 21st Army Group had shorter supply lines than the Americans to the south, Montgomery had not been experiencing serious supply problems to that point.[51]

Montgomery was focused on the Ruhr, and the operations plan of August 25–26 established the next objectives. Crerar's Canadian First Army was to push along the coast all the way to Brügge; Dempsey's British Second Army was to push via Amiens–Lille toward Ghent–Antwerp–Brussels; and Hodges's U.S. First Army was to advance from Paris into the Brussels–Lüttich area.[52]

With the point of the main effort shifted temporarily to the Allied left wing, Patton's U.S. Third Army on the right wing was capable of operating only for about another week, when his fuel supplies would run out. During that time the Third Army, apart from the U.S. VIII Corps, was to wheel toward Reims–Châlons–Troyes and then prepare to resume the offensive via Metz to the east, toward the Rhine River crossings between Koblenz and Mannheim.[53]

The Allies never seriously considered the swift attack toward Dijon that Model feared. Eisenhower made the advance to the southeast dependent on the improvement in the supply situation.[54] That at least improved the escape chances of Blaskowitz's units. But the establishment of a main effort along the Allied northern wing created another crisis for Army Group B.

3. The Deterioration of the Situation in Army Group B's Sector

(a) Evacuation of the Bridgehead West of the Seine River

At noon on August 25, the Fifth Army headquarters received OB West's order to retreat across the Seine River. The crossing operation was to be conducted "in one swift move" during the night of August 26 and 27.[55] Model intended to establish a defensive line of reasonable strength behind the Seine River downstream from Paris, but the German position was already in doubt by the next day, August 26.[56] The Canadians and British jumped off for the attack across the river south of Rouen faster than the Germans had expected.[57] They formed additional bridgeheads at Vernon and in the area of Elbeuf, which the Germans had evacuated that morning.[58]

That clearly defined the turning point along the Seine River Front between Rouen and Paris. The German units on the east bank were no longer strong enough to mount effective counterattacks.[59] During the hard fighting on August 27 the Luftwaffe 17th Field Division did manage to reduce the size of the Canadian bridgehead at Elbeuf, knocking out twenty-six Allied tanks in the process.[60] But there was no hope of ever throwing the enemy back across the river. At the same time, the Americans reinforced their units that had crossed at Mantes. SS-Obergruppenführer and General of the Waffen-SS Georg Keppler and his I SS Panzer Corps were finally and definitely forced on the defensive.[61] He anticipated heavy attacks from the enemy bridgeheads in the coming days.[62] The left wing of the Fifth Panzer Army was already being pushed eastward and away from the Seine River. Simultaneously, the units on the right wing were still fighting across the river between its mouth and Rouen.

It proved impossible to evacuate the west bank of the Seine in one swift move during the night of August 26–27, as had been planned. As Obstfelder, the commanding general of the LXXXVI Army Corps reported,[63] the number of ferries available at Caudebec, La Mailleraye, Duclair, and Rouen was too small to accommodate the troops that were crowding in rapid succession into the three loops of the Seine River.[64] In some places bomb strikes temporarily produced a complete halt of the ferry traffic.[65]

Chaotic situations sometimes arose in the course of the desperate search for crossing points.[66] Small detachments of soldiers using amphibious Volkswagens or even rowboats reached the opposite bank in the area of the river mouth, where the Seine is up to five hundred meters wide.[67]

Apart from some temporary pauses because of the threat from the air, ferry transport operations were now conducted around the clock, with a daily average of some six hundred motor vehicles making it to the east bank.[68] The crossing operations continued only because the Canadian First Army, consisting of the British I Corps and the Canadian II Corps, failed to achieve any immediate success while attacking concentrically toward the mouth of the river. In that sector the German lines west of the Seine were forced back only slowly.[69]

On August 27 the rear guard units of three German infantry divisions,[70] supported by twenty-three Panzers and sixty artillery pieces,[71] were still covering the Seine River loops south of Caudebec, Duclair, and Rouen.[72] But the Allies did not attack with the anticipated strength against the rear guard positions between the

Risle River and the towns of Pont Audemer and Bourg Achard, nor against Forêt de la Londe.[73, 74] Accordingly, Gause anticipated being able to get all the men and all the important fighting vehicles to the opposite bank.[75] On the other hand, many passenger cars and almost all horse-drawn vehicles would have to be left behind.[76]

Gause had figured it correctly. Before the last German units were across the river, Model ordered a message sent to the Wehrmacht operations staff reporting: "The crossing along the lower Seine River was essentially successful, although equipment losses were heavy."[77] The fight along the mouth of the Seine River now had to be finished as quickly as possible, because the situation of Army Group B to the southeast of Rouen had worsened considerably.

The Allies enlarged and reinforced their bridgeheads between Elbe and Mantes.[78] The Canadians and British had already put three divisions across.[79] Maximum artillery preparation indicated that large-scale attacks were coming. The U.S. XIX Corps at Mantes alone was supported by thirty-five artillery battalions.[80] In the meantime, German unit combat strengths had shrunk so severely on the left wing of the Fifth Panzer Army that an enemy breakthrough seemed imminent.[81]

Lieutenant General Hans-Kurt Höcker's Luftwaffe 17th Field Division was able to muster barely four hundred men.[82] The almost destroyed Luftwaffe 18th Field Division could only put three hundred men into the forward line.[83] Höcker, in fact, had sent his regimental commanders home because of nervous breakdowns. Urgent measures were necessary to support the front, although the soldiers, as Höcker wrote, never lost courage.[84]

Model figured that his demands for the assignment of sixteen personnel replacement battalions, 170 Panzers, 100 antitank guns, and 15,000 carbines would not be met quickly enough by the Wehrmacht High Command.[85] He therefore saw his only course of action as the withdrawal of the right wing of his army group from the Seine River.[86]

The elements of the 5th Panzer Division that were still able to fight, and that until then had constituted the backbone of the defenses to the west of the Seine, now had to cross to the opposite bank as quickly as possible. On the morning of August 29 they were to be combined into reserve groups in the area to the northeast of Rouen and at Beauvais.[87]

Only then did the rear guards of the 711th, 346th, and 331st Infantry Divisions cross over during the night of August 29–30. Most of their heavy equipment had to be destroyed.[88] The evacuation of the bridgehead to the west of the Seine River was finally complete. All the divisions of the Fifth Panzer Army had managed to get across the river, but they were now down to an average strength of three thousand men.[89] Each division also had only about 25 to 30 percent of its equipment.[90]

The crossing operation was at least a partial success, especially considering the German starting situation on August 24–25. Both the noteworthy achievements of the controlling headquarters and the troops, as well as the Allies' conduct of their operations, were the basis of that partial success.[91] In the meantime, the situation on Army Group B's southern wing had deteriorated disastrously, which in turn meant that the partial success in the north had no stabilizing effect for the front line as a whole.

(b) The American Breakthrough East of Paris

General von der Chevallerie had been hoping that the Allies would launch their major offensive on the southern wing only after he completed his planned deployment.[92] But that did not happen. Krüger's LVIII Panzer Corps, committed on the First Army's right wing, did manage to maintain contact with the units of the Fifth Panzer Army. Krüger's corps was supposed to intercept the Allied attacks from the Paris area and blockade the city in the north and east.[93] To accomplish that task Battle Group Aulock, the approaching 47th Infantry Division, and the few Panzers available in the First Army sector were placed under Krüger's corps.[94]

The main Allied thrust, however, was not made along the boundary between the two armies, but where the Germans had been forced to assume the greatest risk. The major offensive by the U.S. VII, XII, and XX Corps commenced on August 26 with nine divisions between Melun and Troyes.[95] On the southern wing of the First Army, the Americans merely ran into an extended outpost line defended by the 48th Infantry Division and the 17th SS Panzer Grenadier Division.[96]

The force ratio was overwhelmingly to the Allies' advantage. Despite putting up a bitter resistance, the German troops were able to stop the Allies for only a short time.[97] The 48th Infantry Division, which was attacked from the bridgeheads at Melun, Fontainebleau, and Montereau, was penetrated in multiple places, as its out-of-contact regiments swarmed back on the divisional headquarters.[98] In the sector of the 17th SS Panzer Grenadier Division, Troyes was lost as well. Army Group B headquarters still did not know whether the U.S. XII Corps would advance from there toward Dijon. At any rate, it had to assume an Allied attempt to cut Army Task Group G off along those lines.[99] And as a captured French officer stated, a continuation of the American attack in an easterly direction all the way to the Rhine also appeared possible.[100]

Nonetheless, Model was confirmed in his suspicion that the Allied main thrust was aimed toward the northeast and at Laon–Châlons, in order to collapse the new line of resistance (the Kitzinger Line) and to initiate another envelopment of the German forces between the Seine and the Channel coast.[101]

The Americans attacked on a broad front, but their intentions on the extreme left wing of German First Army remained unclear. That made it impossible for the few German troops available to concentrate effectively. The newly arriving units of the 15th Panzer Grenadier Division were tied down in the fighting near Troyes, and the first trains bringing the 3rd Panzer Grenadier Division from Italy were still unloading at Bar-le-Duc.[102]

On the morning of August 27, Lieutenant General Walter Feyerabend, chief of staff of the First Army, reported to Speidel that "no continuous defensive line exists any longer between the Marne and the Seine Rivers."[103] Chevallerie's intention of offering at least a delaying resistance in that sector had failed.[104]

The withdrawing units, including the 48th Infantry Division, fragmented into individual fighting battalions and were therefore able to delay the American advance only locally wherever antitank weapons were still available.[105] But events developed so quickly that Model's orders no longer had their original purpose. Model had ordered the interception of the enemy along the Meaux–Epernay–Châlons line.[106] Above all, he wanted the blocking or destruction of the Marne River crossings.[107]

In the meantime, Model had conducted an inspection of the Kitzinger Line in the Soissons area on the morning of August 28.[108] The result was quite sobering. At noon, he arrived at Eberbach's Seventh Army headquarters at Metz-en-Conture, northeast of Péronne, to discuss Army Group B's further combat operations with Dietrich and the chiefs of staff of the Fifteenth Army, the Fifth Panzer Army, and the Seventh Army.[109]

It was only during that conference that Model received reports clearly indicating the extent to which the situation had deteriorated. About one hundred American tanks had pushed far across the Marne River and northward, approaching Soissons and Reims to within a few kilometers.[110] That split the LVIII Panzer Corps off from the First Army. An approximately fifty-kilometer-wide gap south of Soissons opened up between Krüger's LVIII Panzer Corps and Chevallerie's remaining weak units.[111] The Germans had underestimated the speed of advance of the American combat units, facilitated by outstanding tactical support from their fighter-bombers.[112]

The headquarters of the First Army and the LVIII Panzer Corps were barely able to avoid capture when they were taken by surprise near Montmirail and Villers-Cotterets by the American tanks that appeared quite suddenly.[113] Model's two command posts also were displaced from the immediately threatened area only at the last moment on August 28. OB West headquarters withdrew to Habay, near Arlon, while the command post of Army Group B moved to Castle Havrincourt, southwest of Cambrai.[114]

Army Group B's war diary recorded the American tank breakthrough across the Marne River to the north as "the most important event of the day."[115] Indeed, it was the overture to the Allied pursuit phase that led to the climax of the German crisis.

(c) Field Marshal Model and the Gap at Reims

The fears that Model had already expressed in his situation estimate of August 24—the worst-case scenario—now became a reality. The Allies, starting with the Americans, shifted over to aggressive operations. The plan that Model had developed at noon on August 28 at the command post of the Seventh Army fell apart within a few hours. The field marshal's intent had been to pull his army group's right wing back from the Seine River to the Somme River.[116] That would then allow him to gradually withdraw his forces for the threatened left wing, and thereby gain eight days' time for the improvement of the Somme–Marne line.[117] That now was no longer possible.

Because of the gravely threatening operational thrust made by the Americans, Model found himself that evening forced to order all available units that were capable of conducting mobile combat operations to move off in the direction of the breakthrough sector.[118]

Schwerin's and Bittrich's reserve groups were to leave their assembly areas behind the Seine immediately and push east via Soissons–Laon, while the 3rd and 15th Panzer Grenadier Divisions under the XLVII Panzer Corps were to push toward Reims from the south.[119] In total, however, the Germans had no more than fifty Panzers that could be sent against the American main-effort offensive thrusting to the northeast.[120]

The other hastily ordered measures, including the withdrawal of the 347th and 348th Infantry Divisions from the Channel coast, offered "little prospect for achieving any major change in the situation."[121] As Model tried to make clear to the Wehrmacht High Command, those measures could only involve the attempt to contain the enemy breakthrough by attacking it on both flanks. Model ordered that Jodl be informed that the enemy—like the Germans in 1940—was free to push "where he wants to go," thanks to his unopposed air superiority. "Everything that can be done here has been ordered."[122]

The coordinated commitment of the still-available Panzer units offered the last chance of intercepting the Allied breakthrough. Model was fully aware of the attendant risk. Although Schwerin's and Bittrich's forces consisted only of severely attrited units, their Panzers nevertheless were effectively able to brace the German Seine River front northwest of Paris.[123] With their departure to the east, the infantry divisions were left on their own without any support. Model therefore ordered the withdrawal of the German right wing to the Somme River to be carried out considerably faster than planned originally.[124] Compared with the fully motorized Allied units, the German horse-drawn infantry divisions were not only almost immobile, they hardly had any antitank weapons left. Several times Eberbach alerted Model to the resultant danger in the terrain, which was excellent tank country between the Seine and Somme rivers. Model agreed with the commanding general of the Seventh Army on that score, but he saw no other option than to accept the risk.[125]

Dietrich's recommendation that all units of the Fifteenth Army and the Fifth Panzer Army be withdrawn behind the Somme in one swift move during the night of August 30–31 was of no value because the necessary truck capacity was not available.[126] The only chance was the possibility that the Allies would pause at night during their attacks, which would give the Germans the opportunity to withdraw and to close the developing gaps.[127] Although Model emphatically stressed and clearly described the seriousness of the situation to the Wehrmacht operations staff, the orders that arrived from Rastenburg the next day showed how little the people there were in a position to understand the rapidly changing situation in the west.

In the afternoon of August 29, Army Group B headquarters received Hitler's order to defend as a fortress the Wolf's Gorge II command post, which had been established in 1940 to serve as the command post for Operation SEA LION, the aborted invasion of Britain.[128] But Wolf's Gorge II had already been evacuated by that point, and besides, it had been little more than a billeting facility with no fortifications. The order, therefore, made little military sense.[129] But because the command post, which was in Margival, near Soissons, was in the area that the Panzer groups coming from the west were supposed to reach, Hitler's demand did not run completely counter to Model's intentions.

Another Führer Order arrived at Havrincourt that evening. Hitler directed that all available mobile units, meaning those available south of the Reims–Metz line, be assembled on the Langres Plateau. From there they were to go on the offensive between the Marne and Seine against the deep flank of the Americans in order to threaten in the rear the enemy's attack toward Belgium.[130] The concept itself appeared highly promising operationally, but the decisive factor once again was the failure to consider the relationship between time and space.

Colonel Zimmermann, the OB West operations officer, immediately saw a similarity to the Avranches plan, the attempted counterattack that had failed early in August with such disastrous consequences.[131] A rapid assembly of the designated units was impossible, which is why Hitler's directive was impractical in terms of time.[132] Moreover, if the 3rd and 15th Panzer Grenadier Divisions had diverted to Langres, that would have exposed the sector southeast of Reims. And if the 105th and 106th Panzer Brigades were assembled as ordered, that would have tied down prematurely the fresh Panzer units that were to be sent to OB West by the middle of September. Hitler's order to send the 11th Panzer Division toward Langres immediately and to commit the two divisions of the LXIV Army Corps via forced marches against the rear of the American army group would have led inevitably to the annihilation of the infantry units of Army Task Group G.[133]

Model, however, would not allow himself to be disoriented by this Führer Order. He stuck to the measures he already had initiated and that he considered to be correct. Largely disregarding the content of the Führer Order, the headquarters staff of Army Group B prepared a detailed situation estimate during the night in which Model justified his course of action. Talking to Speidel, he commented that his directives were "the utmost that could be done at this moment . . . but anything more would be impossible."[134]

To create the impression that the situation estimate was drafted before Hitler's directive had been received, Speidel attached a note to the teletype message dating the receipt of the Führer Order at 0700 hours on August 30.[135] That afternoon, Model ordered a message sent to the Wehrmacht operations staff in response to their query on whether the Panzer Grenadier divisions had been ordered already to wheel toward Langres. Model noted that his order to have both divisions start out toward Reims—in other words, in the opposite direction—was in conformance with the Führer Order, based on the developments in the tactical situation.[136]

The field marshal was able to prevail against Hitler's impossible order, but neither Model's very independent command style nor the early recognition of the enemy's intent sufficed to prevent a further deterioration of the situation along the front. By August 30 it was clear that the plan aimed at intercepting the Americans by combining the Panzer units would fail. The flanking thrust by the II SS Panzer Corps toward Reims bogged down north of the Aisne River near Chauny. Attacking from the west, Bittrich's Panzer corps assumed command of the combat-capable remnants of the 1st, 2nd, 9th, 10th, 12th SS, and 116th Panzer Divisions.[137] But he quickly was forced on the defensive "by superior enemy pressure."[138] The American offensive continued in northerly and easterly directions at an undiminished tempo. Pushing up to fifty kilometers beyond the Soissons–Reims line, the Americans had already taken Raum and had reached the area of Montcornet–Rethel.[139] (See Map 13.)

The German flank attack that was to be launched from the south between the Aisne and the Marne rivers against Reims also failed. General of Cavalry Hans von Funck, commander of the XLVII Panzer Corps, was unable to effectively coordinate the two Panzer Grenadier divisions because their units had been detrained in widely separated unloading areas.[140] Nor had all of the transports arrived from Italy.[141] The German attack, therefore, did not even advance beyond the preparatory stage. The offensive by the U.S. Third Army aimed at the Meuse River crossings from the Châlons area to the east had beaten Funck's Panzer corps to the punch.

Model's stabilization effort was risky, but it was the only practical course of action. Nonetheless, it misfired. Bittrich's few Panzers had been unable to accomplish much against the American penetration; but now they were absent from the right wing of the army group, where the situation was getting increasingly worse.

At that point it was no longer possible to carry out the step-by-step withdrawal behind the Somme River that Hitler had approved on August 31.[142] The German infantry units that were withdrawing in the sector of the Fifth Panzer Army were unable to put up any worthwhile resistance against the British Second Army that was pursuing them across the Seine River. The German soldiers in those hard-pressed units were armed with little more than carbines and similar small arms.[143]

Now the dramatic days of the pursuit phase began for the British as well.[144] On August 30 they managed to break through the front of General of Panzer Troops Adolf Kuntzen's LXXXI Army Corps in two places and advance beyond Beauvais. The units of the 49th Infantry Division that were deployed in the breakthrough area were encircled and wiped out by tanks. Only Lieutenant General Siegfried Macholz's divisional headquarters and the artillery regiment reached the opposite bank of the Somme River.[145]

All General Kuntzen could do was report, "Reserves . . . are no longer available, so the enemy's armored spearheads can push north rather at will."[146] An attack direction toward Abbeville also appeared to be most likely to General Gause.[147] In so doing, the British would have been able to cut off the route of retreat across the Somme for eight German divisions, including one army corps of General of Infantry Gustav von Zangen's Fifteenth Army that was now involved in the fighting.[148]

But Lieutenant General Sir Brian Horrocks's XXX Corps had a different objective. To the surprise of the Germans, the British immediately exploited the resultant breakthrough and continued their advance during the night.[149] Early in the morning of August 31, armored units of the Guards Armoured Division overran the command post of Fifth Panzer Army at Saleux, near Amiens. Dietrich was barely able to escape with his headquarters.[150] General Eberbach and his chief of staff, Colonel Gersdorff, were both taken prisoner.[151]

Model's intention to recommit the Seventh Army and to give Eberbach the Somme River sector between Amiens[152] and the Oise River had thus come to naught.[153] Dietrich's staff, therefore, was unable to concentrate fully on the "gap between the Oise River and the Marne River."[154] Instead, it retained for the time being the responsibility for the entire sector all the way down to the Rethel–Charleville line.

Because the front was broken up, the Fifth Panzer Army headquarters was no longer in a position to execute any command functions. "The troops were on their own."[155] The forces of Army Group B were totally exhausted. As clearly indicated by the chain reaction of unending disaster messages on August 31, there was no longer talk of any "planned retreat."

On the German right wing the British reached Amiens, crossed the Somme River, and pushed about another thirty kilometers farther north, all the way to Albert.[156] In the meantime, the U.S. First Army expanded the American breakthrough area in a northerly direction all the way to Vervins.[157] Its spearheads were only about ninety kilometers away from those of the British Second Army at Albert.

On Army Group B's left wing the U.S. Third Army continued its operational thrust to the east, punched through the Argonne Forest, and established several bridgeheads across the Meuse River between Verdun and Commercy.[158]

The Allies had run over the Kitzinger Line—probably without even noticing it—on a broad front and had thus preempted the ambitious expectations the German High Command had for that position.[159]

In the evening Model asked his chief of staff to report to the Wehrmacht High Command that the enemy situation had developed as had been feared. "The tactical breakthrough by the British, the operational breakthrough by the Americans. There are no forces left with which to oppose them."[160] Even the outwardly unflappable Model showed signs of deep depression—only, of course, in strict privacy. He surprised Blumentritt by questioning what could still really be done to restore the situation.[161] Dietrich expressed his doubts more drastically. While Gause, his chief of staff, constantly tried to establish phone contact with the subordinate corps, Dietrich merely said: "Stop that. It makes no sense."[162]

Considering the "absolute tactical inferiority of the available formations," as Model saw it, the only thing left to do was to try to prevent Army Group B from being totally wiped out before reaching the Western Position.[163] But the push by the U.S. Third Army seemed to be threatening that position already. According to a message from the Third Air Fleet, American tanks were already twenty-five kilometers away from Metz.[164]

Although the entire front line showed signs of breaking up, Model decided to concentrate the fresh units expected from the Reich—initially the 553rd and 559th Grenadier Divisions followed by the 106th Panzer Brigade—in the area between Thionville and Nancy to establish a main effort.[165] Model asked the Wehrmacht High Command to see to it that the still existing gap between Army Group B and Army Task Group G—which in the meantime had shifted dangerously close to the Reich—be screened at the minimum by replacement units at the Vosges mountain passes between Nancy and Belfort.[166]

But most immediately, as Model repeated over and over again, the most important thing was to do everything possible to speed up the efforts to make the existing West Wall positions properly defensible and to man them with divisions from the Reich.[167] Only along the "Western Position" and its nucleus, the West Wall,[168] did the field marshal consider it possible to establish a strong defense, supported by a national levy muster.[169] There, he thought, it was at least possible to emplace light antitank obstacles and establish some protection against Allied carpet bombing.[170]

(d) The Western Position

It took several appeals before Hitler yielded to OB West's urging. The orders to "establish defensive readiness" and to "secure the Western Position and the West Wall" went out on September 1.[171] Only then were the defensive preparations started in the area of the Reich border. The tempo of the Allied advance obviously had taken Hitler by surprise. During the noon situation briefing at the Wolf's Lair, he remarked to Jodl: "They just about came racing at us. . . . What impudence!"[172]

Additionally, Hitler's mistaken belief that not much was needed to be done in the West Wall probably contributed to the fact that the decision was made so late.[173] The Wehrmacht High Command was also confused about the state of the West Wall.[174] Headquarters apparently had fallen victim to its own propaganda of the years 1939–1940 about the invincibility of the world's greatest and most modern fortification system.[175]

In fact, the West Wall in the summer of 1944 resembled a "broken-up warship."[176] After the end of the 1940 campaign in France, weapons and interior furnishings were removed from the line of pillboxes that stood between Kleve and Lörrach, while ammunition and rations were stored elsewhere. The field positions that supplemented the permanent facilities had fallen into disrepair, and wire obstacles and minefields had been removed. The West Wall was essentially demilitarized by 1941.[177]

The remaining fortifications no longer met the requirements of modern 1944 weapons technology. The concrete was not thick enough in a large percentage of the approximately nine thousand bunkers.[178] That even included the more heavily fortified sector of the line south of Trier.[179] The original antitank positions had been designed for the 37mm gun, which was not effective against the tanks of 1944. Moreover, the technically improved German machine gun, the MG-42, could not be mounted into the pillboxes, which had been designed for the older MG-34.

The dragon's teeth obstacles, too, were no longer insurmountable for battle tanks and therefore had to be reinforced with additional antitank ditches.[180] Despite the existing line of bunkers, the West Wall was not at all in a defensible state, and most of the other sectors of the German Western Position were in no better shape.[181] There were no permanent fortifications along the Antwerp–Albert Canal line or in the line of the planned extension of the West Wall all the way to Lake IJssel. The Thionville–Metz area had only obsolete groups of defensive works. The defensive positions of the French Maginot Line, which were also included in the plan, faced the wrong way and were therefore of doubtful benefit to the Germans. Precipitous defensive preparations were now started because the crucial shortcomings had not been addressed early enough—in other words, with adequate lead-time for the anticipated arrival of the enemy armored spearheads in front of the German Western Position.[182]

Complications were bound to arise in the zone of the Western Position because of a clash of the spheres of authority between OB West and Reichsführer-SS Himmler, who was the commander of the German Reserve Army. The various gauleiters throughout the zone also exercised authority as Reich defense commissars.

After the July 20 attempt on Hitler's life, the existing structure of areas of authority of the Wehrmacht and the Nazi Party for the preparation of the defense of the Reich[183] was invalidated.[184] The influence of the military was restricted and further undermined by Himmler's appointment to command of the Reserve Army. Himmler, however, was not completely successful in his grasp for power. He had wanted to give the Reich defense commissars in their respective party districts the most extensive powers, including the authority to convene summary courts-martial and to exercise control through his orders over the commitment of the police, the Reserve Army, and all other available Wehrmacht units.[185] Himmler's efforts were typical of his attempt to broaden the Nazi Party's influence over the Wehrmacht, even in the strictly military sphere of national defense.

The Nazi Party also tried, with limited success, to exploit the opportunities to consolidate power that arose after July 20. The authority of the Reich defense commissars now went beyond what Chief of the Nazi Party Chancellery Martin Bormann had described in May as the most urgent task, "The mobilization of all forces on the home front in order to make them available . . . to the Wehrmacht."[186]

But these questions remained unresolved at that point.[187] Thus, the orders for defense preparations issued at the end of August and the beginning of September were only transitional, with complicated individual provisos that could be interpreted in various ways.

One thing, however, was clear at the time: Himmler held the overall military command in the zone of the Western Position. Supported by an operations staff under General of Engineers Walter Kuntze, Himmler was responsible for security and defense, for establishing the layout of the tactical line, and for establishing the priorities and methods of improvement of the various positions.[188] But it was the gauleiters who were "responsible for directing the efforts to develop and improve the positions." They were in charge of the recruitment of civilian labor under the "national emergency levy" that was to accomplish all of the actual digging and entrenching.[189]

Those forces included members of the Hitler-Jugend (HJ—Hitler Youth), the Bund Deutscher Mädel (BDM—League of German Girls), and 137 detachments of the Reichsarbeitsdienst (RAD—Reich Labor Service), with the paramilitary Todt Organization providing the machinery and the technical supervision.[190] The gauleiters also were given the authority to issue directives to military stations and units on matters of "pure labor employment."

According to Hitler's orders, the initial priority for the digging and entrenching work was the establishment of continuous antitank obstacles and linking them with the existing "permanent installations" to form a positional system echeloned in depth. Tactical and technical combat experience was to be the basis for establishing and orienting the "improvised installations."[191] But the accomplishment of that goal was questionable from the start, because OB West headquarters, which did have expertise in such matters, was expressly barred from involvement in the preparations.[192]

The Fortress Engineer headquarters in the Reich, however, had neither the organizational nor the personnel capacities to execute within the short time available its assigned tasks of plotting the tactical line layout and establishing the priorities for the improvement of the positions.[193] The entrenching work, therefore, was started during the first days of September, in most cases under the direction of the gauleiters, who considered the entire affair to be an opportunity to acquire military skills.[194] The political leadership in the Jülich district, for example, did not have any specific instructions from the Fortress Engineer headquarters. They simply detailed a survey engineer from the city administration and then started to establish the positions thought to be suitable.[195]

During this initial phase there was nothing done in the way of planned entrenching work. Ditches dug with tremendous manpower effort were almost completely worthless from a military perspective. Positions *in front of* the dragon's teeth obstacles were laid out along the long tactical pattern.[196] In many cases there were no proper fields of observation and fire.[197]

The local population, which had been "emergency serviceconscripted," was willing to work but skeptical, according to the reports of the Sicherheitsdienst (SD—the SS Security Service). Typical of the reported comments: "If the Atlantic Wall did not hold, then how can these piles of dirt and ditches accomplish anything?" Other such reports indicated a widespread belief that the construction work had begun too late.[198]

Indeed, the initial calculations on paper showed that it would take at least another seven weeks to put the Western Position into a defensible state.[199] The most critical days now began for the German army on the Western Front. Army Group B faced the almost impossible task of using its exhausted units to gain the necessary time for the development of the positions. The Wehrmacht High Command likewise did not entertain any illusions. The possibility that the Allied offensives might continue swiftly and sweep over the Western Position and the West Wall was a threat that could be met only with improvisations.

All the 88mm antitank guns and any other artillery pieces available in the Reich that were capable of antitank fire were moved immediately to the western border. For the time being, however, there were no fully capable units available to man those guns. As a stop-gap measure the units ordered to the front included the replacement units from Military Districts VI, XII, and V, quickly organized fortress troop units, divisions that were in the process of being organized, and entire classes from various army schools.[200]

As ordered by OB West, the main effort centered in the area between Trier and Nancy. With the spearheads of the U.S. Third Army already in front of Metz, the 19th, 36th, 553rd, and 559th Grenadier Divisions[201] were concentrated in that area.[202] Those were the first reinforcements worth mentioning since Model took command.[203] Plugging the gap between Nancy and Belfort in time depended on bringing the units of Army Task Group G up from the south. Hitler himself was skeptical about that possibility. "If Blaskowitz pulls that off," he said in a comment to Jodl, "then I will only be too happy to apologize to him."[204]

4. From the Crisis at Montélimar to the Initial Consolidation of the Western Front's Left Wing

(a) The Nineteenth Army's Breakthrough of the Rhône River Valley

Following Eisenhower's decision of August 24, the U.S. Third Army was restricted to a limited radius of action. Patton's objectives were placed generally to the east, but an offensive toward Dijon–Belfort was not seriously considered. That reduced the threat of Army Task Group G's being cut by an Allied operational thrust from the north, although the Germans did not immediately recognize that. An essential prerequisite for Blaskowitz's units to link up with Army Group B was the immediate resolution of the crisis in the Rhône River Valley.

On August 25, the Germans tried in vain to push the U.S. 36th Infantry Division to the east, away from the Rhône Valley road. The poorly coordinated attack of the corps grouping under Lieutenant General Wend von Wietersheim failed.[205] That force consisted of the 11th Panzer Division, the 198th Infantry Division, and the 18th Antiaircraft Artillery Regiment.[206] The divisions pushing east from Montélimar to open up a retreat route did not reach their objective.

That afternoon the Americans managed to block the valley road with tanks and infantry north of the city at La Coucourde.[207] The headquarters of the Nineteenth Army was encircled, along with the LXXXV Army Corps, consisting of the 198th and 338th Infantry Divisions and elements of the 11th Panzer Division.

Wietersheim immediately took action. That evening he voluntarily relinquished control of the 198th Infantry Division.[208] He then ordered all the available elements of his Panzer units to attack the enemy from the move before the only possible escape route was finally blocked.[209]

After tough fighting, the road was cleared again by the morning of August 26.[210] The 11th Panzer Division had even taken some of the commanding heights east of La Coucourde. Wiese and his chief of staff, Botsch, urged everyone to pass through the eye of the needle at Montélimar as quickly as possible because they expected the U.S. 36th Infantry Division to attack again.[211] The Nineteenth Army headquarters was also afraid that the Americans might advance from the Grenoble area and continue their encircling pursuit with the objective of blocking the Rhône River Valley farther north.[212] It therefore was critical to disengage the 11th Panzer Division from its combat mission along the pass and to free it up for further flank screening actions to the north and east.[213]

Under American artillery fire the traffic movements started, but only sluggishly. Four American artillery battalions were firing on the valley road from the La Coucourde area alone.[214] Covered by the 111th Panzer Grenadier Regiment, which beat off the American attacks against the position on the heights to the east of the retreat route, only a few units of the Panzer division managed to get through the bottleneck. The two infantry divisions were still to the south at Montélimar.[215]

The situation continued to deteriorate during the night leading to August 27. The Drôme River, a few kilometers north of the pass, had been flooding since late evening, sweeping away an improvised bridge at Loriol.[216] Several of the reconnoitered possible fords were impassable.[217] (See Map 14.)

The Nineteenth Army headquarters had the impression that the Americans now wanted to finish the encirclement, because they continued their attacks with three divisions in daylight.[218] The U.S. 36th Infantry Division pressed the attack near La Coucourde–Loriol, while the U.S. 3rd Infantry Division stepped up the pressure from the south against the blocking position that was defended only by the German 669th Army Engineer Battalion. The thrust by the U.S. 45th Infantry Division, however, was the most serious threat. It was pushing toward Allex–Livron-sur-Drôme along the north bank of the Drôme River, opposed at first by only a few companies of the 11th Panzer Division. The two German infantry divisions were coming up too slowly, while elements of Wietersheim's Panzer units were still tied down at the Montélimar bottleneck.

Botsch, the chief of staff of the Nineteenth Army, had himself gone through the eye of the needle under direct American fire. In Botsch's opinion, Kniess, the commanding general of the LXXXV Army Corps, did not seem to have recognized the seriousness of the situation.[219] Botsch's appeals to get the infantry divisions through at any price, because the army's fate depended on it, produced no results initially.[220] The units that had crossed the Montélimar area with heavy equipment losses were now congested along the Drôme River.[221] The crisis in the south had reached its climax.

When it turned out on August 28 that the main elements of the infantry divisions were still in their old positions, Wiese ordered the commanding general of the LXXXV Army Corps to report for a conference, which, in addition to Kniess, was also attended by Botsch and Wietersheim.[222] Kniess was convinced that the hopeless congestion on the highway and the precise enemy artillery and mortar fire made it impossible to get the infantry elements out unless the Panzer division provided a screen for another two days south of the Drôme River.[223] Wietersheim's force was already needed to the north. Wiese criticized Kniess for obviously still thinking in terms of an orderly withdrawal. He directed the LXXXV Army Corps immediately to form battle groups and to fight its way through to the far side of the Isère River.[224] The 11th Panzer Division's 61st Antitank Battalion, reinforced by one Panzer company, would provide a screen along the Drôme River for several more hours.[225]

What Wiese later called "almost as a miracle" now came to

pass.[226] The last German troops crossed the Drôme River on August 30. By that evening the main body of the LXXXV Army Corps and the 11th Panzer Division were already on the opposite side of the Isère River.[227] Even so, nearly superhuman march efforts were still required.[228] The Lyon area had to be reached by the night before September 1.

In the meantime, the Luftwaffe IV Field Corps had established a bridgehead position around Lyon—also on the east bank.[229] Although the threat from French partisans was still quite serious, General Petersen's units had been able to cross over rapidly from the west bank of the Rhône River and were the first forces available at Lyon.[230] The uprising of the FFI in the city was suppressed within a few hours.[231] Lyon continued to remain wide open for the withdrawal movements, with the FFI in the area constituting no serious threat.

Although the overall situation was starting to look unexpectedly favorable, the Germans nevertheless suffered heavy losses in the Montélimar Pocket.[232] The 198th Infantry Division was able to get all of its personnel through with the exception of the supply trains of the divisional artillery regiment. The 338th Infantry Division managed to get about 60 percent of its troops out to the north.[233] But the combat strength of the regiments of both divisions now was only about four hundred to five hundred men.[234]

Major General Otto Richter, the commanding general of 198th Infantry Division, was captured during the breakout, while his operations officer, Lieutenant Colonel Olof von Lindequist, was killed. Lieutenant General Johannes Baessler, who was in charge of regulating traffic along the valley road, was seriously wounded.[235] Some two thousand motor vehicles, one thousand horses, and forty-five artillery pieces remained behind on the Rhône River road.[236]

The withdrawal march to the north and the final escape of the Nineteenth Army was the result in large measure of the manner in which the American forces conducted their operations. Although the spearheads of the U.S. VI Corps were already northeast of Montélimar on August 21, they never blocked the valley road permanently. The final decisive factor was that the Americans did not establish a definite main effort of attack, but rather conducted piecemeal assaults in several places with resulting weaker forces.[237] The attempt to stop the German withdrawal movements primarily with artillery fire failed. Major General Lucian K. Truscott, commanding general of U.S. VI Corps, was not at all satisfied with the results.[238] In Blaskowitz's opinion, the German breakout was the result of the achievements of the local chains of command[239] and the self-sacrificing, heroic fighting spirit of the troops.[240]

(b) Establishment of the Dijon Bridgehead

The Nineteenth Army's successful breakout established for the first time the necessary conditions for the merger of Army Task Group G's march columns in the Dijon area. In the meantime, Blaskowitz had ordered the formation of a reserve line along the Chaumont–Châtillon–Autun–Châlons–Dôle–Swiss border. The Nineteenth Army, the LXIV Army Corps, and the Ottenbacher March Group were to converge there. It was only an improvised and thin security screen, however. The few available units, which included SS-police, security, and eastern battalions, the Autun Artillery School, and two engineer companies, were insufficient to defend this broad area against any major attacks.[241]

The commanding general of Army Task Group G believed that the real main threat of being cut off would come from the U.S. Third Army thrusting from the north toward Belfort, to close the Belfort Gap. But so far there appeared to be no indicators of such an action by the Americans.[242] Blaskowitz reported to Model that developments along his northern flank "would determine the possibility of getting some one-quarter of a million Germans out."[243]

The important thing for the moment was to reinforce the bridgehead around Dijon with strong combat units and to pass the remaining units of Army Task Group G through as quickly as possible. Blaskowitz now believed that the enemy pressure against the Nineteenth Army was basically no longer as threatening.[244]

The success of the entire withdrawal operation, however, was still in doubt because the march columns of the LXIV Army Corps were still trailing far back.[245] To gain the time to let the corps get through, it became necessary to slow down the smooth withdrawal movement of the Nineteenth Army.[246] As Blaskowitz made clear to the LXIV Army Corps commander, General Sachs, that meant that the Nineteenth Army, which had moved up rapidly after a tremendous fighting and marching effort, would once again have to be placed at risk.[247] Because of telecommunications problems, the commanding general of Army Task Group G received a full briefing on the difficulties encountered by the LXIV Army Corps only during the last days of August and via a liaison officer.[248]

At Hitler's demand, Sachs was removed as the corps commander, but that action did not produce any immediate results. As an "Aryanized" officer, Sachs was still always suspect in the eyes of the Army's Personnel Office.[249] After Sachs's successor, Lieutenant General Otto Lasch, took command on September 3, he remarked that he could not have carried out the difficult assembly phase any faster than Sachs had.[250] Blaskowitz's main concern now was to withdraw the last two divisions safely.[251] Regrettably, however, "one would simply have to accept the fact that individual groups will no longer be able to link up and will be cut off."[252] Pulling the combat units out and moving the mobile forces forward toward Dijon as ordered meant that the three big march groups of the LXIV Army Corps were deprived of their screen.

Major General Botho Elster believed that the situation of the rear march group, which was now under his command, was utterly impossible.[253] The withdrawal of the 159th Infantry Division from the Southern Group deprived him of most of the vehicles and much of the weapons and ammunition. At the conferences on September 1 and 2 in Poitiers, Elster made it perfectly clear that he considered it senseless under such conditions to continue the movement of his twenty-eight-thousand-man force.[254, 255] But the officers present in Poitiers were not convinced by his threadbare argument that the Châteauroux–Bourges–Nevers–Dijon withdrawal route was "occupied by three regular French armies."[256] Colonel Ernst von Bauer, who earlier had fought his way through from Pau to Poitiers with a battle group numbering just about ten thousand men, rejected Elster's argument.[257] And in fact, elements of that group eventually reached the reserve positions around Dijon.[258]

Elster, nonetheless, entered into negotiations with FFI representatives and on September 10 he capitulated with 19,200 men at Issoudun to Major General Robert C. Macon, the commanding general of the U.S. 83rd Infantry Division.[259] The defeatism of the German general, which was recognizable early on, played at least as important a role as the military action of the Resistance in this one and only quantifiable major victory of the FFI. But even during the surrender negotiations General Macon did not concede that the capitulation had been forced by the FFI.[260] Militarily the event was one of relatively minor significance. In military respects the decisive event was the arrival at the Dijon bridgehead of the first German units withdrawing from southwestern France.

Marching up from the Massif Central via Moulins–Autun, Group Ottenbacher arrived on September 2.[261] Ottenbacher's unit, which had covered the shortest distance, was followed by the march columns of the LXIV Army Corps' combat units, which had been ordered to move at the head of the column. The first elements of the 16th Infantry Division reached Langres on September 3.[262] Just two days later, the main body of the 16th and 159th Infantry Divisions entered the perimeter of the bridgehead.[263]

The most immediate task was to reinforce the northern flank, so that the some sixty thousand remaining German troops who had started the march from the southwest under command of the LXIV Army Corps could withdraw into the German lines.[264] Blaskowitz believed that the primary mission of Army Task Group G was to secure the line between Nancy and Châtillon.[265] Therefore, Ottenbacher's units, including the 19th SS Police Regiment, the 1000th Security Regiment, the 1000th Security Reconnaissance Battalion, the units of the 95th, 192nd, 194th, 195th, and 198th Security Regiments,[266] and the 16th Infantry Division were placed under the LXVI Army Corps.[267] That corps was under the command of General of Artillery Walther Lucht.[268] (See Map 15.)

On September 4, Lucht managed to establish initial contact with the First Army's left wing, and thus with Army Group B. The remaining elements of the 21st Panzer Division,[269] which Model had placed under Army Task Group B for refitting in the area of Charmes (Mosel), also established contact with the newly arriving 553rd Grenadier Division, gradually reinforcing the defensive strength of the northern flank.[270] Simultaneously, the reinforcement of the Dijon bridgehead on the southern flank was proceeding smoothly. After the rear guard of Luftwaffe IV Field Corps had evacuated Lyon according to plan, Botsch could see that the Nineteenth Army would be able to make it through in just a few days.[271]

The infantry units that were withdrawing to the north had something of a head start as a result of the extensive demolitions ordered by General Kaliebe, the engineer commander of Army Task Group G. All thirty-three bridges around Lyon across the Rhône and the Saône rivers had been blown.[272] The 11th Panzer Division reported inflicting heavy losses on the American forces that were attacking on the eastern flank. At Meximieux, northeast of Lyon,

Wietersheim's unit smashed a regiment of the U.S. 45th Infantry Division, and at Montrevel, it broke up an American reconnaissance squadron.[273] In the process, the Americans reportedly lost twelve hundred men, thirty tanks and armored scout cars, and sixty-four motor vehicles.[274] The U.S. Army's official history of World War II, however, reports a significantly different outcome.[275]

In the meantime, Lieutenant General Alexander Patch, commanding the U.S. Seventh Army, had yielded to U.S. VI Corps commander Truscott's urging and had postponed the planned regrouping of his forces.[276] But that decision was made too late to ruthlessly exploit the last opportunity to block the German withdrawal to the north.[277] Effective September 3, the Nineteenth Army assumed command of the southern sector of the bridgehead.[278] Its lead infantry units, including the Luftwaffe IV Field Corps with the 716th Infantry Division and the LXXXV Army Corps with the 198th Infantry Division, crossed the Doubs River on the next day and moved into their positions between Châlons and Dôle. The 11th Panzer Division continued to be earmarked for screening the eastern flank in the Besançon area.[279]

Blaskowitz moved his headquarters to Gerardmer in order to organize the defensive preparations in the rear areas.[280] That immediately created difficulties with Himmler resulting from the confused command structure in the zone of the Western Position. Blaskowitz failed to receive the authority to issue tactical directives to the units of the Replacement Army along the Vosges mountain passes and in the Belfort area.[281] Blaskowitz, however, was able to prevent the Reichsführer-SS from expanding his sphere of influence even further.[282] Responding to a message from Defense District V commander Lieutenant General Rudolf Veiel that Himmler intended to take command of all troops up to the Nancy–Epinal–Belfort–Swiss border line, Blaskowitz immediately asked OB West to get the Wehrmacht High Command to veto that decision.[283]

Blaskowitz was probably afraid that Himmler wanted to influence directly the conduct of combat operations in the west, and he emphatically referred to the impossible overlap of military authority that would be the result.[284] The Wehrmacht High Command supported Blaskowitz. For the time being,[285] Himmler's authority was limited to the "Vosges Position."[286] Aside from that relatively secondary problem, it was now becoming apparent that the situation was beginning to stabilize as a whole on the left wing of the front line. But there was no way of telling at that time whether or not the bridgehead that extended far to the west could be held until such time as all the march units of the LXIV Army Corps reached the door that was being held open for them at Dijon.[287]

Nevertheless, according to the summary in the OB West war diary as of September 5, Army Task Group G had for the most part already accomplished its difficult task of moving its units into the area between the left wing of Army Group B and the Swiss border. It was an accomplishment despite the vast number of difficulties, a success justifiably attributed to the "outstanding performance of the troops and their clever and energetic leadership."[288]

The fact that German troops had been able to reach and occupy unopposed the bridgehead at Dijon was partly facilitated by Eisenhower's operational decisions, which forced the U.S. Third Army to stand down and do nothing. The Germans exploited to an almost optimum degree that brief span of time during which Patton's hands were tied. The German First Army's Mosel Front, adjacent to the north of Blaskowitz's command sector, was stabilized within a few days.

(c) The Establishment of the Defensive Line along the Mosel River

The Germans initially believed that the establishment of a defensive line along the Mosel would be impossible. On September 1, Blumentritt reported to Speidel that the U.S. Third Army was continuing its advance to the east.[289] Army Group B headquarters feared that the Third Army would break through all the way to the West Wall area.[290] It thus seemed doubtful at the time that the First Army, with its ragged forces, would be able to accomplish its mission of holding at all costs the line from the Meuse River (Charleville–Stenay) via Diedenhofen (Thionville) and Metz, all the way to a point south of Nancy.[291] Of the promised reinforcements, only one regiment of the 559th Grenadier Division had arrived east of Metz. But the anticipated major American offensive did not materialize. Patton's fuel shortages restricted him to merely conducting a reconnaissance in force across the Meuse River to the east.

The German defensive line, which was just being established, still had considerable gaps. The American cavalry units, therefore, caused considerable confusion when on September 2 they showed up near Longuyon along the Mosel River in the Thionville and Pont-à-Mousson area and occupied Toul.[292]

Chevallerie reported that Gauleiter Gustav Simon had left his post in Luxembourg and that uncontrollable refugee movements in Lorraine impaired the German troop transfers.[293] Because of the "shameless flight" of German civilian agencies—according to a report by the deputy chief of staff at OB West headquarters—"the entire supply management structure was endangered." In the resulting confusion some fifteen hundred cubic meters of fuel and ninety-one eastern-model tractors that had been earmarked for moving the artillery batteries simply disappeared.[294]

Quite apart from such problems, the commanding general of the First Army had quite a bit of trouble as a result of Himmler's involvement in military command functions. As the commanding general of the Replacement Army, Himmler forbade the planned displacement of the First Army's command post to Wittlich.[295] During the period of confusion there was considerable doubt that Chevallerie would get command authority over the new divisions that were being moved into the area of the Western Position and that were thus under either Himmler or Defense District XII. Model requested that Defense District XII be removed immediately from Himmler's authority for the purposes of frontline employment.[296] But the Wehrmacht High Command worked out a compromise that gave the First Army the authority to issue directives, although it would have to do so through Defense District XII, which remained under Himmler.[297] A more sensible way to resolve this problem was not reached until Hitler decided that Model should determine the exact moment at which the First Army would assume operational command in the Western Position.[298]

In the meantime, things continued to remain quiet in front of the First Army's main line of resistance. There were no major combat operations there for almost a week. The initial position of the defenders improved with every passing day. The panicked mood in Thionville and Luxembourg abated, and the mess in Metz was straightened out.[299]

The LXXX Army Corps, under General of Infantry Dr. Franz Beyer, established only a thin outpost line between Charleville and Thionville with the help of the remnants of various units returning from the west.[300] Those units included elements of the 48th Infantry Division, the Panzer-Lehr Division, the 5th Parachute Division, the

1st Security Regiment, and elements of the 15th Panzer Grenadier Division.[301] A regular front was established along the Mosel River to the south within a very short time following the arrival of new units from the Reich.

General of Artillery Johann Sinnhuber and his LXXXII Army Corps took over the sector from Thionville to a point south of Metz.[302] He had two infantry divisions available.[303] The arrival of the 559th Grenadier Division was completed on September 4.[304] Major General Johannes Krause, the commanding general of the 462nd Replacement Army Division committed in the Metz area, had reorganized his unit quickly for combat operations. His regiments now were manned by troops from the VI Officer Candidate School (eighteen hundred men), the Noncommissioned Officer Training Course of Defense District XII (fifteen hundred men), and about twenty-five hundred stragglers from the army in the west.[305] The battle group of 17th SS Panzer Grenadier Division that was being held in readiness east of Metz as a mobile reserve was also placed under the 462nd Division.[306]

First Army's left wing was formed by the XLVII Panzer Corps under General von Funck, with the 3rd and 15th Panzer Grenadier Divisions and the 553rd Grenadier Division. Not all of these three units, however, had yet arrived at the Mosel River in full strength.[307]

Meanwhile, the 19th and 36th Grenadier Divisions were assembled behind the front line in the Trier–Saarbrücken area, while the 106th Panzer Brigade was moved into the area southwest of Luxembourg as a shock reserve unit.[308] The situation was mostly stabilized in that area by September 4. In the evening, Speidel noted that the safest sector in the Army Group B front was the Mosel River line.[309] That meant Chevallerie's First Army for the first time had a clearly organized front line with effective units. Feyerabend, Chevallerie's chief of staff, reported that contact had been established not only with the Fifth Panzer Army,[310] but also with Army Task Group G to the south.[311] The First Army's weak points were on its outer wings. The tenuous contact with the bridgehead at Dijon was a key problem, as was the situation along the boundary with the Fifth Panzer Army. Model, therefore, intended to launch a locally limited attack to relieve the pressure on the LXXX Army Corps, which consisted of heavily mixed units.[312] The 106th Panzer Brigade, teamed up with one regiment from the 15th Panzer Grenadier Division, was to reach the line from Longuyon to Briey and on to the bridgehead, thereby straightening out the front line.[313]

Such reserves were not available to the I SS Panzer Corps that linked up with the First Army to the north. Waffen-SS General Keppler and the remnants of four Panzer divisions, the 1st SS Panzer, 2nd SS Panzer, 12th SS Panzer, and 2nd Panzer Divisions, defended the approximately ninety-kilometer-long line between Namur and Charleville.[314] Keppler's battle groups did succeed in denting the American bridgeheads on the Meuse River at Dinant and Givet, but the I SS Panzer Corps' combat strength was reduced significantly in the process. It was now down to only about one thousand troops with four armored combat vehicles.[315]

For that reason alone, the German commanders considered the constantly increasing activities of the Resistance in the area along the French-Belgian border to be a threat.[316] During the withdrawal of the Panzer-Lehr Division behind the Meuse River the division's soldiers had seen some of the gruesome results of partisan attacks on individual German vehicles.[317] Model urged caution, because the Resistance movements in Belgium and northern France were now planning to stage an open uprising.[318] On September 5, it became crystal clear that the Allied operational pause along the southern wing of Army Group B was nearing its end. The U.S. First Army resumed its offensive to the east, establishing several bridgeheads against the extremely thinly held Meuse River Front, occupied by the I SS Panzer Corps.[319]

On the other hand, the intentions of the U.S. Third Army remained unclear. By September 6, however, OB West headquarters expected Patton's attack to commence within the next several days. This and the assumption that he intended to attack to the east turned out to be correct.[320] The Third Army's offensive was bound to hit the Mosel River Front, where the German defenses were the strongest in the Western Front. (See Map 16.)

5. The Climax of the Crisis in the West

(a) The Mons Pocket

The situation on the left wing of the Western Front had consolidated somewhat within a few days. That was significant for future developments, but at the same time the fact that the Fifth Panzer Army had been almost destroyed cast a long shadow. The continuation of the British offensive across the Somme River drove a wedge between

Zangen's Fifteenth Army and the units of Dietrich's Fifth Panzer Army. Advancing from Amiens–Albert via Arras, the British XXX Corps on September 1 had already reached the area south of Lille, and was thus deep in the rear of the Fifteenth Army.[321] The British Second Army was screened on its right flank by the XIX Corps of the U.S. First Army, which was advancing on Cambrai from Péronne.

The Allied offensive initially smashed the Fifth Panzer Army's western wing. Obstfelder's LXXXVI Army Corps,[322] whose units were still in the process of crossing the Somme River, was pushed into the Fifteenth Army's sector.[323] In Kuntzen's LXXXI Army Corps the corps headquarters itself was about the only element still operational.[324] The Fifteenth Army now faced the danger of being forced back against the coast with a reversed front and being annihilated there. OB West headquarters immediately recognized that the final disintegration of the German front could be prevented only by closing the gap in the front line between the Fifteenth and Fifth Panzer armies.[325] Model ordered both armies to expend all means at their command to effect that closure, but Gause, the chief of staff of the Fifth Panzer Army, referred to that order as a mere "war diary order." A unit "that is no longer a unit," Gause continued, cannot "be given any impossible orders" and "there is no normal front line anymore."[326]

Gause's blunt words described the facts as they were. The Fifth Panzer Army's right wing had been shattered. Command and control contact had been lost with the army's other corps that were fighting in the Péronne (Somme)–St. Quentin–Hirson–Charleville (Meuse) area.[327] Dietrich's headquarters had no way whatsoever of influencing the action and averting the renewed encirclement that was threatening the main body of his army's units.

Lieutenant General Omar N. Bradley, the commanding general of the U.S. 12th Army Group, hoped to block the retreat route for twelve German divisions.[328] To accomplish that the U.S. XIX Corps was to continue attacking in a northeasterly direction via Cambrai as the U.S. First Army's left pincer arm, while U.S. VII Corps was now to wheel north heading toward Mons.[329]

U.S. VII Corps now punched through the line that was held only by strongpoints.[330] Coming from Vervins, the Americans reached the area of Avesnes-sur-Helpe on September 1.[331] As a result, the I SS Panzer Corps was pushed to the east, and Keppler's corps, which was the left wing of the Fifth Panzer Army, thus escaped the pocket and withdrew behind the Meuse River.

Only about fifty kilometers now separated the spearheads of the U.S. VII Corps and U.S. XIX Corps, the latter of which was pushing into the gap in the German front at Cambrai.[332] Three German corps with ten divisional-size battle groups were between the two offensive arms of the U.S. First Army that were aiming at the Mons area.[333]

Krüger's LVIII Panzer Corps command post at St. Quentin was receiving only outdated orders from the Fifth Panzer Army, but no up-to-date situation reports. Krüger therefore agreed with the recommendation from Bittrich's II SS Panzer Corps to take independent action based on the situation.[334] A quickly scheduled conference with the LXXIV Army Corps commander, General of Infantry Erich Straube, confirmed the assessment that the Americans were pursuing only lightly against the middle of the front line of the three corps.[335] Reconnaissance patrols and Allied radio intercepts confirmed that the main threat was on both flanks.[336]

On September 1, the two corps commanders together decided on a breakout to the northeast, all the way into the area of Nivelles, twenty-five kilometers south of Brussels.[337] Despite their swift action, taken entirely on their own responsibility, the chances were poor of successfully making the almost seventy-kilometer-movement through the Mons area, especially for the cumbersome infantry units.

By the next day, when Krüger assembled the commanders and general staff officers for the purpose of issuing his verbal orders, the Americans had already thrust from Avesnes all the way to the Sambre River (Maubeuge) and via Valenciennes into the vicinity of Mons.[338] That city was still being defended by a battle group of the 9th SS Panzer Division.[339] As Bittrich commented to the commanding general of the 47th Infantry Division, the basic idea was to save as many men as possible through this "pipeline."[340] But that pipeline was only about twenty kilometers wide between Mons and Maubeuge.

The breakout attempts began on September 2. The motorized units were able to escape, including the battle groups of the 1st SS Panzer, 12th SS Panzer, and 116th Panzer Divisions that were under Bittrich's corps. Those units reached the area east of Maubeuge–Beaumont, partly by pushing through the American columns that were pursuing to the north.[341]

The headquarters of the LVIII Panzer Corps broke out under

Krüger's personal leadership on September 3, bypassing the last open position in the enemy encirclement north of Maubeuge.[342] The headquarters of the LXXIV Army Corps and the II SS Panzer Corps were also able to escape the encirclement. But then the U.S. VII Corps moved into position along the Maubeuge–Mons highway and blocked the escape route. The U.S. 1st Infantry Division thrust forward into the pocket, trapping in the process six German divisions— the 3rd Parachute Division, the 6th Parachute Division, the Luftwaffe 18th Field Division, the 47th Infantry Division, the 275th Infantry Division, and the 348th Infantry Division.[343] (See Map 17.) Belgian Resistance groups cooperated effectively in the subsequent mopping up.[344] Lieutenant General Joachim von Tresckow, the commanding general of the Luftwaffe 18th Field Division, did manage to fight his way back through his own lines with a few men after a fourteen-day march.[345]

Some twenty-five thousand Germans were captured.[346] The Fifth Panzer Army's front line ceased to exist after that serious defeat. On September 3, the British Guards Armoured Division entered the Belgian capital.[347] With the exception of scattered groups, there were no longer any German forces in the area between Lille and north of Charleroi.[348]

Model ordered the gap in the front line closed by General of Panzer Troops Erich Brandenburger, who he had appointed commanding general of the Seventh Army.[349] That attempt, however, was doomed to failure from the start. With the exception of the headquarters of the LXXIV and the LXXXI Army Corps, Brandenburger had no troops available.[350] He finally was given the order to establish an outpost line between Leuven and Namur.[351] The headquarters of Lieutenant General Friedrich Schack's LXXXI Army Corps and Straube's LXXIV Army Corps were to organize the remnants of scattered units into battle groups and gradually form a defensive front that faced west.[352] But there was no way of telling whether and when that could be accomplished.[353]

The heavy losses during the fighting in the Falaise area, during the crossing of the Seine River, and on the retreat to the Somme River had claimed much equipment. At Arenberg (near Koblenz), the new headquarters of OB West, the success of the enemy was summarized by the lack of German antitank weapons. As a result, the exhausted German infantry units were being "delivered up to enemy tanks."[354] Model ordered a report sent to Wehrmacht High Command detailing the depressed state of morale among his troops.[355]

Likewise, in the German First Army sector there were signs of deterioration in the northern France-Belgium and Dutch areas. Numerous stragglers, administrative elements, and headquarters were flooding east along the retreat routes. Panic in the rear areas caused premature destruction of supplies and weapons. The officer maintaining the war diary for the LXXXIX Army Corps recorded a situation that in his view was "a picture that is unworthy and disgraceful for the German army."[356] Primarily, it was the personnel of the Luftwaffe ground support organization who took flight and withdrew to the east—even from the area around Amsterdam.[357]

Model tried to counter the panic by appealing to the "honor and steadfastness of the individual."[358] An *Appeal to the Soldiers of the Army of the West* was distributed along the routes of the retreat. In it, the field marshal urged everyone to seize the initiative wherever the command had lost control. Addressing the soldiers personally as "your commanding general," he emphasized that everybody had to be prepared to assume responsibility. "We have lost a battle, but I tell you we will still win this war!"[359] As incredible as this might seem in retrospect, it was not merely an appeal to stick it out from somebody who should have known better. Model's letters to his son document that he had not yet lost his basic confident attitude despite all of the setbacks.[360] The field marshal closed his appeal with the words: "Remember that, at this moment, the most important thing is to gain time," in order to move more reinforcements to the west. "Soldiers, we must give the Führer that time!"

But the Germans seemed to be losing that race. The breakthrough wedge the Allies established as the result of the Mons Pocket and the smashing of the German units had resulted in a gap of seventy-five kilometers that was almost impossible to close. During the previous few days the Allies had been able to exploit fully the high degree of mobility of their divisions along the good highway and road network.

Speidel reported to Warlimont that these were not just the spearheads of overextended enemy units. The Army Group B chief of staff foresaw clearly that strong enemy tank forces would mount a thrust to Antwerp to encircle the Fifteenth Army.[361] That meant that the crisis on the Western Front was approaching its climax.

(b) The Fall of Antwerp

Model was forced to stand by almost helplessly and watch the dramatic deterioration of the situation on September 4. OB West headquarters at Arenberg believed that it would only be possible to prevent an encirclement of the Fifteenth Army if several Panzer brigades could be brought up.[362] But it was far too late for that. Model's order to have the only available unit, the 105th Panzer Brigade, attack from the east toward Mechelen to hit the British in the flank had no chance of success.[363] As of that moment, only the headquarters and one company had arrived in the area of operations.[364] Besides, it had no fuel.[365]

The pace of the British advance that exploited the gap in the German front made it no longer possible to establish even a provisional defensive ring around Antwerp. Model had assigned that mission just a few hours earlier to General of Aviation Friedrich Christiansen, the Wehrmacht commander in the Netherlands.[366] But before Christiansen was able to move up the 719th Infantry Division, the spearheads of British XXX Corps were at the outskirts of the city. At about 1000 hours, when scout cars from the 11th Armoured Division showed up at Boom,[367] ten kilometers south of Antwerp, the main body of the 719th Infantry Division[368] was still approaching.[369]

The weak resistance south of Antwerp finally faded out two hours later.[370] At 1425 hours Major General Christoph zu Stolberg[371] reported to Army Group B headquarters that Allied tanks had penetrated into the city.[372] It was impossible to conduct any delaying defensive action with Stolberg's meager units, which consisted of two battalions and one antiaircraft artillery heavy battery. Model, therefore, decided to give up the city and instead to concentrate the available forces on blocking the Albert Canal.[373]

The thrust into Antwerp by the 11th British Armoured Division was mounted so quickly that the Germans no longer had any time to destroy the infrastructure of the international port. Demolitions in the Antwerp docks were prevented by a Belgian engineer reserve lieutenant who worked for the harbor administration.[374] As a result of what was probably the most significant act by the Belgian Resistance, the Allies seized the harbor installations and the docks on the north bank of the Scheldt River almost intact.[375] Incomprehensibly, the commander of the 11th Armoured Division, Major General George Roberts, failed to seize immediately the bridges across the Albert Canal in the northern part of the city.[376] Nonetheless, the Allies claimed a brilliant feat of arms.

Only one week had passed since the Allies pushed across the Seine River. During that time, the British had covered a distance of about 370 kilometers and had seized the international port of Antwerp without any destruction. Apart from that, however, only the ring around the German Fifteenth Army had been closed.[377] Montgomery estimated the strength of Zangen's army[378] at about 150,000.[379]

(c) Defensive Measures in the Rear Position in the West and Model's September 4 Estimate of the Situation

OB West no longer had any available reserves. The situation at the end of August and the beginning of September was so critical that the Wehrmacht High Command now authorized Model to draw personnel from other Wehrmacht components. Long-standing institutional barriers had fallen. But, for example, the 150,000 Luftwaffe recruits of the 1st Air Training Division, who were now immediately available to OB West as personnel replacements, amounted to no more than a drop in the bucket.[380]

Therefore, the organization of the defensive rear position assumed an increased significance. A barrier line to round up the army of refugees flowing east[381] was established from the Swiss border along the Western Position to Aachen and then north along the boundary of the Reich.[382] With the help of the III Military Police Command, the Army High Command I and II Special Staffs, and all other available elements of the Wehrmacht Patrol Service, the flood of retreating soldiers were to be disarmed and then made ready to return to combat as quickly as possible.[383] The responsibility for the defensive rear position measures that Model had initiated shortly after his arrival in the west was now transferred to Himmler.[384] The resulting extreme ruthlessness was quite deliberate. Keitel, for example, advised the commander of the III Military Police Command, General of Infantry Hans Karl von Scheele, to proceed most severely "against malingerers and cowardly shirkers, including officers . . . and to execute [death sentences] immediately for the purposes of deterrence."[385] The Wehrmacht operations staff had no objections to employing Nazi Party functionaries to round up stragglers. The proposal itself had come from General of Infantry Walter Schroth, the commanding general of Defense District XII.[386]

The crisis in the west undoubtedly gave the Party and the Nazi ideologues another opening to penetrate deeper into the military sphere. Some two hundred National Socialist Leadership Officers, for example, were dispatched to Defense Districts V and XII to influence "the attitude of troops returning from the West."[387] The Wehrmacht High Command was already considering converting the German military entirely to a Soviet-style commissar (political officer) system.[388] The mission of the National Socialist Leadership Officer was to promote education that turned out fanatical soldiers of National Socialism.[389]

Fanaticism now was to replace what the Wehrmacht had lost in personnel and materiel strength. The catastrophic situation in the west, however, was not the result of any lack of fighting spirit on the part of the soldiers. Breakdown phenomena primarily occurred where the front line had broken apart and where the command links were lost to those tactically inferior troops that increasingly were becoming burned out with each passing day.[390]

The crisis now had gripped the entire northern wing of the German front following the encirclement of Zangen's Fifteenth Army. There was no longer a continuous defensive line in the sector between Antwerp and Namur. Lieutenant General Heinz-Helmut von Wühlisch, the chief of staff of the Wehrmacht commander in the Netherlands, reported that the first outposts could be established along the Albert Canal by September 6 at the earliest.[391] To the south the Germans had nothing that could have seriously obstructed the continuation of the Allied offensive. After the headquarters of the Fifth Panzer Army was pulled out of the line, the Seventh Army took over the entire sector all the way down to Charleville.[392] The Seventh Army commanding general was now fully occupied with the task of forming battle groups from the scattered units.[393] His immediate problem was to reestablish command and control in the area south of the Albert Canal all the way to Namur.[394] A viable front line existed only on the left wing of the Seventh Army, behind the Meuse River between Namur and Charleville, where it was extremely thinly manned by the battered I SS Panzer Corps.[395]

The situation was such that Model believed it was possible that the enemy armored spearheads might at any moment punch through to the east and out of the Seventh Army sector. It therefore was urgently necessary to man the West Wall defenses immediately.[396] But the commitment of the Replacement Army units that had been mobilized just the day before could only be a stopgap measure.[397] The Army Group B chief of staff even doubted that the outposts along the border would be strong enough to stop a push by the British into the industrial region of the Ruhr.[398] Something had to be done on the northern wing as quickly as possible.[399] (See Map 18.)

Model passed his demands on to the Wehrmacht High Command on September 4, insisting that his original message be submitted directly to the führer. The field marshal estimated the effective combat strength of the Seventh Army at only three-quarters of a Panzer division and one-and-a-half to two infantry divisions.[400] By September 15, therefore, Model had to have at least ten infantry divisions and five Panzer divisions. He concluded, ". . . *otherwise, the gateway to Northwest Germany is wide open.*"[401] It was an accurate description of the desperate situation. Model's assessment remained valid for at least the next several decisive days because the forces he requested were simply not available—and Model most likely knew that.

General Legend Part I

A. Order of Groups and Units

▨	Oberbefehlshaber, Heeresgruppe, Armeegruppe	Supreme Commander, Army Group, Army Task Group
▨	Armee	Army
⊠	Panzergruppe	Panzer (Tank) Group
⊠	Korps, Armeekorps	Corps, Army Corps
▷	Division (Div)	Division
▷	Brigade (Brig)	Brigade
▮	Regiment (Rgt)	Regiment
▶	Bataillon (Btl)	Battalion

B. Numbers and Letters

Co.	Kompanie	Company
D	Divisionsfüsilier-	Fusilier Division
Elem.	Teile	Elements
F	Festungs-	Fortress-
FErs.	Feldersatz-	Field Replacement
Fs.	Fallschirmjäger-	Parachute-
Ind	Indisch	Indian
K.Gr.	Kampfgruppe	Battle Group
Kos.	Kosaken-	Cossack
LL	Luftlande-	Airborne-
Ls.	Landesschützen-	Territorial Defense
Lw.	Luftwaffe	Air Force
LXXXV	Armeekorps, Korps	Army Corps, Corps
Ma.	Marine-	Navy-
Ob.	Oberbefehlshaber	Supreme Commander
Pz.	Panzer-	Panzer- (Tank-)
PzGren	Panzergrenadier-	motorized infantry
Pz. Lehr	Panzerlehr-	Panzer (Tank) training-
Remn.	Reste	Remnants
Res.	Reserve	Field Replacement
244	Division	Division
Sich	Sicherungs-	Security-
SSF	Spezialeinsatzkräfte	Special Service Force
SS-Pz.	SS Panzer-	SS Panzer- (SS-Tank-)
VD	Freiwilligen Div.	Volunteer Depot Division

C. Auxiliary Signs

▱	Panzer-	Panzer- (Tank-)
⚇	Fallschirmjäger-	Parachute-
∞	motorisiert/ Panzergrenadier-	motorized, mobile, Panzergrenadier-
⋈	Luftwaffe	Luftwaffe, Air Force
↑	Flugabwehr-	Air Defense
⫴	Artillerie-	Artillery
↑	Pionier-	Engineer-
⟱	Panzerjäger-	Anti Tank-

D. Movements and Special Signs

⌒⌒	Stellungen	Symbol for positions
∿	Hauptkampflinie	Main line of Resistance
∙-∿-∙	Lageentwicklungen	Development of Situation
⬅	Angriff/Bewegung	Direction of Movement
↲	Rückzug in neue Stellung	Withdrawal to new position
↘	Angriff abgeschlagen	Attack Repulsed
? ←	Richtung/Position unbekannt	Exact location currently unknown
◄∙∙∙∙∙	beabsichtigte Richtung	Intended direction of Movement
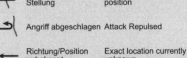	Bewegungsrichtung 15. PzGrenDiv mit vorgeschobener Aufklärung	Direction of Movement 15th Panzer Grenadier Division with recon. forward
	Sammel-/ Verfügungsraum	Billeting or assembly area
✕	gesprengte Brücke	Blown bridge
2 Battr.	Zwei Batterien Haubitzen	Two batteries of howitzers
▽	Fallschirmlandung	Parachute drop zone

General Legend Part II

E. Boundaries

——XXXXX—— Army Group boundary

——XXXX—— Army boundary

——XXX—— Corps boundary

——XX—— Division boundary

F. General Information

Black colored flags, lines, or arrows display German and Axis forces.

Gray colored flags, lines, or arrows display Allied forces.

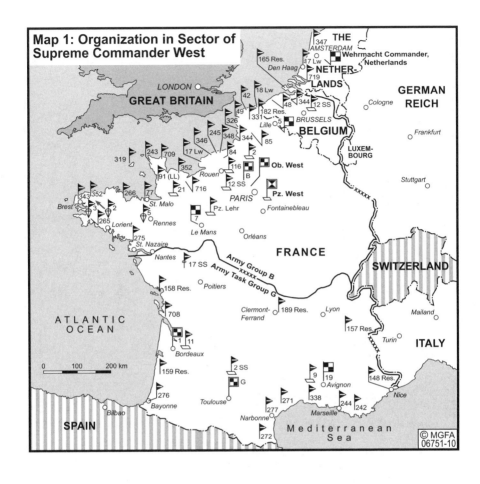

Map 1: Organization in Sector of Supreme Commander West

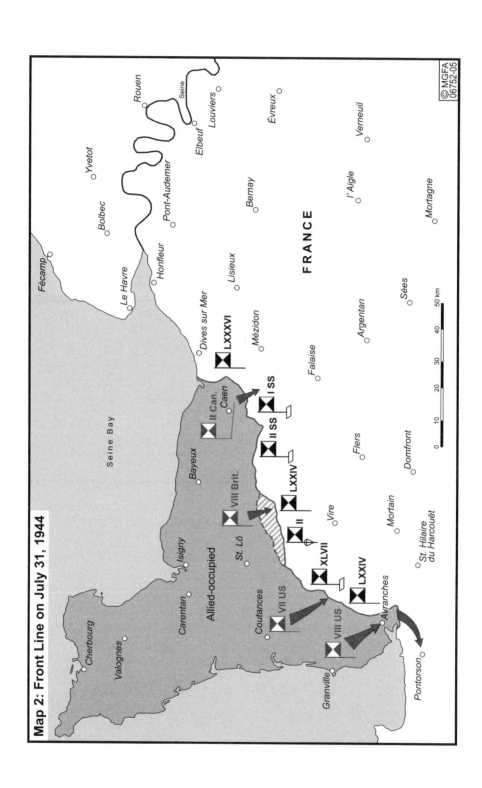

Map 2: Front Line on July 31, 1944

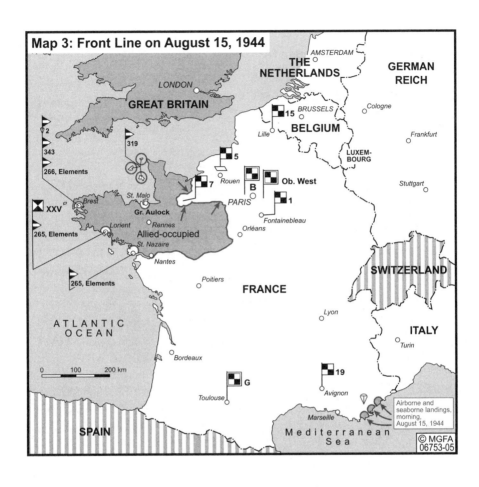

Map 3: Front Line on August 15, 1944

AMSTERDAM

THE NETHERLANDS

GERMAN REICH

LONDON

GREAT BRITAIN

BRUSSELS

Cologne

BELGIUM

Lille

Frankfurt

LUXEM-BOURG

15

5

Ob. West

Stuttgart

319

266, Elements

343

2

7

Rouen

B

PARIS

1

St. Malo

Brest

XXV

Gr. Aulock

Fontainebleau

Rennes

Lorient

265, Elements

St. Nazaire

Orléans

Allied-occupied

SWITZERLAND

Nantes

Poitiers

FRANCE

Lyon

ITALY

265, Elements

ATLANTIC OCEAN

Turin

Bordeaux

0   100   200 km

19

G

Toulouse

Avignon

Marseille

Airborne and seaborne landings, morning, August 15, 1944

SPAIN

Mediterranean Sea

© MGFA
06753-05

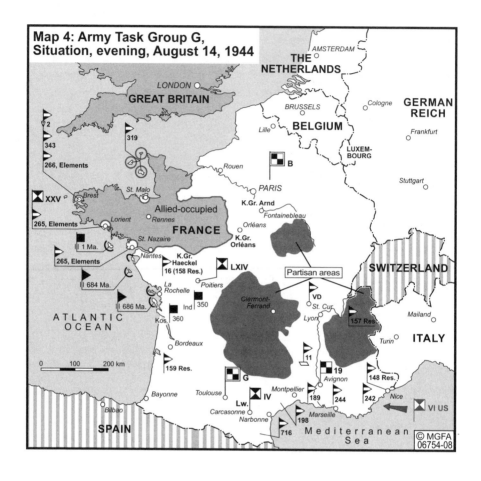

Map 4: Army Task Group G,
Situation, evening, August 14, 1944

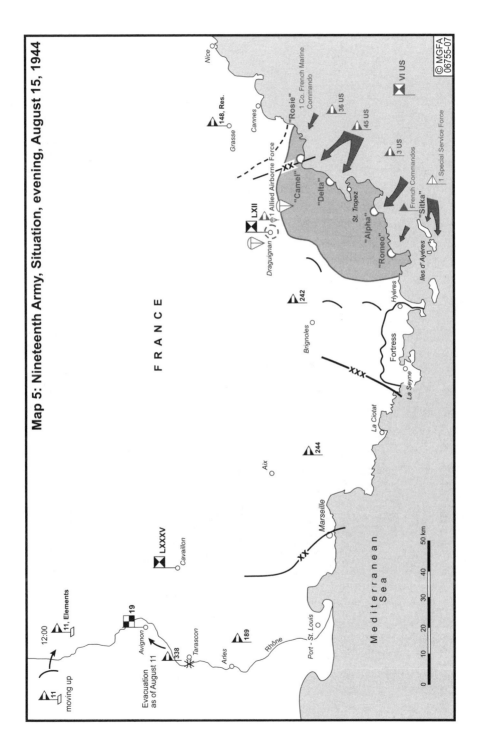

Map 5: Nineteenth Army, Situation, evening, August 15, 1944

FRANCE

Mediterranean Sea

Nice

Cannes

Grasse

148, Res.

"Rosie"
1 Co. French Marine Commando

36 US

45 US

"Camel"

XX

LXII

1 Allied Airborne Force

Draguignan

"Delta"

St. Tropez

3 US

French Commandos

"Alpha"

"Sitka"

"Romeo"

Iles d'Ayères

1 Special Service Force

VI US

242

Hyères

Brignoles

Fortress

XXX

La Seyne

La Ciotat

Aix

244

Marseille

XX

LXXXV

Cavaillon

12:00

11, Elements

11

moving up

19

Evacuation
as of August 11

Avignon

Tarascon

338

Arles

Rhône

189

Port - St. Louis

0 10 20 30 40 50 km

© MGFA
06755-07

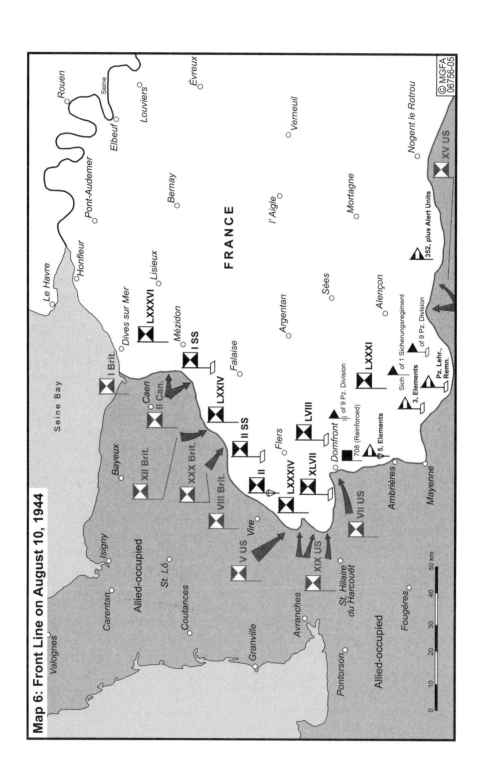

Map 6: Front Line on August 10, 1944

FRANCE

Seine Bay

Allied-occupied

Allied-occupied

Rouen
Seine
Elbeuf
Louviers
Évreux
Pont-Audemer
Verneuil
Bernay
Honfleur
Le Havre
l'Aigle
Dives sur Mer
Lisieux
Mézidon
Nogent le Rotrou
Mortagne
Falaise
Sées
Argentan
Alençon
Flers
Domfront
Ambrières
Mayenne
Vire
St. Hilaire du Harcouët
Avranches
St. Lô
Coutances
Granville
Pontorson
Fougères
Isigny
Bayeux
Caen
Carentan
Valognes

I Brit.

XII Brit.

XXX Brit.

VIII Brit.

V US

XIX US

VII US

II Can.

LXXXVI

I SS

LXXIV

II SS

LXXXIV

II

XLVII

LVIII

LXXXI

XV US

352, plus Alert Units

Sich of 1 Sicherungsregiment

of 9 Pz. Division

Pz. Lehr., Remn.

3, Elements

Sich Elements of 9 Pz. Division

5, Elements

708 (Reinforced)

0 10 20 30 40 50 km

© MGFA
06756-05

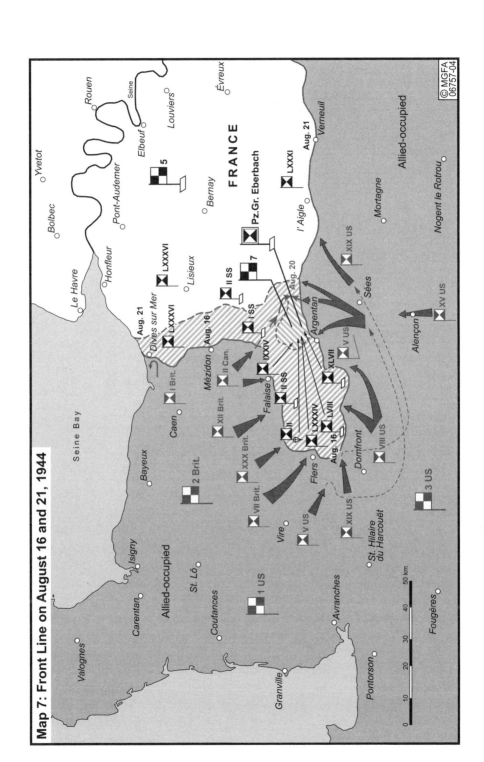

Map 7: Front Line on August 16 and 21, 1944

FRANCE

Seine Bay

Allied-occupied

Allied-occupied

Rouen
Yvetot
Bolbec
Le Havre
Honfleur
Pont-Audemer
Elbeuf
Seine
Louviers
Évreux
Verneuil
Bernay
Lisieux
l'Aigle
Mortagne
Nogent le Rotrou
Dives sur Mer
Mézidon
Falaise
Argentan
Sées
Alençon
Caen
Bayeux
Isigny
St. Lô
Carentan
Coutances
Valognes
Granville
Pontorson
Avranches
Fougères
Vire
Flers
Domfront
St. Hilaire
du Harcouët

Pz.Gr. Eberbach

5

LXXXVI

II SS

7

LXXXI

Aug. 21

Aug. 20

Aug. 21

Aug. 16

Aug. 16

LXXXVI

I SS

II Can.

XII Brit.

II SS

LXXXIV

XLVII

V US

XIX US

XV US

LVIII

LXXXIV

II

XXX Brit.

VII Brit.

V US

XIX US

VIII US

I Brit.

2 Brit.

1 US

3 US

© MGFA
06757-04

0   10   20   30   40   50 km

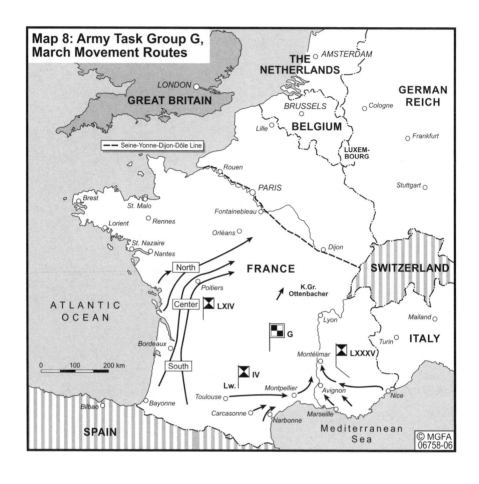

Map 8: Army Task Group G,
March Movement Routes

AMSTERDAM
THE NETHERLANDS

LONDON

GREAT BRITAIN

GERMAN
REICH

BRUSSELS
Cologne

Lille
BELGIUM

Frankfurt

LUXEM-
BOURG

Seine-Yonne-Dijon-Dôle Line

Rouen

PARIS

Stuttgart

Brest

St. Malo

Fontainebleau

Lorient
Rennes

Orléans
Dijon

St. Nazaire
Nantes

North

FRANCE

SWITZERLAND

Poitiers

K.Gr.
Ottenbacher

ATLANTIC
OCEAN

Center
LXIV

G

Lyon

Mailand

Bordeaux

Montélimar
LXXXV

Turin

ITALY

0   100   200 km

South

IV

Lw.

Montpellier
Avignon

Nice

Bilbao
Bayonne

Toulouse

Marseille

Carcasonne
Narbonne

SPAIN

Mediterranean
Sea

© MGFA
06758-06

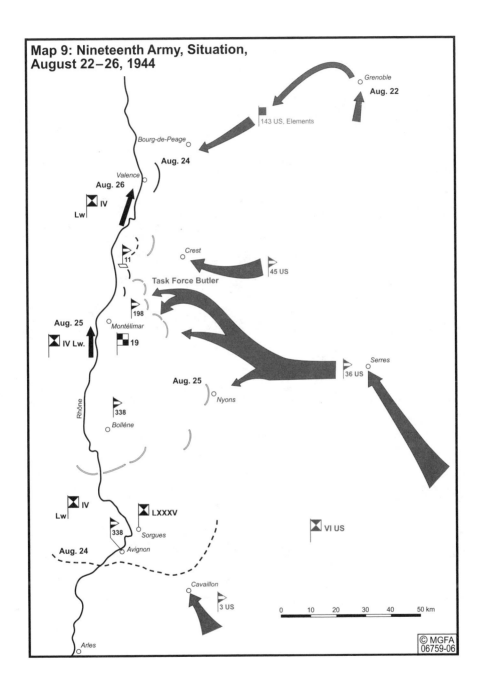

Map 9: Nineteenth Army, Situation, August 22–26, 1944

Grenoble
Aug. 22

143 US, Elements

Bourg-de-Peage
Aug. 24

Valence
Aug. 26

IV
Lw

11

Crest

45 US

Task Force Butler

198

Aug. 25
IV Lw.

Montélimar

19

36 US

Serres

Aug. 25

Nyons

Rhône

338

Bolléne

IV
Lw

LXXXV

VI US

338

Sorgues

Aug. 24

Avignon

Cavaillon

3 US

0   10   20   30   40   50 km

© MGFA
06759-06

Arles

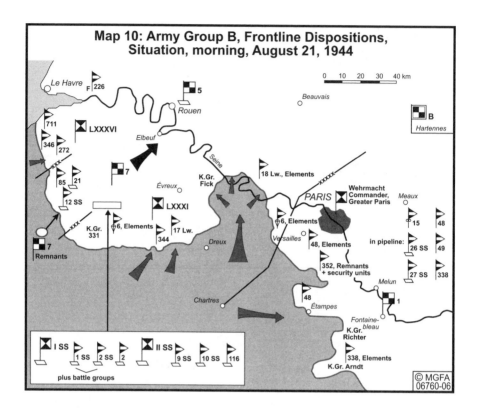

Map 10: Army Group B, Frontline Dispositions, Situation, morning, August 21, 1944

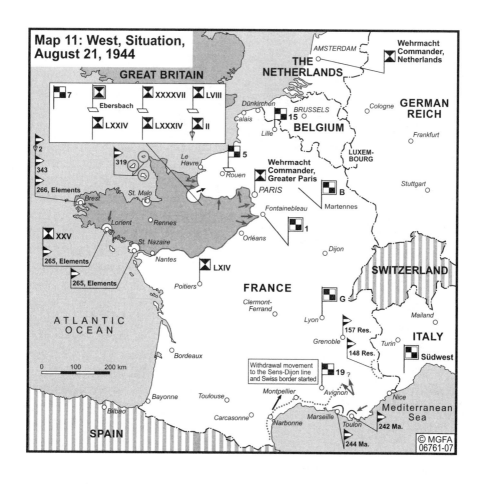

Map 11: West, Situation, August 21, 1944

GREAT BRITAIN

7
Ebersbach
XXXXVII
LVIII
LXXIV
LXXXIV
II

THE NETHERLANDS
AMSTERDAM

Wehrmacht Commander, Netherlands

GERMAN REICH

Dünkirchen
Calais
Lille
BRUSSELS
BELGIUM
Cologne

Frankfurt

2
343
266, Elements
Le Havre
Rouen
319
St. Malo
Brest
LUXEM-BOURG
5
Wehrmacht Commander, Greater Paris
PARIS
Martennes
B
Stuttgart

XXV
Lorient
Rennes
St. Nazaire
265, Elements
265, Elements
Nantes
LXIV
Poitiers
Fontainebleau
Orléans
1
Dijon

FRANCE
Clermont-Ferrand
Lyon
G
SWITZERLAND

ATLANTIC OCEAN

0   100   200 km

Bordeaux

Bayonne
Bilbao
SPAIN
Toulouse
Carcasonne
Montpellier
Narbonne
Grenoble
157 Res.
148 Res.
19
Avignon
Marseille
Toulon
244 Ma.
242 Ma.
Nice
Mailand
ITALY
Turin
Südwest
Mediterranean Sea

Withdrawal movement to the Sens-Dijon line and Swiss border started

© MGFA
06761-07

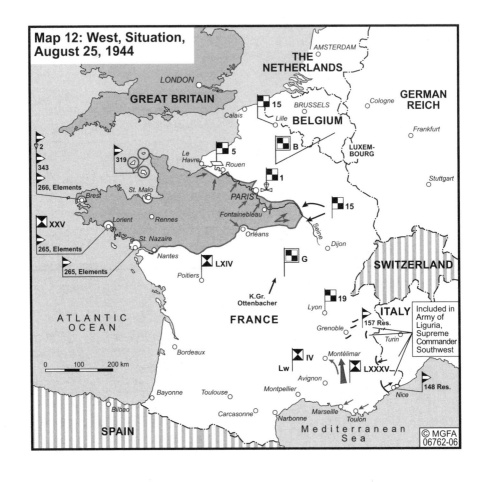

Map 12: West, Situation, August 25, 1944

GREAT BRITAIN

LONDON

THE NETHERLANDS

AMSTERDAM

GERMAN REICH

Cologne

BRUSSELS

BELGIUM

15

Calais

Lille

Frankfurt

B

LUXEM-BOURG

2

343

266, Elements

319

Le Havre

Rouen

5

1

Stuttgart

Brest

St. Malo

PARIS

15

XXV

Lorient

Rennes

Fontainebleau

Seine

Dijon

SWITZERLAND

265, Elements

St. Nazaire

Orléans

G

265, Elements

Nantes

LXIV

Poitiers

K.Gr. Ottenbacher

19

Lyon

ITALY

Included in Army of Liguria, Supreme Commander Southwest

FRANCE

Grenoble

157 Res.

Turin

ATLANTIC OCEAN

0   100   200 km

Bordeaux

IV

Lw

Montélimar

Avignon

LXXXV

148 Res.

Nice

Bayonne

Toulouse

Montpellier

Marseille

SPAIN

Bilbao

Carcasonne

Narbonne

Toulon

Mediterranean Sea

© MGFA
06762-06

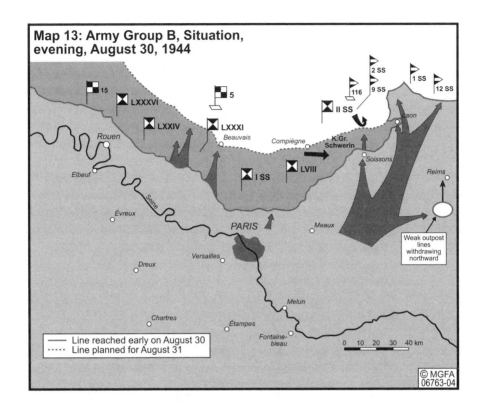

Map 13: Army Group B, Situation, evening, August 30, 1944

15

LXXXVI

5

2 SS

1 SS

116

9 SS

12 SS

II SS

LXXIV

Rouen

LXXXI

Beauvais

Compiègne

K.Gr. Schwerin

Laon

Elbeuf

I SS

LVIII

Soissons

Évreux

Seine

Reims

PARIS

Meaux

Weak outpost lines withdrawing northward

Versailles

Dreux

Melun

Chartres

Étampes

Fontaine-bleau

0 10 20 30 40 km

——— Line reached early on August 30
- - - - Line planned for August 31

© MGFA
06763-04

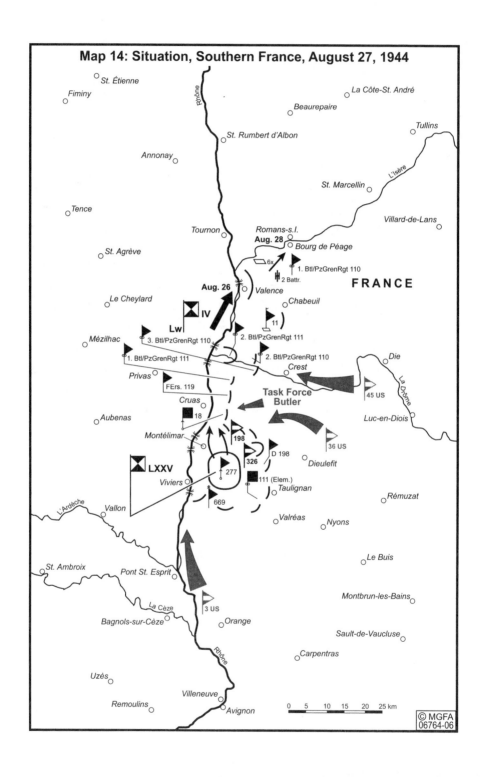

Map 14: Situation, Southern France, August 27, 1944

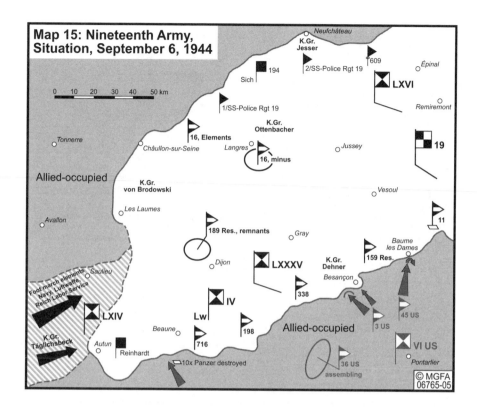

Map 15: Nineteenth Army, Situation, September 6, 1944

0 10 20 30 40 50 km

Neufchâteau

K.Gr. Jesser

194 Sich

2/SS-Police Rgt 19

609

Épinal

LXVI

Remiremont

1/SS-Police Rgt 19

16, Elements

Tonnerre

Châullon-sur-Seine

Langres

K.Gr. Ottenbacher

16, minus

Jussey

19

Allied-occupied

K.Gr. von Brodowski

Les Laumes

Vesoul

Avallon

189 Res., remnants

Gray

11

Baume les Dames

159 Res.

Dijon

LXXXV

K.Gr. Dehner

Besançon

338

45 US

Foot march elements Navy, Luftwaffe, Reich Labor Service

Saulieu

LXIV

IV

Lw

3 US

Beaune

198

Allied-occupied

VI US

K.Gr. Täglichsbeck

Autun

Reinhardt

716

36 US assembling

Pontarlier

10x Panzer destroyed

© MGFA
06765-05

Map 16: First Army, Situation, September 6, 1944

Seventh Army
xxxx
First Army

LUXEMBOURG

Trier

GERMAN REICH

K.Gr. Hauser

LXXX

1.

Moving up

Sedan

15, Elem.

15, Elem.

106, Elements
Sept. 7– 8

5

48

19

Mosel

Moving up

559

36

Moving up

Lehr

Saarbrücken

462

LXXXII

Reims

XX US

Verdun

17 SS

Metz

FRANCE

15, minus one regiment

Meuse

Châlons

Pont-à-Mousson

3

553

XLVII

XII US

Nancy

First Army
xxxx
Nineteenth Army

St. Dizier

Luneville

21

XV US

Neufchâteau

K.Gr.
Jesser

LXVI

608

© MGFA
06766-06

0 10 20 30 40 km

Map 17: Fifteenth Army, Situation, September 4, 1944

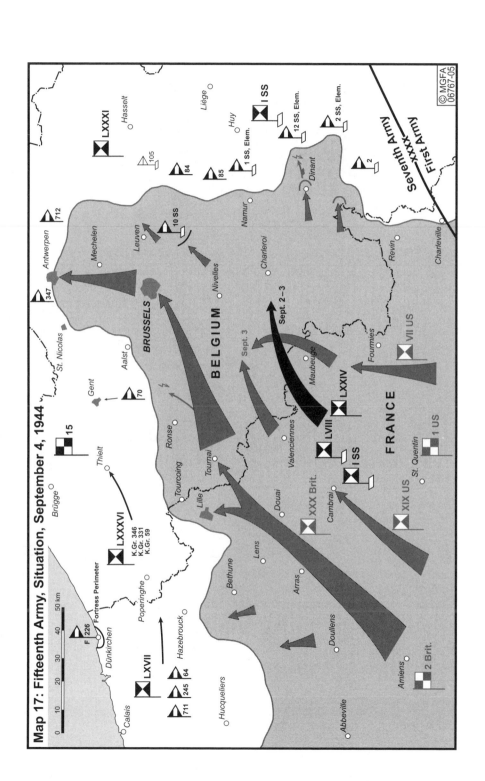

© MGFA
06767-05

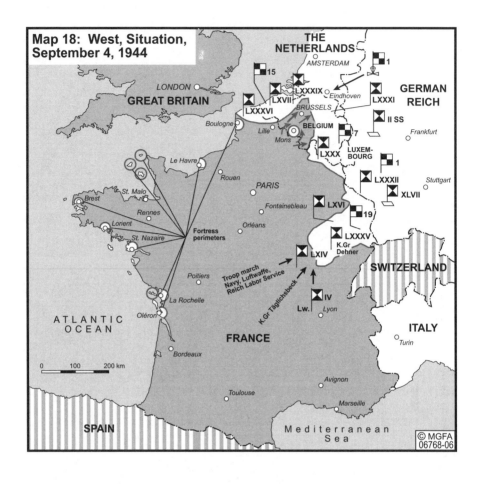

Map 18: West, Situation, September 4, 1944

THE NETHERLANDS

AMSTERDAM

LONDON

GREAT BRITAIN

1

15

LXXXIX

Eindhoven

GERMAN REICH

LXVII

LXXXI

LXXXVI

BRUSSELS

II SS

Boulogne

BELGIUM

Frankfurt

Lille

7

Mons

LXXX

LUXEM-BOURG

1

Le Havre

LXXXII

Stuttgart

Rouen

XLVII

PARIS

Fontainebleau

LXVI

19

St. Malo

Brest

Rennes

Orléans

LXXXV

K.Gr Dehner

Lorient

St. Nazaire

Fortress perimeters

LXIV

SWITZERLAND

Poitiers

Troop march Navy, Luftwaffe, Reich Labor Service

IV

La Rochelle

Lw.

Lyon

Oléron

K.Gr Täglichsbeck

ATLANTIC OCEAN

FRANCE

ITALY

Turin

0   100   200 km

Bordeaux

Avignon

Toulouse

Marseille

SPAIN

Mediterranean Sea

© MGFA
06768-06

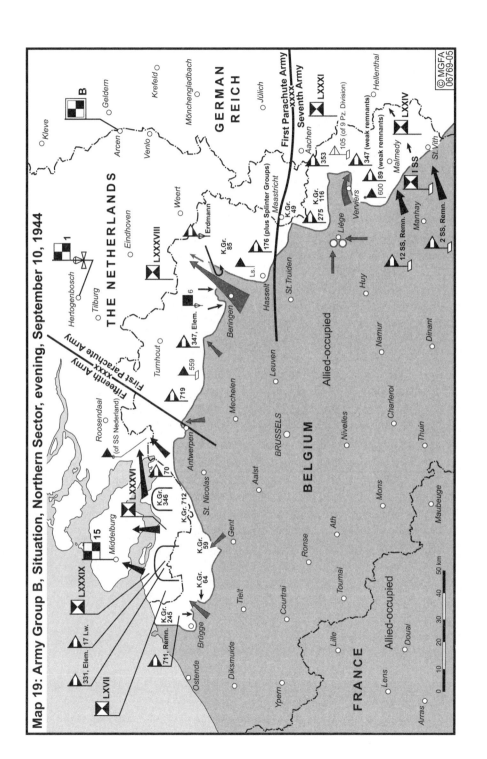

Map 19: Army Group B, Situation, Northern Sector, evening, September 10, 1944

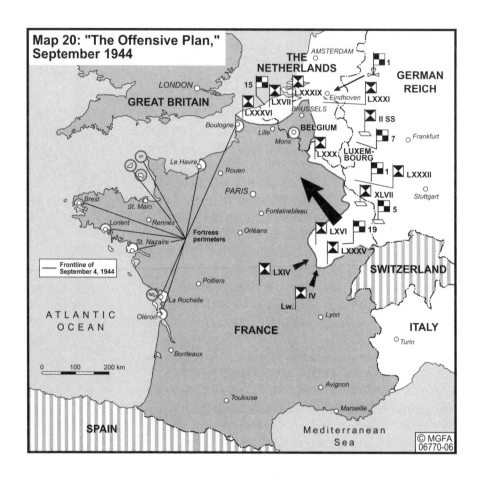

Map 20: "The Offensive Plan,"
September 1944

AMSTERDAM
THE NETHERLANDS
LONDON
GREAT BRITAIN
15
LXVII
LXXXIX
Eindhoven
GERMAN REICH
LXXXI
LXXXVI
BRUSSELS
II SS
Boulogne
Lille
BELGIUM
7
Frankfurt
Mons
Le Havre
LXXX
LUXEM-BOURG
1
LXXXII
Rouen
LXXXII
PARIS
Stuttgart
Brest
St. Malo
Fontainebleau
XLVII
5
Lorient
Rennes
Orléans
19
St. Nazaire
Fortress perimeters
LXVI
LXXXV
SWITZERLAND
Frontline of
September 4, 1944
Poitiers
LXIV
ATLANTIC
OCEAN
La Rochelle
Oléron
IV
Lw.
Lyon
ITALY
FRANCE
Turin
0   100   200 km
Bordeaux
Avignon
Toulouse
Marseille
SPAIN
Mediterranean
Sea
© MGFA
06770-06

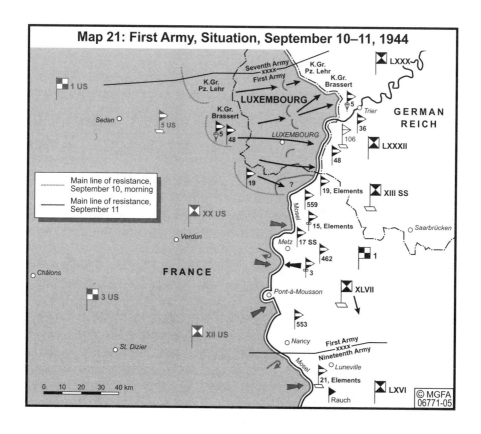

Map 21: First Army, Situation, September 10–11, 1944

LXXX

K.Gr. Pz. Lehr

Seventh Army
————xxxx————
First Army

K.Gr. Pz. Lehr

K.Gr. Brassert

1 US

K.Gr. Brassert

Sedan

5 US

LUXEMBOURG

5

Trier

GERMAN REICH

K.Gr. Brassert

5
48

LUXEMBOURG

36

106

LXXXII

48

Main line of resistance, September 10, morning

Main line of resistance, September 11

19

?

19, Elements

XIII SS

Saarbrücken

XX US

559

Verdun

15, Elements

Metz

17 SS

Châlons

462

1

FRANCE

3

XLVII

3 US

Pont-à-Mousson

XII US

553

St. Dizier

Nancy

First Army
————xxxx————
Nineteenth Army

Luneville

21, Elements

LXVI

0 10 20 30 40 km

Rauch

© MGFA
06771-05

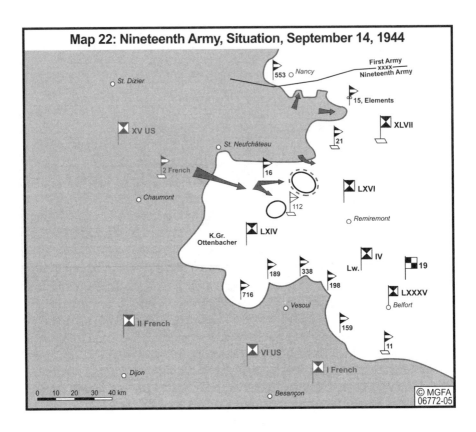

Map 22: Nineteenth Army, Situation, September 14, 1944

St. Dizier

553 ○ Nancy

First Army
xxxx
Nineteenth Army

15, Elements

XV US

XLVII

St. Neufchâteau

21

2 French

16

LXVI

Chaumont

112

Remiremont

K.Gr.
Ottenbacher

LXIV

IV

Lw.

19

189

338

198

LXXXV

716

Belfort

II French

Vesoul

VI US

159

11

Dijon

I French

0 10 20 30 40 km

Besançon

© MGFA
06772-05

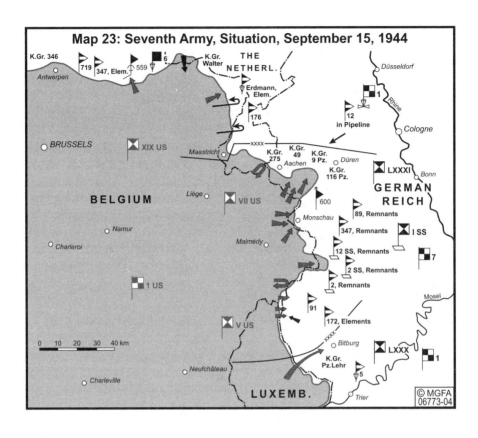

Map 23: Seventh Army, Situation, September 15, 1944

K.Gr. 346

719

347, Elem.

559

6

K.Gr. Walter

THE NETHERL.

Erdmann, Elem.

176

Düsseldorf

1

12 in Pipeline

Rhine

Cologne

Antwerpen

BRUSSELS

XIX US

Maastricht

XXXX

K.Gr. 275

K.Gr. 49

K.Gr. 9 Pz.

Aachen

Düren

K.Gr. 116 Pz.

LXXXI

Bonn

BELGIUM

Liège

VII US

600

GERMAN REICH

89, Remnants

Namur

Monschau

347, Remnants

I SS

Charleroi

Malmédy

12 SS, Remnants

7

2 SS, Remnants

1 US

2, Remnants

Mosel

V US

91

172, Elements

LXXX

1

0 10 20 30 40 km

Bitburg

Charleville

Neufchâteau

K.Gr. Pz.Lehr

5

LUXEMB.

Trier

© MGFA
06773-04

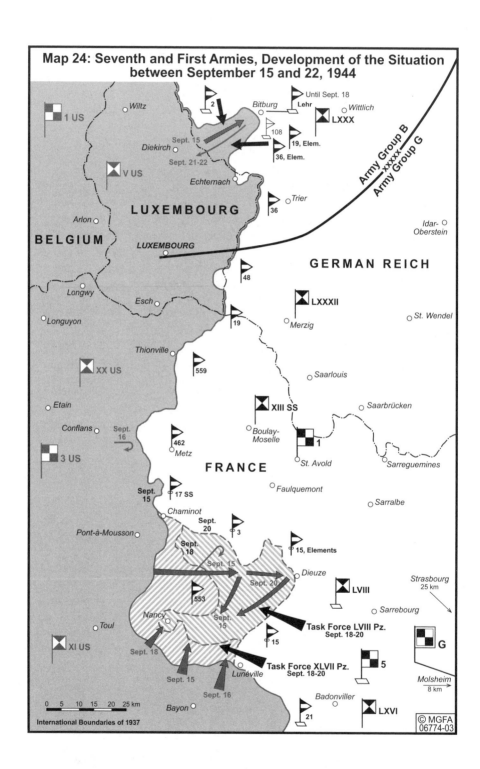

Map 24: Seventh and First Armies, Development of the Situation between September 15 and 22, 1944

1 US

○ Wiltz

Diekirch ○

Sept. 15

Sept. 21-22

2

108

Bitburg ○

Until Sept. 18

Lehr

19, Elem.

36, Elem.

○ Wittlich

LXXX

V US

Echternach ○

LUXEMBOURG

36

○ Trier

Arlon ○

BELGIUM

LUXEMBOURG

Army Group B

xxxxx

Army Group G

Idar- ○
Oberstein

GERMAN REICH

Longwy ○

○ Longuyon

Esch ○

48

19

LXXXII

○ Merzig

○ St. Wendel

Thionville ○

XX US

559

○ Saarlouis

○ Etain

Conflans ○

3 US

Sept.
16

462

Metz

XIII SS

○ Boulay-
Moselle

1

○ St. Avold

○ Saarbrücken

○ Sarreguemines

FRANCE

○ Faulquemont

Sept.
15

17 SS

Chaminot ○

○ Sarralbe

Pont-à-Mousson ○

Sept.
18

Sept.
20

Sept. 15

3

553

Sept. 20

15, Elements

○ Dieuze

LVIII

Strasbourg
25 km

○ Sarrebourg

Nancy ○

Sept.
15

15

Task Force LVIII Pz.
Sept. 18-20

G

Toul ○

XI US

Sept. 18

Sept. 15

Lunéville ○

Task Force XLVII Pz.
Sept. 18-20

5

Molsheim
8 km

Sept. 16

Bayon ○

0   5   10   15   20 25 km

International Boundaries of 1937

21

Badonviller
○

LXVI

© MGFA
06774-03

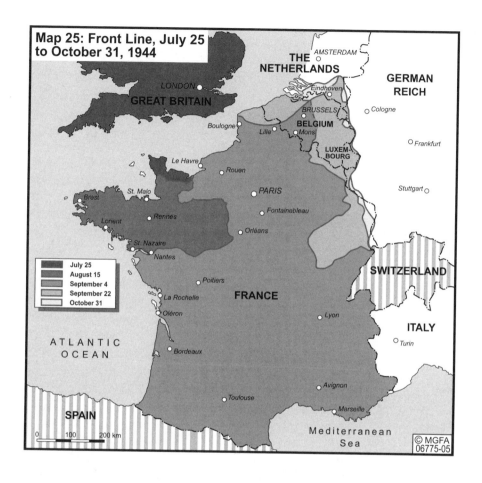

Map 25: Front Line, July 25 to October 31, 1944

July 25
August 15
September 4
September 22
October 31

Chapter 9

The Basis for Continued Combat Operations

1. The Allied Estimate of the Situation and Decision

The objectives that Eisenhower had established for his armies on August 24 had mostly been achieved during the first few days of September. The ease of the Allied advance and the signs of breakup on the German side boosted the Allied camp's confidence in victory. According to the weekly enemy situation estimate prepared by SHAEF headquarters on September 2, the German army represented only "a number of fleeing, disorganized and demoralized battle groups."[1] Nor were major difficulties anticipated on the southern wing. Although the situation of the German First Army along the Mosel River had been consolidated for the time being, Patton expected to run into major but surmountable resistance only in the area of the West Wall.[2] General Patch, the commanding general of the U.S. Seventh Army, even hoped to cut the German Nineteenth Army off before it reached the Belfort Gap.[3] The Allied strategy controversy erupted anew as an immediately impending victory seemed to be coming.

Bolstered by the successes achieved during the August 24–September 4 phase of the establishment of a definite main effort, Montgomery again urged the adoption of the concentrated single-thrust option that had been discussed in the earlier post-OVERLORD planning.

Without going into the details of the long and drawn-out inter-Allied disputes, the key factor at this point was Eisenhower's general skepticism about the single-thrust concept.[4] Those concerns were based on the heavily intertwined combination of factors discussed previously.[5] Eisenhower seemed determined to stick to the original post-OVERLORD planning, even though the assessment of Germany's capabilities to resist had changed considerably.

Eisenhower was convinced that there were clear signs of collapse along the entire front of an enemy who had begun to run.[6,7] He therefore concluded that the important task was to break through the West Wall—what the Allies were calling "The Siegfried Line"— as soon as possible and to take both of the key industrial regions in the Ruhr and the Saar.[8] By establishing main efforts so far apart, he wanted to force the Germans to overextend their remaining weak units.[9] The Allies anticipated that the Germans would probably try to establish a defense along the West Wall, but they obviously thought that the Germans had hardly any chance of succeeding. At any rate, the objectives established for the Allied armies early in September were already located along the Rhine River.[10] The key element of this final phase of the campaign, which in Eisenhower's opinion had started already, was the resumption of Patton's U.S. Third Army's supporting offensive along the southern wing.[11]

This not only meant that the establishment of a definite Allied main effort in the north had been abandoned, but it also implied that the advance would generally slow down. The rapid Allied pursuit had exacerbated the already existing logistical problems, widening the gap between the original operational plan and the support of the actual advance.[12] According to the plan, twelve American divisions were to be in position along the Seine River on September 4. Instead, elements of sixteen American divisions had already pushed 240 kilometers to the east, beyond the river.[13] The establishment of intermediate supply dumps simply did not keep up with the tempo of the advance. Although the U.S. Third Army had paused in its offensive on August 31, the supplies for the Allied left wing that continued to attack were inadequate despite all remedial efforts.[14] Receiving some three thousand tons per day, the U.S. First Army was getting less than half of what it required.[15] On September 2, fuel shortages forced two of its three corps to halt—V Corps temporarily and XIX Corps for a period of four days in Belgium.[16] Lieutenant General Miles Dempsey also had to halt the VIII Corps of his British Second Army for two weeks west of the Seine River, waiting for additional transportation priority space for supplies moving to the front.[17] But Eisenhower's decision now to resume the offensive also on the southern wing was not based on the stabilization of the logistics system. Instead, it was based on a change in the method of allocating the all-too-limited supplies.

As noted earlier, transportation was the basis of the critical logistics problem. The main unloading facilities, Cherbourg and the

Normandy beaches, were more than seven hundred kilometers from the front lines. The ports that the Allied troops had captured since the start of the invasion were still no help at this point. Those included the Seine River ports; the Channel ports of Rouen, Fécamp, and Dieppe; and Toulon and Marseille on the Mediterranean.[18]

Contrary to the hopes of the German command, the two defensive perimeters along the Mediterranean withstood the pressure of the siege only a few days.[19] On the morning of August 28 both positions surrendered to the French. Lieutenant General Hans Schaefer capitulated in Marseille, and Rear Admiral Heinrich Ruhfus surrendered Toulon.[20]

The additional harbor capacity had been a key argument for the Allied advocates of Operation DRAGOON. In the event, Marseille and Toulon were taken considerably earlier than planned.[21] But the exceptionally thorough demolition of the harbor facilities carried out by the Germans prevented the immediate resumption of port operations.[22] The first Allied Liberty ships did not dock in Marseille until September 15.[23] Thus, neither Marseille nor Toulon were of any use to Allied combat operations during the decisive first half of September 1944. The other captured ports were either too far from the front or their capacity was too low or German demolitions had made them at least temporarily useless as unloading points.

Antwerp was different. Its unloading capacity could have easily supplied fifty-four divisions daily.[24] That could have covered both British and American requirements.[25] But before the port could be put into operation, the estuary of the Scheldt River mouth had to be cleared of German forces. That task could have been executed easily during the first days of September if a main effort had been established quickly and consistently. But such was not the case.

In hindsight, therefore, it is difficult to understand why Eisenhower continued to assign high priority to the capture of Brest, at the far end of the Brittany peninsula.[26] The offensive against the Breton port city tied down a reinforced U.S. corps plus air force and naval units.[27] Total U.S. casualties for the operation amounted to some ten thousand men.[28] In the opinion of many American logistics officers, those were unnecessary losses caused by blind adherence to an already outdated plan.[29] Bradley and Patton were of the opinion[30] that once the U.S. Army began an operation, it would have to complete it.[31] That may have carried great weight considering the Allies' confident belief in victory during the first few days of September. But it also indicates that the capture of Brest even then was not considered operationally important and that the port was basically useless.

One possible explanation was that the Allies wanted to eliminate General of Parachute Troops Hermann Ramcke's "fanatical" fortress troops deep in their rear area.[32] Another explanation was that the Allies wanted to secure a reserve port.[33] Neither explanation, however, holds water.[34] The key fact remained that even an undestroyed Brest would not have mitigated the supply problems in any way because at a distance of eight hundred kilometers from the front lines it was even farther away than Cherbourg.

By September 3, Admiral Sir Bertram Ramsay, the commander-in-chief of the OVERLORD naval forces, had already emphatically pointed out the importance of maritime access to the port of Antwerp, as well as the need for mopping up the Scheldt River estuary.[35] In fact, ULTRA information a short time later confirmed that the Germans were beginning to establish a barrier position precisely in that area.[36] Nevertheless, the Scheldt estuary was mentioned only in passing in Eisenhower's rather verbose but otherwise vague orders and comments. That may have been the result of the fact that an analysis of the causes of the logistics difficulties had not yet been developed. Such an analysis almost certainly would have demanded the establishment of a main effort in the Antwerp area. On the other hand, Eisenhower seemed to be convinced that securing the Scheldt estuary could be handled "as a side show" during the advance into Germany.[37] As he wrote to Montgomery, once the Saar and the Ruhr were occupied, then "Le Havre and Antwerp" (note the sequence) should be available.[38] For Eisenhower—who apparently was hoping for a replay of the events of autumn 1918 and who believed that the Germans were just about to collapse—the opening of the port at Antwerp at that point in time was only a secondary objective.[39]

But the British field marshal likewise did not use his critical decision-making prerogatives to address the situation. Montgomery, as the commander of the 21st Army Group, had such prerogatives within the context of Eisenhower's Broad Front strategy.[40] Montgomery's directives show that the significant operational opportunities to alter decisively the course of the war in the west along the Scheldt estuary went unrecognized. Thus, Dempsey's British Second Army was ordered to push as quickly as possible toward Arnhem–Wesel in the direction of the Rhine River. The missions assigned to the Canadian First Army remained unchanged. It was ordered to mop up the coastal sector all the way to Brügge, and eliminate the threat from the V-1 launching sites.[41] Only then was it to clear the Scheldt estuary.[42] Crerar's Canadians, therefore, were sent first against the Channel ports of Le Havre, Boulogne, Calais, and Dunkirk, although it developed rather quickly that those positions could not be taken without hard fighting.[43]

Considering that Montgomery was the most seasoned and experienced of the senior Allied commanders, the sole explanation for what in hindsight appears to have been such a great oversight can only be attributed to the Allies' overwhelming confidence in a short victory that prevailed early in September. Thus, some planners and operations officers even doubted the necessity to open up Antwerp, because the Germans were about to collapse at any moment anyway.[44] The British Joint Intelligence Committee on September 5 went so far as to predict that whatever Hitler might want to do, it was too late for him to influence the outcome of the fighting in the west.[45]

Such thinking shows clearly that the estimate of the enemy situation developed by the Allies since early August increasingly shifted toward underestimating Germany's remaining strength. During the almost euphoric mood of the pursuit phase, any skeptical operational assessments simply found no takers. One of those skeptics was the G-2 of the U.S. Third Army, Colonel Oscar Koch. Despite the enormous losses, Koch warned, the German retreat did not deteriorate into wild flight or mass collapse. Koch made it quite clear that the Germans had not lost control, at least not tactically. Eventually the Allies would have to face the fact that the German troops would continue to fight until they were either wiped out or captured. Koch predicted that the Germans would get strong support from those mightiest of allies, the weather and the terrain. Koch stressed emphatically the importance of the Allies realizing that the Germans for the present were trying to gain time. The first new reinforcements in the German front line had already been identified.[46] But the transition to the Broad Front strategy—without Antwerp—was only possible to accomplish by slowing down the Allied offensive, which of course gave the Germans more time.

One decisive advantage of the Allies' war-fighting capability was mobility. The entire organizational structure of the U.S. Army in particular was built around that concept. But the Broad Front strategy did not maximize that advantage, and at that point the logistical foundations were not there either. Eisenhower therefore considered the Broad Front to be the safest and best possible course of action. In the final analysis, however, the Broad Front did carry a rather considerable level of risk.[47]

2. Hitler's Offensive Plan

At the end of August and the beginning of September, Hitler expressed his conviction that the power and impetus behind the Allied offensive would decrease, like the force of a "wave according to the laws of nature, the more it expands . . . the more it runs on into ever more vast regions."[48] The Wehrmacht High Command also anticipated that the Allies' advance along a broad front would cause them supply problems.[49] Hitler believed that moment was drawing near. Despite the dramatic deterioration in the situation along the front, Hitler therefore focused now on how to change the course of the fighting and regain the initiative.[50]

Within a matter of days the concept of a flanking attack emerged, an attack that would be launched directly from the withdrawal movement.[51] That concept clearly grew out of a proposal that Model had advanced on August 24, albeit based on an entirely different starting situation. The basis of that proposal was to concentrate between seven and eight Panzer divisions on the left wing of the First Army.[52] There was an opportunity for decisive action at that point.[53] Hitler's thinking along those lines had been developing since the end of July and was now coming into focus. Hitler intended to bring about that "big change" by launching a counteroffensive in the west.

Hitler believed that Germany's fate hung on the developments in the western theater of war. Therefore, the strategic main effort and the attempt to achieve a decision through a counteroffensive would have to be made there.[54] Hitler believed that he could achieve a tremendous and decisive success only in the west with the German war-fighting capability that still remained. Compared with the eastern theater of war, the number of enemy divisions in the west was small and the combat zone was geographically limited. Hitler also assumed that the Western Allied leadership would be particularly vulnerable to fracture when faced with a critical situation.[55] His hope for a rupture in the enemy coalition had become a firm conviction.[56]

Hitler's thinking crystallized during the noon situation briefing on September 1. At that point there had not been any talk yet of a Dijon bridgehead. Hitler described the area west of the Vosges Mountains as the strategically most important point where the Germans could assemble an attack force.[57] From there, operational maneuvers could be launched.[58] Hitler hoped that the massing of the German Panzer forces would create a situation that would lead to a major enemy collapse.[59]

The frequent reshuffling in early September of the key leaders in the German Army of the West indicates the significance Hitler assigned to his offensive plan. The new phase in combat operations that he thought was coming had to be launched with "new names" in charge.[60] Field Marshal Gerd von Rundstedt, the German army's most senior officer, was again appointed OB West.[61] His dignified and confidence-inspiring ways gave him tremendous prestige among the troops and the general population.[62] The command structure under which one officer wore two hats, as OB West and as commander of Army Group B, had become increasingly untenable. The separation of those two positions was entirely in keeping with Model's wishes, since he was fully occupied with trying to bring the crisis situation in the northern sector under control.[63] Rundstedt was also considered "one of the cleverest operational brains" in the army, which is why Hitler recalled him precisely at that moment.[64] By virtue of his age, Rundstedt confined himself to commanding primarily from his headquarters and focusing on the big picture. Lieutenant General Siegfried Westphal was assigned as Rundstedt's chief of staff. He was only forty-two years old, but he was promoted unusually early because of his exceptional ability.[65] Through a fresh approach and resoluteness, Westphal compensated for whatever Rundstedt may have lacked because of his age.[66] Speidel, the chief of staff of Army Group B, was also relieved of his position, although Model was able to delay that transfer for some time.[67] Speidel's position was assumed by General of Infantry Hans Krebs, who had long experience working with Model on the Eastern Front.[68] Krebs was thoroughly familiar with Model's difficult style of command.

Rundstedt and the two newly assigned chiefs of staff had been briefed on Hitler's intentions at the Führer Headquarters before they departed to take up their assignments in the west.[69] During the early days of September, Hitler's thoughts revolved exclusively around the projected offensive operation that was to be launched by the middle of the month at the latest from the German southern wing and directed toward Reims.[70]

Westphal received approval from Jodl to prepare an operations plan that was to reconcile the actual situation on the front with Hitler's intent. Westphal's major concern was to preserve the remaining substantive capability of the German Army in the West.[71] The operations plan was signed by Hitler after some hesitation.[72] It was issued on September 3 as *Directive for Continued Combat Operations, Supreme Commander West*.[73] The critical passages noted that because of the "heavily worn-out German forces and the impossibility of quickly providing adequate reinforcements," the most important objective now was "to gain as much time as possible for the organization and transfer of new units and for the buildup of the Western Position." To accomplish that mission, the *right wing*[74] and *center*[75] (including the First Army) of the Army of the West were to engage the enemy by "bitter, delaying action." Simultaneously, the German forces were to avoid being caught in any further encirclements of major groups of units.

"On the *left wing*,"[76] Army Task Group G "was to assemble forward of the Vosges Mountains . . . a mobile group of forces for an attack deep into the eastern flank of the enemy. . . ." The *"first"*[77] mission of Army Task Group G was to screen the withdrawal of the Nineteenth Army and the LXIV Army Corps.

Army Task Group G's subsequent *primary mission* was an "attack with combined forces against the deep eastern flank and the rear of the Americans."[78] Initially the command and control would be assumed by the XLVII Panzer Corps and later by the Fifth Panzer Army. Six Panzer divisions or Panzer Grenadier divisions and six new Panzer brigades were to be massed for this operation.[79] (See Map 20.)

Key personnel reassignments were made in preparation for the operations.[80] General of Panzer Troops Otto von Knobelsdorff was assigned to command the First Army, which had a delaying-defensive mission. Knobelsdorff had distinguished himself while commanding the XLVIII Army Corps and the XL Panzer Corps during the retreat and the defensive battles on the Eastern Front.[81] An even more important reassignment was the decision to relieve Dietrich, who was in over his head as Fifth Panzer Army commander.[82]

Dietrich was replaced with recently promoted General of Panzer Troops Hasso von Manteuffel, who had served successfully on the Eastern Front as the commander of Panzer divisions.[83] His experience in commanding mobile units led Hitler to consider the former cavalryman as the right man to command the offensive operation to be executed by the Fifth Panzer Army. The fact that Manteuffel had never before commanded either at the corps or the army level and was not a trained and qualified General Staff officer was immaterial to Hitler.[84]

Like most of the Panzer divisions in the west,[85] the headquarters staff of the Fifth Panzer Army had to be reconstituted.[86] Until Fifth Panzer Army was operational again, the XLVII Panzer Corps was responsible for conducting the initial mobile combat operations. But there was key personnel turbulence even at that level. Funck was replaced as commander by General of Panzer Troops Heinrich von Lüttwitz, who also had come from the cavalry and who was recognized as an able Panzer leader even by the Allies.[87]

The German commanding generals all along the front met Hitler's plan to launch an offensive from the area of the Vosges Mountains with skepticism, if not with open rejection.[88] Blaskowitz immediately noted the time requirement to mass the Panzer units. He reported to Wehrmacht High Command that they could assemble at the earliest by September 12.[89] What appeared even more than questionable to him was whether or not the assembly areas forward of the Vosges Mountains could be held that long.

Model, who had learned of Hitler's intent even before the directive arrived, was even more plainspoken with Jodl, the chief of the Wehrmacht operations staff: "I just have General Krebs here with me. From his statements I gather that the assessment of the situation from topside is different than what it is here. There seems to be a belief that it is still possible to mount attacks here. Were my situation estimates not submitted to the Führer? . . . I simply cannot keep commanding this way."[90]

If the plan was to be carried out at all, then in Model's opinion radical measures were necessary. Accordingly, he immediately requested authorization to reinforce von Manteuffel's Fifth Panzer Army with three Panzer divisions from the East by September 10.[91]

Model probably made his request assuming it would be rejected by Colonel General Heinz Guderian, the chief of the Army General Staff. That in turn would force Hitler to modify his concept. But the gambit didn't work because Guderian shared Hitler's convictions. Guderian lectured Krebs that "success on the left wing would . . . certainly have an effect on the center and the northern wing." Therefore, all Panzer forces would have to be committed en masse on the southern wing.[92] Guderian's primary concern was with "his front"—the Eastern Front—and he wanted to make sure that any attack operation in the west would be executed as quickly as possible to free up reserves for the east before the start of the frost and the anticipated Soviet winter offensive.[93] That also explains why by the end of August and the start of September Hitler already was pushing for preparations for a "decisive" strike, even though the future development of the situation was still completely uncertain and there was no secured foundation for planning.[94]

In contrast to the Allies, the Wehrmacht High Command assessed the "utterly unexpected" fall of Antwerp[95] as an operational event of the first order.[96] Hitler also had realized that his entire fortress concept threatened to fail following the seizure of the port, and that his hope that the Allies would have to halt their advance because of supply problems was becoming illusory.[97] Accordingly, he ordered OB West to make sure that Antwerp remained unusable by the Allies for as long as possible. With Antwerp in operation, the Allies would be able to unload vast volumes of supplies along the Western Front, which would cancel out the effect of the defense of the ports in Biscay, Brittany, and along the Channel coast that was expending such tremendous resources. OB West, he stated, must block the entry to the mouth of the Scheldt River by stubbornly defending the islands of Walcheren and Schouwen and the batteries around and to the west of Breskens.[98]

Although the crisis in the west had undoubtedly reached its climax with the fall of Antwerp, Hitler nevertheless hesitated once more at discarding his new grand concept—the establishment of a definite Panzer main effort in front of the Vosges Mountains.[99]

As a result of the focus on the Vosges operation, there was only a muddle of battalions from the Replacement Army that were available to support the Antwerp–Albert Canal line.[100] Those units included antiaircraft batteries from the Reich, replacement and training units, and the remnants of three parachute divisions that were in the process of reconstituting.[101] That conglomeration of units was now to be thrown forward against the enemy. A "defensive front," a strong fighting army, was now to be established as rapidly as possible under the command of Colonel General Kurt Student's First Parachute Army.

The chiefs of staff of the higher headquarters in the west thought that undertaking had little chance of success. Blumentritt noted that the "closing of the open door into the Rhineland" was presently not possible because Model's requests for fresh reinforcements to support the northern wing had been disapproved as the result of the führer's directive.[102] Krebs too told the Wehrmacht operations staff that the attack in the south would have no effect on an Allied thrust aimed northeast across the Albert Canal. "The current occupation of the Albert Canal . . . is woefully inadequate."[103]

Although the Wehrmacht High Command was aware of the scope of the crisis on the right wing, OB West headquarters was allocated only weak forces to cope with that crisis. The defense had to rely mostly on skill and improvisation. The grave significance of Eisenhower's and Montgomery's directives becomes even clearer against the background of the critical situation on the German side. During those first days of September, both Allied commanders missed the opportunity to force a final and decisive turning point to the combat operations in the west—one that most probably would have saved time and blood.

3. Field Marshal von Rundstedt and the Strength Situation in the West

"On orders of the Führer, I again assumed command this day as OB West. I am convinced that every man . . . knows what is at stake! I put my trust in you, just as our homeland puts its trust in you."[104] Rundstedt addressed that appeal[105] to all the soldiers of the German Army in the West after arriving at the Arenberg command post near Koblenz early in the evening of September 5.[106] The troops welcomed his return. The verbal mission given to Rundstedt at Führer Headquarters was brief. The important thing above all was to stop the enemy's advances as far to the west as possible. Simultaneously, however, the offensive from the area forward of the Vosges Mountains had to be prepared.[107]

The German strength situation was frightening, of course. Only thirteen infantry divisions, three Panzer divisions, and two Panzer brigades were still rated fully combat effective. Forty-two infantry and thirteen Panzer divisions were battered and worn out, including seven infantry divisions that had been broken up and nine infantry and two Panzer divisions that were being reconstituted.[108] Army Group B had only about one hundred battle tanks left.[109]

Apart from Allied control of the air, the enemy's superiority on the ground was also quite clear. In the judgment of the new OB West, Army Group B in Belgium and northern France faced as many as fifty-four Allied divisions totaling some twenty-five hundred tanks. According to German estimates, at least another thirty divisions, including the Allied First Airborne Army with six divisions, were in Britain and ready for commitment on the Continent.[110]

Although the German estimates were too high, the fact of Allied superiority still remained. At that point Eisenhower had thirty-nine major units, including twenty American, thirteen British, and three Canadian divisions, as well as one Polish and one French division.[111] The Operation DRAGOON forces moving up from the south included another three American and five French divisions.[112] As of August 31, Allied losses came to about 220,000 men.[113] OB West had lost 289,000 men since the start of the invasion.[114] If the Scheldt River estuary were to fall into Allied hands, then the 185,000 men who were still holding out as ordered in the fortresses and defensive perimeters along the coast would represent a useless sacrifice of fighting strength without achieving the intended purpose of the force.[115]

The SHAEF G-2 section estimated with noteworthy accuracy that the Germans would then have only about fifteen effective combat divisions left.[116] According to that estimate, the Germans for the time being would have only around three hundred thousand troops to oppose the Allied offensive that was aimed at the Reich. As the SHAEF G-2 estimated, that would not be enough to hold the West Wall, let alone the entire Western Position, even if reinforcements were brought forward from Germany.[117] Indeed, the crushing of the German units and the losses in combat strength inflicted upon the German Army of the West could no longer be compensated for by ad hoc measures.

In the meantime, Josef Goebbels, the Reich Plenipotentiary for the Total War Effort, had managed with the apparent general support of the German population to round up for the Wehrmacht some 170,000 men by September 1.[118] He did it by means of drastic intervention in the economy, the armaments industry, the government administration, and the cultural institutions.[119] That process culled out those who until then had been classified as essential in their positions.[120] By squeezing out the last reserves in August, some three hundred thousand more augmentees were added to the Replacement Army.[121] But the manpower potential thus gained was used primarily to organize new infantry divisions in the Reich, rather than replace the losses at the front. That meant that the combat-seasoned frontline units were increasingly worn down.[122] But as Field Marshal Erich von Manstein later sarcastically described it, Hitler kept insisting that the "flood of statistics" be used to establish new units "out of thin air."[123]

There was a general expectation that there would be an increase in the combat efficiency if these newly formed Volksgrenadier (People's Grenadier) divisions were placed under Himmler's administrative command.[124] Himmler, in the process, would advance one step closer to his goal of a National Socialist People's Army.[125] The new Volksgrenadier divisions, however, were each only 11,200 men strong.[126] At Himmler's request, the selection of their officer cadres was subject to a personnel screening process independent from the rest of the army.[127] These new divisions were not especially well equipped, and it was predictable that they would suffer significant growing pains that naturally result when the chain of command and the troops are not a team.[128] The newly formed Panzer brigades that Hitler wanted to use in his Vosges offensive had similar problems.[129]

The critical reality for the German command in the west, however, was that they could not expect any noticeable immediate relief along the Western Front, because the organization of the forty-one new infantry divisions had started only in July and August.[130] All Rundstedt had immediately available was the already assigned units from the Replacement Army plus a few so-called fortress battalions. Since the end of July 1944, those units had consisted of soldiers and draftees classified as fit for only limited service, but who could still be used to garrison permanent fortifications.[131] Nine of the more than two hundred fortress battalions that were finally organized had in the meantime arrived in the west.[132]

Based on the information Rundstedt was receiving from Führer Headquarters, he could not expect any significant reinforcements before the middle of September. By then he would receive four infantry divisions and seventeen fortress battalions. He also would receive the 107th, 108th, 111th, 112th, and 113th Panzer Brigades, but those units were earmarked specifically to support the planned offensive on the southern wing.[133]

Part 3

Developments from the Climax of the Crisis until the Transition to Positional Warfare in the West

Combat Operations in September 1944

Chapter 10

From the Climax of the Crisis to the First Indications of a Stabilization of the Western Front

1. Developments on the Northern Wing

(a) Commitment of the First Parachute Army between Antwerp and Maastricht

At first, there were no indications of any major offensive by the 21st Army Group across the Albert Canal, contrary to the fears of the German command in the west.[1] For two and a half days, until late in the evening of September 6, things were mostly quiet along the front between the mouth of the Scheldt River and Maastricht.

The British apparently were not going to immediately exploit the "open door leading into the Rhineland." Likewise, there was no indication of any swift establishment of a main effort near Antwerp with the objective of gaining control of the mouth of the Scheldt River and the isthmus of Woensdrecht, although the Germans had absolutely anticipated the Allies would attempt to do so.[2] Such a move would have had a decisive operational impact on the retreat of the Fifteenth Army.[3]

Indeed, the main body of Montgomery's divisions was located in the area west of Antwerp. The Canadian First Army turned toward the German fortresses along the channel and simultaneously with the XII Corps of the British Second Army pushed Zangen's trapped units concentrically against the coast or the south bank of the Scheldt River.[4] Only Horrocks's British XXX Corps with three divisions was left for the offensive across the Albert Canal.[5]

At first, Horrocks's units operated there only very hesitantly, partly because the bulk of the heavy and medium artillery was still along the Seine owing to transportation problems.[6] On Horrocks's right flank the U.S. XIX Corps likewise had no way of advancing briskly. The main reason in that case was the fuel shortage. Lieutenant General Courtney Hodges, the commanding general of the U.S. First Army, decided on September 3 that the most important thing for the time being was to provide the fuel required by the U.S. V Corps and VII Corps. The U.S. XIX Corps, which was to attack the left wing of the German First Parachute Army between Hasselt and Maastricht, remained inactive therefore for several days.[7] An Allied cavalry group did not reach the Albert Canal until September 7. Another three days went by until all of the corps' units had closed up there.[8] As had happened along the Mosel Front, every passing day in that sector was to the advantage of the Germans. As major defensive improvisations began to take effect, the "open door" was gradually closing, at least between Antwerp and Maastricht.

On September 5, however, the situation had still looked entirely different: By noon only two of the seventeen bridges across the Albert Canal at Antwerp had been blown.[9] At that point four battalions of the 719th Infantry Division were in the area. To their left was a battle group that had been patched together from the hastily retreating stragglers of several units by the commanding general of the almost completely destroyed 85th Infantry Division, Lieutenant General Kurt Chill.[10] The first four battalions of the 176th Replacement Army Division had just arrived farther to the south, between Hasselt and Maastricht.[11]

When Colonel General Student—who had left Berlin by plane early that morning—arrived at the command post of Army Group B in the vicinity of Verviers near Lüttich to meet Field Marshal Model, the combat strength along the approximately one hundred-kilometer-long Albert Canal sector amounted to no more than one reinforced infantry division. For that reason alone it seemed doubtful whether Student would be able to accomplish his mission, which was to defend the canal line and, above all, to keep the "isthmus at Woensdrecht" open for the withdrawal of the Fifteenth Army.[12] But until September 7 it remained possible to further consolidate the situation of the First Parachute Army because the British were probing forward only cautiously.[13] In the meantime, the so-called "Valkyrie units," the remaining six battalions of the 176th Infantry Division, plus forty antiaircraft batteries from the VI and XI Air Defense Districts, had been inserted into the front line or were just at the unloading areas at Utrecht and Tilburg.[14] The same was true of some twenty thousand paratroopers.[15] That force included new soldiers from the very youngest birth-year classes, and also battle-seasoned soldiers who had been plucked out of deployed positions in Bitsch, Güstrow (Mecklenburg), and Köln-Wahn and were shipped to the west in "blitz transports."[16] The 559th Army Antitank Battalion had been involved in the fighting just the day before, September 6, and had broken up a small bridgehead that the British had established near Merxem, just four kilometers south of Antwerp.[17]

The indicators of collapse that earlier had emerged in the central and southern sectors of Holland disappeared with the first successful defensive operations conducted along the initially provisional defensive line. That resulted in no small measure from the energetic efforts of Student, who went to the front lines every day. The turning point came around September 6–7, according to a report filed by the German naval commander, Netherlands.[18]

The British XXX Corps launched its offensive along the Albert Canal a short time later. Near Beeringen the Guards Armoured Division seized an intact bridge and established a foothold on the east bank. Despite heavy tank losses,[19] the British on September 8 were able to consolidate against the defending German unit.[20] The Guards Armoured Division then continued its advance into the area of Leopoldsburg–Hechtel against Battle Group Chill, which was supported by two companies of the 559th Antitank Battalion.[21] Thus, contrary to the fears of General Krebs, the chief of staff of Army Group B, the enemy main effort was not directed against the Antwerp area.[22]

Instead, Major General George Roberts on that day was ordered to suspend the attacks by his British 11th Armoured Division along the northern edge of the port city, and instead attack farther to the east, supporting the Guards Armoured Division on his right flank.[23] The decisive factor here was Montgomery's concern for his eastern flank, which was still exposed because the U.S. XIX Corps was hanging back.[24]

Model repeatedly urged that the Allied bridgeheads[25] be mopped up with the help of all available forces.[26] But the bitter counterattacks by Parachute Division Erdmann and the 6th Parachute Regiment did not achieve that objective.[27] It was, however, possible periodically on September 10 to retake Hechtel and to push all the way into Beeringen.[28] According to Student's reports, fifty British tanks alone were destroyed there in close-quarters combat.[29] (See Map 19.)

But that also meant that the German forces were pretty much exhausted. Student doubted that he could eliminate the enemy bridgehead without adequate Panzer and artillery support.[30] Because the British had moved up reinforcements, he asked Model to give him the proper order to move his own forces back behind the nearest water obstacle, the Meuse–Scheldt Canal, so he would no longer have to waste his troops in the penetration area.[31] The commander of Army Group B, however, only authorized Student to make initial preparations for a defense along the canal.[32]

But now something that Model initially had wanted to prevent from happening was forced by the British. During the night leading up to September 11, the spearheads of the Guards Armoured Division reached Neerpelt and crossed the Meuse–Scheldt Canal.[33] That indicated the threat of an operational breakthrough.[34] But no such breakthrough came. Suddenly, all was quiet along the entire front line of the First Parachute Army, whose left wing was now withdrawn behind the Meuse–Scheldt Canal.[35] Once again, the British regrouped their forces at a moment that was critical for the Germans, and thus gave them a breather.[36] Dempsey's British First Army had gained ground, but the decisive fact remained that the Albert Canal line at Antwerp was still in German hands. Thus, the eye of the needle for the withdrawal of the trapped Fifteenth Army from the south bank of the Scheldt via Walcheren and Südbeveland continued to be secured.

(b) The Start of the Fifteenth Army's Retreat across the Westerschelde

Originally, General von Zangen's plans looked different. Crossing the Scheldt appeared to him to be a rather unpromising escape option.[37] The width of that arm of the river's mouth, the fact that the British were only about fifteen kilometers from the isthmus at Woensdrecht, and especially the Allied control of the air all militated against that course of action.[38] General Warlimont, deputy chief of the Wehrmacht operations staff, phoned Army Group B at noon on September 5 and informed Krebs that the führer likewise did not believe that it was possible to extricate the Fifteenth Army from the encirclement ring via Vlissingen. In Warlimont's opinion, it was therefore important to break through toward Antwerp with all available forces and to hit the Allies in the flank.[39]

In the meantime, Zangen's staff had developed a plan that completely coincided with those assessments. Eight of his divisions were to break out to the east from the Oudenaarde area and then push toward Diest and north past Brussels, to link up there with Army Group B.[40] Of the two remaining divisions, the 70th Infantry Division was earmarked for the occupation of Walcheren, and the 226th Infantry Division for the reinforcement of Fortress Dunkirk.[41]

It seems that Field Marshal Model initially left the decision between a breakthrough or a crossing operation to General von Zangen. Model merely urged that a final decision be made soon and that it then be executed resolutely.[42] However, his new chief of staff, Krebs, was able to convince him that a breakthrough was hopeless and that it therefore would be necessary to attempt to head north across the Westerschelde.[43] Krebs was not deterred by Warlimont's repeated remark that Hitler believed that extrication via Vlissingen was not feasible.[44]

Krebs's estimate was confirmed when it became clear that the enemy apparently had no major offensive intentions in the Antwerp area. The Allied attacks at Merxem were beaten off on September 6 and there was no immediate threat to the critical isthmus at Woensdrecht. In the evening of the 6th, Zangen received the order "to cross his army over to Walcheren, holding on to a bridgehead along the Leopold Canal."[45]

In Krebs's words, the Army had to "manage the retreat by water." Therefore, he simultaneously ordered the establishment of contact with the German navy headquarters of the Admiral, Netherlands. Krebs asked that the ship runs on the Scheldt be increased to the highest possible extent because the survival of the Fifteenth Army depended on it.[46] The army already had established the prerequisites for this operation through the independent actions of the lower command echelons. While Zangen was still thinking about a breakthrough, Lieutenant General Eugen Schwalbe, the commanding general of the 344th Infantry Division—which no longer existed as such—had established the crossing organization in a very efficient fashion.[47]

Schwalbe initially ordered the formation of a blocking line that would be ten to fifteen kilometers away from Breskens and Terneuzen. That line was completed by September 6.[48] The crossing units were to be received and provided with rations on that line and they then were to be organized for the crossing and called forward individually. From the very beginning Schwalbe thus prevented the convoys from becoming caught in traffic jams in front of the two main ferry sites.[49] That also prevented any repetition of the semi-chaos that had developed during the Seine River crossing. There would be no heavy concentrations of troops that would have catastrophic consequences considering the Allies' control of the air.

The crossing traffic moved smoothly. According to German navy reports, around twenty-five hundred men had already reached Walcheren and Südbeveland by 1755 hours on September 8.[50] Along the front south of the Scheldt River mouth, enemy action was limited to preventing breakout attempts and concentrically squeezing the pocket that opened toward the sea.[51] And because no serious crises developed at the crossing sites, Zangen was able to lead his units according to plan back into the Boulogne, Calais, and Dunkirk bridgehead positions after he had reinforced as ordered the fortress detachments at Brügge–Ghent–St. Niklaas.[52]

On the morning of September 9, the 712th Infantry Division was the last of the nine remaining divisions of the Fifteenth Army to enter the bridgehead.[53] OB West headquarters was obviously surprised by the favorable developments in that sector. At any rate, after the Fifteenth Army had made such progress despite all of the mobility shortcomings, it was now possible to conduct a delaying defense at the mouth of the Scheldt River.[54] Moreover, OB West headquarters now concluded that it would be possible to reinforce the defensive front of the First Parachute Army.[55]

Lieutenant General Crerar's First Canadian Army hardly had any opportunity of advancing more aggressively. His hands were tied because his army, which was operating from the Seine River mouth all the way into the Ghent area, was ordered to turn primarily toward the German fortresses. Four of his six divisions were tied down in front of Le Havre, Boulogne, Calais, and Dunkirk.[56] On the left wing of the British Second Army, however, the XII Corps had been committed to the concentric attack with four divisions against the mouth of the Scheldt River. But the XII Corps had been shifted into the Antwerp–Geel area on September 7.[57] The remaining two armored divisions, the Polish 1st Armored Division and the Canadian 4th Armoured Division, were committed at Brügge and Ghent and were not a sufficient force to seriously threaten the German bridgehead positions that were screened by artificial flooding.

Thus, the Germans had no problems extricating the forward regimental battle groups from the front and holding them in reserve along the blocking line in front of Terneuzen and Breskens. By September 9 the units that were being transported to Vlissingen and Hoedekenskerke were mostly supply elements and rear-echelon services with a strength of some thirty-one thousand men.[58] The crossing operation for the Fifteenth Army's combat units, starting with the 346th and 711th Infantry Divisions, started the following night.[59]

It quickly turned out that the main threat came from the air. Delays in the ferrying operation across the Scheldt River were unavoidable, with as many as six bombing raids against the assembly areas.[60] On September 10 alone Allied fighter-bombers temporarily put two ferries out of action and sank two barges.[61] On September 11 the reported crossing throughput had dropped by 40 percent.[62] But as had been the case during the retreat across the Seine River, such ferrying operations could be restricted and delayed by air attacks, but they could not be stopped completely. On those days the Allied air forces also were heavily committed at both Le Havre and Brest, where the fighting neared its climax. During a ninety-minute air raid on the afternoon of September 10, some one thousand four-engine bombers dropped five thousand tons of bombs on Le Havre.[63]

Colonel Eberhard Wildermuth,[64] the Le Havre fortress commandant, finally capitulated to the attacks by the British I Corps at noon on September 12.[65] By that time, however, the harbor had been rendered mostly inoperable.[66] At approximately the same time as when Wildermuth laid down his arms, Lieutenant General Rudolf Hofmann, the chief of staff of the Fifteenth Army, briefed Army Group B that the first two infantry divisions had reached the far bank.[67] On that same evening, the LXVII Army Corps under General of Infantry Otto Sponheimer, was to be committed along the Albert Canal with the 346th and 711th Infantry Divisions.[68]

That report was a function of the events around Le Havre, both in terms of time and in some respects content. The commitment of the Canadian First Army against sectors that were 320 kilometers apart clearly illustrates the absence of any Allied thought of establishing a main effort. That, in turn, undoubtedly facilitated the retreat of the Fifteenth Army. Following the first interim assessment that Hofmann had reported to Krebs, it was only a matter of hours until Student's First Parachute Army would receive its first relief elements. Considering future combat operations on the Western Front, the consolidation of the German right wing was probably more significant than the capture of Le Havre was for the Allies.

2. Actions in the Center of the Western Front

(a) The Seventh Army's Retreat to the West Wall

The gradual consolidation on the right wing relieved the German command staffs in the west of only a part of their worries. To use Model's metaphor, the gateway to Germany was for the time being closed between Antwerp and Maastricht, but only tenuously. To the south, however, in the area all the way down to the Charleville–Luxembourg line, there was hardly any prospect of a delaying action gaining the time required for the refitting of the West Wall fortifications.

The superiority of the Americans in this sector of the front was entirely too obvious. General Hodges, commanding the U.S. First Army, had eight intact divisions with about 110,000 troops and 850 tanks.[69] On the other hand, there was no single fully combat-effective division left in the sector of the German Seventh Army after the 347th Infantry Division had been almost completely destroyed within forty-eight hours during the fighting at Namur on September 4–5.[70] The state of the other eight divisions fighting in the sector of General Brandenburger's Seventh Army early in September was desolate. Four of those divisions consisted of the headquarters of infantry divisions that largely had been wiped out during the retreat from France and were then given control of some quickly formed battalions of stragglers, plus the supply trains of other destroyed divisions. It was not uncommon to find more than one hundred different Army field postal numbers represented within these "divisions."[71] In fact, it was only the names of those units that survived for the most part.[72] The Seventh Army also had the remnants of the 116th Panzer Division and the 9th Panzer Division, which was being refitted, plus the battle groups of the 2nd SS Panzer Division and the 2nd Panzer Division of the I SS Panzer Corps. The 105th Panzer Brigade had most of the still-operational fighting vehicles, with forty PzKpfw V Panther tanks and assault guns.[73] On the whole, Brandenberger's army had no more than about thirty thousand men and sixty Panzers.[74]

On September 6, OB West's war diary recorded that it was critically important for the buildup of a new general front line to move up new forces to support the Seventh Army, especially since events might develop there quickly.[75] The anticipated American attack to the east started on that same day.[76] Considering the rather precarious strength situation, Brandenberger was now primarily concerned only with preserving his remaining units in as compact a fashion as possible for the coming defensive battle within the West Wall.[77] During the day the Americans pushed unhindered from Namur through the Meuse River Valley toward Lüttich.[78] In the evening, Model approved the Seventh Army's withdrawal to the Hasselt–Huy–Bouillon line.[79] The German command was surprised by the fact that Hodges also mounted a heavy attack with his right wing against the Meuse River position of the I SS Panzer Corps. Both Jodl and the commanders in the west had assumed instead that the enemy would finally establish a definite main effort on the Allied left wing.[80]

In the event, however, the U.S. VII Corps attacked with three divisions from the Namur–Givet area to the northeast. On the VII Corps' right flank, the U.S. V Corps also attacked with three divisions, punching through the Ardennes Forest along an eighty-kilometer-wide sector.[81] During a conference held in the pharmacy of the town of Stadkyll in the Eifel at noon the following day, September 7, Field Marshals Rundstedt and Model agreed that the main threat from the American offensive launched along a broad front lay in the direction of the thrust line via Lüttich and Aachen, toward the Rhein-Westphalia industrial region of Germany.[82] Accordingly, Rundstedt reported to the Wehrmacht High Command that he could see there the acute danger that threatened the rear of the West Wall, which lay directly to the south. According to Rundstedt's report, there was now a compelling necessity to immediately move up at least five or, better still, ten divisions.[83]

The Wehrmacht operations staff countered by noting the impossibility of shifting forward the major units already scheduled to move up.[84] Hitler, however, did give OB West "Wehrmacht authority" to commit as he saw necessary all available combat forces and resources of the Wehrmacht and Waffen-SS elements available in his sector.[85] But at that point in time it hardly did any good. Model, therefore, was determined to act on his own initiative to correct the situation. Going outside official channels, he telephoned Armaments Minister Albert Speer and requested the allocation as soon as possible to Army Group B of thirty PzKpfw V Panthers, thirty PzKpfw VI Tigers, and some assault guns.[86]

In the meantime, the German situation deteriorated further. By noon on September 8, Brandenberger's right wing had to withdraw to or behind the Meuse River. The Americans already had pushed into Lüttich. Graf von Schwerin, the commanding general of the 116th Panzer Division deployed in that area, was no longer willing to see his remaining six hundred men and eighteen Panzers destroyed there.[87] If necessary, he fully intended on his own initiative to withdraw his division as unscathed as possible toward the Reich.[88] Brandenberger's situation became increasingly hopeless and he therefore demanded that Schwerin be relieved.[89] The 105th Panzer Brigade, which was to intercept the American thrust across the Ourthe River, remained without fuel and stuck on the defensive in the area of Herve, north of Verviers. In the Ardennes to the south, strong Allied forces punched through the I SS Panzer Corps, which then was forced to withdraw farther to the northeast, to the Ourthe–La Roche–Libramont line.[90]

On the afternoon of September 8, Rundstedt once again contacted the Wehrmacht High Command and forwarded a situation estimate by Model, which was to be submitted to Hitler verbatim. Because of the deterioration of the particularly threatening situation, the available remnants could at best hold only temporarily the Meuse River line from Maastricht to a point north of Lüttich. On Model's immediate southern flank, there remained merely a thin and completely inadequate outpost line. There the Allies were already capable of moving all the way to the West Wall at will. At that time the West Wall to the rear of the Seventh Army was held by only seven or eight battalions covering a distance of about 120 kilometers. Model and Rundstedt now believed that the final moment had come to brace the Seventh Army. "If three infantry divisions and one Panzer division are not moved up in the shortest possible time, then one can be certain that the expended major units will again be shattered, as happened southwest of Brussels [Mons], but this time, completely. That will automatically and immediately give the enemy his desired operational hole at the German border."[91]

In the meantime, the Wehrmacht High Command had briefed the headquarters of Army Group B that the first of the major units scheduled to be moved up in September, the 12th Infantry Division, could not possibly arrive before September 16–17.[92] But at least the approval finally was given for the withdrawal to the West Wall—"if there is no other possibility."[93] There was, of course, no other such possibility, considering the way the situation was developing.

After the Meuse River had been forced, the last natural obstacle before the border of the Reich, Rundstedt expected the Seventh Army to swing back into the Western Position. He therefore demanded that he receive tactical command over the Western Position and the West Wall, including all of the screening forces, to give him oversight of the defensive preparations and to establish clear lines of command authority.[94] Although such a transfer of authority was long overdue, another two and a half days went by before Hitler agreed to OB West's demand.

In the meantime, the U.S. First Army, minus the U.S. XIX Corps, which was still assembling along the Albert Canal, was able to make such swift progress that Brandenberger was afraid the Americans would reach the West Wall before the German troops.[95] Major General J. Lawton Collins's U.S. VII Corps pushed on, took Verviers on September 9, and its attacking spearheads were already at Limbourg.[96] Gerow's U.S. V Corps simultaneously closed up along the St. Vith–Echternach line by September 10.[97] (See Map 19.) As had been feared, an approximately forty-kilometer-wide hole immediately before the border of the Reich gaped toward the German First Army, on the left wing of Brandenberger's Seventh Army.[98]

The attack by Gerow's units had pushed Keppler's I SS Panzer Corps farther and farther northeast during its retreat through the Ardennes. On the right wing of the German First Army, meanwhile, the LXXX Army Corps during the night leading up to September 11 had been able to withdraw according to plan to the east to the West Wall, between Wallendorf and the Mosel River.[99] To the north of Wallendorf, the Reich border lay unprotected in front of the Americans. (See Map 21.)

Keppler ordered Colonel Adolf von Nostitz-Wallwitz,[100] the commanding officer of the 2nd Panzer Division, to cross the Our River as quickly as possible and then to move into the West Wall sector east of Heinerscheid–Wallendorf.[101] At that point it appeared extremely doubtful whether the division would beat the Americans to that sector. On the evening of September 11, the lead American patrols crossed the Reich border unopposed in the area between St. Vith and Vianden.[102]

On the immediate left flank of the I SS Panzer Corps, General of Infantry Franz Beyer's LXXX Army Corps was the first to face the negative consequences of the muddled command channels in the Western Position sector. Until the evening of September 9, neither

Beyer's headquarters nor the headquarters of the First Army had received any maps or documents on the line of fortifications. Preparations had hardly been made to turn the position over to the front-line troops. The incoming divisions themselves had to assume the job of assigning and allocating West Wall positions to their various units.[103] That, of course, was an extremely problematic task without a precise knowledge of the layout of the line.

Characteristic of this kind of trouble was Himmler's order requisitioning all individual vehicles and officers in the rear area of the LXXX Army Corps for the purpose of organizing and forming alert units. Beyer's chief of staff, Colonel Rolf Wiese, immediately demanded that "this nonsense be stopped, because otherwise it will be impossible to provide supplies and handle communications in the combat zone."[104] Similar problems also made it difficult to command combat operations on the right wing of the Seventh Army.

Brandenberger, of course, already had withdrawn the headquarters of the 353rd Infantry Division from the front on September 8 to organize the defense of the West Wall in the Aachen area.[105] But the division commander, Lieutenant General Paul Mahlmann, was prevented by Reich defense commissar Rainer Grohe[106] from initiating "hasty and premature" measures there.[107] The improper emplacement of barriers and mines behind the front meant that any attempt to intercept the American thrust west and southwest of the old imperial city by mobile combat operations would yield little success.[108] First of all, hardly any fuel had reached the front.[109] And besides, the plan had failed to organize a provisional Panzer unit in front of Eupen that was supposed to come under the command of Major General Gerhard Müller's 9th Panzer Division. The 394th Assault Gun Brigade was approaching from the Reich. With its thirty fighting vehicles it was to form the main body of the major unit, which would consist of the remaining ten Panther tanks of 105th Panzer Brigade and the first arriving infantry elements of the 9th Panzer Division.[110] But the 394th did not arrive on time because of direct interference by Nazi Party functionaries.[111] The forces available were thus unable to prevent the American breakthrough toward Eupen on September 11. On the evening of that same day, Battle Group Müller, still being assembled at Eynatten, consisted of only forty men and three Panzers.[112]

The Americans had thus pushed Brandenberger's Seventh Army back near Aachen and in the area adjoining to the south to within a few kilometers of the Reich border. The battle groups of the Seventh Army at that time were positioned in a line that ran from the Meuse River at Visé (Eijsden, about ten kilometers south of Maastricht), along the Voer River to the east, then via Hombourg, Hergenrath, and all the way to Eynatten.[113] After that the line turned south and ran through the Hürtgen Forest (Hürtgenwald) west of Monschau, via Butgenbach east of Malmedy.[114] From there it ran from St. Vith to Reuland Castle on the Our River.[115, 116]

During the week since he took command, Brandenberger had been able to establish control of his army under the most difficult conditions. But his units were now so weakened, despite the constant surrender of terrain, that they were hardly able to offer any resistance to the American breakthrough attack toward Aachen and Cologne that was anticipated at any moment.[117]

The hope that the front line of the Seventh Army might still at the last moment be reinforced all the way to the Mosel position had surfaced before, but now it vanished. With this situation, Field Marshal von Rundstedt finally was given overall command of the Western Position.[118] His initial assessment was very sobering. He ordered a message sent to the Wehrmacht High Command reporting the "current state of the West Wall . . . in no way meets the requirements."[119]

Apart from the previously noted weak points in the fortifications,[120] Rundstedt initially criticized the fact that the number of some 170,000 trench diggers reported for the entire Western Position was much too small.[121]

The Reich defense commissars tried to neutralize Rundstedt's criticisms immediately. Gauleiter Josef Bürckel, for example, ordered a quadruple increase in the manpower commitment. Now, women up to the age of forty, and personnel from hitherto "protected" factories were to be used.[122] They were to work at the construction sites daily in two shifts of ten hours each.[123]

Considering the situation, all that seemed to be too late for the Seventh Army, because the Americans in places had already approached the West Wall to within artillery range. The West Wall screening force behind Brandenberger's army consisted of about twenty thousand infantrymen, who had been transferred into the Aachen–Wallendorf sector, ten kilometers northwest of Echternach, in response to the Valkyrie appeal. Those troops came from the 406th Special Purpose Replacement Army Division,[124] the 526th Replacement Army Division,[125] and the 172nd Replacement Army

Division.[126] They undoubtedly could have reinforced Brandenberger's thinned-out ranks as they moved into the West Wall. But the Replacement Army units alone were not adequate to reinforce a sector width of some 120 kilometers.

On the evening of September 11, Model returned to his headquarters in Arcen, north of Venlo.[127] He had just made an extensive tour of the front, visiting the LXXXI Army Corps at Weiden, the Seventh Army headquarters at Monschau, the I SS Panzer Corps at Schönberg, and finishing at Düren. He reported to the Wehrmacht operations staff, ". . . the defense of the West Wall with current forces cannot be assured."[128]

That assessment coincided completely with that of OB West. At that point Rundstedt absolutely expected the U.S. First Army to launch a breakthrough attempt, which he was certain would be completely successful.[129] To the astonishment of the German command in the west, however, the enemy did not immediately jump off in the attack.

General Krebs believed that the cause of the American hesitation might have been the proximity of the West Wall and the suspicion that strong German forces were behind it.[130] But Krebs's assumption was only partly correct. The decision by Hodges, the commanding general of the U.S. First Army, to commence the major offensive at the earliest on September 14 was due neither to the fact that the West Wall was considered a difficult obstacle nor that the Allies suspected strong German forces behind it.[131] On the contrary, like most American officers, Hodges shared the view that the "Siegfried Line" could withstand an attack for a maximum of only three days.[132] The enemy situation estimate prepared by the U.S. V and VII Corps did not contradict that. The G-2 sections estimated only about fourteen thousand Germans along that sector of the front.[133]

That again was the product of underestimating the enemy's capability for resistance, which obviously was inseparably tied to the feeling of optimism that the situation seemed to justify. Hodges decided, in spite of everything, to wait for the replenishment of artillery ammunition, remaining content for the moment to conduct a reconnaissance-in-force.[134] That decision was probably prompted by psychological factors, including the heady days when the French and Belgians euphorically cheered and feted their liberators. But those days were drawing to an end. The American troops now faced the real objective of their "Crusade in Europe"—the thrust into German territory.[135] Indications of stiffening resistance along the Albert Canal and the Mosel River positions made obvious to Hodges the necessity for preparing the coming attack carefully to ensure its success. Simultaneously, the still largely unresolved supply problems also dictated a more cautious approach to the American generals. But that consideration by itself was not decisive, because Hodges was convinced that he still had on hand enough fuel for an offensive all the way to the Rhine and ammunition for about five days of fighting.[136]

The pursuit phase had finally ended in that sector of the front, although the commanders on both sides did not yet realize it. The temporary halt to the Allied offensive also made it possible for the Germans to beef up their defenses significantly in a very short time. Rundstedt learned by September 14—the day Hodges wanted to launch his offensive—that a total of thirty-two fortress battalions (or fortress artillery battalions) with a total of some sixteen thousand men would be made ready for commitment for the West Wall in the sector of Army Group B.[137]

(b) Initial Fighting along the First Army's Mosel River Front

The U.S. Third Army was able to resume its "supporting offensive" following Eisenhower's decision to stick to the original basic plan of the Broad Front strategy. Patton assumed that the Germans would merely fight a delaying action along the Mosel River and would then withdraw to the West Wall.[138] The Americans obviously failed to note that the Germans had used the almost one-week pause in the fighting to beef up their positions along the Mosel River quite significantly. In the event, the Americans did not establish a main effort at any point. The U.S. Third Army launched its offensive on September 6 along a wide front.

That fact and the selected direction of the attack, which pointed east, turned out to be a stroke of luck for the German First Army.[139] Patton at that point had only six divisions, because the U.S. XV Corps with the U.S. 79th Infantry Division and the French 2nd Armored Division did not enter the line until September 11.[140] Patton's six divisions attacking in the area between Thionville and Nancy ran into the strongest German defensive sector, which also was defended by six divisions under the command of General von der Chevallerie.[141]

The outer wings, which were the weak points of the German

First Army, were not attacked initially. The LXXX Army Corps, committed to the right along the boundary with the Seventh Army, was able to withdraw according to plan through Luxembourg, although it did not have a single intact major unit.[142] (The Grand Duchy had been integrated into the German Gau of Koblenz–Trier.) General Beyer managed to disengage his corps—which consisted of only about five thousand to six thousand men and sixteen Panzers—from the 5th Armored Division of the U.S. First Army just in time.[143] Beyer then led his force without any difficulty into the West Wall sector between Wallendorf and Trier during the night leading up to September 11.[144]

That withdrawal movement by the German right wing meant that the almost four-week-long American pursuit had come to an end, at least for the U.S. First Army. The combat operations that developed from Patton's Third Army offensive launched farther to the south also differed noticeably from the heady events of August.

On September 7–8 the 106th Panzer Brigade, reinforced by elements of the 19th Grenadier Division and the 15th Panzer Grenadier Division, conducted locally limited attacks "to improve the positions."[145] The attacks were mounted from the right wing of the German First Army in the Audun–Briey area, which at that time was still echeloned far forward, and thrust into the assembly areas of the U.S. XX Corps. The U.S. 90th Infantry Division was taken by surprise and their lines were quickly pierced.[146] After that initial success, Colonel Franz Bäke's brigade clashed in a series of fierce meeting engagements with the U.S. 7th Armored Division.[147] Both sides suffered heavy losses. The 106th Panzer Brigade lost almost half of its forty-seven fighting vehicles.[148] (See Map 16.) Although the attack did not achieve its intended objective, it nevertheless brought considerable relief for the frontline sector between Thionville and Metz.[149]

On September 7, the Americans pushed all the way to the Mosel River at Hagondange, north of Metz.[150] But they made no attempt at all to force the river crossing, because they were afraid of more German Panzer attacks.[151] Offensive actions along the northern wing of the U.S. Third Army instead were confined initially to a week-long artillery duel with the fortress guns at Metz.[152]

The first few days of the American offensive also were unsuccessful in the Mosel River sector all the way down to Nancy. The frontal attack against the German positions at Metz by the U.S. 5th

Infantry Division, supported by tanks, did not succeed. The 462nd Replacement Army Division was able to stop the American advance on the old 1870 battlefields along the western approaches to the cities of St. Privat, Amanvillers, and Gravelotte. There again both sides suffered considerable losses, with the Americans alone losing thirty-five tanks.[153] The Americans obviously were baffled by the outstanding fighting spirit of the bitterly resisting regiments of the German division that consisted mostly of officer candidates and noncommissioned officer students.[154] According to a contemporary Reuters report, the Americans confirmed that the "corps of cadets fought the way only the fresh SS units would normally fight. Hardly any prisoners were taken, and the few who were captured would thrash about and bite."[155] But that was only small comfort for the German Army Personnel Office, considering that the young officers and noncommissioned officers had been sent as a body straight into the enemy fire.

For Gruppenführer and Lieutenant General of the Waffen-SS Hermann Priess, the commanding general of the XIII SS Corps, which had relieved Sinnhuber's LXXXII Army Corps on September 7, the most important task at that point was to hold the Metz bridgehead.[156] The Americans, of course, did manage to cross the Mosel River a few kilometers farther south at Dornot at noon on September 8. The small Allied bridgehead, however, was immediately and severely attacked by units of the 17th SS Panzer Grenadier Division and the 3rd Panzer Grenadier Division.[157] Major General S. Leroy Irwin, the commanding general of the U.S. 5th Infantry Division, gave up hope of holding the bridgehead.[158] His unit had lost around one thousand men during the first few days of the offensive.[159] That penetration of the Mosel River position, which was doomed to failure, was the U.S. Third Army's only tactical success, and it was bought at a high price.

The attacks by the U.S. XII Corps also had been beaten back. The units of Major General Hans Hecker's 3rd Panzer Grenadier Division inflicted a bloody setback on the American attempt to establish a bridgehead at Pont-à-Mousson, sinking thirty-eight of the sixty-four assault boats that were supposed to carry one regiment of the U.S. 80th Infantry Division. The German counterattack during the forenoon of September 6 then cleared up the situation once and for all. The Americans left 160 dead and wounded on the east bank, while the losses to the German Panzer Grenadiers were minor.[160]

In reaction, Major General Manton Eddy, commanding general of the U.S. XII Corps, refrained for the moment from making any additional crossing attempts. He instead ordered the preparation of a combined attack so that his three divisions would establish bridgeheads initially south of Nancy and immediately thereafter north of the city in order to split the German defending forces. That operation was scheduled for September 11.[161]

Chevallerie's German First Army had thus successfully beaten off the first onslaught of the U.S. Third Army and gained valuable time. Nevertheless, Hitler now acted on his decision to relieve Chevallerie, which he had already made in conjunction with the planned offensive operation.[162] The opportune moment to take that action sprang from intrigues that were hatched by the gauleiters. As one example, they hinted to Himmler that some sixty-four thousand stragglers were clustering around in the First Army's immediate rear areas. OB West headquarters had no doubt that these leaks to the Reichsführer-SS had no credibility.[163] Nonetheless, they were the foundation of the verdict from Führer Headquarters about the commanding general and the chief of staff of the First Army: "Chevallerie and Feyerabend are no good."[164] The false information undoubtedly had been floated by Reich defense commissar Gustav Simon, who was thrusting for personal revenge. Early in September Chevallerie had reported to the Wehrmacht High Command that gauleiter's rather inglorious flight from Luxembourg.

The new commanding general, General of Panzer Troops Otto von Knobelsdorff, arrived at the command post of the First Army in Schrassig near Schuttrange east of Luxembourg on September 10.[165] Rundstedt, unaware of the underhanded background of this personnel change, immediately lodged a protest with the Wehrmacht High Command. He simply would not have any such interferences in the future without his agreement, especially since he had no criticism to make of the way in which the First Army had been commanded until then.[166] Although it was not the personal responsibility of von Knobelsdorff, his tenure as commander thus began under a cloud. He also had problems with events along the front, although not to the northern sector of the Mosel River line. The situation there continued to be stable. The attacks against the German positions in front of Metz abated after the Allies suffered more heavy losses. The Allied attacks were finally suspended on September 14.[167]

A few kilometers south of Metz, the U.S. 5th Infantry Division on September 10 managed to put troops across the river at Arnaville. That, however, did not aggravate the German situation because the Americans at almost the same time were forced to abandon their bridgehead at Dornot.[168] The OB West morning report on September 11 stated that there had been only "actions of local significance" in the First Army's sector.[169] On urging from Wehrmacht High Command, Knobelsdorff withdrew the headquarters of the XLVII Panzer Corps from his command sector and sent it south to link up with the Fifth Panzer Army.[170] In the evening of September 11 the situation became serious in the frontline sector, requiring the commitment of the XIII SS Corps. An American crossing attempt south of Nancy had been beaten off that afternoon. Colonel Erich Löhr's 553rd Grenadier Division had been able to capture 250 men of the U.S. 35th Infantry Division.[171] But then the U.S. XII Corps reached the initial objective established by Major General Eddy. The U.S. 35th Infantry Division, reinforced by one combat command of the U.S. 4th Armored Division, formed a 5–7-kilometer-wide bridgehead at Bayon, south of Nancy.[172] The attack by the left pincer arm of the XII Corps was also successful on the following day, and the Americans crossed the Mosel River at Dieulouard, north of Nancy. (See Map 21.)

Knobelsdorff's situation had worsened considerably within a very short time. On September 12, the U.S. Third Army already had three bridgeheads that were in the process of being consolidated. Behind a smokescreen, the Americans were able to build a military bridge at Arnaville and put tanks across the river.[173]

The German nighttime attack against the Dieulouard bridgehead on September 12–13 caused heavy losses on both sides. But the Germans were stopped shortly before the objective, the Le Mont crossing site, and the attack had to be broken off because there were no shock force reserves.[174] The 15th Panzer Grenadier Division, which was to advance against the American units south of Nancy, was unable to jump off immediately because of fuel shortages.[175] The Americans, therefore, continued their advance with almost no resistance from the Bayon bridgehead, pushing all the way into the Gerbévillers area, ten kilometers south of Lunéville.[176] On September 11 the U.S. XV Corps, with its U.S. 79th Infantry Division and French 2nd Armored Division, was committed on the right wing of the U.S. Third Army, bringing the German Mosel River position now under increasing pressure.

With the simultaneously increasing threat to the Nineteenth Army in the salient in front of Dijon, Rundstedt saw the chances dwindling for the planned offensive of the Fifth Panzer Army.[177] (See Map 20.) Nonetheless, the Germans had prevented the U.S. Third Army from achieving its ambitious attack objectives.[178] Although the fighting along the Mosel River started to show the general indicators of bogging down in static warfare, Patton remained optimistic. He assumed the Germans had neither a deep defense nor the necessary reserves to conduct a defensive delaying action. Thus Patton on September 12 told Bradley that he saw a clear road ahead to the Rhine River as soon as the expected final breakthrough came off successfully within the next several days.[179]

Chapter 11

The Situation Estimate Prepared by the Operations Staffs and the Failure of the Concept of a German "Counteroffensive from the Move"

1. Situation Estimates and Decisions toward the End of the First Ten-Day Period in September

(a) The Allies and the "Terminal Phase" of the Fight against the German Reich

In his September 9 situation report to the Combined Chiefs of Staff, Eisenhower emphasized among other things that although German resistance had been believed close to collapse in recent weeks, it had "become somewhat stiffer" following the shift of combat operations to the vicinity of the Reich border. Moreover, he now saw the danger that the continuation of Allied operations might be considerably restricted because of the blockage of the Scheldt River estuary, which was still in German hands.[1] That meant that the situation was now being assessed in a new light at Allied headquarters. There were many indications that Eisenhower now wanted to give the Broad Front strategy the logistical foundation that it had been lacking until then.

In contrast to what American official historian Forrest Pogue has written, no new phase in Allied operations planning began following that reference to the significance of Antwerp.[2] For the time being, in fact, there was nothing more than a verbal reference to the importance of the Scheldt estuary. The emphasis in Eisenhower's September 13 directive, issued shortly thereafter, was instead on a new element, the airborne and ground joint operation designated MARKET-GARDEN, as proposed by Montgomery. The plan called for Lieutenant General Lewis H. Brereton's First Allied Airborne Army to commit the U.S. 82nd and 101st Airborne Divisions, the British 1st Airborne Division, and the Polish 1st Separate Airborne

Brigade in order to seize the bridges across the Meuse, Waal, and Nederrijn rivers and some of the canals in the Grave–Nijmegen–Arnhem area.[3] The airborne assault phase was designated Operation MARKET. The British Second Army was given the objective of attacking across the Meuse–Scheldt Canal and then pushing across the bridges seized by the paratroopers, all the way to IJsselmeer. That phase was designated Operation GARDEN. The advantages expected to accrue from this coordinated operation were quite obvious. The Allied forces would be able to cut off all German forces in western Holland while at the same time outflanking the West Wall and reaching a favorable position for the thrust into the North German Plain.[4] The fact that the British population would be freed from the threat of the V-2 missiles that the Germans had been firing from that area since September 8 also played a role in the decision to launch Operation MARKET-GARDEN.[5] Eisenhower was fully aware that this operation, scheduled to be launched on September 17, could lead to a delay in the opening of the Scheldt River.[6]

Another factor in this decision was the temporary improvement in the supply situation. Eisenhower's assessment of September 9, therefore, now assumed a secondary significance in the order-issuing procedure. Neither the U.S. First nor the U.S. Third Armies suffered from any acute supply shortages at the start of the second ten-day period in September. On September 12, Hodges and Patton told Bradley that the fuel supplies of their armies would suffice for a push all the way to the Rhine, and they even had artillery ammunition for as much as four to five days of combat.[7] The frontline commanders undoubtedly were not getting all of the supply tonnage they had requested, although they often inflated their figures. But the overall situation remained. And as Eisenhower now began to realize, without Antwerp, the cause of the logistical problems could not be eliminated entirely. Because of the unplanned swift advance and the ever-longer transportation distances, it would have been impossible to establish a regular supply and depot system.[8] But the tremendous series of improvisations that the Allied command was able to patch together would have made it possible for the central group of armies—i.e., the 12th Army Group—to conduct a large-scale offensive with one of its two American field armies.[9] The prerequisite for that, however, was that the other army would have to assume a defensive posture during that period.

At that time the supply situation of the northern group of

armies—i.e., the 21st Army Group—also did not justify Ruppen-thal's subsequent assessment that the Allies were in an "almost desperate supply situation."[10] A difficult situation did exist, but only in relation to the Broad Front strategy. As Montgomery, who continued to oppose that strategy, described that complex problem so very aptly: "It is basically a matter of rail and road and air transport, and unless this is concentrated to give impetus to the selected thrust then no one is going to get very far."[11]

Montgomery, believing that he had convinced the Supreme Commander of the invasion forces, reported to the British Chiefs of Staff on September 12 that Eisenhower had given in and that the offensive toward the Saar would be discontinued. Hodges's U.S. First Army, Montgomery hoped, would now get the majority of the supplies of the American 12th Army Group. But his conclusion that "so we have gained a great victory" proved premature.[12] The two single-spaced typed pages of Eisenhower's directive of September 13 corresponded at best to Montgomery's intentions only in selected passages. The timing of the Allied operations, according to Eisenhower, was now of the utmost significance, because there were not sufficient resources available to pursue multiple goals simultaneously.[13]

Eisenhower apparently intended once again to establish a definite main effort on the Allied northern wing, at least temporarily. According to his scheme of maneuver, the 21st Army Group, supported by the Allied First Airborne Army, was to establish a bridgehead across the lower Rhine (Nederrijn) and then prepare to push into Germany's Ruhr region from the north. Montgomery's army group would have its right flank covered by the U.S. First Army. Hodges was given the mission of crossing the Rhine River in the Cologne–Bonn area and then advancing toward the Ruhr region, coming from the south.

While that was taking place, Eisenhower's general plan specified that Montgomery's army group would simultaneously clear the approaches to Antwerp or Rotterdam and also clean out the additional Channel ports. Montgomery's issued orders and the deployment of his forces up until then showed and continued to show that he saw no major problems in seizing those ports in passing.[14] Those additional missions, therefore, were not instrumental in making it clear to the British commander that his arguments against the Broad Front strategy had once again failed.[15] What did make it clear to Montgomery was the fact that Eisenhower had no intention of halt-

ing Patton's offensive. Eisenhower's scheme of maneuver directed
the U.S. Third Army to assume a defensive posture—a "holding and
threatening action"—until such time as the Allied left wing had attained its objectives. Eisenhower then established a key exception
to that clear rule: The logistical main effort would be shifted to U.S.
First Army only after Patton's Third Army had seized the Mosel
River bridgeheads with a large enough force to constitute a constant threat to the Germans. But based on his past experiences with
Patton, Eisenhower figured that the Third Army commander, who
was driven by his unrestrained urge to keep advancing, would use
those exceptions to his own advantage. Eisenhower's directive even
pointed to a way that it could be done: "After the attainment of
the Moselle bridgeheads above directed, operations on our left will,
until the Rhine bridgeheads are won, take priority in all forms of
logistical support except for . . . adequate measures and continuous
reconnaissance by forces on the right." Patton later on admitted that
he always looked for such loopholes in Eisenhower's orders.[16]

In the final analysis, Eisenhower's reaction to the slowing Allied advance and the increasing German resistance in at least some
sectors of the front resulted in the execution of Operation MARKET-
GARDEN. It was actually the new element in his directive of September 13 which otherwise retained the Broad Front strategy. That
strategy was reflected in the new Allied command structure. The
Operation DRAGOON forces, consisting of Lieutenant General
Jacob Devers's southern group of armies now came under Eisenhower's command. Devers's 6th Army Group included the French
First Army and the U.S. Seventh Army. But the Allied strategy still
lacked the necessary logistical foundation. Opening the maritime
access ways to the port of Antwerp had assumed great significance
for Eisenhower, but not in the way he issued his orders.

The Allied Supreme Commander undoubtedly knew certain key
factors that should have militated against the success of MARKET-
GARDEN. He expected the bad-weather phase to set in at the latest
on September 20. As he said, that would seriously hinder all airborne
operations and would cause them to become "spasmodic."[17] But Operation MARKET-GARDEN, which was intended to last between
seven and ten days, was not to commence until September 17.

Eisenhower accepted a delay in Antwerp's opening, although
according to his own statements, even a one-week autumn storm
along the Channel coast would reduce the supply transloading op-

erations that were still taking place across the Normandy beaches to such an extent that Allied combat operations would be paralyzed.[18] The decisive element of Eisenhower's September 13 directive was the trend toward an optimistic situation assessment based on wishful thinking, which continued to prevail in the Allied camp.[19] The conviction of the G-2 of the British 1st Airborne Division is a typical example: The enemy was still bound to be disorganized after the lengthy, hasty, and bloody retreat. German resistance, therefore, seemed to be ruled out.[20]

Under such apparent conditions, Eisenhower's decision to venture on a "last major battle" and then push ahead across the Rhine River, regrouping there and consolidating the supply system, was to some extent logical.[21] On September 13, General George C. Marshall, chief of staff of the U.S. Army, informed his senior field commanders that the termination of the war in Europe might be expected by November 1944.[22] The Western Allies' Second Quebec Conference (OCTAGON), held on September 11–16, 1944, began against this background.

The Soviets likewise seemed to be convinced that their partners in the "Anti-Hitler Coalition" were just about to win final victory. Previously they had long refused to approve a protocol for the allocation of the occupation zones until the Americans and British first decided who would get the northern of the two western occupation zones. The Soviets now waived that precondition.

Based on the war situation, Fedor Gusev, the Soviet representative to the European Advisory Commission, was instructed by his government on September 12 to sign that protocol. That left the allocation of the western occupation zones still unsettled, but it assured the Soviets of the demarcation line that the British had suggested in January 1944.[23]

The war against the Third Reich seemed to be drawing to a close. Quebec, therefore, focused primarily on the continuation of combat operations against Japan.[24] Under the heading of European Affairs, however, Roosevelt and Churchill on September 15 signed a draft prepared by the U.S. secretary of the treasury, Henry Morgenthau Jr.[25] Known as the Morgenthau Plan, it called for imposing a "Carthaginian peace" upon Germany.[26]

The disclosure of Allied occupation intentions undoubtedly facilitated Goebbels's efforts to manipulate the mood of the German people, previously characterized by depression and fatalism.[27] The hopes entertained by German "bourgeois circles" that an occupation by the Anglo-Americans would not result in the ruination of Germany thus received a serious blow.[28] Talking about the Morgenthau Plan later on, Goebbels said that "we need not add a single word to its publication in order to enflame the spirit of resistance of our people."[29] One therefore can understand that, considering the always close reciprocal relationship between the mood on the home front and the battlefront, the publication of the plan did not fail to have an effect on the morale and spirit of sacrifice of the combat soldiers.[30] Orders aimed at the "fanaticization of the defensive struggle" thus fell on more fertile soil. Morgenthau's plan, however, did not become known in Germany until the end of September.[31] At that point the German front line in the west had already been consolidated and positional warfare had started.

(b) The Start of German Offensive Preparations

Roughly at the same time when Eisenhower was discussing future operations with his field commanders, Führer Headquarters also made a decision that was important for future events. The point of departure on both sides certainly was the same: The Allied advance had lost impetus and had not in recent days achieved any major successes.

Following the loss of Antwerp, Hitler's offensive plan had for the moment receded into the background. Stunned by this operational event of the first order,[32] the führer now agreed with Jodl that a decisive, large-scale German offensive would not be possible in the west before November 1.[33] Hitler's fear was that the Allies might launch a main effort on the northern wing within a very short time. That would cause his entire fortress concept to fail, and simultaneously it would lay the foundation for the consolidation of the Allied logistics system. But that fear did not materialize. Contrary to expectations, the estuary of the Scheldt River continued to remain in German hands, and the enemy for the time being was unable to use Antwerp. And so the German offensive plan again became feasible, and Hitler now saw an opportunity to seize the initiative earlier than November.[34] The moment seemed favorable inasmuch as the Allies continued to operate along a broad front and there was no need to abandon the hope that their advance would be stopped by supply problems.[35]

An offensive launched directly from the retreat would produce an operational-level turning point.[36] The plan was to thrust from the Dijon bridgehead to the northwest, between the Marne River and the Argonnes via Bar-le-Duc, hitting the U.S. Third Army in the deep southern flank and in the rear.[37] There was, of course, one problem still outstanding. That was whether the salient that protruded far to the west could be held until such time as the Panzer units were assembled. Time was short. OB West was ordered on September 7 to make sure the units earmarked for the attacking element of Army Task Group G sped up their deployments into their designated areas, and in full strength.[38]

Rundstedt initially was concerned with establishing at least the organizational structure for this effort. The 17th SS Panzer Grenadier Division, the 3rd and 15th Panzer Grenadier Divisions, and the 106th Panzer Brigade that were to conduct the offensive were still fighting under the command of the First Army, which in turn was under Model's Army Group B. Rundstedt changed this chain of command and now put the German First Army under Army Task Group G.[39]

That seemed to make more sense, since Blaskowitz henceforth had to make his decision as to whether and when those units were to be withdrawn from the Mosel River sector and could then be moved south. In keeping with the significance of the planned operation, the attacking Fifth Panzer Army was to get its orders directly from OB West headquarters.[40] Rundstedt issued the deployment order on that very evening of September 7.[41] Five Panzer or Panzer Grenadier divisions plus six Panzer brigades were to be combined under Manteuffel's Fifth Panzer Army.[42] Those forces had to be ready in the bridgehead by September 12.[43]

Rundstedt, however, expressly alerted the Wehrmacht High Command to other preconditions for the offensive, including the immediate delivery of ten thousand cubic meters of fuel and the restriction of Allied control of the air by the commitment of all available air assets, stripping the other fronts to do so.[44] But those two demands were hardly possible to meet. That kind of fuel volume simply could not be found in such a short time.[45]

Rundstedt also saw no solution to the problem of establishing an air umbrella for the offensive. According to the forecasts of the meteorologists, there would be a high-pressure system—in other words, good flying conditions—during the time between September 12 and 20.[46] But that was bound to benefit the Allies primarily,

considering the weakness of the Luftwaffe. The disastrous consequences that might result from this for any German Panzer offensive had already been demonstrated early in August during the
failed counterattack at Avranches.[47] Another aggravating factor was
that the attacking units were being readied only sluggishly. In the
evening of September 10, OB West headquarters informed Rastenburg that so far only the 21st Panzer Division and the lead transports of the 111th, 112th, and 113th Panzer Brigades had arrived in
the designated areas. Combat operations in the German First Army
sector had made it impossible to pull the Panzer Grenadier units out
of the front line.[48]

Hitler, of course, suspected that this was primarily traceable to
Blaskowitz. Although the disparity in the strength ratio at the Dijon bridgehead area was known to everyone, Hitler believed that
Blaskowitz was the main culprit in bringing about a situation where
this deployment area kept shrinking constantly. Hitler's belief that
Army Task Group G was not fully aware of its mission was supported primarily by so-called "information reports" from one particular
gauleiter.[49] Here again, the particular Reich defense commissar involved did not fail to use his opportunity to discredit the military
establishment.[50]

Despite everything, Hitler stuck to his plan undeterred. He
ordered Blaskowitz to use draconian methods to stamp out any
thoughts among his units of withdrawing to the Vosges Mountains
or to the West Wall. Army Task Group G must hold the area that it
held during the night between September 10 and 11.[51] Addressing
the chief of the Wehrmacht operations staff, Hitler in the evening
of September 11 demanded that the Fifth Panzer Army must in all
circumstances attack against the rear of the enemy, exploiting favorable opportunities as they arose.[52]

2. The Situation on the Southern Wing

(a) The Fight for the Dijon Bridgehead: The End of the Retreat from Southwestern France and the Prerequisites for the Counteroffensive

The situation in the Dijon bridgehead had deteriorated considerably during the past several days. The area intended as the pivot
for the offensive operation kept shrinking, the result of the enemy's

superior pressure and not of the inability of the German generals. It was Blaskowitz, above all, who constantly urged that the exposed salient in the front line be defended as long as possible in order to be able to take in additional march columns withdrawing from south-western France.

The critical aggravation of the situation, however, did not begin along the northern flank, as Blaskowitz had anticipated, but rather in the south of the bridgehead.[53] The Nineteenth Army headquarters had firmly believed since September 4 that the Allies intended to exploit the last possibility of effecting a passing pursuit maneuver before reaching the Belfort Gap.[54] The second pressure point against the southern flank came from an attack by the French II Corps' 1st Infantry Division and 1st Armored Division along the Saône River. The French were able to liberate Châlons on September 5. But they then were stopped for the time being after the German units were successful in achieving a major antitank victory.[55] During the fighting in the Chagny area fifteen kilometers south of Beaune, the 716th and 189th Infantry Divisions under the Luftwaffe IV Field Corps attacked fourteen out of the twenty-five advancing Allied armored vehicles.[56] The retreat routes of the columns marching from the southwest to the bridgehead were not threatened directly. Between Moulins and Beaune, however, they were screened only by the 360th Cossack Regiment under Lieutenant Colonel Ewert von Renteln.[57]

The Allied main thrust actually came in the area between Besançon and Switzerland, heading toward Belfort.[58] The four Allied divisions, the U.S. 3rd, 36th, and 45th Infantry Divisions and the Algerian 3rd Infantry Division, attacked at the base of the German frontline salient. That pressure point was the critical operational threat to the entire Nineteenth Army. The German countermeasures seemed to come too late. The 11th Panzer Division, which was to block the Montagnes de Lomont between Doubs and Switzerland and running laterally to the enemy attack, did arrive in time to prevent the Algerian 3rd Division from getting to Montbéliard and Belfort.[59] At Besançon, however, the Americans only ran into the weak screening detachment.[60] That force consisted of the provisionally organized Corps Dehner, which included the 18th Antiaircraft Artillery Regiment, the 669th Army Engineer Battalion, and the 608th Mobile Battalion.[61] By the afternoon of September 6 the Americans were able to establish an eight-kilometer-deep bridgehead across the Doubs River.[62] The 159th Infantry Division, earmarked to support Corps Dehner as Army Task Group G reserve, was no longer able to stabilize the situation in the Besançon area.[63] That unit, which had just completed its retreat from the southwest shortly before going into action along the Doubs River, lost its commander, Lieutenant General Albin Nake, as a result of a car accident.[64] The American attack commenced before the former senior field commandant of Lyon, Lieutenant General Otto Kohl, who had been temporarily appointed the division's commander, was able to familiarize himself with the situation and before the division had completely occupied its positions.[65]

On the other hand, there were no reserves available any longer. Nonetheless, Blaskowitz the previous day had turned down a request from Nineteenth Army chief of staff Lieutenant General Walter Botsch to shorten the frontline salient, with the order that the Nineteenth Army should if at all possible hold out longer so that the remaining march columns from the south could still be recovered.[66] As during the past weeks, however, Blaskowitz was primarily concerned with the situation in the rear of the front line. Based on his past experiences with Himmler, Blaskowitz had little confidence in the latter's capability to command in the area of the Western Position. Blaskowitz, therefore, ordered the LXXXV Army Corps to pull its headquarters out of the front line and move to Belfort. General of Infantry Baptist Kniess and his staff were to round up stragglers there, organize emergency reaction groups,[67] and ensure the smooth and above all timely transfer of command authority.[68]

But with the Allied penetration in the vicinity of Besançon, the Nineteenth Army headquarters now insisted on a more far-reaching decision.[69] Early in the morning on September 7, Lieutenant General Walter Botsch suggested that the 198th and 338th Infantry Divisions be withdrawn from their positions along the Doubs River on both sides of Dôle during the night and that they deploy against the American penetration area toward the east. The headquarters of the Luftwaffe IV Field Corps was to command the attack.[70] According to Botsch, however, the planned shift to the east would also require moving the LXIV Army Corps back in the western and southwestern sectors[71] of the frontline salient.[72]

Major General Hans von Gyldenfeldt, chief of staff of Army Task Group G, initially approved only the attack plan.[73] Blaskowitz arrived at the command post of the Nineteenth Army in Lure at

0900 hours. He stated that a major withdrawal was out of the question, considering the subsequent operation of the Panzer forces. The "longer pivot" must be held in all circumstances.[74] Thus, it was possible to reduce the size of the frontline salient in the west and southwest only up to the Chaumont–Langres–Dijon–Dôle line.[75]

On the one hand, Blaskowitz's hands were tied by directives from the Supreme Command. On the other hand, he hoped to be able to keep open the door at Dijon for some time yet. The Nineteenth Army headquarters felt that this decision was not adequate, emphasizing that the almost two hundred-kilometer-long position between Langres and Switzerland could not be defended for long with the currently available forces, which amounted to six divisions that were all weak in personnel and equipment.[76] "One must, therefore, anticipate [Allied] breakthroughs everywhere."[77] That estimate of the situation was essentially confirmed during the fighting over the course of the following days.

The attack launched by the Luftwaffe IV Field Corps failed and Besançon fell to the Allies that same day, September 8.[78] The 159th Infantry Division lost two of its regimental headquarters and about twelve hundred men during the fighting for the city.[79] The failure of that operation showed that even locally limited offensive thrusts could no longer be mounted with the exhausted German infantry units. The equipment losses since August 15 had become intolerable. Those losses included 1,316 out of 1,481 artillery pieces lost during the fighting retreat from southern France.[80]

On the evening of September 8, Botsch requested that the Nineteenth Army be moved back to a narrow bridgehead position around Belfort.[81] But Blaskowitz was unable to approve that request for the reasons noted. The front line of the Nineteenth Army was stretched to the breaking point.[82] But even so, any withdrawal movements could be carried out not over a span of several days, but only when hard-pressed by the enemy.[83] The requirement to reinforce the German forces along the southern front was operationally decisive.[84] Blaskowitz, however, now approved the suggestion of allowing the southwestern section of the salient to withdraw relatively rapidly. The Doubs River line also had to be abandoned after the fall of Besançon. Only the 11th Panzer Division was able to hold its defensive positions along the south bank of the river from L'Isle-sur-le-Doubs all the way to the Swiss border at Blamont.[85]

As a result of the outstanding work done by the maintenance

services, Wietersheim's units still had twenty-five operational Panzers, although they all had exceeded the normal service life of their engines by more than double the standard number of hours.[86] The LXIV Army Corps evacuated the southwestern corner of the frontline salient, and by September 10 it had withdrawn to the Langres–Gray–Frétigney line, twenty-five kilometers north of Besançon.[87] Some units of the 716th Infantry Division, however, were left in Dijon, which was now in front of the German lines. Their mission was to hold open the route of retreat for the last withdrawing march element,[88] which numbered about ten thousand men.[89] The day before, the French II Corps had mounted flanking attacks against the Autun–Dijon road, and there seemed little prospect of that last retreat column escaping destruction or captivity. By midnight between September 9 and 10, traffic through Dijon had dwindled to a trickle.[90]

The following night the 716th Infantry Division was ordered to reestablish contact with the German lines.[91] Dijon's evacuation on September 10–11 then took place roughly at the same time when a patrol of the French 1st Armored Division coming from the south near Sombernon, twenty kilometers west of Dijon, ran into a reconnaissance unit from the French 2nd Armored Division. That established the link up of the OVERLORD and DRAGOON forces.[92] The main concern of the German operational staffs now, however, was the southern sector of the frontline salient. In his personal war diary Botsch noted that there was reason to anticipate that the front would be split in the sector of the Luftwaffe IV Field Corps.[93] As Botsch noted: ". . . if the enemy mounts a somewhat reasonably spirited attack."[94] Wiese, the commanding general of the Nineteenth Army, was afraid that the Allies might manage to break through to Belfort on September 9.[95]

Contrary to expectations, however, Wiese's fear did not materialize, although the Allies reinforced their attack group in that sector to a strength of five divisions—the U.S. 3rd, 36th, and 45th Infantry Divisions, and the French 3rd Algerian Division and 9th Colonial Division. But the defenders were helped by Blaskowitz's foresighted measures. Kniess accomplished his assigned tasks in the rear of the German lines with great improvisational skill. He was able to form battle groups several times within a few hours, leading blocking battalions[96] behind the critical points of action in the front line.[97] Reporting on the events of September 10, the Nineteenth Army headquarters noted that the intention of the far superior enemy to open the way to the Belfort Gap was frustrated during the course of the fierce back-and-forth fighting.[98] Both sides suffered heavy losses. The companies of the 198th Infantry Division, for example, now averaged only twenty men.[99] The Luftwaffe IV Field Corps had been pushed back, but it had preserved a coherent front line, which ran from the boundary to the LXIV Army Corps at Frétigney via Montbozon, fifteen kilometers northwest of Baume-les-Dames, all the way to L'Isle-sur-le-Doubs. That was the beginning of the sector of the 11th Panzer Division, which continued to maintain contact with the Swiss border. In the evening, Botsch noted that the picture was the same as the day before: "Worn out troops . . . and penetrations here and there, which have been sealed off everywhere."[100]

The Nineteenth Army headquarters expected the situation in the southern sector to deteriorate rapidly, anticipating the "continuation of enemy attacks via Vesoul to the north and Villersexel and Montbéliard, with the objective of breaking into the Belfort Gap."[101] When Dijon was evacuated during the night, the German retreat from southwestern France was essentially completed. In the process, some sixty thousand men had established contact with the German lines.[102] In his reply to the previously noted charges leveled by the gauleiter, Blaskowitz emphasized to the Wehrmacht High Command that his troops had fought well and for the most part heroically during the as much as one thousand-kilometer-long retreat.[103] Rundstedt agreed, and he requested that the Wehrmacht High Command designate Army Task Group G as Army Group G in recognition of its accomplishments during that period of particularly difficult fighting.[104]

As Blaskowitz noted, the evacuation of the frontline salient and the occupation of a shortened line from the Mosel River to the Belfort Gap was now long overdue because of the Allies' constant superiority in personnel and equipment. General Wiese was still puzzled why the enemy had not long before mounted a concentric breakthrough attack against Belfort.[105] Botsch, his chief of staff, believed that the American tactics were mostly responsible for the fact that the German front was still holding, despite all the worries. In his opinion, the Americans were advancing too hesitantly, focusing almost exclusively on security.[106] The Americans always attacked at the same time of day, never attacked at night, and never attacked without tank support. The attacks also had rather shallow objectives, which is why the Americans often did not exploit opportunities. Again and again the Germans managed to close up the breaches in their lines.[107] Nonetheless, the last moment now seemed to have come for pulling the Nineteenth Army back.

But it was Hitler's holding order of September 11 that once again jeopardized the success of the retreat operations from the south and southwest of France. Hitler obviously was prepared to continue to risk the Nineteenth Army in its still exposed position, rather than abandoning his plan for an offensive. But by the evening of that day it had become crystal clear how shaky an undertaking that really would be. The situation also deteriorated very quickly on the northern wing of the frontline salient, against which the U.S. XV Corps had so far only been probing.[108] The French 2nd Armored Division broke through at Andelot, twenty kilometers northwest of Chaumont, penetrating the approximately one hundred-kilometer-long flank that was screened only by the 16th Infantry Division and Ottenbacher's regional defense battalions. The French pushed southeast into the rear of the 16th Infantry Division and reached the towns of Contrexéville and Lamarche, southwest of Vittel.[109] This meant that the French had penetrated deeply into the German deployment area. That thrust, however, did not trigger the concentric main-effort attack on Belfort that Rundstedt feared.[110] The objectives of the U.S. XV Corps were instead the Mosel River crossings in an easterly direction.

The enemy's pressure abated somewhat in front of the southern flank of the frontline salient. Lieutenant General Alexander Patch, the commanding general of the U.S. Seventh Army, ordered the Allied forces to regroup.[111] After a retreat of almost incredible proportions, Blaskowitz had won the race to the Belfort Gap—but he could not yet be sure of that fact.[112] It was clearly recognizable, however, that the situation in the sector of the Nineteenth Army's salient offered no guarantee at all for any orderly deployment of Panzer units. The conditions just were not there for Hitler's offensive.

(b) The Failure of the Offensive Concept: Defeat at Dompaire and Its Consequences

The preparations for the offensive nevertheless continued at the urging of the Supreme Command.[113] Field Marshal von Rundstedt, however, was fully aware of the awkward situation on the left wing of the Western Front, which was still echeloned far forward. He therefore gave Army Group G a free hand in committing the approaching Panzer units. The most immediate task was to stabilize the frontline salient in order to be able to secure the deployment area for the planned offensive.[114] The 112th Panzer Brigade was the first unit earmarked for that offensive that had arrived at full strength.[115] Blaskowitz thereupon put the brigade under Lucht's LXVI Army Corps.[116]

Since no Panzer Corps headquarters was as yet available, Lucht had the job of straightening out the situation along the northern wing with the 112th Panzer Brigade and the battle group of the 21st Panzer Division. That latter element consisted only of two reinforced Panzer Grenadier battalions, and the actual tanks were not as yet on the scene.[117] At that point Field Marshal von Rundstedt obviously no longer believed that the Fifth Panzer Army would arrive in time for the planned major offensive operation. Therefore, he placed Manteuffel's army, which was just being assembled, under Army Group G.[118]

Hitler did not agree with the organization for combat as it was being established. The Fifth Panzer Army, he noted, must not be used up in frontal counterattacks. Instead, it must repeatedly launch thrusts into the deep flank and rear of the enemy.[119] Rundstedt, however, was undeterred. He reported rather laconically that the situation made it necessary to commit the Fifth Panzer Army initially by corps for lesser blows in order to preserve the maneuver space forward of the Vosges Mountains that would be needed for the subsequent concentrated attack.[120] In the meantime, the preparations for that operation had begun, but the indicators were not favorable.

General Lucht initially believed that the French, who had broken through the northern flank all the way to Contrexéville–Vittel, consisted only of a relatively weak armored task force.[121] That enemy element was to be engaged and beaten back from the southeast and east with all available force. Lieutenant Colonel Horst von Usedom's 112th Panzer Brigade was assigned two assembly areas that were twenty-five kilometers apart. The 2112th Panzer Battalion, with about forty-five PzKpfw IV Panzers, was sent to Darney. The 1st Battalion of the 29th Panzer Regiment, with about forty-five PzKpfw V Panthers, was assigned the area around Dompaire.[122]

But when General Wiese, the commanding general of the Nineteenth Army, arrived at the command post of the LXVI Army Corps in Bains-les-Bains to issue orders between 1800 and 2000 hours on

September 12, events now showed that the assumptions upon which Lucht had based the starting point of his assessment were no longer valid.[123] The corps headquarters estimated that the enemy force in the north consisted of sixty to eighty tanks from the French 2nd Armored Division.[124] The spearhead of that force had already probed beyond Vittel to the east and southeast.[125] That thrust not only cut off the battalions of the 16th Infantry Division from the rear, but also seriously threatened the German attack preparations. The French had beaten their opponents to the punch and inflicted losses on one of the two German Panzer battalions even before it had reached its assembly area. Five Panthers of the 1st Battalion, 29th Panzer Regiment, driving one behind the other on the way to Dompaire were "knocked out by novel phosphorus ammunition."[126] The French 2nd Armored Division obviously had approached to within a few kilometers of the assembly areas. And Usedom's brigade still had only a little fuel, which is why the situation quickly turned critical.[127]

Neither the headquarters of the LXVI Army Corps nor the 112th Panzer Brigade believed there now was any sense in trying to execute the planned offensive operation. Both Usedom and Colonel Siebert, the chief of staff of the LXVI Army Corps, believed that the best course of action would be to pull the Panzers back to protect Epinal on the Mosel River and immediately order the 16th Infantry Division to break through to the southeast.[128] Citing Hitler's stand fast order, however, Wiese forbade any pullout.[129] He was not satisfied with the measures and intentions so far. He also sensed a general feeling of nervousness rather than élan in Lucht's headquarters.[130] Wiese concluded that a Panzer headquarters had to lead the attack. Lieutenant General Edgar Feuchtinger, the commanding general of the 21st Panzer Division, was the prime candidate for that assignment, but to Wiese's frustration all communications with Feuchtinger had been lost.[131] After a long discussion, General of Panzer Troops Heinrich von Lüttwitz, the commanding general of the XLVII Panzer Corps, agreed to take over.[132] He did so under protest, pointing out that the plan he was to execute was not his.[133] He also expressly pointed out that he did not have the necessary information. Nevertheless, he would assume command of the attacking group the following day, on September 13.[134]

It was now too late, of course, to make any changes in the rather dubious deployment plan. The mounting of the concentrated Panzer thrust required the 2112th Panzer Battalion to attack initially toward

Dompaire—as soon as it had enough fuel. In the event, the hope of thus combining both Panzer battalions and then going into the actual attack failed in the afternoon of September 13.[135] While on its way to Dompaire, at Ville-sur-Illon the 2112th Panzer Battalion was forced on the defensive by a superior Allied force.[136] At that point the situation of the 1st Battalion, 29th Panzer Regiment, in Dompaire had already become hopeless. Even before the fuel arrived, the Panthers were hit by a heavy fighter-bomber attack at 0845 hours, which knocked out ten tanks immediately.[137] Two subsequent air strikes followed a few hours later. Around noon, elements of the French 2nd Armored Division were able to encircle at Dompaire the remnants of the German tank force that were still able to fight.[138]

The operations staffs of Army Group G, the Fifth Panzer Army, and the Nineteenth Army agreed in the evening that there was no longer any hope of success if the attacks were to be continued with the objective of preserving the frontline salient for the offensive.[139] Speaking to his chief of staff, Lieutenant General Walter Botsch, Blaskowitz noted that the time had now come to request approval to pull out and establish a bridgehead at Epinal–Belfort.[140] Botsch agreed that it was now necessary to make the decision to withdraw from the bulge that protruded so far to the west.[141]

The Nineteenth Army headquarters, however, thought that an attempt should be made to first reassemble the battered 112th Panzer Brigade and to have it attack once more to help the cut-off 16th Infantry Division to escape.[142] But that effort failed too. Only four Panthers were able to escape from Dompaire and join the 2112th Panzer Battalion.[143] The attack that bogged down as soon as it started had to be broken off once and for all on September 14 because of the unexpectedly heavy Panzer losses.[144] (See Map 22.)

The attempt to hold the area intended as the pivot for Hitler's offensive from the retreat, which had little chance of success from the very beginning, had now failed with heavy losses. The 112th Panzer Brigade lost about five hundred men and sixty-one of its ninety Panzers.[145] The battalions of the 16th Infantry Division that had been salvaged laboriously from southwestern France were destroyed almost completely or captured.[146] Blaskowitz agreed with Botsch, who once again phoned higher headquarters to request authorization to shorten the front line.[147] By noon on September 14 Army Group G headquarters in Molsheim, near Strassburg, was working on the development of a new course of action and decision.[148]

At 1230 hours Blaskowitz reported to OB West that his army group was trying with all the means at its command to preserve the salient forward of the Vosges Mountains. But because of the unfavorable developments along the northern and southern flanks of that bulge, the lead elements of the Allied spearheads were now only forty kilometers apart. Blaskowitz and Manteuffel thus believed that the area forward of the Vosges Mountains had become so narrow that the planned operation from that area no longer seemed feasible.

Instead, the commander of Army Group G recommended that the units of the Fifth Panzer Army that still could be assembled should mount an attack east of the Mosel River from the St. Dié–Rambervillers–Epinal area to the north, with the objective of hitting in the flank the Allied forces that had crossed the river on both sides of Nancy. And, according to Blaskowitz, the Nineteenth Army would finally receive authorization to fight its way back to the Charmes–Epinal–forward of Belfort line.[149]

Field Marshal von Rundstedt agreed with this assessment and that afternoon he ordered it to be transmitted to Führer Headquarters with the emphasis that "an immediate decision is requested."[150] During that night Hitler finally yielded to this clear and resolute recommendation.[151] At that very moment when Hitler generally agreed with Blaskowitz's and Rundstedt's recommendations, two things were basically decided.[152] First of all, the left wing of the Western Front, the Nineteenth Army, which until then had been echeloned far forward, could now pull back and withdraw to a shortened position that extended from the Mosel River at Nancy all the way to the Belfort Gap. In addition, Hitler now all but abandoned his notions of mounting a counteroffensive directly from the retreat. But looking at it overall, the military situation undoubtedly had changed in favor of the Germans during the days leading up to the start of the second ten-day period in September. Considering the disastrous situation in which the German Army of the West had been at the start of the month, the situation at the halfway point now seemed encouraging enough.

The German front line, however, was not yet consolidated to the point where it would be possible to hold the necessary reserves back for a large-scale counteroffensive and to deploy them in an orderly fashion. That operation, which did not get beyond its initial stage, once again proved the importance of the weather and its influence on the Allies' control of the air—something that Field Marshal von Rundstedt previously had pointed out in vain.

Looking at it in retrospect, it becomes even clearer how important such an operation was in Hitler's strategy. Its execution would have resulted in the heaviest concentration of German Panzers in the West to that point. The failure of the attempt to shift from the retreat movement directly into a flanking offensive was a major factor in Hitler's decision to launch the Ardennes Offensive later, both in terms of timing and force structure.[153] The realization that such a vast operation could be launched only from a consolidated, solid, and compact front line had finally prevailed. In General Heinz Guderian's opinion, the reconstitution of the Panzer units necessary for this operation could commence only in October.[154] Considering the coming period of bad weather, it thus appeared that the last two months of 1944 would be the time span that could be considered as the earliest for a decisive major German offensive.

Chapter 12

The End of the Retreat Operations in the West and the Transition to Positional Warfare

1. The German Army of the West's Defensive Fight between Aachen and Nancy

Hitler and the Wehrmacht High Command entertained plans for an offensive through the end of 1944. But the various operations staffs in the west were fully occupied with preventing the defense line between Antwerp and Belfort from collapsing again in the face of the pressure from the Allied offensives. As Field Marshals Rundstedt and Model had made clear as early as September 7, the point of acute danger was located in the Aachen area. Both commanders expected an enemy thrust via the old imperial city toward the Rhein-Westphalia industrial region.[1]

That fear seemed to be confirmed when on the evening of September 12 American troops occupied the first West Wall pillbox south of the city. In the event, however, that was not the beginning of a large-scale breakthrough offensive. As noted earlier, Lieutenant General Hodges, commanding the U.S. First Army, had decided to advance cautiously. But he did allow the two corps near the Reich border to conduct a reconnaissance-in-force.

Major General Collins, commanding the U.S. VII Corps west of the Aachen–Monschau line, was satisfied with that concession for the moment. His G-2 section assumed that the Germans could only fight a delaying action there. Collins, therefore, wanted to punch through the West Wall during the reconnaissance phase.[2] He ordered three divisions—the U.S. 3rd Armored and 1st and 9th Infantry Divisions—of his corps to line up for the attack along a thirty-kilometer sector. The city of Aachen itself was to be spared, but from the very beginning, no plans had been made to establish a definite main effort. A certain concentration of American forces developed only in what was known as the "Stolberg Corridor," through which the 3rd Armored Division was supposed to move with its flanks screened by infantry.[3]

The preparations for a thrust into the territory of the Reich proceeded in a similar manner on the right wing of the U.S. First Army. The estimate of the enemy situation developed by Lieutenant General Gerow's U.S. V Corps agreed essentially with that of the VII Corps. The American planners estimated some seven thousand Germans in the sector of the U.S. VII Corps and perhaps only six thousand Germans in the forty-kilometer-wide sector of the U.S. V Corps, which ran west of the line from Prüm to Bitburg.[4] Gerow had the U.S. 5th Armored and the 4th and 28th Infantry Divisions. He intended to have one of his divisions advance in the direction of Prüm–Bitburg. He picked September 14 as the date for the V Corps attack.[5] Combat operations near Aachen began earlier.

The LXXXI Army Corps, which held the positions on the German side, was very weak. Lieutenant General Friedrich Schack had only the worn-out 275th and 49th Infantry Divisions on the right wing between Maastricht and Aachen.[6] The battle groups of the 9th Panzer Division[7] and 116th Panzer Division, with about forty battle tanks, were located in the Aachen–Roetgen area, about ten kilometers north of Monschau.[8] The 353rd Infantry Division was behind them.

The sector against which Collins intended to send his tanks was still one of the strongest defensive positions along the entire Seventh Army front, but there was little prospect that it could withstand an American attack for any length of time.[9] The German military command also faced a problem that was mostly beyond its control. On September 11, Hitler ordered the evacuation of the population in the threatened territories in the west, including the city and rural areas around Aachen.[10] The Nazi Party officials as well as the police stations that were responsible for conducting the evacuation, however, simply pulled out without first making it clear to the population that anybody who did not leave the city immediately would be considered a traitor. That resulted in the eruption of an immediate panic behind the German lines, as the disorganized civilian population was driven into the streets with no guidance.[11]

By that point American units had taken the first West Wall pill-box along the outskirts of the city. Farther south, the Americans had passed the little town of Roetgen, closing to the front of the line of dragon's teeth antitank obstacles that formed the "Scharnhorst Line."[12] Then things became quiet again in this sector. When the U.S. VII Corps launched its attack on the morning of September 13, Aachen was virtually unprotected. The 116th Panzer Division was not yet in the position that it was ordered to occupy to the west and southwest of the city, because the minefields and the barriers made the terrain difficult to traverse. Lieutenant General von Schwerin, therefore, ordered his division to assemble and refit north of Aachen, after it withdrew through the West Wall.[13]

The division was able to move into the front line at the earliest in the afternoon of September 14. In the meantime, the division commander tried to bring the panic in Aachen under control. With the help of the military police and some officers, he stopped the "evacuation." Then, assuming that the American troops would be moving into the city shortly, Schwerin posted a letter in English at the city's telephone exchange asking the American commander to treat the population in a humane fashion.[14]

On that same day, General Brandenberger, the commanding general of the Seventh Army, anticipated Aachen's fall at any moment.[15] But the American division's axis of attack ran past the southern edge of the city. By the evening the two combat commands of the 3rd Armored Division were able to break through the Scharnhorst Line at Kornelimünster and Roetgen.[16] By noon on September 14, the Americans were already five kilometers south of Stolberg.[17] Major General Müller's 9th Panzer Division resisted them stubbornly, but the German forces no longer had the combat power to maintain a successful defense.[18] In the meantime, Schwerin's division had reached its frontline positions.

Field Marshal Model now urgently requested additional reinforcements in addition to the Replacement Army units and the five fortress battalions that already had arrived in the LXXXI Army Corps sector.[19] He believed that Aachen would be lost unless he received those forces.[20] But the deterioration of the situation could hardly be prevented with the immediate support that OB West was able to provide—which amounted to one artillery battalion.

Rundstedt, meanwhile, ordered the speedup of the rail deployment of the 12th Infantry Division. He also sent thirty-one Panzers to the Düren area, and put the 107th and 108th Panzer Brigades on hold for Army Group B.[21] Those actions, however, would only produce effects over the course of the next several days. The crisis in this sector of the front line reached its climax on September 15. (See Map 23.)

The U.S. 3rd Armored Division had already broken through the "Schill Line" on both sides of Stolberg by that evening, and the U.S. 9th Infantry Division also had penetrated that line.[22] Colonel von Gersdorff alerted General Krebs to the dangerous fact that the Aachen–Cologne autobahn started in the penetration area and would make an ideal avenue of advance to the Rhine.[23] Hitler reacted to the threat in the LXXXI Army Corps sector in his typical way. In his notes, Jodl recorded the führer's order[24]: "Every inch of ground in the West Wall was to be treated like a fortress."[25]

Subsequent orders were ever tougher. On September 15, Westphal alerted Army Group B headquarters that Hitler ordered each individual house in Aachen to be defended exactly the way the Russians had defended Stalingrad.[26] On the following day, Rundstedt announced the receipt of yet another Führer Order. The fact that the enemy had reached the territory of the Reich must "fanaticize the fighting to the utmost degree of toughness in the battle zone, employing every physically capable man.[27] Every pillbox, every city block, . . . every German village must become a fortress. Commanders of all ranks are responsible to make sure that this fanaticism will be constantly increased among the troops and the *population*. . . . Anybody . . . regardless of whether he is a leader or a plain soldier, who does not do his job by fully committing his very own life, will be eliminated."[28]

It is impossible to reconstruct realistically the effect such orders actually had on the fighting spirit of the troops. On a previous and extensive visit to the front, Rundstedt had already noted that in contrast to armament and training, the esprit and morale of the troops was good.[29] The officer maintaining the LXXX Army Corps war diary noted on September 10 that the order to move into the West Wall did give the troops a particular boost. "The Officers and enlisted men feel, perhaps without knowing it, that the fighting . . . is now entering a new phase."[30]

Similar testimony came from the LXXIV Army Corps in the Monschau–Ormont sector. Colonel von Gersdorff found there a considerable incremental improvement in fighting spirit resulting from the stable situation along the West Wall, which had been occupied on September 13–14.[31] Obviously, the worn-out combat units of the German Army of the West regained control of themselves quickly after the hardships of the retreat. Simultaneously, the units of the Replacement Army that were transferred from the home front to the battlefront acquitted themselves well.[32] Only the provisionally assembled Luftwaffe fortress battalions—which consisted primarily of Luftwaffe personnel with hardly any infantry training—had practically no combat value.[33] In general, the German Army of the West by the middle of September 1944 was lacking in trained personnel and equipment, but not in fighting spirit. Nonetheless, the crisis south of Aachen could not be resolved without manpower and equipment reserves.

There were no indications that the Americans would move against the weakest sector in the defense line north of the city. The U.S. XIX Corps attacked north from the Maastricht–Aachen line. Major General Charles Corlett was for the time being forced to stick to that axis of advance because he was worried about his left flank, with the British Second Army heading toward Eindhoven.[34] Lieutenant General Friedrich Schack's right wing did keep withdrawing, but he was able to maintain contact with the First Parachute Army, which had evacuated Maastricht during the night between September 13 and 14.[35] So far there was no danger in that sector of an Allied breakthrough into the territory of the Reich. September 15 was a particularly critical day for the German command in the west, and not only because of the situation at Stolberg. Gerow's infantry units had come to a halt at the West Wall in front of Prüm, but to the south armored units of the U.S. V Corps had broken deeply through the German lines.[36]

On the afternoon of September 14 the Americans hit a particularly weak point at Wallendorf, along the boundary between the two German army groups. There the U.S. 5th Armored Division was facing little more than a German battalion of stragglers that had moved into the position just a few hours earlier. The commanding officer, Major Heutelbeck, had known his men for just three days.[37] Nevertheless, the battalion defended itself bravely and withdrew only after Wallendorf was in flames.[38] Exploiting the opportunity, the Americans had eighty tanks and one infantry regiment within five kilometers of Bitburg by the evening of September 15.[39]

The third dangerous threat developed in the Army Group G sector along the still weak boundary between the First and Nineteenth Armies. On September 14 one combat command from the U.S. XII Corps had advanced from the Dieulouard bridgehead all the way to Arracourt.[40] From there that unit established contact with the American units that had crossed the Mosel River south of Nancy. Nancy was now cut off. The 553rd Grenadier Division in Nancy was trapped, and the 15th Panzer Grenadier Division was isolated in its positions at Lunéville.[41] (See Map 24.)

Meanwhile, Patton's forces were in motion again. South of Metz they struck a wide gap between the two German field armies. Based on Eisenhower's directive of September 13, the moment had now come to shift the logistical main effort to the north and to have the U.S. Third Army go on the defensive.[42] But that did not happen.

Patton had already achieved the operational objective established for him by the Supreme Allied Commander.[43] But during the following week of September 16–22 the two American field armies continued to receive the same supply tonnage.[44] Patton, therefore, was able to pursue his ambitious offensive plans farther.[45] Eisenhower obviously saw no reason to interfere and correct that situation. The successes achieved over the past forty-eight hours misled him on September 15 to the conclusion that the Allies would probably soon take both the Ruhr and the Saar regions. In a key letter to Montgomery, Eisenhower already addressed the subject of the thrust to Berlin.[46]

Within a few days, however, it turned out that Eisenhower was wrong about the German resistance. OB West headquarters concentrated primarily on the two crisis points in the north. At Aachen, everything depended on whether the reinforcements directed to that area would actually arrive before the Allies were able to exploit their success. General Krebs also thought that the events of September 16 would indicate how things would play out southeast of Aachen.[47]

Krebs was right. The situation began to stabilize in the afternoon with the arrival of the first battle groups of the 12th Infantry Division.[48] The action of a fresh, solid, and cohesive major unit boosted the defenses of the LXXXI Army Corps, and not only numerically.[49] The OB West war diary noted that the arrival of the 12th Infantry Division had an encouraging effect on the troops and the population.[50]

Major General Collins, on the other hand, had to abandon his hope of widening the breach in the West Wall and continuing his push into the Reich.[51] He decided that any combat operations initially would have to be limited to the improvement of his existing positions.[52] According to their own estimate, the Americans now were not strong enough to continue the attack. The U.S. 3rd Armored

Division had seventy Shermans left, barely more than one-third of its authorized tank strength.[53] The Germans, too, had suffered heavy losses. During the continuous counterthrusts launched by the 12th Infantry Division the combat strength of one of its regiments dwindled down to some four hundred men within just a few days.[54] Collins now assigned the main effort to an infantry division, an indicator that the fighting had entered a new phase.

U.S. 9th Infantry Division was given the mission of advancing east from Zweifall, mopping up the wooded area up to the Kleinhau–Hürtgen–Germeter line, and in the process screening the flank of the American forces at Stolberg.[55] The fighting in that area started on September 20.[56] The men of Major General Lewis Craig's U.S. 9th Infantry Division were the first Americans to experience the horrors of operating in the Hürtgen Forest, a name now synonymous with some of the worst combat on the Western Front. By September 21, the U.S. VII Corps had enveloped Aachen in a semicircle from the south. The Americans had reached the center of the city of Stolberg and the southern outskirts of Eschweiler. From there the front line trace ran through the Hürtgen Forest into the Monschau area.[57] But the Americans had come to a standstill along that line, failing to attain Collins's objectives.

To the north of the old imperial city the advance of the U.S. XIX Corps sped up only on September 17. Corlett's two widely strung-out divisions reached the area of the German-Dutch border between Sittard and Kerkrade.[58] But the stiff German resistance at Stolberg caused Corlett to hesitate in ordering his relatively weak corps to attack the West Wall.[59] That pause again gained valuable time for the Germans. The 183rd Volksgrenadier Division had left Linz, Austria, on September 16.[60] Its first elements engaged in the fighting on the 19th, and it finally was able to establish a linkup with the First Parachute Army in the area of Waldenrath, twenty-five kilometers north of Aachen.[61] With the arrival of that division the crisis in the sector of the front line near Aachen was over for the time being. That was the second fresh major unit sent to OB West since the end of August.

But General von Schwerin's problems were just beginning. His letter to the American commander had fallen into the wrong hands. Himmler immediately jumped to the absurd conclusion that the correspondence with the Americans had prevented the evacuation of Aachen.[62] That question was cleared up relatively quickly when it became obvious that the confusing events in the city were caused by the failure of the Nazi Party officials. Hitler had no thoughts of taking any punitive actions against Schwerin.[63] Himmler, however, would not let it go.[64] In the meantime, the defensive battle against the Allies' MARKET-GARDEN Operation was the new crisis point in Army Group B. That situation pushed Model to the very limit of his capacity. But with all that on his hands, he was forced by Himmler's interference to deal with the relatively minor issue of Schwerin.

Model undoubtedly did not condone Schwerin's action, which the field marshal described as a "piece of clowning."[65] But protected by the men of his division, Schwerin went into hiding for several days after the charges against him were first lodged.[66] Model ordered Schwerin taken before an army court-martial and then to the judge advocate general at OB West headquarters.[67] General Brandenberger was detailed to assemble the points of the investigation. Model knew that the latter had from the very beginning ruled out any suspicions against Schwerin.[68] Model's order to relieve as well Schwerin's superior, Lieutenant General Friedrich Schack, obviously served the same purpose of "side-stepping any further differences with the Reichsführer-SS."[69]

Other generals of the German Army of the West shared fates similar to that of Schack, who had made a considerable contribution to the initially successful defensive fighting at Aachen.[70] Himmler kept trying to push through personnel changes with no military justification. General of Infantry Franz Beyer, the commander of the LXXX Army Corps, also ran afoul of Himmler. The Reichsführer-SS requested an investigation of Beyer on the absurd basis that the general's estimate of the situation had been "too little optimistic."[71] That happened just a few days after the American breakthrough at Wallendorf, in Beyer's frontline sector. But there again, the Americans were unable to exploit their initial success, even though the result had been an approximately six-kilometer-wide breach in the German border fortifications along the boundary between the two army groups. As an immediate response, OB West ordered the long-range action group of the III Antiaircraft Artillery Corps with eleven batteries that originally had been earmarked for Aachen to divert toward Bitburg.[72] By the evening of September 16, the LXXX Army Corps had established a thin blocking line, but the local counterattacks were unsuccessful. Rundstedt then took additional measures.

In order to delineate clearly the chain of command in that sector, he placed Beyer's corps under Army Group B's Seventh Army. Rundstedt also urged the launching of a concentric counterattack.[73] But the units allocated for that mission, including the 108th Panzer Brigade and elements of the 19th and 36th Grenadier Divisions, were not completely assembled until September 19.[74]

In the meantime, Gerow had already ordered a halt to the American thrust to Bitburg. The objective of the U.S. 5th Armored Division, reinforced by infantry units, was now merely to defend the Wallendorf bridgehead.[75] Gerow realized that the Wehrmacht was not yet at the end of their tether, and that caused him to move more deliberately. The main body of his infantry units was tied down west of Prüm, which left little possibility for reinforcing his right wing. But the concentric counterattack also inflicted heavy losses on the Germans. By the first day of the action on September 19 the 108th Panzer Brigade had lost half of its Panthers.[76]

After the first days of heavy fighting the American troops were ordered to evacuate the bridgehead on the far side of the West Wall and to return to the west bank of the Sauer River, or of the Our River that flowed in at Wallendorf.[77] By September 22 the crisis at Wallendorf had been overcome by the Germans. The main line of resistance as well as the West Wall were once again firmly in German hands. German losses totaled 900; the Americans left forty-one tanks and 530 dead on the east bank.[78] (See Map 24.) By the middle of September the American generals were still thinking in terms of pursuit and underestimating their enemy.[79] They therefore continued to push the attacks on a broad front, but with relatively little penetration force.

The American troops now faced the new conditions of pillbox and forest fighting, where their tank superiority and higher mobility gave them less of an advantage. The start of the autumn foul-weather period also limited the operations of the Allied air forces to a greater extent than during the previous months.[80]

All those factors made it easier for the German command to shift the available reserves in a timely manner to the particular focal points of combat operations. The 183rd Volksgrenadier Division was one example of this flexibility, while another involved the 12th Infantry Division, which within two and a half days was transported from the Gruppe Exercise Area near Graudenz some nine hundred kilometers to Aachen.[81] Thus the German command was able to reinforce the Seventh Army by September 20 with two fresh major infantry units, the 108th Panzer Brigade, an additional sixty Panzers, and twenty-five fortress units of battalion strength.[82]

On September 22, Hodges was forced to admit that his U.S. First Army had been brought to a halt along the entire front line.[83] The U.S. Third Army likewise was not able to reach the objectives that had been established by its commanding general. In the evening of September 20 Patton admitted for the first time that his expectations had been too optimistic.[84] But the situation in that sector of the front had not developed as Rundstedt had hoped. OB West's intention to eliminate the dangerous threat at Nancy by offensive operations and again to stabilize the Mosel River Front along the entire line as the ultimate objective simply was not possible. Rundstedt earlier and with a certain degree of confidence had ordered an attack in the general direction of Lunéville, at the latest on September 18. After smashing the Allies there, the German forces were immediately to push on toward Pont-à-Mousson. Apart from the planned combined attack by the Fifth Panzer Army on the east bank of the Mosel River, OB West also ordered the continuation of the defense of the Diedenhofen-Metz Proving Grounds.[85] That latter mission, at least, was accomplished fully. The U.S. XX Corps was not able to make any significant headway there during the static fighting and suffered heavy losses in the process. The U.S. 7th Armored Division alone lost twelve hundred men and fifty-five tanks.[86]

On September 17, Major General Walton Walker ordered his XX Corps to discontinue its attack.[87] That sector of the front remained quiet for the rest of the month. The Germans then saw an opportunity to eliminate the threat at Nancy, located farther south. There were still some armored reserves available there that could be thrown in against Patton's main attack. The battle-seasoned 3rd and 15th Panzer Grenadier Divisions were in that area, and after the arrival of their divisional Panzer battalions their combat power had increased considerably.[88] On September 17 the XIII SS Corps was able to withdraw south of Metz from the Mosel River to the east, over a distance of some ten kilometers, to the Seille River. The 3rd Panzer Grenadier Division, meanwhile, managed to regain contact with the German troops that were encircled at Nancy.[89] But in order to maintain that regained contact, Colonel Löhr was forced to withdraw his 553rd Grenadier Division to the northeast, initially to the outskirts of the city.[90]

An approximately forty-kilometer-wide hole gaped in the German front between the left wing of the First Army at Nancy and the right wing of the Nineteenth Army at Charmes–Rambervillers.[91] Isolated in the middle of the penetration area, the 15th Panzer Grenadier Division defended itself in the sector of Lunéville–Forêt de Parroy. The American thrust between Forêt de Parroy and Nancy had pushed a wedge all the way into the sector around Chateau-Salins.[92] Patton intended to conduct the offensive toward Sarreguemines–Saarbrücken from there. That operation was scheduled to commence on September 18, which was the same day Rundstedt had set for the offensive by the Fifth Panzer Army.[93] The two opposing armored forces were set on a collision course.

The German attack plan called for advancing simultaneously out of the Rambervillers–Baccarat area to the north and via Sarebourg–Blamont westward toward Lunéville. The initial task was to extract the 15th Panzer Grenadier Division from its pocket there. After the two attacking elements merged at Lunéville, the push was to continue in the direction toward Nancy to establish contact with the 553rd Grenadier Division, and then close up the front along the shortest line.[94] Considering the forces available, however, the ultimate objective of the operation, the restoration of the Mosel River line, was now only a remote possibility.

The 107th and 108th Panzer Brigades, which originally had been allocated to the operation of Manteuffel's Fifth Panzer Army, were held back with Army Group B in response to the situation in the north. The 11th Panzer Division likewise was unable to go into action because it was still tied down in the Belfort area. For the time being, then, Manteuffel's army only consisted of the battle group of the 21st Panzer Division with attached remnants of the 112th Panzer Brigade, plus the 111th and 113th Panzer Brigades.[95] A total of only about one hundred battle tanks were operational in the evening of September 17.[96]

Manteuffel and his corps commanders, therefore, looked forward to the next day with skepticism. Success was generally considered doubtful at the headquarters of Krüger's LVIII Panzer Corps, which was to launch the thrust to Blamont with the 113th Panzer Brigade.[97] The attack nonetheless started on a promising note. (See Map 24.) Group Lüttwitz, consisting of the 21st Panzer Division and the 111th Panzer Brigade, jumped off at 0745 hours from the Baccarat area and reached Lunéville about noon.[98] A littler later Colonel Heinrich Bronsart von Schellendorff's 111th Panzer Brigade penetrated into the city against tough resistance and occupied the southeastern section.[99] They established contact with the 15th Panzer Grenadier Division, thereby allowing General Krüger to assign another objective to the 113th Panzer Brigade. Colonel Erich von Seckendorff was now no longer to send his Panzers to the outskirts of the city of Lunéville, but rather was to march north of the Rhine-Marne Canal toward Champenoux, ten kilometers northeast of Nancy.[100]

Von Manteuffel now prepared to launch the thrust toward Nancy after the first attack objective had been reached with surprising speed. Initially, General of Panzer Troops Heinrich von Lüttwitz's XLVII Panzer Corps was given the mission of using the 21st Panzer Division with remnants of the 112th Panzer Brigade to establish a flank screen between Forêt de Parroy–Lunéville and the Baccarat area.[101] For this task Manteuffel also gave the XLVII Panzer Corps the 15th Panzer Grenadier Division. But the 111th Panzer Brigade was withdrawn from Lunéville. It was to cross the Rhine-Marne Canal at Parroy and reinforce Krüger's Group.[102] That attack toward Nancy began the next morning.[103]

Initially the LVIII Panzer Corps made good progress, but then came to a halt about five kilometers short of Arracourt in the afternoon of September 19.[104] Manteuffel ordered the high plateau east of the town to be seized from the enemy, but that was no longer possible.[105] The Americans quickly brought up reinforcements.[106] Toward the evening, the German Panzer brigades were hit by a flanking attack mounted by sixty Shermans that inflicted heavy losses.[107] Krüger's chief of staff, Colonel Hans-Jürgen Dingler, reported during the night that there was no longer any possibility of continuing the attack.[108] With about two hundred tanks, the American numerical superiority was now too great.[109] On the request of the LVIII Panzer Corps headquarters, Manteuffel gave the approval to shift to the defensive.[110]

During the course of September 20, Dingler's suspicion was confirmed. The spearheads of four Allied units were in the penetration area. The U.S. 4th Armored Division had broken off its main attack to the north and had turned against the LVIII Panzer Corps.[111] That afternoon the Americans coming from Chateau-Salins reached Hampont and penetrated Dieuze, but they withdrew back to the south again in the evening.[112] The tank battle at Arracourt had claimed considerable losses on both sides. Krüger's brigades only had forty-five operational battle tanks left.[113] Some sixty-five had been either destroyed or were temporarily out of action. According to German reports, the Americans lost fifty-four Sherman tanks.[114]

The attack by the Fifth Panzer Army did not achieve the desired success, but it had made it possible to establish a secure defensive front along the Dieuze–Forêt de Parroy–(eastern outskirts of) Lunéville–Rambervillers line and to intercept the American offensive heading northeast, thereby preventing the breakthrough.[115] The limited operation carried out by Manteuffel's army was now over. On September 21, the Fifth Panzer Army was assigned a solid defensive sector between the First and Nineteenth Armies.[116]

Blaskowitz, of course, gave Manteuffel a mission that was not restricted entirely to defense. Manteuffel's next objective was to close the small gap in the front line in the Vic sur Seille–Moyenvic area from the right wing, by concentrically coordinating with the left wing of the First Army. Manteuffel was promised reinforcements for that mission. But above all, as Blaskowitz emphasized, the mission was to engage the enemy again and again and to deprive him of his operational freedom.[117]

Patton's comment to the U.S. XII Corps commander, Major General Manton Eddy, also makes it clear that the German objective had been accomplished at that point. "It may be impossible to complete the mission which we started out on, but we could kill a lot of Germans trying."[118] But the information Eisenhower had obviously did not correctly reflect the true situation at the end of the second ten-day period in September. As he wrote to General Marshall concerning the operations of the U.S. First Army: "Hodges is going well. His operations are coordinated with those of Montgomery. Hodges is driving straight on to Cologne and Bonn."

There was as little truth there as there was in the statement with which he tried to inform Montgomery about the operations of U.S. Third Army: "You may not know that for four days straight Patton has been receiving serious counterattacks . . . *without attempting any real advance himself.*"[119]

Montgomery, on the other hand, obviously had realized already that the attempts to break through the center of the German Western Front in the first onrush had failed. He kept demanding that Patton be ordered to go on the defensive: "It seems clear that 12 Army Group has been allowed to outstrip its maintenance and as a result *we have lost flexibility throughout the battle area as a whole.*"[120]

2. The End of the Retreat: The Success of the Withdrawal Operations along the Outer Wings of the German Western Front

During the second ten-day period in September, the focal points of combat operations were located in the area between Arnhem and Nancy. The development of the situation along the outer wings of the front, however, turned out to be no less significant for the further course of events in the Western theater of war. In contrast to the front's center, where positional warfare had already stabilized along extensive sectors, the German lines were still fluid both in the north and in the south.

The retreat operation from southern France was halted in the Dijon bridgehead on orders from the High Command. After Hitler's plan to shift directly to a major offensive from the protruding frontline salient had failed, Blaskowitz finally was given approval to withdraw the exposed left wing of the Western Front. The corresponding Wehrmacht High Command order, however, included the restriction that the withdrawal movement could be carried out only under enemy pressure.[121] But the Allied pressure against the Nineteenth Army abated precisely at that very moment.

The Allied Operation DRAGOON units coming from the south were ordered to go into a laborious regrouping operation on September 14. The two French corps were to be combined on the right wing before Belfort. General Truscott's American units were to take over the left wing, which was oriented toward Strassburg.[122] For the time being, there were no major offensive operations along the U.S. Seventh Army's northern wing.

The advance of the U.S. XV Corps became more hesitant after the major success at Dompaire. Patton had instructed Major General Wade Haislip to postpone his thrust across the Mosel River. The commanding general of U.S. Third Army believed that a cautious advance was in order, obviously in response to the appearance of the 112th Panzer Brigade.[123]

Quiet for the first time prevailed along the front line of the Nineteenth Army on September 16.[124] But that meant that there was no decisive situation upon which the Wehrmacht High Command could have based the completion of the withdrawal. The German headquarters in the west, however, were justified in believing that it made no sense militarily to wait until the Allied attack preparations had been completed in that sector of the front. Lieutenant General Walter Botsch, chief of staff of the Nineteenth Army, noting the army's overextended lines, judged that the security screen was so thin, ". . . that one need not wonder if it simply snaps one fine day."[125]

Rundstedt and Blaskowitz, therefore, agreed to have the Nineteenth Army withdraw more rapidly into a shortened position.[126] The commander of Army Group G hoped that this would allow him to constitute some reserves and to send the resultantly released forces of the Fifth Panzer Army to close the frontline gap in the Nancy area.[127] In the evening of September 17, without enemy pressure, General Wiese issued the orders.[128] His Nineteenth Army would finally evacuate the frontline salient the following night.[129] Hitler issued a counterorder that an accelerated withdrawal was out of the question; but that order arrived too late—at least according to Rundstedt—to stop the movement.[130]

Throughout September 18, Wiese's units moved back into a frontline trace that ran roughly north-south from the Mosel River at Châtel via Epinal–Remiremont to the Belfort area.[131] The operational-level threat of the Nineteenth Army being cut off was over, and the final stage of the great retreat operation from southern and southwestern France was finished. Blaskowitz had played a decisive role in the final outcome. What had started with a catastrophic initial situation produced impressive results in the end. The southern sector of the German front line had been stabilized—at least for the time being.

Of the some 235,000 soldiers who had started on the march back, more than 160,000 reached the Dijon bridgehead.[132] On September 20, the Nineteenth Army headquarters still reported a ration strength of 130,000 troops.[133] Like OB West, Hitler at the end of August also had doubted that Blaskowitz would accomplish the difficult operation successfully. But Hitler no longer felt obligated by his comment at the time that he would ask Blaskowitz's pardon if he pulled it off.[134] Blaskowitz's "mistake" in not holding the deployment area for Hitler's offensive from the move overshadowed the success of the withdrawal. The die was now cast for a change in command. Himmler and some other Nazi Party functionaries apparently had long been preparing the ground for Blaskowitz's removal.[135] The justification for that action was based on the speed of the Nineteenth Army's withdrawal, which had been too fast to suit the führer's taste.

Rundstedt supported Blaskowitz with the very clear statement that all the withdrawal actions had been unavoidable considering the relative strength situation. There was, therefore, no blame that could be laid against the commander of Army Group G, and furthermore Rundstedt himself bore full responsibility for everything that was happening in his area of command.[136] Hitler nonetheless refused to change his decision. Even before the change in command became official, rumors were rife at Army Group G headquarters in Molsheim.[137] The background may not have been known, but the incident that cost Blaskowitz his position certainly was.

The reaction of the chief of staff, then, was only logical. Gyldenfeldt told Colonel Friedrich Schulz, the Nineteenth Army operations officer, that in the future there should be a little more verbiage in the reports on enemy activities so as to justify to the High Command any gradual withdrawal to the Vosges Mountains that would become necessary sooner or later.[138] According to the activity report of the chief of the Army Personnel Office, Hitler made his decision on September 19. Blaskowitz's relief was ordered, the report states with unintended irony, because the retreat operations had not been conducted in the manner intended.[139] That undoubtedly was true, but in a sense completely different from what had been meant. The Germans, in fact, had expected the worst as soon as the Operation DRAGOON forces began their campaign of maneuver in Provence. It was primarily to Blaskowitz's credit that the worst-case scenario did not occur. The campaign of maneuver had now drawn to an end in the south. On September 21, General of Panzer Troops Hermann Balck arrived in Molsheim to take command of Army Group G.[140] He would lead the army group during the new phase of the fighting.

In the meantime, there were no major Allied attacks in the Nineteenth Army sector or on the right wing of the Western Front prior to the start of Operation MARKET-GARDEN. The relative quiet in front of the main line of resistance of the Fifteenth Army and the First Parachute Army was tied to Montgomery's impending major offensive. The intelligence section of Army Group B had analyzed the objectives of the British commander early and accurately. Since September 8 the Germans had assumed that Montgomery's center of gravity was no longer in the area of the Scheldt River estuary. The preparations of the 21st Army Group now indicated an offensive by way of Eindhoven into the area of Arnhem–Nijmegen–Wesel.[141] Just five days later the German assessment was confirmed by reports of minor enemy attack activity against the bridgehead south of the Westerschelde River. The Allies obviously were planning to conduct a major offensive "in a northeasterly direction to encircle all German forces *in depth*[142] in Western Holland."[143]

Accordingly, the main effort had to be on the eastern wing of the 21st Army Group. That was indicated by the fact that Dempsey's British Second Army tried to extend on both flanks the wedge that was pointing toward Eindhoven, since that wedge probably was intended as the springboard for the offensive. The British were successful, forcing the center and left wing of Colonel General Kurt Student's First Parachute Army to withdraw and evacuate the area between the Albert Canal and the Meuse–Scheldt Canal.[144]

The Canadian advance toward the bridgehead south of the Scheldt River, however, became even more hesitant. The attempt to cross the Leopold Canal at Moerkerke failed with bloody losses on September 14. Lieutenant General Guy Simonds, the commander of the Canadian II Corps, then confined himself "to maintain contact . . . *without sacrificing forces* in driving out an enemy, who may be retreating."[145] Montgomery's instructions to the Canadian First Army contained the misleading instruction that the opening of the Scheldt River mouth "will be a *first priority* for Canadian Army" and "The *whole energies of the army* will be directed towards operations designed to enable full use to be made of the port of Antwerp."[146] That, however, was irrelevant, at least for the next several weeks. Instead, Montgomery at the same time ordered Lieutenant General Crerar to capture the ports of Boulogne and Calais.[147] Thus, only the Canadian 4th Division and the Polish 1st Armored Division up to that point were available for the task of attacking the German bridgehead along the Scheldt River. According to Montgomery's enemy order of battle estimate, there were only relatively weak forces on the western wing of his army group in the Brügge–Antwerp–Herentals area.[148]

That explains why General of Infantry Gustav von Zangen considered the Canadian units that followed his Fifteenth Army to be just one of his problems. The question of whether the major retreat operation of the Fifteenth Army across the Scheldt River could in the end help stabilize the German Western Front depended on other factors. The very feasibility of the difficult crossing operation itself even remained in doubt for the time being. But that crossing offered the only prospect at all of supplying the First Parachute Army with additional forces in time before the anticipated British offensive achieved an operational-level breakthrough in that sector. Furthermore, it was important for Zangen to block the Scheldt River mouth in such a lasting fashion that the Allies would be denied the logistic exploitation of the harbor of Antwerp for as long as possible. The immediate plan, therefore, was to leave four divisions, in other words half of the Fifteenth Army, back in that area. The 64th Infantry Division was to defend the Breskens bridgehead; the 70th Infantry Division was to defend Walcheren; the 245th Infantry Division was to defend Südbeveland; and the 331st Infantry Division was to defend the islands located to the north and all the way to the mouth of the Meuse River.[149]

The remaining four divisions were earmarked for commitment on the mainland to support the main front of Army Group B. Besides the 64th Infantry Division, which remained behind on the south bank of the Scheldt River, seven major units had to cross the five-kilometer-wide estuary.[150]

Two of those units reached the mainland by September 14. General of Infantry Otto Sponheimer's LXVII Army Corps with the 346th and 711th Infantry Divisions had already reinforced the right wing of the First Parachute Army in the Antwerp area. Nevertheless, the forces of Student's army, in Field Marshal Model's estimation, would not suffice to beat back the impending British offensive—even after the arrival of the hastily refitted 10th SS Panzer Division.[151]

There was, however, no way to speed up the retreat operation across the Scheldt River. Earlier, Allied aircraft had been able to block temporarily the harbor exit at Terneuzen by sinking several barges.[152] A second major ferry connection also was interrupted temporarily by air raids on September 15. Allied bombers heavily damaged the Breskens landing.[153] In addition to the two main ferries, the Germans since September 12 also had been using the passage between Doel and Lillo, about fifteen kilometers northwest of Antwerp.[154] But that ferry link was within the range of Canadian artillery. On September 16, the artillery fire was so heavy that all crossing traffic came to a halt.[155] There was, however, never a complete standstill. Because of the threat from the air, the movements of troops and equipment and the berthing operations of the boats now took place only during the hours of darkness or in fog.[156] Despite the tremendous difficulties, the retreat operation continued. The very possibility of such an operation was a masterpiece of coordination by the German army and navy elements involved.[157]

The indirect but hardly voluntary support from the Dutch also played no inconsiderable role. Krebs, for example, ordered a delay in the demolitions at the ports of Amsterdam and Rotterdam, although clearance had already been given by OB West. Krebs was afraid that the otherwise expected change in the mood of the Dutch population would have negative consequences for the Fifteenth Army. He emphasized that Zangen's forces depended on Dutch vessels, at least until September 21.[158]

The key point to remember here is that any Allied main efforts were now somewhere else—not in the area of the Scheldt estuary and Antwerp. Even the Canadian II Corps, which was operating against the Fifteenth Army's bridgehead with two divisions, opened another effort on September 17, with the attack on Fortress Boulogne.[159] After a heavy bombardment of the port city, the Canadians jumped off with one infantry division and two tank regiments, supported by 330 artillery pieces.[160] On the German side, Lieutenant General Ferdinand Heim faced the attackers with just about ten thousand men.

At just about the same time, Operation MARKET-GARDEN, the long-anticipated Allied major offensive, started some three hundred kilometers farther to the northeast. By that point two corps headquarters and five infantry divisions of the Fifteenth Army had already crossed the Westerschelde River.[161] Three of those units were in the meantime committed on the mainland.[162] That undoubtedly facilitated Model's defensive measures at the new focal point of crisis in Army Group B. Considering the situation, the field marshal also requested the commitment of the 712th and 245th Infantry Divisions.[163] Those two units were still waiting to cross the river to be moved into the Tilburg area.[164] The crossings were accomplished, although the situation south of the Scheldt River was now becoming critical. Advancing along the Ghent–Terneuzen Canal, Lieutenant General Simonds's tank units penetrated deeply into the German defensive positions on September 19.[165]

The eastern part of the German bridgehead had to be abandoned, and the ferry transport operations were shifted entirely to Breskens. The German units, including the 712th Infantry Division, that were stationed between the Ghent–Terneuzen Canal and in the area northwest of Antwerp were able to cross at Doel. Once that was accomplished, the ferrying operations were finally halted there as well.[166] The Canadian attack, however, had come too late and failed to produce any decisive results.

By September 22 the last units of the 245th and 712th Infantry Divisions had evacuated the bridgehead.[167] Nonetheless, eleven thousand troops of the 64th Infantry Division remained behind to defend Fortress Scheldt-South.[168] Altogether, about eighty-five thousand German troops and more than 530 artillery pieces, 4,600 vehicles, and 4,000 horses had been ferried across the Westerschelde River.[169]

Compared to the impressive numerical results of this German "little Dunkirk," any success achieved by the Canadians hundreds of kilometers farther to the west were rather insignificant.[170] The capture of Boulogne did not produce any direct advantage for the Allies. The approximately ninety-five hundred German soldiers taken prisoner there left behind harbor facilities whose infrastructure had been paralyzed to such an extent that it was useless for Allied logistics operations for the immediate future.[171]

By far, the most decisive aspect of the combat operations on September 22, 1944, was the successful completion of the German withdrawal movement across the Scheldt River according to plan. That most probably would not have happened if the Canadians had not diverted so much of their combat power to the capture of Fortress Boulogne. The net result was that the major retreat operations of the German Army of the West had now come to a halt.[172] And as a direct result, the Germans were able to shorten their front lines on the two outer wings, thereby freeing up forces that were badly needed at other critical points in the fighting.

Five divisions of the Fifteenth Army had reached the mainland since the middle of the month. In the judgment of General of Infantry Gustav von Zangen, those soldiers still retained an absolutely strong fighting spirit after the successful retreat operation.[173] And those five divisions reinforced Model's Army Group B at just the right moment. Those reserves facilitated Model's defensive measures during the extremely critical phase of reactions to Operation MARKET-GARDEN.

3. The Failure of Operation MARKET-GARDEN

Operation MARKET-GARDEN, the largest airborne operation of World War II, has already been the subject of numerous studies and works of history.[174] We can, therefore, dispense with a detailed description of that operation here. We should, however, examine the reasons why it failed.

According to Eisenhower, the primary objective of MARKET-GARDEN and the main effort in Allied combat operations was the establishment of a bridgehead on the north bank of the Rhine River (Nederrijn).[175] That bridgehead, then, would be used as a base of departure for the offensive against Germany's industrial Ruhr region. As noted previously, the Allies planned to commit airborne units behind the German front lines to seize the most important bridges in the sector between Eindhoven and Arnhem, and thus facilitate the rapid thrust by the British XXX Corps toward IJsselmeer. The airborne landings were to commence at 1400 hours on September 17. The U.S. 101st Airborne Division would drop in the Eindhoven–Veghel area; the U.S. 82nd Airborne Division would land south of Nijmegen; and the British 1st Airborne Division would land northwest of Arnhem.[176] According to the plan, Horrocks's XXX Corps would jump off for the breakthrough attack one hour after the start of the drops. The Allies obviously hoped that the shock effect of the operation might also trigger a rapid German collapse.[177]

The crucial reason why MARKET-GARDEN failed is that the Allies' estimate of the enemy situation upon which it was based was no longer accurate by the time the operation started. During the first ten-day period in September, while MARKET-GARDEN was in its final planning phase, the Allied command believed that the Germans were on the brink of defeat. Indicators of stiffening resistance had, of course, been identified; but there was hardly anything to indicate what force the Germans might be capable of mustering to oppose the offensive.

When Eisenhower approved the operation on September 10, the estimate of the enemy situation was still valid, at least for the northern sector of the front.[178] It is only against the background of the situation as of that moment that the Allied optimism can be justified, which in turn explains why certain risks were not identified and the weaknesses inherent in the basic operational concept were not credited with any special significance.

The Allied command knew that the II SS Panzer Corps was in the southern Holland area for refitting with the 9th and 10th SS Panzer Divisions. But Eisenhower and especially Montgomery were so sure of success that this intelligence from ULTRA and the report[179] confirmed by information from the Dutch Resistance did not result in a modification to the operations plan.[180]

The assumption that MARKET, the airborne phase of the operation, could be executed within the three successive days of September 17–19 undoubtedly carried a significant risk based on the generally uncertain weather conditions at that time of year.[181] Another assumption was that the element of surprise was not really necessary. The presumably safer course of action was preferred over the bolder option in the Nijmegen–Arnhem area because the Allied command was not anticipating any major German countermeasures. To avoid the fire of the German antiaircraft guns, the U.S. 82nd Airborne Division and the British 1st Airborne Division were to drop well outside both cities—in other words, at a considerable distance from the bridges that were their objectives.[182]

Another serious weakness in the basic concept was the fact that GARDEN, the ground operation by the XXX Corps, had to run almost entirely along a single route of advance that led via Eindhoven–St. Oedenrode–Veghel–Grave–Nijmegen.[183] The corps' twenty thousand motor vehicles were restricted largely to this single highway link because of the numerous drainage ditches, canals, and rivers throughout the sector.[184] Nevertheless, the overly optimistic Allies expected that the spearhead of the XXX Corps would thrust more than ninety kilometers to reach Arnhem by the evening of September 20, and reach IJsselmeer two days later.[185]

Lieutenant General Horrocks did not even reach Arnhem. The overall failure of MARKET-GARDEN, however, can be blamed only to a limited extent on its conceptual weaknesses and risks. The resultant problems undoubtedly made it difficult for the Allies to conduct combat operations. The bad flying weather disrupted the airborne landings starting on the second day of the operation.[186] Those difficulties, however, could certainly have been overcome if the Germans at that point in time were still really as weak and disorganized as the Allied commanders assumed. The Allies were obviously taken by surprise by the German defensive reactions, and especially by the speed with which they reacted. But even before the operation started, information was available that could have challenged Montgomery's assessment that "the enemy is expecting our attack at that point last of all."[187] ULTRA intelligence could have been analyzed to conclude that the Germans were absolutely preparing for an offensive in the vast Eindhoven–Arnhem sector.[188] As discussed in the preceding chapter, that indeed was the fact.

Army Group B headquarters anticipated major airborne landings by the Allied First Airborne Army based in Great Britain in conjunction with Dempsey's offensive that had been feared for days.[189] Of course, the exact time and place were unknown. The Army Group B Intelligence Section believed that the area east of the Rhine between Wesel and Hamm was particularly vulnerable.[190] The shortest distance between that area and the actual landing zones was about fifty kilometers—Wesel–Groesbeek near Nijmegen.

A few days earlier the Netherlands had still been considered a potential target area and the Germans initiated certain precautions there as well. For example, the war diary officer of Army Group B recorded on September 10: "Because an enemy landing operation cannot be ruled out based on reliable indicators, all required measures have been taken in the Netherlands."[191] The pertinent orders went out during the night leading up to September 11. All the German units in the Netherlands initially were put on Alert Level II. The II SS Panzer Corps was ordered to prepare all available forces to defend against any enemy airborne landings or for operations along the coast.

Bittrich's corps also was ordered to maintain close liaison with the Wehrmacht Commander, Netherlands. The latter's headquarters was ordered to hold in readiness transportation assets for the units committed along the Waal River to facilitate a rapid movement to the center of gravity sectors.[192]

Then the appropriate headquarters of the Replacement Army, Defense District VI, also was alerted. General of Infantry Franz Mattenklott's staff was to evaluate the extent to which Defense District VI could release supporting forces in the event of an Allied operation in the Netherlands.[193] Thus, the German command authorities that would have to react to any airborne landings behind the front were alerted early on that such an operation was possibly impending. That was one of the key measures that facilitated the rapid reaction to the crisis by the German forces. The Wehrmacht Senior Officer, Wesel, for example, was able to report that prepared defensive measures had been launched even while the first Allied airborne wave was landing.[194] But just how effective those measures would prove hung in the balance during the first hours. By around 1520 hours some twenty thousand Allied soldiers were already on the ground behind the German front lines.[195]

Model personally experienced Operation MARKET from close up. Army Group B's command post at Oosterbeek near Arnhem was practically in the jump zone of the British 1st Airborne Division. The field marshal issued the terse order to his staff, "Let's get out of here—Assembly point: Terborg!" Then he went to Bittrich's II SS Panzer Corps in Doetinchem.[196] From there he personally directed the first German countermeasures.[197]

Just three-quarters of an hour after the start of the airborne landings, Army Group B headquarters marched in a calm and orderly manner through Arnhem heading for Terborg, about ten kilometers northeast of Emmerich.[198] The Allied intentions were estimated quite clearly within a short period of time. An officer from the U.S. 101st Airborne Division was captured carrying documents that yielded important conclusions.[199] That undoubtedly facilitated the rapid coordination of the defensive action.

German counterattacks were under way by the morning of September 18 throughout the entire sector between Eindhoven and Arnhem.[200] The units committed there varied widely in their combat effectiveness. Battle-seasoned units of the Wehrmacht and the Waffen-SS[201] fought side by side with soldiers of the Replacement Army[202] as well as the battle groups pulled together from navy and Luftwaffe personnel.[203]

The decisive fact, however, was the resistance the Allies quickly encountered everywhere, which prevented them from developing their attack fully. Field Marshal Model, therefore, was rather confident in the beginning. The thrust by the British 1st Airborne Division toward Arnhem had been blocked and the unit itself was now surrounded in Oosterbeek and under concentric attack by German forces.[204] Only one British battalion was able to fight its way through to the north end of the bridge, but it was soon pushed back.[205]

Horrocks's XXX Corps likewise had not achieved any major successes by September 18 and was still in the Eindhoven area.[206] The situation in Nijmegen, therefore, was not immediately threatening because the bridges were still in German hands. General of Infantry Hans Krebs hoped that the U.S. 82nd Airborne Division could be held in check by the German counterattack that was progressing well.[207] Model now wanted to close up the front south of the Waal River again.[208] He therefore ordered the bridges at Nijmegen not to be blown.[209] That turned out to be a mistake.[210] During the night leading up to September 21, American paratroopers supported by tanks of the British Guards Armoured Division were able to overwhelm the German troops in Nijmegen. When the demolition order was finally issued, it was too late.[211]

Nevertheless, German forces did manage to block the Allied advance a few kilometers north of Nijmegen.[212] The advance was halted there amid heavy losses on both sides.[213] Operating off the main road to Arnhem, the British were still able to establish contact with the Polish 1st Separate Airborne Brigade, which had landed at Driel on the south bank of the Rhine. But it was no longer possible to reinforce the remnants of the 1st Airborne Division on the north bank after it had been squeezed by German pressure into an area of 1,500 meters by 500 meters.[214] That meant it was now impossible for the Allies to establish a bridgehead beyond the Nederrijn.

The concentric counterattacks that Model ordered at the base of the narrow corridor extending from Eindhoven all the way to before Arnhem decisively contributed to the failure of the XXX Corps to punch its way through and cross the Rhine. North of Eindhoven the Germans repeatedly managed to cut Horrocks's only access of advance and main supply route. One unit of the Fifteenth Army constituted the nucleus of the forces that attacked the Allies from the West.[215] Lieutenant General Walter Poppe's 39th Infantry Division had escaped across the Scheldt River estuary just a few days before.[216] The LXXXVI Army Corps headquarters, which also had recently escaped across the river, coordinated the thrust from the east.[217] It commanded some parachute units, elements of the 10th SS Panzer Division, and the 107th Panzer Brigade.[218]

Major Joachim-Wilhelm von Maltzahn's 107th Panzer Brigade was en route to the Aachen operations area, but it was then diverted and moved relatively quickly to the Netherlands. Maltzahn's Panzers were unloaded in Thorn only on September 16, but the unit managed to enter the fighting between Eindhoven and St. Oedenrode by September 19.[219] The Allied air forces for the most part were not able to interdict the German reinforcements moving toward the point of the crisis.

That evening the supply movements for the British XXX Corps were disrupted for the first time.[220] The Germans managed to do that several times for at least a few hours each time over the course of the following days during the back and forth fighting.[221] The

German concentric attack launched before noon on September 22 actually produced a more than twenty-four-hour blockage of the highway between Uden and Veghel.[222] The British now began to realize that Operation MARKET-GARDEN would not achieve its objectives.

On the evening of September 23, Lieutenant General Dempsey, with Montgomery's approval, agreed that the 1st Airborne Division should be withdrawn from the north bank of the Rhine if the situation so required.[223] Although the new airborne landings on that day caused great concern for the German side, the main purpose of the drops was actually defensive.[224] The additional forces were necessary to stabilize the frontline salient that the British had established.[225] In retrospect, however, it is clear that Allied offensives along the entire Western Front stalled or were blocked by September 23, 1944. (See Map 25.)

Horrocks's next attempt to salvage success at Arnhem despite everything also failed.[226] On September 25, the survivors of the British 1st Airborne Division were ordered to fight their way through to the south across the Rhine River.[227] At noon on the next day, Bittrich, the commanding general of the II SS Panzer Corps, reported to Army Group B that the situation at Arnhem had been straightened out.[228] Operation MARKET-GARDEN had failed.

Both sides had fought with great self-sacrifice.[229] The British in Oosterbeek defended themselves "bitterly to the very last," as Bittrich's staff reported with respect.[230] Field Marshal Model passed the appreciation from OB West on to his soldiers with the words: "I fully subscribe to those words with my special thanks to all officers, noncommissioned officers and men for the attitude displayed during this fighting."[231]

The ten-day battle claimed heavy losses. More than 15,500 Allied soldiers, including 7,500 men of the British 1st Airborne Division, were killed or captured.[232] In the Arnhem area alone 3,300 German soldiers were killed or wounded.[233] The Allies did not realize that the situation along the front had changed significantly in the favor of the Germans in the period between the planning of the operation and its execution. They failed to detect that the Germans had assembled the means with which to close what earlier in the month had been a wide-open door to northwest Germany.

The large-scale Allied offensive had been based on a flawed estimate of the situation. It was executed in the wrong place and at the wrong time.[234] The last attempt to crown the war of movement with a decisive blow had failed. Positional warfare along the entire Western Front now became the reality for the coming months in the wake of MARKET-GARDEN's failure.

Conclusion

Toward the end of August 1944, the Americans had punched through the wobbly front line of Army Group B in the area east of Paris. Early in September, the Allies had managed to form the Mons Pocket. It seemed that the breakup of the German defense lines, which had barely been averted following the losses at Falaise and during the Seine River crossing, was now inevitable. The center of Army Group B had been shattered. The breakthrough led to the climax of the war of maneuver. Attacking toward Antwerp, the British on September 4 seized for the first time an undestroyed major port. Simultaneously, they encircled the German Fifteenth Army on the south bank of the Scheldt River. Both the Germans and the Allies at that point reached similar assessments on the future of combat operations. Field Marshal Model believed that "the gateway to northwest Germany was open."

During those first few days of September the Germans could not have blocked a large-scale Allied offensive between Aachen and Trier. At OB West headquarters there was even talk of an operational-level hole between the Meuse and Mosel rivers. General Eisenhower saw signs of a German collapse all along the front. Convinced that the defeat of the German armies was complete, he concluded that the Allies could push wherever they wanted. The final German collapse in the west, and even the end of the war, seemed to be just around the corner. But things did not happen that way. The presumed imminent defeat of the Germans did not materialize. By three weeks after the capture of Antwerp the situation had changed completely. The Germans had consolidated their situation to the point where Field Marshal von Rundstedt, without knowing about the decision that Hitler had already made to launch the Ardennes Offensive, himself began to think about staging a major counterattack.[1]

On September 29, Eisenhower had to admit to the Combined Chiefs of Staff that the Germans had managed to form a "relatively stable front."[2] Although it was, of course, only a temporary stabilization of the front in the west, what were the reasons for that accomplishment? What were the reasons for the transition from a war of maneuver to positional warfare? There was neither a so-called "miracle at the West Wall," nor a similarly inexplicable phenomenon that led to the surprising consolidation of the German front that ran from the southern Netherlands, to Aachen, to the Mosel River area, and to Belfort. Rather, it was the interplay of several factors and decisions that caused the abrupt change in the nature of the fighting.

On the German side, Hitler's counteroffensive plans and the resulting preparations do not supply an adequate explanation. But as Hitler had told Jodl on July 31, a change in the situation in the west was essential to bring about because that was where "Germany's destiny will be decided." As he spelled it out in the basic concept of *Führer Directive 51*, it was only in the west that Hitler saw any possibility of achieving with the still-available forces and resources a far-reaching military success that could be exploited at the overall strategic level.

Hitler therefore ordered that the forces generated through Germany's second "total mobilization" be concentrated in the west. But those new forces only started to influence the situation some two weeks after the climax of the German crisis in the west. The first of the twenty-five Volksgrenadier divisions, whose raising Hitler had ordered in conjunction with his intent to launch a counteroffensive, did not enter combat in the west prior to September 16–17. But the indicators that the situation was starting to stabilize were already unmistakable by September 11.

By the end of the month another five Volksgrenadier divisions plus numerous fortress units had entered the front lines. Those reinforcements undoubtedly contributed to the stabilization of the situation. But the decisive prerequisites for that stabilization had already been established. Thanks to the operational readiness of the troops and the ability of the chain of command, the German Army of the West had been pulled back in better condition than originally expected. Model's and Blaskowitz's achievements, therefore, must be rated particularly high, because it was already too late for the execution of orderly withdrawal operations by the time Hitler on August 16 gave the approval for the long-overdue retreat from the occupied French territory in the west.

When the Eastern Front defensive expert Field Marshal Model assumed command as OB West, the German Army of the West was only fighting to survive. The Allies dictated the general conditions for that fight with their absolute control of the air and their over-whelming superiority in personnel and materiel. The clearly greater mobility of the Allied units proved decisive above all.

Hitler's style of command, the frequent interference by the Wehrmacht High Command in the command authority of OB West, the adherence to missions that were no longer relevant to the situation, and the issuing of orders already overcome by events on the ground all contributed to the coming of a grave defeat for Army Group B at Falaise and an apparently fatal crisis for Army Task Group G in the Montélimar Pocket. As the action reached its climax around Paris on August 25, the problems facing the commander on the ground were compounded by having to answer to a Supreme Command that acted contrary to the military realities of the situation. The responsible generals there, especially Choltitz and Dessloch, circumvented Hitler's utterly irrational destruction orders, his "rubble field vision." And Model, too, once again proved that he was not prepared to follow blindly the directives that were coming from Führer Headquarters.

Model's thinking and actions were completely guided by the basic principles of military effectiveness. This consciously exclusive focus on only the purely military factors—as problematic as such an approach appears by today's standards—enabled Model to impose his will on the defensive operations. That, combined with his self-confident leadership style, gave Model a relatively wide degree of independence in his command prerogatives that Hitler generally tolerated.

Model certainly was not a man who saw things in terms of vast concepts. But the time was already past when far-reaching operational-level decisions could still have opened up more favorable opportunities. Such opportunities would now only be possible for Hitler to exploit if the front in the west could be stabilized. Thus, during the retreat operation that began in northern France under the most difficult conditions, Model once again proved his talents as a "frontline patchwork artist of the first order."[3]

Model's skilled conduct of defensive combat and his ruthless stripping of nonthreatened frontline sectors to reinforce the acute crisis points prevented the Allies from establishing a second pocket along the Seine River that would have led inevitably to the collapse of Army Group B while still on French soil. Of course, after crossing the river the German troops were at the end of their tethers, and the

Panzer units especially were now little more than burned-out shells. The anticipated Allied breakthrough, which reached its climax point with the capture of Antwerp, could no longer be prevented.

The uncontrolled panic retreats at the end of August and the beginning of September and the incidents of breakup and dissolution are unsurprising considering the heavy losses, the constant Allied air raids, and the German helplessness in dealing with the swiftly advancing Allied tank units. What is considerably more noteworthy is that the German military leadership managed to bring these situations under control within a few days.

Model's quickly improvised formation of reserve lines were a major factor in the stabilization. Another key factor was Model's practice of constantly seeking contact with the common soldiers and leading from the front, in contrast to Rundstedt's style of commanding from a headquarters. Thus, Model's tremendous optimism and his confidence inspired the troops, even under such seemingly hopeless conditions.

The lower and middle German command echelons also managed to adapt quickly to the abrupt situation changes and reach the necessary decisions. It was only through this high degree of individual initiative, for example, that it was possible to establish in a very short time a viable albeit weak resistance line north of Antwerp and along the Albert Canal. The German leadership, including the field army and corps commanders, had recognized immediately the operational-level significance of the Antwerp area for future operations. Such swift and resolute action based on individual responsibility had far-reaching consequences. It was the precondition for leading the Fifteenth Army back across the Scheldt River estuary and denying the Allies the use of the port of Antwerp for such a long time. Through maximum improvisational measures, the Germans by the end of the first ten-day period in September had been able to establish a relatively strong defensive line running from Antwerp to Belfort.

The German Army of the West, of course, suffered heavy losses during the retreat. For the first time in the war the loss statistics in the west exceeded those of the Eastern Front.[4] But in the process, the essential foundations necessary for a reorganization of the defense were preserved. Most important among those were the efficient operations staffs.

Contrary to Allied expectations, the German fighting spirit did not collapse. Instead, there was a definite stiffening of the resistance as the fighting moved closer to the Reich border. The mobilization of the very last available resources was driven by the fact that the fighting was now aimed at defending and protecting the homeland, one of those "primary values of traditional soldiering."[5] The fighting in the West, therefore, assumed a completely new character on September 11, when American troops first entered German soil in the Eifel Mountains near Prüm.

The improvement and reinforcement of the German Western Position had been started too late—only after Model repeatedly insisted on such actions. As the center of this position, the West Wall had no special defensive value because of its obsolete fortress engineering and its inadequate armament. That it nevertheless became a nucleus for the country's defense resulted primarily from psychological factors. Inadequate as the West Wall was, it was the first prepared position that the German troops reached after weeks of nonstop marching and fighting.

Toward the end of the first ten-day period in September the front of Model's Army Group B was defended by only a motley collection of troops of the most varied origins. The backbone of that line was manned by battalions of stragglers, soldiers from other Wehrmacht components, and especially by units of the Replacement Army. The whole thing was held together by the still intact command structure of the German Army of the West and its decimated divisions.

At that point, however, the strength situation would have made it quite impossible for the Germans to beat off any Allied main-effort offensive launched anywhere in the area between Antwerp and Trier. The crisis south of Trier, however, had been stabilized for the most part. Soon after taking command, Model decided to concentrate the reinforcements he was promised during the retreat operation on the left wing of his Army Group B. That was the sector most important in operational terms. Model's decision produced positive results. The rapid establishment of the firm defensive position between Trier and Nancy during the first days of September was easier for the Germans because Patton's U.S. Third Army, which was already in front of Metz, had to interrupt its offensive for a short time because of fuel shortages. That pause gave the approaching German divisions enough time to occupy their defense sectors.

Model's establishment of a defensive center of gravity in the south was risky because of the deterioration in the situation in the north. But considering the overall situation, it was the only viable alternative he had. Stabilizing the Mosel River sector of Lorraine was the prerequisite for enabling Blaskowitz's units to link up. And that in turn made it possible to combine the hitherto separated army groups into a contiguous Western Front.

The units of Army Task Group G reached the Dijon bridgehead by September 10–11. Despite the losses suffered in the process, the retreat movement from southern France was a success because of Blaskowitz's leadership. The results surprised both Hitler and Model. One important reason for this success was the relatively free hand that Blaskowitz had in conducting the operation that had started with the most unfavorable prospects. The catastrophic losses in telecommunications capabilities severely limited the Wehrmacht High Command's ability to interfere with Blaskowitz. Model, for his part, gave Blaskowitz the necessary freedom of action. Thus, Blaskowitz's leadership style, which was based on the principal of Auftragstaktik [mission orders], was most effective in this situation.

Like Blaskowitz, Model identified early on the Allies' intentions and operational objectives. Considering the vastness of the space involved, however, the disparity between the German and the Allied forces in northern France was entirely too great, especially in terms of personnel strength, equipment, and mobility. Thus, even the correct estimate of the Allied situation would not have been sufficient to establish there a defensive center of gravity at the decisive moment. That disadvantage was mitigated in southern France to some extent, because the terrain was not ideal for the Allies to fully exploit their mechanized capabilities. Similar terrain conditions had a similar effect later on in the Eifel and the Vosges mountains.

The special factors in southern and southwestern France included the French Forces of the Interior, which operated in greater force in that part of the country. The FFI's military effectiveness, however, remained relatively minor, contrary to German fears. The FFI did, of course, create pockets of uncertainty along the German march routes, but they were not able to restrict the withdrawal in any significant manner.

The breakthrough of General Wiese's Nineteenth Army to the Rhône River Valley, which was blocked at Montélimar, was of decisive significance for the successful retreat of Army Task Group G. Without the resolute fighting spirit of the units that were cut off and the nimble commitment of the 11th Panzer Division, the only Panzer force available, the breakthrough would have been impossible. And that failure, of course, would have prevented the stabilization of the southern sector of the German Western Front.

The German field army and corps commanders again and again managed to quickly establish the necessary defensive and counterattack centers of gravity during the fighting in the Rhône River Valley. The American forces were definitely outmatched during this fighting. As in the Falaise sector and during the Seine River crossing in northern France, the Allies did not fully exploit the opportunities they had at Montélimar.

The greatest danger to the success of the German retreat from the south was Hitler's obsession with mounting a major counteroffensive against Reims directly from the retreat. Of course, the prerequisites for such an operation did not exist. The preparations for the stillborn operation would have required extensive personnel reshuffling of the operations staffs, which indicates the great significance Hitler attached to this offensive. But to execute his far-reaching intentions for what he believed would be a new phase of the fighting, Hitler needed the Wehrmacht's oldest field marshal. Field Marshal von Rundstedt thought exclusively in strategic terms, but at the same time he was considered one of Germany's "cleverest operational brains." Thus, Rundstedt again became OB West. Model, who was the dynamic force needed to master the crisis in the north, retained command of Army Group B.

The impracticability of Hitler's counteroffensive from the retreat became obvious by September 14. The German front had not yet been consolidated to the point where longer-term preparations would have been possible. The instability of the front was the main reason for the failure of the timely formation of the reserves and especially the assembly of the required Panzer units. By September 16, Hitler had decided instead to launch the Ardennes Offensive. The idea of the "left hook" would now be executed from a solid front line.

The frontline salient at Langres could now finally be evacuated and the Nineteenth Army could be moved back to a shortened position in the area between Nancy and Belfort. That marked the completion of the withdrawal of Army Task Group G. Quite contrary to expectations, the withdrawal operations to pull back the far-forward-echeloned wings ended successfully by September 21–22. The German Western Front was now stabilized and any surprise operational-level breakthrough by the Allies was highly unlikely. Like the Nineteenth Army in the south, the Fifteenth Army in the north had been able to slip out of the encirclement. A total of some 215,000 troops from those two field armies that were assumed lost returned to the German lines during the second half of September. And that made a decisive contribution to the stability of the positional warfare during the following months.

The German generals largely agreed that if the Allies had been more resolute in the conduct of their operations, it would have been impossible for the Germans to recover such a large number of their forces. A strong case in point is the retreat of General von Zangen's Fifteenth Army across the Westerschelde River. Although the Allies by September 4 had advanced to the Woensdrecht isthmus and were almost within artillery range, the Germans still managed over the course of the next two weeks to move some eighty-five thousand soldiers through the eye of this needle and deploy those forces on the mainland behind the German right wing. That beefed up Model's defensive strength during the fighting along the West Wall, and especially during the battle at Aachen, where Army Group B was hard pressed. These additional forces also were the foundation for Model's defensive operations that caused the Allies' Operation MARKET-GARDEN to fail.

The consolidation of the German front, however, had been possible only because the Allies were not prepared to exploit the operational-level opportunities that arose during the campaign of maneuver in August and September 1944. The supply problems that surfaced as the Allies crossed the Seine River only grew worse the faster the advance to the east continued. It was not so much a shortage of harbor capacity that restricted their ability to conduct operations during the critical period; rather, it was the fact that the supply lines constantly grew longer between Cotentin and the front lines. The transportation capacity was insufficient to meet the requirements of the Allied commanders. Because of their high level of mechanization, the Allied forces were particularly dependent on an efficient logistical system.

The logistical plans prepared prior to the start of OVERLORD had been based on the assumption of a steady, slow advance. But things did not play out that way. Initially the Allies were pinned down for almost two months in the Normandy bridgehead. Then the campaign of maneuver broke wide open with the breakout at

Avranches. As a result, Allied logisticians did not have the time necessary to develop a well-balanced supply dump system between the unloading ports and the front lines.

The Allied command, of course, did recognize the logistical problems. But it did not manage to analyze them accurately or to take the necessary actions to solve the problems. The major attack against Brest is a typical example. The attack was senseless, because even if the harbor had been captured undestroyed, it was much too far away from the front lines to ease the supply situation in the short run.

There had been practically no base of experience upon which the Allied operations staffs could have developed the planning for a landing operation on such a massive scale. The Allies, however, did manage to come up with some innovative improvisations, such as the Red Ball Express and the frontline fuel airlift. Those improvisations undoubtedly reduced the immediate effects of the supply crisis. But on the other hand, they probably contributed to the Allies' failure to recognize more quickly the necessity of capturing and clearing Antwerp as soon as possible. Nevertheless, it is difficult to understand even in retrospect why neither Eisenhower nor Montgomery recognized the opportunities that were available to them in that sector. The timely establishment of a main effort with the twin objectives of clearing the maritime access to the port of Antwerp and blocking the last retreat route of the Fifteenth Army never happened.

ULTRA intelligence indicating that the opportunities along the Scheldt River estuary were dwindling with every passing day apparently influenced the Allied command decisions. The conclusion, therefore, must be that the Allies' ULTRA advantage was of little help to them from about the middle of August on. Key information was decoded and forwarded to the senior commanders at the front, but it was not used in a decisive manner.

The Allied logistical advantage that had been such a dominant factor during the invasion planning phase in the spring of 1944 progressively lost its importance through the decisions of the senior Allied ground commanders as their estimate of the German situation changed. Opportunities to strike a decisive blow against the Germans arose repeatedly during the campaign of maneuver, but were never fully exploited. The pace and ease of the advance created a situation in which the initial overestimation of German capabilities gradually yielded to an underestimation of their ability to establish a stable and coherent defense.

Anticipating that the German collapse was just around the corner, the Allied ground commanders concentrated entirely on the question of the suitable strategy for what they presumed to be the terminal phase of the war. And while that debate raged back and forth and consumed valuable time, the broader logistical problems and their solution at Antwerp assumed second priority. The question of whether the single thrust, as advocated in vain by Montgomery, could have ended the war successfully in 1944 remains speculative. That question should be assessed with a great deal of skepticism because Montgomery repeatedly failed to exploit the opportunities that opened up to him under the Broad Front concept.

On the other hand, the failure of Eisenhower's strategy to live up to its expectations is quite obvious. Eisenhower's strength lay in the difficult field of defusing the internal frictions within the coalition forces, rather than in developing and consistently implementing operational-level command decisions. Because of his personal lack of field command experience, Eisenhower constantly tried to work out a consensus, or at least to fashion the conflicting views of his generals into an acceptable compromise solution. The results, however, were not always consistent with the principle of military efficiency.

The final great victory apparently at hand, combined with the high expectations among the publics of the western democracies, made it extremely difficult for Eisenhower to completely halt one or the other wing of his front. Halting either the British or the Americans to establish a single main-effort offensive focused in one sector seemed almost impossible. Eisenhower, therefore, decided to return to the basic operational concept that had been drafted by the British-American planning staff prior to the start of the invasion—a broad front advance running along two main offensive axes. But because the supply problems continued to exist, the return to and rigid adherence to that concept could only result in an overall slowdown of the Allied advance.

The exact moment at which the Broad Front strategy was re-implemented was very important to the German stabilization efforts. On September 4, at the very point when the crisis in the north reached its climax, Patton's U.S. Third Army was allocated so much fuel that it was able to resume its offensive in the south against the German Mosel River Front, which in the meantime had grown stronger. The overall slowdown of the advance toward the Reich gave the Germans valuable time to further strengthen the defenses of the Western Position.

The transition to the Broad Front strategy, which was not sufficiently supported logistically, deprived the Allies of what until then had been a decisive advantage. The organizational structure of the U.S. Army was based completely on fully motorized, mobile combat forces. But from that point onward, the mobility of the Allied units lost much of the operational significance that had dominated the fighting during the previous month. And as that advantage was lost, the Allied weakness that first became evident during the pursuit phase became increasingly significant. Undoubtedly, the logistical difficulties were a serious impediment to Allied operations. But those difficulties to that point had not determined the line along which the brisk advance of the pursuit phase actually came to a halt.

The ability to exploit opportunities by quickly establishing main efforts presupposes a degree of military combat experience that was lacking, at least among American generals from the top levels down to the division commanders. The German generals, on the other hand, had no such lack of experience. The Allied field army and corps commanders were acting from a completely different psychological foundation as well. Being fully aware of the certainty of their ultimate victory, they were therefore far less inclined to take risks. The Americans' lack of experience only reinforced their security-oriented thinking. They launched ever smaller thrusts only after tremendous expenditures of ammunition and fuel, which in turn further strained their already overburdened supply system.

But the Allied command only seriously addressed their logistics problem after Operation MARKET-GARDEN. That operation had failed in its objective to seize the Rhine River bridges at Arnhem as a point of departure for the follow-on offensive toward the Ruhr region. And that failure was mostly caused by the fact that one of its key planning assumptions about the collapsing state of the German army was no longer valid by the time the offensive started on September 17.

When the fighting ended at Arnhem, the phase of the brisk Allied advance came to its final and spectacular end. The opening of the Scheldt River estuary now gradually assumed an overriding importance for the Allied senior commanders. But even so, three more weeks passed after Eisenhower realized that access to the port of Antwerp would be tantamount to a "blood transfusion" for Allied combat operations.[6] The actual main-effort offensive to clear the Scheldt only started in the middle of October.

One of the causes of that delay was Eisenhower's style of issuing orders. His directives tended to be very voluminous, but not at all precise. They also were framed in such a manner as to invite the type of independent actions taken by Patton. Early in September, a main-effort offensive to free up Antwerp could still have unhinged Hitler's entire fortress concept with one blow. Based on Hitler's concept, roughly a quarter million German soldiers had been left behind to block the ports along the Channel, Atlantic, and Mediterranean coasts. Allied hesitation in completely seizing the Antwerp area, however, made it possible for the Germans to establish Fortress Scheldt. Because of the stubborn resistance offered by the remaining two German divisions there, the harbor was not available for Allied supply shipments until the end of November—in other words, three months after the port had been seized intact.[7]

In the final analysis, Hitler's fortresses concept succeeded for a period of time only because of faulty operational-level decisions on the Allied side. But that relative success was bought at the price of considerable German personnel sacrifices.

By November the Allies no longer had any prospects of ending the war in Europe in 1944. Their ambitious expectations at the end of August and the beginning of September had not materialized. The static positional warfare that now raged along the Western Front since October and that caused heavy losses on both sides justify Montgomery's realistic observation on November 30 that the Allies had suffered a "strategic setback."[8]

The German military accomplishments that had been bought at such a high price in blood and the fighting spirit of the soldier can be attributed primarily to the military mission that had boiled down to a single point—the defense of the borders of the Reich. There was no alternative to that mission. That was the case even for an officer such as General Blaskowitz, who in 1939 had first confronted the horrible consequences of the racial ideology objectives of the Nazi regime, and who had protested in vain against the atrocities in Poland. He was bound to have known the kind of humanity-despising system he was defending. But even Blaskowitz at that time did not consider something that now seems very clear by the standards of today, ". . . that the state of injustice that destroyed all legal standards . . . could no longer make any legitimate claim to obedience, and that resistance had long since become an ethical duty."[9]

On the question of the determination of the occupation zone boundaries, which was so important for the Germans, the war situation at the end of August and at the beginning of September 1944 seemed to have offered the Western Allies an opportunity to establish a more favorable East-West demarcation line. The chance was slim, but it was not grasped. The Soviets, however, did realize that the Lübeck–Helmstedt–Eisenach–Hof line, which generally had been accepted since the spring of 1944, might again come into question because of the rapid advance of the western invasion forces starting in August. Subsequently, the Soviets were now ready to abandon their past reservations against an agreement that would once and for all establish the zones. On September 12, Gusev, the Soviet representative to the European Advisory Commission, signed the first occupation zone protocol. Apart from the fact that this question still had relatively little significance for the two Western Allies at that point, it was probably Roosevelt's policy of cooperation with the Soviet Union that worked against any possibility of urging a shift of the zone boundary to the east on the basis of military successes in the west. The rapid reorganization of the German Army of the West, however, created a situation where only a narrow window of opportunity was left for any such initiative.

Following the stabilization of the German front, any opportunities to alter the occupation zone boundaries vanished once and for all. Thus, the bitter defensive fighting in the west may cast some light on the widespread ambivalence of many of the German military leaders. By mustering all of their technical skills and the very last ounces of strength in the shattered front lines, they managed again and again to stabilize the situation and to win defensive battles. But in doing so they only contributed to the prolongation of a war that had been lost long before. That was the tragedy of the German military leadership in the west. Repeatedly and frequently, without being aware of it, they facilitated through October 1944 the continuation of one of the greatest crimes in the history of mankind, the genocide of the Jews of Europe.

Notes

1. Ose, "Entscheidung" [Decision].

2. Jung, "Ardennenoffensive" [Ardennes Offensive].

3. The German troops did not enter the part of France that was left unoccupied in 1940 (Operation ANTON) until November 11, 1942. The territory to the east of the Rhône River was occupied after the Italian Armistice (September 8, 1943). Some "fortresses" along the French coastline and the Channel Islands remained in German hands until the end of the war.

4. For example, the chief of staff of the U.S. Army, General George Marshall, on September 13, 1944, informed his senior commanders that one could figure on finishing the war in Europe by November 1944; cf., *Eisenhower Papers*, IV, p. 2117. On the German side, for example, see Colonel General Alfred Jodl's comment in Nürnberg, in "Der Prozess" [The Trial], XV, p. 441 f, and Albert Speer's comment, also in "Der Prozess" [The Trial], XVI, pp. 533 ff.

5. Klein, "Militärgeschichte" [Military History], p. 193.

6. Groote, "Militärgeschichte" [Military History], p. 18.

7. Schreiber, "Der Zweite Weltkrieg" [World War II], p. 453.

8. Showalter, *German Military History 1648–1982*, p. 239.

9. Haupt, "Rückzug" [Retreat].

10. For example, Johannes Nosbüsch, "Bis zum bitteren Ende—Der Zweite Weltkrieg im Kreis Bitburg-Prüm" [To the Bitter End—World War II in the County of Bitburg-Prüm] (Bitburg, 1978); id., "Damit es nicht vergessen wird. Pfälzer Land im Zweiten Weltkrieg" [Lest We Forget—The Palatinate during World War II] (Landau, 1982); Adolf Hohenstein and Wolfgang Trees, "Hölle im Hürtgenwald" [Hell in Hürtgen Forest] (Aachen, 1981); Manfred Gross, "Der Westwall zwischen Niederrhein und Schnee-Eifel" [The West Wall between the Lower Rhine and Schnee-Eifel] (Cologne, 1982); Rolf Dieter Müller, Gerd R. Ueberschär, and Wolfram Wette, "Wer zurückweicht, wird erschossen" [Anyone Who Retreats Will Be Shot] (Freiburg, 1985).

11. The unprinted sources cited in this study, as a rule, come from the Federal Archives-Military Archives or from the Military History Research Institute. The place of origin of the documents is indicated separately only where this is not the case.

12. RW 4/Vol. 34.

13. Cf., among others, Joachim Ludewig, "Stationen eines Soldatenschicksals: Generalfeldmarschall Walter Model" [Waystations in a Soldier's Destiny: Field Marshal-General Walter Model], in "Militärgeschichtliche

Beiträge" [Military History Contributions] 5 (1991): pp. 69–75.

14. These were studies prepared from memory, mostly without access to sources, by German officers after 1945, by direction of the "Historical Division." Depending on the aptitude and interest of the particular author, their quality varies, and in the following, they will be cited with the author's name and the corresponding "MS" identification number.

15. *United States Army in World War II,* Office of the Chief of Military History, Dept. of the Army, Washington 1947 ff.; *History of the Second World War,* United Kingdom Military Series, London 1952 ff. The individual works in this series will be cited in the following only under the names of the authors. The bibliography contains further information.

16. This involved the ongoing decoding of secret German radio codes by British cryptologists. Originally, ULTRA was the security classification for radio messages or teletype messages that were used to transmit the knowledge gained from these sources to Allied operations staff.

17. Literature used in this connection: Ralph Bennett, Ultra in the West—The Normandy Campaign 1944/45, London 1980; Ronald Lewin, "Entschied Ultra den Krieg?" [Did Ultra Decide the War?], Koblenz Bonn, 1981; F.H. Hinsley with E.E. Thomas, C.F.G. Ransom, R.C. Knight, *British Intelligence in the Second World War,* 3, Part I, London, 1984.

18. Schreiber, "Der Zweite Weltkrieg," p. 473.

1. The German Reich's Military-Political Situation

1. War Diary, Wehrmacht High Command, IV/2, pp. 1530 ff.

2. Hillgruber, *Der Zweite Weltkrieg,* p. 128.

3. War Diary, Wehrmacht High Command, IV/1, p. 12.

4. Reich Minister of Armament and Ammunition in 1942; Reich Minister of Armament and War Production since 1943.

5. Hitler, *Mein Kampf,* p. 741 f.

6. Proclaimed by the Western Allies at the January 1943 Casablanca Conference. Stalin joined in May 1943.

7. Hansen, *Aussenpolitik,* p. 118.

8. Hillgruber, *Der Zweite Weltkrieg,* p. 166.

9. Hildebrand, *Drittes Reich,* p. 96.

10. Ibid., p. 105.

11. Ibid.

2. The Initial Situation on the Allied Side

1. Joint Western Allied general staffs in Washington since 1942. The Combined Chiefs of Staff (hereafter abbreviated: CCS) consisted of the U.S. Joint Chiefs of Staff (hereafter abbreviated: JCS), reinforced by the liaison officers of the British Chiefs of Staff (hereafter abbreviated: COS).

2. Leighton, "OVERLORD versus the Mediterranean at the Cairo-Tehran Conferences," in *Command Decisions,* p. 208.

3. Matloff, *Strategic Planning for Coalition Warfare 1943–1944,* p. 475.

4. Ehrman, *Grand Strategy*, V, p. 180.

5. Matloff, *Strategic Planning for Coalition Warfare 1943–1944*, p. 179 ff.

6. The actual strength figure, however, was only eighty-nine divisions by the end of the war; see ibid., p. 183, footnote 56.

7. Ibid., p. 522.

8. Matloff, "The ANVIL Decision, Crossroads of Strategy," in *Command Decisions*, p. 286 ff.

9. This approach was charted by Field Marshal Sir Alan Brooke, Chief of the Imperial General Staff. In 1943, Churchill considered the establishment of a major Balkan front as a substitute for the invasion of France; cf., Hillgruber, "Problem der Zweiten Front," pp. 339 ff.

10. Matloff, "The ANVIL Decision, Crossroads of Strategy," in *Command Decisions*, p. 298 f.

11. Hillgruber, "Problem der Zweiten Front," pp. 348 ff.

12. Matloff, "The ANVIL Decision, Crossroads of Strategy," in *Command Decisions*, p. 285.

13. Ehrman, *Grand Strategy*, V, p. 368.

14. Churchill's letter to Roosevelt, July 1, 1944, in: Ehrman, *Grand Strategy*, V, p. 355 f.

15. The title of a book by the then chief of the United States military mission in Moscow, Major General John R. Deane.

16. Matloff, *Strategic Planning for Coalition Warfare 1943–1944*, p. 532 f.

17. Pogue, *The Supreme Command*, p. 225.

18. Matloff, *Strategic Planning for Coalition Warfare 1943–1944*, p. 532.

19. Hillgruber, "Problem der Zweiten Front," p. 348.

20. Ibid., p. 346.

21. George Catlett Marshall held this position from 1939 to 1945.

22. Matloff, *Strategic Planning for Coalition Warfare 1943–1944*, p. 412.

23. Ibid., p. 410 f.

24. Lieutenant General Sir Frederick Morgan.

25. Ruppenthal, *Logistical Support of the Allied Armies*, I, p. 178.

26. OVERLORD was to be terminated by D+90. Considering June 6, 1944, as D-Day, D+90 would be September 4, 1944. The Allied documents relating to the subsequent operations come under the heading of "Post-OVERLORD Planning."

27. Eisenhower, *Crusade in Europe*, p. 343; Ruppenthal, *Logistical Support of the Allied Armies*, II, p. 173, gives a figure of 840 tons, including 280 for reserves. Wilmot, *The Struggle for Europe*, p. 564, points out that this figure, taken from the *Operations Field Manual*, is too high. An Allied division could have been able to get along with 500 tons in combat during the advance and half of that on the defense. This excessively high figure, he noted, contained all normally present items that, however, are not absolutely necessary. The decisive factor, however, is how the Allied field army commanders, who were accustomed to this normal rate, judged the action capabilities of their own formations when less supplies were available.

28. Liddell Hart, *History of the Second World War*, p. 700.

29. The supreme command was made up of air, ground, and naval units. Air Marshal Sir Arthur W. Tedder became Eisenhower's deputy. There will be no discussion of the naval forces chain of command because it is not relevant to our topic.

30. The COSSAC planning staff constituted the core of Eisenhower's staff at Supreme Headquarters, Allied Expeditionary Forces (SHAEF). Major General Walter Bedell Smith was Eisenhower's chief of staff.

31. Eisenhower's letter to Montgomery on July 10, 1944, in: Blumenson, *Breakout and Pursuit*, p. 346.

32. Twenty-three infantry, ten armored, and four airborne divisions.

33. Matloff, *Strategic Planning for Coalition Warfare 1943–1944*, p. 170.

34. Blumenson, *Breakout and Pursuit*, p. 348.

35. Eisenhower's letter to Montgomery early in June 1944, in: Ruppenthal, *Logistical Support of the Armies*, I, p. 474.

36. Blumenson, *Breakout and Pursuit*, p. 346 f.

37. Ruppenthal, *Logistical Support of the Armies*, I, p. 288.

38. Prefabricated in Great Britain, they were to be towed across the Channel and were then to be set up along the beaches of Normandy at Arromanches and St. Laurent so as to substitute for the large harbor docks that were not available there.

39. Matloff, *Strategic Planning for Coalition Warfare 1943–1944*, p. 170.

40. From Port en Bessin (north of Bayeux) or from the Isle of Wight, with the help of PLUTO (Pipeline under the Ocean) via Cherbourg; see also Ruppenthal, *Logistical Support of the Armies*, I, p. 322 f.

41. Ibid., p. 319.

42. Ibid., p. 189.

43. Ibid., p. 327.

44. Ruppenthal, *Logistical Support of the Armies*, I, p. 485.

45. Pogue, *The Supreme Command*, p. 249.

46. See also and hereafter: Caspar, *Kriegslage*, pp. 173–183.

47. Apart from East Prussia, its zone thus covered 40 percent of the surface area, 36 percent of the inhabitants, and 33 percent of the economic capacity of Germany.

48. Hillgruber, *Problem der Zweiten Front*, p. 346.

49. Ruppenthal, *Logistical Support of the Armies*, I, p. 178.

50. Matloff, *Strategic Planning for Coalition Warfare 1943–1944*, p. 170.

51. Greenfield, *Command Decisions*, p. 273.

52. Ehrman, *Grand Strategy*, VI, p. 8.

53. Ibid., V, pp. 291 ff, and Wilmot, *The Struggle for Europe*, p. 221.

54. In addition, the Allies also had two strategic bomber forces, so that a total of about 12,800 Allied aircraft were available; see Galland, *Die Ersten und die Letzten*, p. 299.

55. Ose, *Entscheidung im Westen*, p. 119, and Galland, *Die Ersten und die Letzten*, p. 301.

56. As Eisenhower's deputy, Air Chief Marshal Sir Arthur Tedder took care of the rather difficult job of coordinating.

57. Wilmot, *The Struggle for Europe*, p. 221 f, and Galland, *Die Ersten und die Letzten*, p. 295 f.

58. See also the data in Wegmüller, "Die Konzeption," p. 236 f.

59. Ose, *Entscheidung im Westen*, p. 115.

60. Ibid., p. 84, and Galland, *Die Ersten und die Letzten*, p. 299.

61. Because of their wide dispersion pattern against the target, the V-weapons were not suitable for employment against military targets. Instead, they were used only as terror weapons; see Hölsken, *Die V-Waffen*, p. 206 f.

62. Ibid., pp. 181 ff.

63. Ibid., p. 120 f.

64. Ehrman, *Grand Strategy*, VI, pp. 9 ff, and Wilmot, *The Struggle for Europe*, p. 220.

65. On November, 1, 1944, Harris noted that in spite of the "invasion diversions," he was still able to destroy about "two-and-a-half German cities" each month; see also *Eisenhower Papers*, IV, p. 2248.

66. The first raids against the oil refineries and hydration plants in Ploesti, Vienna, and Budapest as well as in Upper Silesia had been carried out in April.

67. War Diary, Wehrmacht High Command, IV/1, pp. 942 ff.

68. Ehrman, *Grand Strategy* , VI, p. 12.

69. Galland, *Die Ersten und die Letzten*, p. 299.

70. War Diary, Wehrmacht High Command, IV/1, p. 955.

71. The first memo was dated June 30, 1944; another one was dated July 28, 1944; see Hillgruber, "Hümmelchen, Chronik," p. 225. See also Speer's testimony in "Der Prozess," XVI, p. 534 f, and Speer, *Erinnerungen*, pp. 360 ff.

72. Ehrman, *Grand Strategy*, V, p. 396, and VI, p. 9.

73. New priorities were set on September 25, 1944. But this plan likewise gave the bomber generals a measure of freedom and was less comprehensive; see Ehrman, *Grand Strategy*, VI, pp. 6 ff.; Ellis, *Victory in the West*, II, pp. 150 ff.

74. This is only too understandable considering the "importance of the liberation of France to the French themselves," in light of the significance of the Resistance in the way the French viewed themselves after the war, as Henri Michel stated in 1974. See Henri Michel, "Sur la Résistance" (October 1974 Conference in Paris) in: RHDGM [French Historical Review of World War II] 99, (1975), pp. 101 ff. In the following, however, we will only take up the military effectiveness of the Resistance and its influence on operations.

75. Ose, *Entscheidung im Westen*, p. 118.

76. Staiger, "Rückzug," p. 38.

77. Eisenhower to 21st Army Group on May 24, 1944, quoted by Pogue, *The Supreme Command*, p. 154.

78. Beaufre, "Revolutionierung," p. 147.

79. Hahlweg, "Typologie," pp. 29 f and 47.

80. Knipping, "Konzeptionen," p. 127.

81. See also Goyet, "Unification," RHA 4/1974, pp. 104–121.

82. Knipping, "Konzeptionen," pp. 129 ff.

83. See also de Dainville, "ORA" [Army Resistance Organization], in: RHA 3/1974, pp. 11–36.

84. Knipping, "Konzeptionen," p. 137; Pogue, *The Supreme Command*, p. 156; Ehrman, *Grand Strategy*, V, p. 326.

85. The example of the French Forces of the Interior units operating around Lorient and St. Nazaire (August to December 1944) is very interesting on that score; see Mordal, "Bastionen," pp. 82 ff.

86. Ehrman, *Grand Strategy*, V, p. 321; Knipping, "Konzeptionen," p. 128.

87. De Gaulle, "Memoiren" [Memoirs], p. 238 f.

88. Roosevelt, to the Joint Chiefs of Staff on November 15, 1943. Matloff, *Strategic Planning for Coalition Warfare 1943–1944*, p. 339.

89. Roosevelt recognized the French National Liberation Committee on July 11, 1944, of course, only as a "de facto" authority. The "provisional government" was not recognized until October 1944.

90. Knipping, "Konzeptionen," p. 135.

91. Ibid., pp. 135 ff.

92. Eisenhower's letter to the Combined Chiefs of Staff, dated June 4, 1944, in: *Eisenhower Papers*, III, p. 1906 f.

93. Pogue, *The Supreme Command*, p. 236.

94. The reaction to de Gaulle's radio address and an inquiry at the Wehrmacht High Command did not produce any change in the German attitude at that time; see: "Der Prozess," XXI, p. 36.

95. Ehrman, *Grand Strategy*, V, p. 324 f.

96. Eisenhower's letter to the Combined Chiefs of Staff, dated May 11, 1944, in: *Eisenhower Papers*, III, p. 1857 f.

97. Ehrman, *Grand Strategy*, V, p. 321.

98. Eisenhower's letter to d'Astier, dated March 17, 1944, *Eisenhower Papers*, III, p. 1771 f.

99. On June 5, 1944, Eisenhower took the precaution of drafting an announcement for public consumption that was to be broadcast in case the invasion failed; see: Ibid., p. 1908.

100. Ehrman, *Grand Strategy*, V, p. 325.

101. Pogue, *The Supreme Command*, p. 156.

102. SHAEF Directive to Koenig, dated June 17, 1944, ibid, p. 236 f.

103. Ehrman, *Grand Strategy*, V, p. 325.

104. Eisenhower's letters to d'Astier, dated March 17, 1944, *Eisenhower Papers* III, p. 1771 f.

105. de Jong, "Kollaboration," pp. 256 ff.

106. Pogue, *The Supreme Command*, p. 237 f.

107. Ose, *Entscheidung im Westen*, p. 117 f.

108. War Diary, Wehrmacht High Command, IV/1, p. 315.

109. Ibid., p. 318.

110. Umbreit, "Stratégie," p. 136.

3. Development of the Situation through the Middle of August 1944

1. OB West, Ia, No. 5991/44, dated October 18, 1943, RH 19 IV/145, p. 350.

2. Under his direction, he had the commanding generals for Northeastern France, Lieutenant General Wilhelm Hederich; Northwestern France, General of Infantry Erwin Vierow; Southwestern France, General of Cavalry Kurt Feldt; and starting in August General of Infantry Dietrich von Choltitz, as Wehrmacht Commander of Greater Paris. After German troops occupied southern France, the area of the Commanding General, Army Territory, Southern France, was added as the 5th District, which was at least internally under the Military Commander.

3. Umbreit, "Militärbefehlshaber," [Military Commander], pp. 50 ff. That number includes the 325th Security Division (with four regiments) under the Commandant of Paris and the 74th Security Brigade (with two regiments), which was organized as a fast-moving unit with police squad cars. In the West, there were also two regiments and two regional defense battalions, under the Wehrmacht commander for Belgium/Northern France and under SS-Gruppenführer and Major General of Police Richard Jungclaus, in the Netherlands.

4. For the details of the command chaos, see Ose, *Entscheidung im Westen*, pp. 60 ff.

5. Ibid., p. 159.

6. Mennel, "Schlussphase," p. 74.

7. Schweppenburg called it "bazaar haggling"; cf., "Geschichte der Panzergruppe West," MS-B-258, p. 18.

8. Ose, *Entscheidung im Westen*, p. 270.

9. Ibid., p. 152.

10. War Diary, Wehrmacht High Command, IV/1, p. 19.

11. Ose, *Entscheidung im Westen*, p. 132.

12. *Hitlers Lagebesprechungen, Besprechung mit Jodl, Warlimont et al. vom 31.7.1944*, [Hitler's Situation Conferences, Conference with Jodl, Warlimont, et al., of July 31, 1944], pp. 584 ff, specifically: p. 585.

13. They were part of the 29th activation wave (Organization Order dated July 10, 1944). The divisions were partly still in the process of being organized; others were already en route to the Eastern Front. See Tessin, "Verbände" [Major Formations], I, p. 87.

14. *Hitlers Lagebesprechungen* [Hitler's Situation Conferences], Conference on July 31, 1944, pp. 588 ff.

15. Ibid., p. 590.

16. Ibid., p. 593.

17. Ibid., p. 585.

18. Ibid., p. 586.

19. Ibid., p. 592.

20. Ibid., p. 591.

21. Ibid., p. 599.

22. Ibid., p. 601.

23. Ibid., p. 597.

24. Ibid., p. 598 f.

25. Ibid., p. 602.

26. Ibid., p. 591.

27. Ibid., p. 603.

28. Ibid., p. 586.

29. Ibid., p. 594.

30. Ibid., p. 593.

31. Ibid., pp. 593 and 598.

32. Ibid., p. 594.

33. OB West, Ia, No. 553/44, dated January 20, 1944, RH 19 IV/26, pp. 65 ff.

34. The responsible commander there, Major General Karl-Wilhelm von Schlieben, had capitulated after a short time.

35. *Hitlers Lagebesprechungen,* Conference on July 31, 1994, pp. 594 and 606.

36. Chief of Naval Operations, 1 SKL 1b, No. 1750/44, dated June 13, 1944, in: "Lagevorträge Kriegsmarine," [Navy Situation Briefings], p. 589.

37. *Hitlers Lagebesprechungen,* Conference on July 31, 1944, p. 592.

38. This line had been reconnoitered on October 31, 1943, on Hitler's orders by General of Infantry Fischer von Weikersthal; cf., War Diary, Wehrmacht High Command, III/2, p. 1235.

39. *Hitlers Lagebesprechungen,* Conference on July 31, 1944, p. 595.

40. Office of the Chief of Naval Operations, 1, SKL 1b, No. 1750/44, dated June 13, 1944, in: "Lagevorträge Kriegsmarine," p. 589.

41. The Vosges positions were to be reconnoitered immediately, as per *Hitlers Lagebesprechungen,* Conference on July 31, 1944, pp. 596 and 606.

42. Ibid., p. 607.

43. This involved the new Messerschmitt Me-262 jet aircraft. Each group had sixty-eight aircraft of this type; cf., RW 4/Vol. 34, p. 57, and comments by General of Artillery Walter Warlimont in: Warlimont, "Kommentare," [Commentaries], MS-P-215, p. 314 f.

44. *Hitlers Lagebesprechungen,* Conference on July 31, 1944, p. 607.

45. Ibid., p. 586.

46. Ibid., Conference with Lieutenant General Siegfried Westphal and General of Infantry Hans Krebs on August 31, 1944, p. 616.

47. *Hitlers Lagebesprechungen,* Conference on July 31, 1944, p. 595.

48. *Völkischer Beobachter,* July 26, 1944.

49. For example, the new fighter program with whose help Hitler intended to break the Allied command of the air roughly by November 1944; see also War Diary, Wehrmacht High Command, IV/1, p. 60; or the hope

for a "new submarine war"; see Salewski, "Seekriegsleitung," [Chief of Naval Operations], 2, pp. 483 ff.

50. For the development of the Somme–Marne–Saône–Jura position, see Keitel Wehrmacht High Command/Wehrmacht Operations Staff/Operations (Army), No. 772719/44, dated August 3, 1944, quoted in: OB West, Ia, No. 657/44, RH 19 IV/52, p. 143 f.; concerning the fortresses, see Keitel Wehrmacht High Command/Wehrmacht Operations Staff/Operations (Army), No. 772752/44, dated August 5, 1944, quoted in: OB West, Ia, No. 668/44, RH 19 IV/52, pp. 207 ff.; regarding the effort to secure the French-Italian border, see Wehrmacht High Command/Wehrmacht Operations Staff/Operations (Army), No. 009377/44, dated August 4, 1944, quoted in: OB West, Ia, No. 6393/44, RH 19 IV/52, pp. 165 ff.

51. Ose, *Entscheidung im Westen*, pp. 202 ff and 260 ff.

52. Montgomery, nevertheless, continued to retain his superior position as overall Allied ground forces commander until Eisenhower moved his headquarters to the Continent and on September 1 assumed direct command of the ground forces, as well as retaining overall Allied supreme command.

53. Pogue, *The Supreme Command*, pp. 262 ff.

54. OB West, Ia, No. 6297/44, dated August 2, 1944, RH 19 IV/52, p. 89.

55. Ose, *Entscheidung im Westen*, p. 221.

56. RH 19 IX/8, p. 124 f.

57. War Diary, Headquarters, Fifth Panzer Army, dated August 14, 1944, RH 21-5/52, p. 13.

58. Wehrmacht High Command/Wehrmacht Operations Staff/Operations (H), No. 772801/44, dated August 9, 1944, quoted in: RH 19 IV/52, p. 355.

59. Zimmermann, "Bericht," MS-B-308, IV, p. 89.

60. Wehrmacht Operations Staff/Operations, No. 772864/44, dated August 13, 1944, quoted in: RH 19 IV/53, p. 110 f.

61. Daily Report, Army Group B, dated August 15, 1944, RH 19 IX/9, Part 2, p. 1089 f.

62. See also and below: Ose, *Entscheidung im Westen*, pp. 242 ff.

63. Although OB West in the meantime did not seek any contact with the Allies—as Hitler assumed after he had several days earlier been informed about Kluge's involvement in the events of July 20—this renewed trip to the front indirectly also was tied to the attempt on Hitler's life. See ibid. and Irving, *Hitler und seine Feldherren*, p. 626, footnote 6.

64. Zimmermann, "OB West," MS-T-121, B IV, p. 1571.

65. Ibid., p. 1545.

66. Situation Estimate, Army Task Group G, dated August 12, 1944, quoted in: OB West, Ia, No. 706/44, RH 19 IV/53, p. 60.

67. Telephone conversation between Kluge and Blumentritt on August 16, 1155–1207, RH 19 IV/53, pp. 208 ff.

68. RH 19 IV/53, p. 171 f.

69. *Hitlers Lagebesprechungen,* Conference on August 31, 1944, p. 612.

70. Zimmermann, "OB West," MS-T-121, B IV, p. 1555.

71. Wehrmacht Operations Staff/Operations, No. 772887/44, dated August 15, 1944, quoted according to Headquarters, Army Group B, Operations Section, No. 6073/44, RH 19 IX/7, p. 27 f.

72. Telephone conversation between Blumentritt and Jodl, dated August 15, 1944, RH 19 IV/53, pp. 170 ff.

73. In contravention of Hitler's order, Hausser had his II SS Panzer Corps evacuate Kharkov on February 15, 1943, quite on his own initiative; see: Hillgruber/Hümmelchen, "Chronik," [Chronicles], p. 162.

74. War Diary, Wehrmacht High Command, IV/1, p. 345. The effective date of the promotion was March 1, 1944.

75. Keilig, "Generale," [General Officers], p. 228.

76. War Diary, Wehrmacht High Command, IV/1, p. 466.

4. The Initial Situation in Southern France

1. War Diary, Wehrmacht High Command, III/2, dated June 10, 1943, pp. 1442 ff.

2. Ibid., p. 1025 f.

3. Situation Estimate, dated October 25, 1943, OB West, Ia, No. 550/43, RH 19 IV/1, pp. 71 ff.

4. Ibid.

5. Ibid., p. 287.

6. Ibid., p. 300 f.

7. In addition, there were reservations at the very highest levels about Colonel General Johannes Blaskowitz, who was to be put in charge of it.

8. See Blaskowitz, Headquarters, Army Task Group G, Operations Section, No. 1598/44, August 4, 1944, in: Staiger, "Rückzug," pp. 19 ff.

9. War Diary, Wehrmacht High Command, III/2, p. 508.

10. On June 3, and then, until the middle of August, once again, four divisions, including two Panzer divisions.

11. Zimmermann, "Operationen" [Operations], MS-B-308, IV, p. 89.

12. See Blaskowitz, Headquarters, Army Task Group G, Operations Section, No. 1598/44, dated August 4, 1944, in: Staiger, "Rückzug," pp. 19 ff.

13. The probabilities of a landing in Liguria or southern France or the Adriatic Sea area were estimated at 5:4:1; War Diary, Armed Forces High Command, IV/1, p. 349.

14. Telephone conversation, Major Friedel (Wehrmacht Operations Staff) with Operations Officer, OB West, dated August 5, 1944, 2100 hours, RH 19 IV/52, p. 186.

15. War Diary, OB West, dated August 5, 1944, RH 19 IV/45, p. 40.

16. Order dated August 11, 1944, RH 19 IV/45, p. 90.

17. In 1944 a German infantry division had four to five antitank companies with twelve antitank guns each; Mueller-Hillebrand, "Heer" [Army], III, p. 225.

18. OB West, Ia, No. 6726/44, dated August 10, 1944, RH 19 IV/52, p. 381.

19. War Diary, Wehrmacht High Command, IV/1, p. 512.

20. Telephone conversation of Navy Group West, dated August 11, 1944, 2240 hours, RH 19 IV/53, p. 23.

21. Report, 2nd Air Division, dated August 12, 1944, 0720 hours, RH 19 IV/45, p. 93.

22. War Diary, Wehrmacht High Command, IV/1, p. 512.

23. Ibid., p. 350.

24. Communication from General Warlimont, dated August 12, 1944, 1000 hours, War Diary, Wehrmacht High Command, IV/1, p. 465.

25. Blaskowitz, "Lagebeurteilung," MS-B-421, p. 2.

26. Gyldenfeldt, in: Zimmermann, "OB West," MS-T-121, B V, p. 1676.

27. Bonaparte's Birthday: August 15, 1769.

28. Situation Estimate, Headquarters, Army Task Group G, Operations Section, No. 1800/44, dated August 12, 1944, RH 19 XII/7, p. 145.

29. See Hitler, Wehrmacht Operations Staff/Operations, No. 772864, quoted in: OB West, Ia, No. 712/44, RH 19 IV/53, p. 110 f.

30. War Diary, Wehrmacht High Command, IV/1, p. 511 f.

31. Situation Estimate, Headquarters, Army Task Group G, Operations Section, No. 1859/44, dated August 14, 1944, RH 19 XII/7, p. 177 f.

32. OB West, Ia, No. 6872/44, dated August 14, 1944, RH 19 IV/53, p. 122.

33. Ose, *Entscheidung im Westen*, p. 134.

34. Supplies of bauxite and tungsten, of course, were still ensured for 1944; War Diary, Wehrmacht High Command, IV/1, p. 23.

35. Zimmermann, "OB West," MS-T-121, B V, p. 1715 f.

36. Major General Treusch von Buttlar-Brandelfels, in: Zimmermann, "OB West," MS-T-121, B V, pp. 1721 ff.

37. Ose, *Entscheidung im Westen*, p. 224.

38. This operation was renamed DRAGOON in July probably because Churchill felt "dragooned" (forced) into the landing in southern France. See: *Eisenhower Papers*, IV, p. 2056.

39. Combined Chiefs of Staff, dated August 16, 1943, in: Wilt, *The French Riviera Campaign of August 1944*, p. 5, footnote 1.

40. Pogue, *The Supreme Command*, p. 111.

41. De Gaulle, "Memoiren" [Memoirs], p. 130.

42. Matloff, *Strategic Planning for Coalition Warfare 1943–1944*, p. 422 f.

43. Pogue, *The Supreme Command*, p. 112.

44. Matloff, *Strategic Planning for Coalition Warfare 1943–1944*, p. 425.

45. Wilson's letter to Eisenhower, dated June 19, 1944, in: Matloff, *Strategic Planning for Coalition Warfare 1943–1944*, p. 470, and Pogue, *The Supreme Command*, p. 220.

46. June 24, 1944, letter, Pogue, *The Supreme Command*, pp. 219 ff.

47. Ibid., p. 222.

48. Ehrman, *Grand Strategy*, V, pp. 362 ff.

49. "Hitlers Weisungen" [Hitler's Directives], p. 176.

50. Situation Estimate, OB West, dated October 25, 1943, RH 19 IV/1, pp. 71 ff.

51. War Diary, OB West, dated August 5, 1944, RH 19 IV/52, p. 186.

52. The army corps had only one signal company, whereas the corps units normally would include an entire signal battalion with up to four companies; cf., Tessin, "Verbände" [Formations], 5, p. 258.

53. Wilutzky, "Heeresgruppe G," MS-A-882, Appendix 3c.

54. Tessin, "Verbände," 7, pp. 113 ff, and Wegmüller, "Die Konzeption," p. 199.

55. OB West, Ia, No. 7317/44, dated August 24, 1944, RH 19 IV/54, p. 141, and OB West, Ia, No. 7396/44, dated August 25, 1944, RH 19 IV/54, p. 217.

56. Situation Estimate, OB West, dated October 25, 1943, RH 19 IV/1, pp. 71 ff.

57. Zimmermann, "OB West," MS-T-121, B V, pp. 1670 ff.

58. Blaskowitz, "Armeegruppe G," MS-B-800, p. 9 f.

59. Zimmermann, "OB West," MS-T-121, B V, p. 1678.

60. Situation Estimate, dated August 7, 1944, OB Commander West, Ia, No. 6584/44, RH 19 IV/52, pp. 261 ff.

61. Zimmermann, "OB West," MS-T-121, B V, p. 1758 f.

62. Situation Estimate, Army Task Group G, dated August 14, 1944, RH 19 XII/7, p. 177 f.

63. Wilutzky, "Heeresgruppe G," MS-A-882, Appendix 3c.

64. Staiger, "Rückzug," p. 13 f.

65. Schulz, "19. Armee," MS-B-514, p. 6.

66. In the winter of 1943–1944, most of these battalions were transferred to France, contrary to the original idea, which had been to employ them to "go fight against Stalin"; cf., Tessin, "Verbände," 1, p. 140 f.

67. Schulz, "19. Armee," MS-B-514, p. 7.

68. Tessin, "Verbände," 6, p. 80.

69. At that point in time, Marseille and Toulon had not yet been designated as fortresses. Their commanders were given authority as fortress commandants only on August 21, 1944, RH 19 IV/54, p. 36.

70. Tessin, "Verbände," 8, p. 190, and 9, p. 211.

71. Ibid., 8, p. 183.

72. At that time, thirty-three artillery pieces, including nine from the 338th Infantry Division, were en route to Normandy.

73. Wilt, *The French Riviera Campaign of August 1944*, p. 41, and Schulz, "19. Armee," MS-B-514, pp. 9 ff.

74. Staiger, "Rückzug," pp. 14 ff.

75. See also Lieutenant General Eugen Oberhäuser, in: Zimmermann, "OB West," MS-T-121, B IV, pp. 1768 ff.

76. Headquarters, Army Task Group G, Intelligence Section, No. 636/44, RH 19 XII/31, p. 1.

77. Schulz, "19. Armee," MS-B-514, p. 9.

78. Ibid., p. 11.

79. See von Gyldenfeldt, Headquarters, Army Task Group G, Operations Section, No. 1769/44, dated August 10, 1944, RH 19 XII/7, p. 123.

80. War Diary, OB West, dated August 6, 1944, RH 19 IV/52, p. 215.

81. Calculated according to "Message on Status of Reorganization of 11th Panzer Division," as of August 1, 1944, RH 19 IV/52, pp. 135 ff.

82. See Adolf Hitler, Wehrmacht Operations Staff/Operations Section, No. 772801/44, dated August 9, 1944, quoted in: OB West, Ia, No. 682/44, dated August 10, 1944, RH 19 IV/52, p. 355.

83. OB West, Ia, No. 687/44, dated August 11, 1944, RH 19 IV/52, p. 392.

84. Headquarters, Army Task Group G, Ia, No. 1800/44, dated August 12, 1944, RH 19 XII/7, p. 145.

85. Headquarters, Army Task Group G, Ia, No. 1833/44, dated August 13, 1944, ibid., p. 161.

86. Headquarters, Army Task Group G, Ia, No. 1800/44, dated August 12, 1944, ibid., p. 145.

87. Headquarters, Army Task Group G, Ia, No. 1869/44, dated August 14, 1944, ibid., p. 181.

88. Wiese, "19. Armee," MS-B-787, p. 10.

89. Ibid., p. 12.

90. Wilt, *The French Riviera Campaign of August 1944*, p. 82.

91. Ibid., p. 21 and 75 f.; Staiger, "Rückzug," p. 30.

92. For the planning details, see Wilt, *The French Riviera Campaign of August 1944*, pp. 64 ff and 82 ff.

93. By comparison, five Allied infantry divisions and three airborne divisions totaling around 130,000 men landed in Normandy on June 6. During the first two days, 185,000 men and 19,000 vehicles had been put ashore; cf., Ehrman, *Grand Strategy*, V, p. 284.

94. Wilt, *The French Riviera Campaign of August 1944*, p. 84 f.

95. Staiger, "Rückzug," p. 36.

96. Eisenhower to Wilson, dated July 6, 1944, in: Pogue, *The Supreme Command*, p. 223.

97. By comparison, on June 6, 1944, the Allied landings were supported by eight battleships, twenty-two cruisers, ninety-three destroyers, eight hundred smaller vessels, and about forty-two hundred landing craft.

98. Wilt, *The French Riviera Campaign of August 1944*, pp. 70 f and 83 f.

99. Supreme Commander, Mediterranean Allied Air Forces. His deputy was Air Marshal Sir John Slessor.

100. Wilt, *The French Riviera Campaign of August 1944*, pp. 71 ff.

101. Ibid., p. 74.

102. Blaskowitz, "Reaction," MS-A-868, p. 5.

103. Situation Estimate, OB West, dated July 24, 1944, in: War Diary, Wehrmacht High Command, IV/1, p. 327.

104. Wiese, "19. Armee," MS-B-787, p. 5, and Seiz, "159. Inf. Div.," MS-A-960, p. 3.

105. Pogue, *The Supreme Command*, p. 238.

106. For the first time, six hundred "terrorists" appeared in a cohesive formation on June 2, 1944, at Figeac (north of Toulouse); War Diary, Wehrmacht High Command, IV/1, p. 310.

107. Monthly Report No. 15 of the Control Inspectorate of the German Armistice Commission, July 7, 1944, No. 890/44, quoted in: Wilt, *The Atlantic Wall: Hitler's Defense in the West*, p. 152.

108. Situation Estimate, Headquarters, Army Task Group G, Ia, No. 1859/44, August 14, 1944, RH 19 XII/7, p. 177 f.

109. Activity Report, Intelligence Section, Army Task Group G, for the period of August 1 to August 31, 1944, Intelligence Section, No. 636/44, RH 19 XII/31, p. 1.

110. Wilutzky, "Heeresgruppe G," MS-A-882, pp. 7 ff.

111. Situation Estimate, OB West, Ia, No. 6872/44, dated August 14, 1944, RH 19 IV/53, p. 122 f.

112. Situation Estimate, OB West, Ia, No. 6584/44, dated August 7, 1944, RH 19 IV/52, pp. 261 ff.

113. War Diary entries, Lieutenant General Walter Botsch (Chief of Staff, Headquarters, Nineteenth Army), RH 20-19/85, p. 1.

114. War Diary, Headquarters, Nineteenth Army, RH 20-19/88, p. 40.

115. Report from Navy Group West, dated August 15, 1944, 0315 hours, OB West, Ia, No. 6742/44, RH IV/53, p. 143.

116. Supplement to daily report for August 15, 1944, Headquarters, Army Task Group G, Ia, No. 1909/44, dated August 16, 1944, RH 19 XII/7, p. 193.

117. RH 20-19/85, p. 2.

118. Ibid., and War Diary, Headquarters, Nineteenth Army, RH 20-19/88, p. 40 f.

119. RH 20-19/85, p. 2.

120. War Diary, Headquarters, Nineteenth Army, RH 20-19/88, p. 40.

121. See Keitel, Wehrmacht High Command/Wehrmacht Operations Staff, Operations (H) West, No. 772752/44, dated August 5, 1944, quoted in: OB West, Ia, No. 668/44, RH 19 IV/52, pp. 207 ff.

122. War Diary, Headquarters, Nineteenth Army, RH 20-19/88, p. 42.

123. On August 15, the Allied Air Forces reported 3,936 sorties, while the Luftwaffe reported twenty-one missions.

124. Schulz, "19. Armee," MS-B-514, p. 18.

125. War Diary, Headquarters, Nineteenth Army, RH 20-19/88, p. 41 f.

126. Ibid.

127. See Blaskowitz, Headquarters, Army Task Group G, Operations/Supply, No. 13102/44, dated August 16, 1944, RH 19 XII/7, p. 203 f.

128. Robichon, *Invasion Provence*, p. 109.

129. RH 20-19/85, p. 3.

130. Army Task Group G received the first report as to the landing via OB West telephone report, Intelligence Section, OB West—Headquarters, Army Task Group G, dated August 15, 1944, 1355 hours, RH 19 IV/142, p. 158.

131. Headquarters, Army Task Group G, Ia, No. 1879/44, dated August 15, 1944, RH 19 XII/7, p. 188.

132. RH 19 IV/142, p. 158.

133. Zimmermann, "OB West," MS-T-121, B V, p. 1690.

134. War Diary, OB West, RH 19 IV/45, p. 112.

135. War Diary, Headquarters, Nineteenth Army, RH 20-19/88, p. 45.

136. See Blaskowitz, Headquarters, Army Task Group G, Ia, No. 1598/44, dated August 4, 1944, in: Staiger, "Rückzug," pp. 19 ff.

137. War Diary, Headquarters, Nineteenth Army, RH 20-19/88, p. 42.

138. Wilt, *The French Riviera Campaign of August 1944*, p. 91.

139. War Diary, Headquarters, Nineteenth Army, RH 20-19/88, p. 43.

140. See Blaskowitz, Headquarters, Army Task Group G, Operations Section/Supply Section, No. 13102/44, dated August 16, 1944, RH 19 XII/7, p. 203 f.

141. RH 20-19/85, p. 3.

142. The following had been ordered to the front since August 1, 1944: 48th, 49th, 89th, 344th Infantry Divisions, 6th Parachute Division, and Luftwaffe 17th and 18th Field Divisions.

143. One of these bridges had just been destroyed by bombs, RH 20-19/85, p. 4.

144. RH 20-19/85, p. 4.

145. Zimmermann, "OB West," MS-T-121, B V, pp. 1700 ff.

146. Order, Headquarters, Nineteenth Army, dated August 15, 1944, 2400 hours, RH 20-19/88, p. 44.

147. Telephone connections were still available, War Diary, Headquarters, Nineteenth Army, RH 20-19/88, p. 54.

148. War Diary, Headquarters, Nineteenth Army, dated August 15, 1944, RH 20-19/88, p. 54.

149. Ibid., p. 44.

150. War Diary, Headquarters, Nineteenth Army, dated August 15, 1944, RH 20-19/88, p. 43.

151. Message, Headquarters, Nineteenth Army, dated August 15, 1944, 1340 hours, RH 19 IV/53, p. 156.

152. Zimmermann, "OB West," MS-T-121, B V, pp. 1691 ff.

153. Ibid., p. 1554.

154. Telephone conversation between Jodl and Blumentritt, dated August 15, 1944, 1830 hours, RH 19 IV/53, p. 171 f.

155. War Diary, Wehrmacht High Command, IV/1, pp. 346 and 470.

156. War Diary, Headquarters, Nineteenth Army, dated August 16, 1944, 0620 hours, RH 20-19/88, p. 60.

157. Message, Operations Section, LXII Army Corps, dated August 16, 1944, 0115 hours, War Diary, Headquarters, Nineteenth Army, RH 20-19/88, pp. 58 and 88.

158. General Neuling was at first able to escape, but he was captured farther north on August 18, 1944.

159. Message, Headquarters, Nineteenth Army, dated August 16, 1944, 0930 hours, RH 19 XII/7, p. 164.

160. War Diary, Headquarters, Nineteenth Army, dated August 16, 1944, RH 20-19/88, p. 55.

161. Blaskowitz, Army Task Group G, MS-B-800, p. 12 f.

162. In January 1944, Blumentritt had requested the chiefs of staff of the field armies in the west to comment on the question of employing fast-moving formations against the background of the threatening invasion. The quotations given here are taken from Feyerabend's letter of reply, dated February 4, 1944, and Botsch's letter, dated January 29, 1944, RH 19 IV/1, pp. 26 ff.

163. Colonel Carl Bründel was in command on the spot.

164. Headquarters, Nineteenth Army, Operations Section, No. 8505/44, dated August 16, 1944, RH 20-19/88, p. 68.

165. RH 20-19/85, p. 7.

166. War Diary, Headquarters, Nineteenth Army, dated August 16, 1944, RH 20-19/88, p. 93.

167. Message from Forward Command Post, Army Task Group G, dated August 16, 1944, quoted in: Headquarters, Army Task Group G, Operations Section, No. 1922/44, dated August 17, 1944, RH 19 XII/7, p. 165.

168. War Diary, Headquarters, Nineteenth Army, dated August 16, 1944, 1140 hours, RH 20-19/88, p. 89.

169. Wilt, *The French Riviera Campaign of August 1944*, p. 107.

170. War Diary, Headquarters, Nineteenth Army, dated August 16, 1944, RH 20-19/88, p. 90.

171. Most of the PzKpfw V Panther tanks of the 11th Panzer Division's 15th Panzer Regiment were still stuck at Toulouse, RH 20-19/85, p. 3.

172. Blaskowitz and Gyldenfeldt, however, were at the forward command post at Nineteenth Army headquarters in Avignon.

173. War Diary, Army Task Group G, dated August 16, 1944, Rh 19 XII/5, p. 119.

174. He did, however, agree that Wiese should husband his pontoon equipment that might still be decisive in the course of further developments. He therefore ordered bridging columns to be brought up from the rest of the army task force group sector; Headquarters, Army Task Group G, Operations Section, No. 1913 and 1914/44, dated August 16, 1944, RH 19 XII/7, p. 201 f.

175. See Blaskowitz, Situation Estimate, Headquarters, Army Task Group G, Operations Section/Supply Section, No. 13102/44, dated August 16, 1944, RH 19 XII/7, p. 203 f.

176. Ibid.

177. On August 21, 1944, he took command of French Army B, which, on September 15, 1944, was renamed First French Army.

178. War Diary, Headquarters, Nineteenth Army, dated August 16, 1944, RH 20-19/88, p. 93.

179. Zimmermann, "OB West," MS-T-121, B V, p. 1716.

180. Ibid., pp. 1721 ff.

181. See Keitel, Wehrmacht High Command/Wehrmacht Operations Staff, Operations Section (H), No. 009944/44, dated August 17, 1944, quoted from OB West, Ia, No. 6945/44, dated August 17, 1944, 0320 hours, RH 19 IV/53, p. 252. The date on the order in reference must be in error. The order was issued on August 16, 1944; see Warlimont's communications on August 18, 1944, 2000 hours, War Diary, Wehrmacht High Command, IV/1, p. 466, and RH 19 IV/53, p. 276.

182. Zimmermann, "OB West," MS-T-121, B V, pp. 1715 and 1736 ff.

183. The order arrived at 1115 hours on August 17, 1944, at Headquarters, Army Task Group G, in Rouffiac; War Diary, Army Task Group G, RH 19 XII/5, p. 121. At that time, Blaskowitz and Gyldenfeldt were in Avignon. Communications from Rouffiac had broken down once again; this is why Blaskowitz received the order only in the evening; cf., Wilutzky, "Heeresgruppe G," MS-A-882, p. 16.

184. The 16th and 159th Infantry Divisions on the Atlantic were too far away; the 716th Infantry Division, which was west of Montpellier, was considered to be immobile.

185. Gyldenfeldt, "Armeegruppe G," MS-B-488, p. 1.

186. Zimmermann, "OB West," MS-T-121, B V, p. 1739.

187. See Blumentritt, OB West, Ia, No. 6945/44, dated August 17, 1944, 0320 hours, RH 19 IV/53, p. 252.

188. Telephone conversation between von Kluge and Blumentritt, dated August 16, 1944, 1155–1207 hours, RH 19 IV/53, p. 209.

189. War Diary, Wehrmacht High Command, IV/1, pp. 352 and 471.

190. Gyldenfeldt in: Zimmermann, "OB West," MS-T-121, B V, pp. 1745 ff.

191. See Adolf Hitler, Wehrmacht Operations Staff, No. 772916/44, dated August 18, 1944, quoted in: OB West, Ia, No. 730/44, dated August 18, 1944, RH 19 IV/53, p. 276. The date for Hitler's order is in error, because the order had been signed already on August 16 and was received by Army Group B at 0830 hours on August 17; War Diary, Army Group B, dated August 17, 1944, RH 19 IX/88, p. 18.

192. War Diary, Headquarters, Nineteenth Army, dated August 18, 1944, 1515 hours, RH 20-19/88, p. 185.

193. Schulz, "19. Armee," MS-B-514, p. 21.

194. See Adolf Hitler, Wehrmacht Operations Staff, No. 772916/44, dated August 18, 1944, in: RH 19 IV/53, p. 276.

195. See Jodl, Wehrmacht Operations Staff, Supply Section, No. 009986/44, dated August 19, 1944, quoted in: OB West, Ia, No. 7023/44, dated August 19, 1944, ibid., p. 315.

196. See Adolf Hitler, Wehrmacht Operations Staff, No. 772916/44, dated August 18, 1944, ibid., p. 276.

197. Headquarters, Army Task Group G, Operations Section, No. 42(?)/44, dated August 12, 1944, RH 19 XII/9, p. 19 f.

198. *Hitlers Lagebesprechungen,* Conference on July 31, 1944, pp. 593 ff.

199. See Adolf Hitler, Wehrmacht Operations Staff, No. 772916/44, dated August 18, 1944, in: RH 19 IV/53, p. 276.

200. Blaskowitz, "Armeegruppe G," MS-B-800, p. 15.

201. Zimmermann, "OB West," MS-T-121, B V, p. 1753.

202. War Diary, Army Group B, dated August 17, 1944, 0830 hours, RH 19 IX/88, p. 18.

203. War Diary, Army Task Group G, dated August 18, 1944, 1100 hours, RH 19 XII/5, p. 125.

204. RH 20-19/85, p. 11.

205. General of Engineers Karl Sachs finally was informed of the retreat order via the Navy Duty Station of Admiral, Atlantic; Zimmermann, "OB West," MS-T-121, B V, p. 1749 f.

206. Wilutzky, "Heeresgruppe G," MS-A-882, p. 17.

207. Blaskowitz, "Armeegruppe G," MS-B-800, p. 14.

208. Bennett, *Ultra in the West: The Normandy Campaign 1944–45,* p. 152.

209. Ose, *Entscheidung im Westen,* p. 245.

210. Telephone conversation between Kluge and Jodl, dated August 16, 1944, 1245 hours, War Diary, Headquarters, Fifth Panzer Army, RH 21-5/53, Appendix 24.

211. OB West, Ia, No. 726/44, dated August 16, 1944, RH 19 IV/53, p. 217.

5. The Initial Situation in Northern France

1. War Diary, Wehrmacht High Command, IV/2, p. 466 f.

2. War Diary, Army Group B, dated August 16, 1944, RH 19 IX/88, pp. 4 ff.

3. OB West, Ia, No. 726/44, dated August 16, 1944, RH 19 IV/53, p. 217.

4. RH 19 IX/88, p. 7 f.

5. Conference between OB West and General of Infantry Dietrich von Choltitz (Commanding General and Wehrmacht commander of Greater Paris), General of Aviation Karl Kitzinger (Military Commander in France), on August 17, 1944, 0900 hours, RH 19 IX/88, p. 18.

6. RH 19 IV/53, p. 153 f.

7. Telephone conversation between Blumentritt to Speidel, dated August 16, 1944, 1630 hours, RH 19 IX/88, p. 10.

8. For Operation SEA LION, which was planned against England in 1940 but was never carried out.

9. The consequence of the resultant delay was that this headquarters was able to move only on August 19 under enemy fire; Daily Report, Army Group B, dated August 19, RH 19 IX/88, p. 37 f.

10. War Diary, Army Group B, dated August 17, 1944, 1815 hours, RH 19 IX/88, p. 23.

11. Domarus, "Hitler," II, p. 2141.

12. Liddell Hart, *The German Generals Talk,* p. 503.

13. Kluge would have been arrested immediately anyway; see: *Hitlers Lagebesprechungen,* Conference on August 31, p. 610 f.

14. Ose, *Entscheidung im Westen,* pp. 247 ff. Ose also interprets the farewell letter of August 18, 1944, which Kluge addressed to Hitler. For the text of the letter itself, see RH 19 IV/226.

15. On his very first day in the west, Kluge had a very serious personal dispute with Rommel. See: Ruge, *Rommel und die Invasion,* p. 276.

16. At first, Model wore two hats, as OB West and as Commanding General, Army Group B.

17. Zimmermann, "OB West," MS-T-121, B IV, p. 1596.

18. Ritgen, *Die Geschichte der Panzer-Lehr Division im Westen, 1944/45,* p. 185.

19. Warlimont, *Im Hauptquartier der Deutschen Wehrmacht 1939–1945,* p. 485. The War Diary, Wehrmacht High Command, IV/1, p. 466, on the other hand, mentions a "detailed situation briefing." Warlimont (Deputy Chief, Wehrmacht Operations Staff) explained such deviations by noting that he never had enough time to instruct the War Diary officer in detail; cf., Warlimont, *Im Hauptquartier,* p. 481, footnote 34.

20. Comment by Colonel General Hans von Salmuth, in: BA-MA, N 6/1, "Model," p. 253.

21. Teske, *Die silberne Spiegel,* p. 216 f.; Speidel, *Invasion 1944,* p. 162; Zimmermann, "OB West," MS-T-121, B IV, p. 1594 f.

22. War Diary, Wehrmacht High Command, IV/2, p. 1711.

23. Warlimont's Communications, dated August 26, 1944, 2200 hours, War Diary, Wehrmacht High Command, IV/2, p. 467.

24. *Hitlers Lagebesprechungen,* Conference on July 31, 1944, pp. 586 ff.

25. Ibid., p. 598.

26. Major General Treusch von Buttlar-Brandenfels, in: Zimmermann, "OB West," MS-T-121, B IV, p. 1574 f.

27. U.S. First Army Group.

28. Situation Estimate, OB West, dated July 30, 1944, RH 19 IV/51, pp. 274 ff.

29. On August 1, 1944, Salmuth still had fourteen major units.

30. The 47th, 70th, 136th (Special Missions), 182nd, 245th, 348th, 712th, and 226th Infantry Divisions, which had just arrived in the Army sector. The 136th consisted of only eight companies of personnel with stomach problems. Messages on the status of rail movements between August 15 and August 20, 1944, RH 19 IV/53, pp. 189 ff.

31. The following had been ordered to the front since August 1, 1944: 48th, 49th, 89th, 344th Infantry Divisions, 6th Parachute Division, and Luftwaffe 17th and 18th Field Divisions.

32. Zangen, "15. Armee," MS-B-249, p. 9.

33. In addition to the 226th (see above), also the 59th and 64th Infantry Divisions that arrived in the west by the end of August. Organization Order, dated June 22, 1944, Tessin, "Verbände," 5, pp. 226, 259, and 8, p. 123.

34. Zimmermann, "OB West," MS-T-121, B IV, pp. 1607 ff.

35. Ibid.

36. Walter, "V-Waffen," MS-B-689, pp. 57 ff.

37. The V-1 bases in northern France had been abandoned since August 12, 1944, and most of the rockets were moved into the Belgian area.

38. The fighting had ended in St. Malo on August 18, but the force manning the battery on Ile de Cézembre did not surrender until September 2, 1944.

39. Numerically, with a strength of about two divisions, OB West, Ia, No. 7201/44, dated August 23, 1944, RH 19 IV/54, p. 108.

40. The following units in addition to the eight major formations of Headquarters, Fifteenth Army: 347th and 719th Infantry Divisions from Wehrmacht Commander, Netherlands.

41. RH 19 IV/68 K, Map 8, dated August 16, 1944.

42. Together with Panzer Group Eberbach under command.

43. Headquarters, Army Group B, Operations Section, No. 6078/44, dated August 17, 1944, RH 19 IX/4, p. 322 f.

44. Daily Report, OB West for August 17, 1944, RH 19 IV/53, p. 266.

45. Headquarters, Seventh Army, and the headquarters of Panzer Group Eberbach, which performed functions resembling those of a field army headquarters.

46. Daily Report, OB West, August 16, 1944, RH 19 IV/53, pp. 228 ff.

47. Telephone conversation between Gause and Speidel, dated August 15, 1944, 1240 hours, RH 19 IX/87, p. 241.

48. For example, the 331st and 344th Infantry Divisions, the Luftwaffe 17th Field Division, and some scattered remnants, including from the 352nd Infantry Division.

49. OB West, Operations Section, No. 6598/44, dated August 8, 1944, RH 19/4, p. 254.

50. See Adolf Hitler, Wehrmacht Operations Staff/Operations Section, No. 772830/44, dated August 11, 1944, quoted in: Headquarters, Army Group B, Operations Section, No. 5951/44, dated August 12, 1944, RH 19 IX/8, p. 119 f.

51. Emmerich, "1. Armee," MS-B-728, p. 3.

52. See also: Message to OB West, status as of August 19, 1944, RH 19 IV/53, p. 362 f.

53. The men of the 1010th Security Regiment had neither steel helmets nor entrenching tools; see Emmerich, "1. Armee," MS-B-728, p. 7.

54. War Diary, OB West, Appendix for August 12, 1944, RH 19 IV/53, pp. 52 ff.

55. Daily Report, OB West, for August 17, 1944, ibid., p. 265.

56. War Diary, Army Group B, dated August 17, 1944, RH 19 IX/88, p. 19.

57. Daily Report, OB West, for August 18, 1944, RH 19 IV/53, p. 299.

58. Telephone conversation between Blumentritt and Speidel, dated August 16, 1944, 1540 hours, RH 19 IX/88, p. 9.

59. General of Infantry Erwin Vierow was to develop the barrier belt. Line layout: Poissy–Aigremont–St. Gemme–west of St. Nom–Villepreux–Hill

168–Troux–Saclay–Le Guichel–Palaiseau–Hill 106–Vigeux–Montgeron–Bonneuil–Marne River loop, War Diary, OB West, Appendices, RH 19 IV/53, p. 253.

60. Daily Report, OB West, for August 15, 1944, RH 19 IV/53, pp. 184 ff.

61. War Diary, OB West, dated August 8, 1944, RH 19 IV/45, p. 63.

62. OB West, Operations Section, No. 6335/44, dated August 2, 1944, RH 19 IV/52, p. 99.

63. Fahrmbacher held Wehrmacht authority, OB West, Operations Section, No. 6335/44, dated August 2, 1944, ibid.

64. Army Group B, Operations Section, No. 5101/44, dated August 16, 1944, RH 19 IX/88, p. 15.

65. Only the battery on Ile de Cézembre with about 360 men and three guns continued to fight.

66. Remnants of the 77th Infantry Division and scattered elements of the 91st Air Landing Division (as well as elements of 5th Parachute Division).

67. Brest: 266th and 343rd Infantry Divisions, 2nd Parachute Division. Lorient: Elements of the 265th Infantry Division. St. Nazaire: Remnants of the 265th Infantry Division.

68. 84th, 89th, 271st, 276th, 277th, 326th, 353rd, and 363rd Infantry Divisions, 3rd Parachute Division, 2nd and 116th Panzer Divisions, 1st SS Panzer Division, 10th SS Panzer Division, 12th SS Panzer Division.

69. 243rd, 275th, 331st, 338th, and 352nd Infantry Divisions, 5th and 6th Parachute Divisions, 9th and 21st Panzer Divisions, Panzer-Lehr Division, 17th SS Panzer Grenadier Division; wartime organizational charts, Army General Staff/Operations Section III, dated August 15, 1944, MGFA [Military History Research Institute] Documentation Center.

70. Kluge's letter to Hitler, dated August 18, 1944, RH 19 IV/226.

71. In the area of the 21st Army Group: 21–23 divisions, in the area of 12th Army Group: 24–26 divisions; cf., RH 19 IV/68 K and 69 K as well as Staubwasser, "Feindbild," [Enemy Situation], MS-B-825, pp. 63 ff.

72. Twenty U.S., twelve British, and three Canadian divisions as well as one French and one Polish division each; cf., Ruppenthal, *Logistical Support of the Armies,* I, p. 457, and Eisenhower, *Crusade in Europe,* p. 342.

73. For the German side: Situation Estimate, August 14, 1944, OB West, Operations Section, No. 6872/44, RH 19 IV/53, p. 122 f. For the Allied side: Blumenson, *Breakout and Pursuit,* p. 516.

74. According to German data, by July 31, 1944: 2,395 Allied tanks, 951 German Panzers; by August 13, 1944: 3,370 Allied tanks, War Diary, Wehrmacht High Command, IV/1, p. 329 f.

75. Ruppenthal, *Logistical Support of the Armies,* II, p. 5.

76. Ibid., I, p. 465.

77. Ibid., pp. 413 and 465.

78. Ibid., pp. 468 ff.

79. Ibid., p. 470.

80. Blumenson, *Breakout and Pursuit,* p. 431 f.

81. Ruppenthal, *Logistical Support of the Armies*, I, p. 483.

82. Eisenhower to Marshall, dated August 7, 1944, *Eisenhower Papers*, IV, p. 2059 f.

83. Eisenhower to Marshall and Combined Chiefs of Staff, dated August 2, 1944, ibid., pp. 2048 ff.

84. Blumenson, *Breakout and Pursuit*, p. 431.

85. Ibid., p. 370.

86. Major General Robert Grow, U.S. 6th Armored Division (Brest), ibid., p. 380.

87. Ibid., p. 382 f and pp. 394 ff.

88. Early in August, Brest held about fifteen thousand men instead of the initially assumed three thousand; St. Malo was held by about twelve thousand men instead of three thousand to five thousand; around twenty-five thousand Germans were in Lorient; ibid., pp. 364, 380, 386 ff.

89. Elements of the 266th Infantry Division, reinforced by the 77th Infantry Division in St. Malo and the 343rd Infantry Division in Brest. On August 9, 1944, Brest also received the 2nd Parachute Division of Lieutenant General Hermann Ramcke, who then became the fortress commandant there.

90. Eisenhower's letter to Marshall, dated August 9, 1944, in: *Eisenhower Papers*, IV, p. 2062 f.

91. Blumenson, *Breakout and Pursuit*, p. 633.

92. Bennett, *Ultra in the West: The Normandy Campaign 1944–45*, pp. 117 ff.

93. Eisenhower's letter to Marshall, dated August 9, 1944, in: *Eisenhower Papers*, IV, p. 2062 f.

94. Montgomery, *Normandy to the Baltic*, p. 151.

95. The statistics vary: Ehrman, "Strategy," V, p. 378; Blumenson, *Breakout and Pursuit*, p. 557 f.

96. Wilmot, *The Struggle for Europe*, p. 448.

97. According to German estimates, during the week of August 14–20, 1944: three hundred Allied tanks; Staubwasser, "Feinbild," MS-B-825, p. 82.

98. Eisenhower's letter to Marshall, dated August 17, 1944, in: *Eisenhower Papers*, IV, p. 2071 f.

99. Pogue, *The Supreme Command*, p. 215; Blumenson, *Breakout and Pursuit*, p. 555.

100. Ose, *Entscheidung im Westen*, p. 255.

101. Pogue, *The Supreme Command*, p. 214. The fact that Bradley did not insist on an earlier revision in dealing with his British superior may have partly been determined rather decisively by the need for considering the sensitivities involved in coalition warfare; cf., Blumenson, *Breakout and Pursuit*, p. 508 f.

102. Quoted from: Wilmot, *The Struggle for Europe*, p. 443.

103. Blumenson, *Breakout and Pursuit*, pp. 524 ff. The Canadian Corps, coming from the north, also had problems. At any rate, the commanding general of the Canadian 4th Armored Division was relieved.

104. Montgomery's directive of August 20, 1944; Blumenson, *Breakout and Pursuit*, p. 574 f.

105. War Diary, Army Group B, dated August 19, 1944, RH 19 IX/88, p. 37 f.

106. Eisenhower's letter to Montgomery, dated August 19, 1944, in: *Eisenhower Papers*, IV, p. 2077 f.

107. Eisenhower, *Crusade in Europe*, p. 343.

108. Blumenson, *Breakout and Pursuit*, p. 572.

109. Michel, "Histoire," p. 118.

110. Cf., Pogue, *The Supreme Command*, p. 238.

111. Blumenson, *Breakout and Pursuit*, p. 354.

112. Pogue, *The Supreme Command*, p. 238.

6. The Start of the Retreat in the West

1. Colonel General von Salmuth's impressions, in: N 6/1, "Model," p. 253.

2. Conference with Model, dated August 18, 1944, RH 21-5/53, p. 59, and War Diary, Headquarters, Fifth Panzer Army, dated August 18, 1944, RH 21-5/52, p. 21.

3. See Model, dated August 18, 1944, RH 19 IX/4, p. 339 f.

4. See Model, Headquarters, Army Group B, Operations Section/Operations Officer, Air, No. 1702744, dated August 21, 1944, RH 19 IX/7, p. 42. But on Hitler's orders, those aircraft were to be employed only as "blitz bombers"—in other words, not as fighters.

5. According to Blumentritt in: N 6/1, "Model," p. 239.

6. Discussed for the German side in Ose, *Entscheidung im Westen*, pp. 232 ff.

7. Message, Operations Officer, Headquarters, Fifth Army, dated August 21, 1944, RH 19 IX/88, p. 64, supplemented by Gersdorff, "5. Panzerarmee," MS-B-726, p. 33 f.

8. 47th and 49th Infantry Divisions, 26th and 27th SS Panzer Divisions as well as 352nd Infantry Division and 9th Panzer Division, Headquarters, Army Group B, Operations Section, No. 6303/44, dated August 19, 1944, RH 19 IX/88, p. 40.

9. See Adolf Hitler, Wehrmacht Operations Staff/Operations Section, No. 772956/44, dated August 20, 1944, quoted in: Headquarters, Army Group B, Operations Section, No. 6352/44, RH 19 IX/7, pp. 30 ff.

10. War Diary, Wehrmacht High Command, IV/1, p. 379. That order was held back until August 24.

11. Jodl's War Diary entry of August 19, 1944, p. 57 f.

12. Wehrmacht High Command/Wehrmacht Operations Staff, Operations/West, No. 0010144/44, dated August 21, 1944, quoted in: Army Group B, Operations Section, No. 6378/44, RH 19 IX/7, p. 36 f.

13. OB West, Operations Section, No. 6883/44, dated August 20, 1944, RH 19 IV/53, p. 345 f.

14. According to Model in a letter to his son, dated August 26, 1944; Model's private archives.

15. See Blaskowitz, Headquarters, Army Task Group G, Operations Section, No. 67/44, dated August 21, 1944, RH 19 XII/9, pp. 28 ff, and Order, Army Task Group G, dated August 18, 1944, RH 19 XII/5, p. 125 f.

16. Ibid.

17. Headquarters, Army Task Group G, Operations Section, No. 1960/44, dated August 18, 1944, RH 19 XII/7, p. 223.

18. See Blaskowitz, Headquarters, Army Task Group G, Operations Section, No. 67/44, dated August 21, 1944, RH 19 XII/9, p. 28 ff.

19. That order had been transmitted from Headquarters, OB West. See also Sachs, Headquarters, LXIV Corps, Operations Section, No. 1288/44, dated August 27, 1944, RH 19 XII/7, pp. 363 ff, and Schuster, LXIV, AK, MS-A-885, p. 5.

20. These are individuals who support the combat units in specific functions without being members of those forces. They came under the protection of the First to Third Geneva Conventions and were to be treated as prisoners of war in enemy hands. See also Karl Heinz Fuchs and Friedrich Wilhelm Kölper, "Militärisches Taschenlexikon" [Military Pocket Dictionary], Frankfurt 1961, p. 153.

21. Message, LXIV Army Corps, dated August 25, 1944, RH 19 IV/54, p. 217, and LXIV Army Corps, Operations Section, No. 1200/44, dated August 19, 1944, RH 19 IV/54, p. 50.

22. See Sachs, LXIV Army Corps, Operations Section, No. 1288/44, dated August 27, 1944, RH 19 XII/7, pp. 363 ff.

23. Message, LXIV Army Corps, dated August 25, 1944, RH 19 IV/54, p. 217, and "Lagevorträge Kriegsmarine" [Navy Situation Briefings], p. 609, extract from messages of Supreme Commander Navy Group West.

24. See Sachs, LXIV Army Corps, Operations Section, No. 1288/44, dated August 27, 1944, RH 19 XII/7, pp. 363 ff.

25. Headquarters, Nineteenth Army, Operations Section, No. 9559/44, dated September 20, 1944, RH 20-19/86, p. 46 f.

26. At first, totaling seven thousand men. The number increased after the abandonment of the Fort of Bordeaux to about nine thousand. Cf., OB West, Operations Section, No. 7191/44, dated August 22, 1944, RH 19 IV/54, p. 53, and Hartwig Pohlman, "Fortress Gironde North (Royan) 1944/45," in Feldgrau [Field Gray], 8/1960, p. 14.

27. War Diary, Army Group B, dated August 31, 1944, RH 19 IX/88, p. 211.

28. See Blaskowitz, Headquarters, Army Task Group G, Operations Section, No. 1951/44, August 17, 1944, RH 19 XII/7, p. 169 f.

29. Botsch's entry for August 18, 1944, RH 20-19/85, p. 11.

30. See Blaskowitz, Headquarters, Army Task Group G, Operations Section, No. 2042/44, dated August 20, 1944, RH 19 XII/7, p. 243.

31. Daily Report, August 19, 1944, Headquarters, Army Task Group G, Operations Section, No. 1999/44, ibid., p. 237.

32. See Blaskowitz, Headquarters, Army Task Group G, Operations Section, No. 1933/44, dated August 18, 1944, RH 19 XII/9, p. 21 f.

33. Conference at Headquarters, Nineteenth Army, in Pont d'Avignon, August 19, 1944, 0800 hours, RH 20-19/89, pp. 32 ff.

34. See Gyldenfeldt, Headquarters, Army Task Group G, Operations Section, No. 1970/44, dated August 19, 1944, RH 19 XII/7, p. 232.

35. Situation briefings, Navy, p. 612 f, extract from message from Languedoc Naval Commandant.

36. Conference at LXXXV Army Corps, dated August 18, 1944, RH 20-19/88, p. 201.

37. Wiese, "19. Armee," MS-B-787, pp. 16 ff.

38. Headquarters, Nineteenth Army, Operations Section, No. 8680/44, dated August 20, 1944. The order, however, was issued in Pont d'Avignon already at 0800 hours on August 19, RH 20-19/89, pp. 32 ff and 78 ff.

39. In addition, there were seventy-three hundred naval infantry troops. Headquarters, Nineteenth Army, Operations Section, No. 9559/44, dated September 20, 1944, RH 20-19/86, p. 46 f.

40. Headquarters, Nineteenth Army, Operations Section, No. 8697/44, dated August 20, 1944, RH 19 XII/7, p. 242.

41. The 157th Infantry Division also stayed behind but is not included in these figures because it initially was under the Military Commander and was therefore not considered in the ration strength report of Headquarters, Nineteenth Army.

42. That included 87,000 men under the control of the LXIV Army Corps, 145,000 under the command of Headquarters, Nineteenth Army, as well as 12,000 who were under the commandant in the Southern France Army Legion. Headquarters, Nineteenth Army, Operations Section, No. 9559/44, dated September 20, 1944, RH 20-19/86, p. 46 f.

43. Headquarters, Army Task Group G, Operations Section, No. 1934/44, dated August 19, 1944, and No. 1999/44, dated August 20, 1944, RH 19 XII/7, pp. 224 f and 237.

44. Botsch, "19. Armee," MS-B-696, p. 20.

45. OB West, Operations Section, No. 7150/44, RH 19 IV/54, p. 45.

46. Field Order No. 2 for the U.S. Seventh Army, dated August 19, 1944, cf., Wilt, *French Riviera Campaign of August 1944*, p. 118.

47. See Blaskowitz, Headquarters, Army Task Group G, Operations Section, No. 67/44, dated August 21, 1944, RH 19 XII/9, pp. 28 ff.

48. Ibid.

49. Weekly Report, Headquarters, Nineteenth Army, dated August 20, 1944, RH 20-19/89, p. 54 f.

50. See Blaskowitz, Headquarters, Army Task Group G, Operations Section, No. 67/44, dated August 21, 1944, RH 19 XII/9, pp. 28 ff.

51. Ibid.

52. Headquarters, Nineteenth Army, Operations Section, No. 8729/44, dated August 21, 1944, RH 20-19/89, p. 117 f.

53. The U.S. 36th Infantry Division was then to follow Task Force Butler; cf., Wilt, *French Riviera Campaign of August 1944*, p. 135.

54. See also Daily Report for August 22, 1944, OB West, Operations Section, No. 7212/44, RH 19 IV/54, p. 67.

55. Botsch's entry for August 22, 1944, RH 20-19/85, p. 14.

56. Gyldenfeldt, "Armeegruppe G," MS-B-488, p. 16.

57. Ibid., pp. 10 ff.

58. Botsch's entry for August 22, 1944, RH 20-19/85, p. 14, and Botsch, "19. Armee," MS-B-696, p. 24.

59. Daily Report for August 22, 1944, OB West, Operations Section, No. 7212/44, RH 19 IV/54, pp. 65 ff.

60. See Blaskowitz, Headquarters, Army Task Group G, Operations Section, No. 2112/44, dated August 23, 1944, RH 19 XII/7, p. 273.

61. Botsch, "19. Armee," MS-B-696, pp. 25 ff.

62. Wiese, "19. Armee," MS-B-787, pp. 19 ff.

63. Headquarters, Nineteenth Army, Operations Section, No. 8786/44, dated August 24, 1944, RH 20-19/90, p. 20.

64. See Blaskowitz, Headquarters, Army Task Group G, Operations Section, No. 67/44, dated August 21, 1944, RH 19 XII/9, pp. 28 ff.

65. Daily Report for August 23, 1944, OB West, Operations Section, No. 7259/44, RH 19 IV/54, pp. 100 ff.

66. Daily Report for August 21, 1944, OB West, Operations Section, No. 7149/44, ibid., pp. 28 ff.

67. Daily Report for August 23, 1944, OB West, Operations Section, No. 7259/44, ibid., pp. 100 ff.

68. Ibid., and Daily Report for August 25, 1944, OB West, Operations Section, No. 7360/44, RH 19 IV/54, pp. 182 ff.

69. See Blaskowitz, Headquarters, Army Task Group G, Operations Section, No. 67/44, dated August 21, 1944, RH 19 XII/9, p. 30.

70. Diary entry for August 22, 1944, RH 20-19/85, p. 14.

71. Daily Report for August 24, 1944, OB West, Operations Section, No. 7326/44, RH 19 IV/54, p. 151.

72. Botsch, "19. Armee," MS-B-696, p. 35 f.

73. Daily Report for August 21, 1944, OB West, Operations Section, No. 7098/44, RH 19 IV/53, pp. 353 ff.

74. Daily Report for August 23, 1944, OB West, Operations Section, No. 7259/44, RH 19 IV/53, pp. 100 ff.

75. Belfort, Besançon, Vesoul, Chaumont; see Blaskowitz, Headquarters, Army Task Group G, Operations Section, No. 1962/44, dated August 26, 1944, RH 19 XII/7, p. 310.

76. Daily Report for August 24, 1944, Headquarters, Army Task Group G, Operations Section, No. 2102/44, RH 19 XII/7, p. 288, and War Diary, Army Task Group G, dated August 24, 1944, RH 19 XII/5, p. 147.

77. Schuster, "LXIV AK" [LXIV Army Corps], MS-A-885, Appendix C.

78. Täglichsbeck (former Field Commandant 651 Niort), "Südwestfrankreich" [Southwestern France], MS-A-886, p. 4.

79. Ibid., p. 3 f.

80. Schuster, "LXIV AK," MS-A-885, Appendix C.

81. Täglichsbeck, "Südwestfrankreich," MS-A-886, p. 5 f, and Lieutenant General Ernst Haeckel, 16th Infantry Division, MS-B-245, p. 14.

82. Report, LXIV Army Corps, dated August 19, 1944, quoted in: OB West, Operations Section, No. 7189/44, dated August 22, 1944, RH 19 IV/54, p. 50.

83. That involved the submarines *U-534* and *U-857*. See OB West, Operations Section, No. 741/44, dated August 19, 1944, RH 19 IV/53, p. 312.

84. See Sachs, Headquarters, LXIV Army Corps, Operations Section, No. 1288/44, dated August 27, 1944, RH 19 XII/7, pp. 363 ff.

85. Schuster, "LXIV AK," MS-A-885, p. 6.

86. Nanteuil/Levy, *Elster*, p. 70.

87. Schuster, "LXIV AK," MS-A-885, p. 7.

88. Army, navy, and Luftwaffe alert units, especially the mobile 602nd and 608th Battalions.

89. Haeckel, "16. Inf. Div.," MS-B-245, p. 24.

90. Ibid., p. 11 f, and Seiz, 159th Infantry Division, MS-A-960, p. 3.

91. War Diary, Army Task Group G, dated August 20, 1944, RH 19 XII/5, p. 132 f.

92. Headquarters, Diary, Nineteenth Army, Operations Section, No. 9559/44, dated September 20, 1994, RH 20-19/86, p. 47.

93. Including: 1000th Security Regiment, two battalions of the 19th SS Police Regiment, and several local defense battalions; cf., Ottenbacher, "Rückzugskämpfe" [Fighting Retreat], MS-B-538, p. 1 f.

94. Daily Report for August 23, 1944, OB West, Operations Section, No. 7259/44, RH 19 IV/54, pp. 100 ff.

95. Cf., Daily Reports, OB West for August 22–25, 1944, RH 19 IV/54, pp. 65 ff, pp. 100 ff, pp. 182 ff.

96. Addition to Daily Report, OB West for August 23, 1944, RH 19 IV/54, p. 105.

97. Daily Report, OB West for August 25, 1944, RH 19 IV/54, pp. 182 ff.

98. War Diary, Army Group B, dated August 21, 1944, RH 19 IX/88, p. 59 f.

99. OB West, Operations Section, No. 7189 and 7208/44, dated August 22, 1944, RH 19 IV/54, p. 50 f, and War Diary, Army Task Group G, dated August 22, 1944, RH 19 XII/5, p. 143.

100. War Diary, OB West, dated August 24, 1944, RH 19 IV/45, p. 161 f.

101. See Blumentritt, OB West, Operations Section, No. 759/44, dated August 25, 1944, RH 19 IV/54, p. 175 f.

102. Letter dated August 24, 1944, quoted in: Pogue, *The Supreme Command*, p. 228.

103. Daily Report for August 20, 1944, OB West, Operations Staff, No. 7098/44, RH 19 IV/53, pp. 353 ff.

104. War Diary, Army Group B, dated August 20, 1944, RH 19 IX/88, p. 46.

105. Ibid., pp. 51 and 61.

106. See Model, Headquarters, Army Group B, Operations Section, No. 6390/44, dated August 21, 1944, RH 19 IX/7, p. 33 f, and Frank, "5. Panzer-armee" [Fifth Panzer Army], MS-B-729, pp. 6 ff.

107. LXXXVI Army Corps, with 711th, 346th, and 272nd Infantry Divisions; LXXXI Army Corps, with 331st and 344th Infantry Divisions and Luftwaffe 17th Field Division; I and II SS Panzer Corps, with 1st, 2nd, 9th, 10th, and 12th SS Panzer Divisions and 2nd, 21st, 116th Panzer Divisions. They were supported by the units of Seventh Army that were still able to put up a fight. RH 19 IV 69 K and 139 K (Maps for August 20–25, 1944).

108. Evening Report, dated August 24, 1944, Headquarters, Army Group B, Intelligence Section, No. 3323/44, RH 19 IX/26, Part I, p. 61.

109. Daily Report for August 20, 1944, OB West, Operations Section, No. 7098/44, RH 19 IV/53, pp. 353 ff.

110. War Diary, Army Group B, dated August 20, 1944, RH 19 IX/88, p. 52.

111. See Model, Headquarters, Army Group B, Operations Section, No. 6376/44, dated August 21, 1944, RH 19 IX/4, p. 365 f.

112. War Diary, Army Group B, dated August 21, 1944, RH 19 IX/88, p. 64.

113. Ibid., p. 58.

114. War Diary, Headquarters, Fifth Panzer Army, dated August 21, 1944, RH 21-5/52, p. 24 f.

115. See Jodl, Wehrmacht Operations Staff/Operations Section, No. 772974/44, dated August 21, 1944, RH 19 IX/7, p. 35.

116. Daily Report for August 22, 1944, OB West, Operations Section, No. 7212/44, RH 19 IV/54, pp. 65 ff.

117. War Diary, LXXXI Army Corps, dated August 22, 1944, RH 24-81/97, p. 135/1.

118. Ibid., p. 136/1.

119. War Diary, Army Group B, dated August 25, 1944, RH 19 IX/88, p. 138 f.

120. Ibid., dated August 23, 1944, p. 103.

121. Ibid., dated August 23, 1944, p. 80.

122. Ibid., dated August 23, 1944, p. 107.

123. Ibid., dated August 22, 1944, p. 84.

124. War Diary, Headquarters, Fifth Panzer Army, dated August 22, 1944, RH 21-5/52, p. 26.

125. Daily Report for August 23, 1944, OB West, Operations Section, No. 7212/44, RH 19 IV/54, pp. 65 ff.

126. War Diary, Army Group B, dated August 23, 1944, RH 19 IX/88, p. 89 f.

127. Model's order, dated August 23, 1944, War Diary, Headquarters, Fifth Panzer Army, RH 21-5/52, p. 29.

128. Telephone conversation between Dietrich and Speidel, dated August 23, 1944, War Diary, Army Group B, RH 19 IX/88, p. 105 f.

129. War Diary, Headquarters, Fifth Panzer Army, dated August 23, 1944, RH 21-5/52, p. 30.

130. Telephone conversation between Jodl and Model, dated August 23, 1944, War Diary, Army Group B, RH 19 IX/88, p. 108 f.

131. Headquarters, I SS Panzer Corps, commanded in the Seine sector in place of Schwerin, who had now taken over the job of coordinating the Panzer units.

132. War Diary, Headquarters, Fifth Panzer Army, dated August 23, 1944, RH 21-5/52, p. 31 f.

133. Daily Report for August 24, 1944, OB West, Operations Section, No. 7326/44, RH 19 IV/54, pp. 148 ff.

134. War Diary, Headquarters, Fifth Panzer Army, dated August 24 and 25, 1944, RH 21-5/52, p. 33 f.

135. See Model, Headquarters, Army Group B, Operations Section, No. 6527/44, dated August 24, 1944, RH 19 IX/4, p. 392.

136. War Diary, Army Group B, dated August 25, 1944, RH 19 IX/88, pp. 141 ff.

137. War Diary, LXXXI Army Corps, dated August 25, 1944, RH 24-81/97, p. 147/1.

138. Daily Report for August 25, 1944, OB West, Operations Section, No. 7360/44, RH 19 IV/54, pp. 182 ff.

139. Eberbach, "7. Armee," MS-B-841, p. 3.

140. War Diary, Headquarters, Fifth Panzer Army, dated August 25, 1944, RH 21-5/52, p. 35. Presumably, this is a misprint. The author, at any rate, believes that the figure is quite a bit too high.

141. War Diary, Headquarters, Fifth Panzer Army, dated August 25, 1944, Appendix 50, RH 21-5/53, p. 76.

142. Telephone conversation between Speidel and Gause, dated August 25, 1944, RH 19 IX/88, p. 133 f.

143. Wehrmacht High Command, Wehrmacht Operations Staff, No. 772933/44, dated August 19, 1944, quoted in: OB West, Operations Section, No. 740/44, dated August 19, 1944, RH 19 IX/7, p. 29.

144. See Adolf Hitler, Wehrmacht Operations Staff, Operations Section, No. 772956/44, dated August 20, 1944, quoted in: OB West, Operations Section, No. 745/44, dated August 20, 1944, RH 19 IX/7, pp. 30 ff.

145. Remnants of the 352nd Infantry Division and one regiment of the 338th Infantry Division.

146. The 9th Panzer Division, the Panzer-Lehr Division, and the 17th SS Panzer Grenadier Division.

147. Army Group B, Intelligence Section, No. 3323/44, dated August 24, 1944, RH 19 IX/26, Part 1, p. 61.

148. See Model, Headquarters, Army Group B, Operations Section, No. 6390/44, dated August 21, 1944, RH 19 IX/7, p. 33 f.

149. War Diary, OB West, dated August 21, 1944, RH 19 IV/45, p. 142.

150. Daily Report for August 22, 1944, OB West, Operations Section, No. 7212/44, RH 19 IV/54, pp. 65 ff.

151. The 26th and 27th SS Panzer Divisions. Both of these "Panzer Divisions," however, only had one reinforced infantry regiment each; they did not have any Panzers. They were placed under the 17th SS Panzer Grenadier Division on August 24, 1944. War Diary, OB West, RH 19 IV/45, p. 160.

152. War Diary, Army Group B, dated August 22, 1944, RH 19 IX/88, p. 86.

153. Zimmermann, "OB West," MS-T-121 B IV, p. 1647.

154. War Diary, OB West, dated August 23, 1944, RH 19 IV/45, p. 156.

155. Telephone conversation between Blumentritt and Jodl, dated August 22, 1944, 2300 hours, RH 19 IX/8, p. 87.

156. Zimmermann, "OB West," MS-T-121, B IV, p. 1647 f.

157. War Diary, OB West, Appendix, dated August 22, 1944, (unnumbered), RH 19 IV/54, pp. 69 ff.

158. See Blumentritt, OB West, Operations Section, No. 751/44, dated August 23, 1944, RH 19 IV/54, p. 95.

159. Zimmermann, "OB West," MS-T-121, B IV, pp. 625 ff.

160. See also War Diary, OB West, Appendix, dated August 22, 1944 (unnumbered), RH 19 IV/54, pp. 69 ff.

161. War Diary, Army Group B, dated August 23, 1944, RH 19 IX/88, p. 100.

162. Emmerich, "1. Armee," MS-B-728, p. 10.

163. OB West, Operations Section, No. 7141/44, dated August 22, 1944, RH 19 IV/54, p. 40 f.

164. Krüger, "LVIII. Pz. Korps" [LVIII Panzer Corps], MS-B-157, p. 1.

165. Daily Report for August 23, 1944, OB West, Operations Section, No. 7259/44, RH 19 IV/54, pp. 100 ff.

166. Caspar, "48. Inf. Div.," MS-P-166, p. 11.

167. Daily Report for August 24, 1944, OB West, Operations Section, No. 7326/44, RH 19 IV/54, pp. 148 ff.

168. Daily Report for August 25, 1944, OB West, Operations Section, No. 7360/44, RH 19 IV/54, pp. 182 ff.

169. Telephone conversation between Chevallerie and Speidel, dated August 25, 1944, 0155 hours, RH 19 IX/88, p. 134.

170. War Diary, Army Group B, dated August 23 and 25, 1944, RH 19 IX/88, pp. 102 and 137.

171. Telephone conversation between Chevallerie and Speidel, dated August 25, 1944, 0155 hours, RH 19 IX/88, p. 134.

172. War Diary, Army Group B, dated August 25, 1944, RH 19 IX/88, pp. 133 and 137.

173. Telephone conversation between Chevallerie and Model, dated August 25, 1944, 1740 hours, RH 19 IX/88, p. 144 ff.

174. Daily Report for August 25, 1944, OB West, Operations Section, No. 7360/44, RH 19 IV/54, pp. 182 ff.

175. See Blumentritt, OB West, Operations Section, No. 759/44, dated August 25, 1944, RH 19 IV/54, p. 175 f.

7. The Situation around Paris

1. Michel, *Paris,* p. 293.

2. Hesse, *Paris,* MS-B-611, pp. 12 ff.

3. Elements of the U.S. XV Corps had reached the Seine River between Mantes and Vernon during the night of August 18–19 and had thus cut the last communications west of the river; War Diary, Army Group B, dated August 19, 1944, RH 19 IX/88, p. 37.

4. Choltitz, *Paris,* p. 44.

5. This assumption was also initially supported by the enemy situation estimate prepared by the Intelligence Section of OB West; Intelligence Section Daily Report of August 15, 1944, Intelligence Section No. 5726/44, RH 19 IV/137, pp. 64 ff.

6. Warlimont, *Siegfriedline,* MS-ETHINT 1, p. 43.

7. See Adolf Hitler, Wehrmacht Operations Staff, Operations Section, No. 772956/44, dated August 20, 1944, quoted in: Headquarters, Army Group B, Operations Section, No. 6352/44, RH 19 IX/7, pp. 30 ff.

8. War Diary, Army Group B, dated August 20 and 22, 1944, RH 19 IX/88, pp. 42 and 86.

9. Wehrmacht High Command/Wehrmacht Operations Staff/Operations Section (Army), No. 772989/44, dated August 23, 1944, according to Army Group B, Operations Section, No. 6355/44, RH 19 IX/7, p. 40.

10. Ibid.

11. SHAEF Planning Staff Study of May 30, 1944, "Post-OVERLORD Planning," Blumenson, *Breakout and Pursuit,* p. 590.

12. Blumenson, *Breakout and Pursuit,* p. 632.

13. Ruppenthal, *Logistical Support of the Armies,* I, pp. 483 ff.

14. Blumenson, *Breakout and Pursuit,* p. 590.

15. Pogue, *The Supreme Command,* p. 257.

16. Ruppenthal, *Logistical Support of the Armies,* I, p. 486.

17. Montgomery's Directive M-519, dated August 20, 1944, in: Pogue, *The Supreme Command,* p. 240.

18. Marshall's letter to Eisenhower, dated March 17, 1944, ibid., p. 145.

19. Blumenson, *Breakout and Pursuit,* p. 591.

20. Combined Chiefs of Staff to Eisenhower, dated August 17, 1944, in: Pogue, *The Supreme Command,* pp. 241 ff.

21. Matloff, *Strategic Planning for Coalition Warfare 1943–1944,* p. 501.

22. De Gaulle's statement, dated March 27, 1944: "France, who gave the world freedom . . . does not need any alien advice on the matter of how freedom is to be rebuilt at home." Translation according to Pogue, *The Supreme Command,* p. 145.

23. Michel, *Paris,* p. 294.

24. Ibid., p. 286.

25. De Gaulle, "Memoiren," p. 270.

26. The French 2nd Armored Division was included in the planning

here with Eisenhower's approval since early 1944; see Pogue, *The Supreme Command*, p. 239.

27. Michel, *Paris*, p. 295.

28. Ibid., p. 286.

29. Ibid., p. 264.

30. Ibid., pp. 297 ff.

31. De Gaulle, "Memoiren," p. 277.

32. Michel, *Paris*, p. 312.

33. Blumenson, *Breakout and Pursuit*, p. 602.

34. Michel, *Paris*, pp. 316 ff.

35. De Gaulle's letter to Eisenhower, dated August 21, 1944; see Pogue, *The Supreme Command*, p. 240; Blumenson, *Breakout and Pursuit*, p. 599; de Gaulle, *Memoiren*, pp. 273 ff.

36. Blumenson, *Breakout and Pursuit*, pp. 600 ff.

37. Translated on the basis of Eisenhower's handwritten notes in response to de Gaulle's letter to him, dated August 21, 1944; see Pogue, *The Supreme Command*, pp. 240 ff.

38. Eisenhower, *Crusade in Europe*, p. 348.

39. This was to be made clear to Choltitz by an American intelligence officer sent to contact him; cf., Blumenson, *Breakout and Pursuit*, p. 604.

40. ZDF [German 2nd TV Channel] records, interview with Military Judge Roskothen, p. 12.

41. Hesse, "Paris," MS-B-611, p. 14.

42. Choltitz, "Paris," p. 7.

43. Wilmot, *Struggle for Europe*, p. 409.

44. Choltitz, "Paris," pp. 9 ff, and Choltitz, "Soldat" [Soldier], p. 231.

45. OB West, Operations Section, No. 6454, dated August 8, 1944, RH 19 IV/52, Appendix 1219, pp. 316 ff.

46. RH 19 IV/53, Appendix 1324, dated August 12, 1944, p. 55.

47. Kluge's order, dated August 17, 1944, Army Group B, Operations Section, No. 6232/44, quoted in: OB West, Operations Section, No. 6960/44, dated August 18, 1944, RH 19 IV/53, p. 287.

48. Ziegelman, "352. Inf. Div.," MS-B-741, p. 11.

49. OB West, Operations Section, No. 6960/44, dated August 18, 1944, RH 19 IV/53, Appendix 1505, p. 287.

50. See Choltitz, "Kommandanturbefehl No. 32/44" [Kommandantur Order No. 32/44], dated August 18, 1944, RH 36/51, pp. 40 ff.

51. See Model, Army Group B, Operations Section, No. 6390/44, dated August 21, 1944, RH 19 IX/7, pp. 33 ff.

52. See von Aulock, "Kampfgruppenbefehl No. 2" [Battle Group Order No. 2], dated August 18, 1944, RH 36/51, pp. 42 ff.

53. Telephone conversation between Blumentritt and Speidel, dated August 16, 1944, 1540 hours, RH 19 IV/88, p. 9.

54. Telephone conversation between Blumentritt and Speidel, dated August 17, 1944, 0250 hours, RH 19 IX/88, pp. 17 ff.

55. See also Captain of the Reserve Dr. Cartellieri in: War Diary, Wehrmacht High Command, IV/1, pp. 501 ff.

56. Michel, *Paris*, pp. 287 ff.

57. See Eckelmann, see Dr. Reinhardt (Military Administration), see von Choltitz: Report on the food situation in Paris, dated August 23, 1944, RW 35/1137. The report was sent to Model personally.

58. Michel, *Paris*, p. 289.

59. Conference, Reich Chancellery, July 11, 1944, see Lammers, "Der Prozess" [The Trial], XI, p. 394.

60. The statistics are rather uncertain: Blumenson, *Breakout and Pursuit*, pp. 595 ff, mentions twenty thousand; de Gaulle, "Memoiren," p. 271, speaks of twenty-five thousand; Michel, *Paris*, p. 301, mentions various sources giving figures fluctuating between thirty thousand and seventy thousand members of the French Forces of the Interior for the Paris region. Michel, *Paris*, pp. 303 ff, explains the poor armament, among other things, in the light of a certain reluctance on the part of the Allies to arm the Communist-led urban guerrillas.

61. Tessin, "Verbände," 9, p. 157.

62. Kommandantur Order 32/44, dated August 18, 1944, RH 36/51, pp. 40 ff.

63. Choltitz, "Paris," p. 18.

64. RW 4/Vol. 828, Wehrmacht Operations Staff/Operations (Army) West, Führer Headquarters, dated November 5, 1944; Hesse, "Paris," MS-B-611, pp. 3 and 11.

65. Jäckel, "Frankreich" [France], p. 345.

66. Telephone conversation between Kitzinger and Model, dated August 18, 1944, 0845 hours, RH 19 IX/88, p. 28.

67. Choltitz, "Paris," p. 23.

68. Ibid., pp. 35 ff.

69. A brief cease-fire was already in effect to retrieve the dead and the wounded at the Police Prefecture. Cf., Michel, *Paris*, p. 315.

70. Michel, *Paris*, pp. 310 ff.

71. Telephone conversation, Operations Section, Wehrmacht Commander of Greater Paris, and Orderly Officer, Operations Section, Army Group B, dated August 20, 1944, 1900 hours, RH 19 IX/88, p. 49.

72. Ibid. and RH 19 IV/142, pp. 166 ff, Choltitz phoning Intelligence Section/Supreme Commander West, August 20, 1944, 1110 hours.

73. RH 19 IV/142, pp. 165 ff, telephone conversation between Choltitz and Intelligence Section/OB West, August 20, 1944, 1110 hours, and phone conversation between Major Doertenbach and Lieutenant Colonel Staubwasser at 1117 hours on August 20, 1944.

74. Telephone conversation between Operations Section, Wehrmacht Commander of Greater Paris, and Orderly Officer, Operations Section, Army Group B, dated August 20, 1944, 1900 hours, RH 19 IX/88, p. 49.

75. According to a late order from the Wehrmacht Operations Staff,

dated July 24, 1944, members of the Resistance were to be treated as guerrillas—that is to say, they were to be "liquidated." See Wehrmacht High Command/Wehrmacht Operations Staff/Administrative Section (West), No. 05617/44, Secret, dated July 24, 1944, with reference. See also: RH 19 IV/141, p. 254, OB West, signed by Westphal, Intelligence Section/Headquarters, No. 6330/44, dated September 17, 1944.

76. Telephone conversation between Operations Section, Wehrmacht Commander of Greater Paris and Orderly Officer, Operations Section, Army Group B, dated August 20, 1944, 1900 hours, RH 19 IX/88, p. 50.

77. Hitler had given him the authority of a fortress commandant; OB West, Operations Section, No. 6454/44, dated August 8, 1944, RH 19 IV/52, pp. 316 ff.

78. Telephone conversation between Operations Section, Wehrmacht Commander of Greater Paris and Orderly Office, Operations Section, Army Group B, dated August 20, 1944, 1900 hours, RH 19 IX/88, p. 49. As for the attitude and the differing positions within the French camp, see Michel, *Paris,* p. 315; de Gaulle, "Memoiren," p. 278, and Blumenson, *Breakout and Pursuit,* pp. 596 ff.

79. Choltitz, "Paris," p. 90.

80. Ibid., p. 75.

81. Telephone conversation between Blumentritt and Operations Officer, Army Group B, dated August 21, 1944, 1745 hours, RH 19 IX/88, p. 66, and Daily Report for August 22, OB West, Operations Section, No. 7212/44, RH 19 IV/54, pp. 65 ff.

82. See Adolf Hitler, Wehrmacht Operations Staff/Operations Section, No. 772956/44, dated August 20, 1944, quoted in: Army Group B, Operations Section, No. 6352/44, RH 19 IX/7, pp. 30 ff.

83. See Model, Headquarters, Army Group B, Operations Section, No. 6390/44, dated August 21, 1944, RH 19 IX/7, p. 33 f.

84. Telephone conversation between Blumentritt and Operations Officer, Army Group B, dated August 21, 1944, 1745 hours, RH 19 IX/88, p. 66, and telephone conversation between Choltitz and Operations Officer, Army Group B, dated August 21, 1944, 1815 hours, ibid., p. 67.

85. Communication from Operations Officer, Army Group B to Blumentritt, dated August 21, 1944, 1955 hours, RH 19 IX/88, p. 72 f.

86. Telephone conversation between Choltitz and Operations Officer, Army Group B, dated August 21, 1944, 1815 hours, RH 19 IX/88, pp. 67 ff.

87. Telephone conversation between Choltitz and Speidel, dated August 23, 1944, 2215 hours, RH 19 IX/88, p. 106.

88. Telephone conversation between Choltitz and Colonel Schmidtke, Propaganda Staff Officer, Intelligence Section, OB West, dated August 20 and 22, 1944, RH 19 IV/142, pp. 166 and 173.

89. De Gaulle, "Memoiren," pp. 277 ff, and Choltitz, "Paris," pp. 53 ff.

90. RH 19 IV/54, p. 99, quoted in: OB West, Operations Section, No. 7250/44, dated August 23, 1944.

91. Model's order, dated August 21, 1944, quoted from: Telephone conversation between Operations Officer, Army Group B, and Blumentritt, dated August 21, 1944, 1555 hours, RH 19 IX/88, p. 72.

92. Telephone conversation between Operations Officer, Headquarters, First Army, and Operations Officer, Army Group B, dated August 23, 1944, 1835 hours, RH 19 IX/88, p. 102.

93. Telephone conversation between Model and Plenipotentiary Transportation Officer, Army Group B, dated August 24, 1944, 0920 hours, RH 19 IX/88, p. 116.

94. OB West, Operations Section, No. 6825/44, dated August 22, 1944, RH 19 IV/54, p. 78.

95. Report on the food situation of Paris, August 23, 1944, pp. 1–4, signed by Eckelmann, Dr. Reinhardt, Choltitz, to the attention of the Field Marshal personally, RW 35/1137.

96. Telephone conversation between Operations Officer, Army Group B, and Operations Officer, Headquarters, First Army, dated August 23, 1944, 1745 hours, RH 19 IX/88, p. 101.

97. Daily Report, OB West, dated August 23, 1944, Supreme Commander West, Operations Section, No. 7259, RH 19 IV/54, pp. 100 ff.

98. Model gave orders to the effect that the deputy chief of staff should leave Paris "as quickly as possible" on account of the situation there; see War Diary, Army Group B, August 23, 1944, RH 19 IX/88, p. 107. Choltitz had to relinquish Headquarters, 352nd Infantry Division, and the few Panzers of the Panzer-Lehr Division, which he had kept in Paris; ibid., p. 92.

99. Wehrmacht High Command/Wehrmacht Operations Staff/Operations Section (Army), No. 772989/44, dated August 23, 1944, quoted in: Headquarters, Army Group B, Operations Section, No. 6355/44, dated August 23, 1944, 1100 hours, RH 19 IX/7, p. 40.

100. OB West, Operations Section, No. 7250/44, dated August 23, 1944, and telephone conversation between Choltitz and Model, 1200 hours, RH 19 IX/88, p. 95.

101. Telephone conversation between Model and Jodl, dated August 23, 1944, 2350 hours, RH 19 IX/88, pp. 107 ff.

102. In this connection, it is interesting to note that Choltitz had already given permission for the dispatch of a delegation through the front lines to de Gaulle. According to his "Memoirs," he merely hoped to be able to ensure compliance with the armistice with the help of the French general. But it seems doubtful whether that was the only purpose of this mission. One cannot rule out the possibility that Choltitz instead was trying to persuade the Allies—even if only indirectly—to send troops; see also: de Gaulle, "Memoiren," pp. 280 ff; Michel, *Paris*, pp. 317 ff, and Blumenson, *Breakout and Pursuit*, p. 206.

103. Blumenson, *Breakout and Pursuit*, p. 607.

104. Ibid., pp. 610 ff.

105. Ibid., pp. 613 ff.

106. The French 2nd Armored Division suffered astonishingly heavy losses: By August 29, 1944, it had lost around 300 men, 35 tanks, and 111 vehicles; see Blumenson, *Breakout and Pursuit*, p. 614.

107. Telephone conversation between Choltitz and Speidel, dated August 24, 1944, 1745 hours, RH 19 IX/88, p. 120.

108. Telephone conversation between Choltitz and Blumentritt, dated August 24, 1944, 1855 hours, RH 19 IX/88, p. 123.

109. Michel, *Paris*, p. 316; Choltitz, "Paris," pp. 97 ff.

110. Telephone conversation between Choltitz and Operations Officer, Army Group B, dated August 24, 1944, 2325 hours, RH 19 IX/88, pp. 126 ff.

111. War Diary, Army Group B, dated August 24, 1944, RH 19 IX/88, pp. 112 ff, and telephone conversation between Choltitz and Operations Officer, Army Group B, August 24, 1944, 2325 hours, ibid., pp. 126 ff.

112. Telephone conversation between Choltitz and Speidel, dated August 25, 1944, 0150 hours, ibid., p. 134.

113. RH 19 IX/88, p. 139, telephone conversation between Choltitz and Speidel, dated August 25, 1944, 1100 hours, ibid., p. 139.

114. Telephone call from Headquarters, First Army, Intelligence Section, to Intelligence Section, Army Group B, dated August 26, 1944, 0515 hours, RH 19 IX/21, pp. 43 ff. Copies of the agreement between Leclerc, Rol, and Choltitz as well as Choltitz's order can be found in: RHA No. 3/1974, pp. 103 and 113.

115. Teletype message from Wehrmacht High Command/Wehrmacht Operations Staff, RH 19 IX/7, p. 41, transmitted to Army Group B at 1405 hours on August 25, 1944, First Army Ic from OB West.

116. Hillgruber, "Hitler, König Carol," p. 220.

117. Telephone conversation between Chevallerie and Model, dated August 25, 1944, 1740 hours, RH 19 IX/88, pp. 144 ff.

118. RH 19 IX/88, pp. 144 ff.

119. Teletype message from Wehrmacht High Command/Wehrmacht Operations Staff, RH 19 IX/7, p. 41, transmitted to Army Group B at 1405 hours on August 25, 1944, First Army Ic from OB West.

120. See Model, "Generalfeldmarschall," OB West, Operations Section, No. 770/44, copy on August 28, 1944, 1245 hours, RH 19 IV/54, p. 255.

121. Model and Speidel had promised that to Choltitz; see: Choltitz, "Paris," p. 78.

122. See Model, "Generalfeldmarschall," OB West, Operations Section, No. 770/44, copy on August 28, 1944, 1245 hours, RH 19 IV/54, p. 255.

123. N 6/1, Model, p. 245, Interview with Colonel Freyberg (retired) (former military aide to Commanding General, Army Group B) with H. Model, dated August 19, 1955.

124. Note of Wehrmacht Operations Staff/Operations Section (Army)/ West, dated November 5, 1944, regarding the request of the Presiding Judge of the Reich Court-Martial for an expert report in the Choltitz case, RW 4/Vol. 828, and Conference between Colonel-Judge Rittau with Majors

Doertenbach and Brink, Intelligence Section/OB West, dated September 21, 1944, 1300 hours, RH 19 IV/142, p. 226.

125. RW 4/Vol. 828.

126. The trial in Torgau in 1945 was postponed until Choltitz himself could be heard; see Choltitz, "Paris," pp. 85 ff.

127. Choltitz, "Soldat," pp. 230 ff: "It would naturally have been possible to turn Paris into another Warsaw . . . , but did I have the right to plunge a city of millions into disaster? . . . I was thinking of the future relationship between these two great neighboring nations, and I suddenly found myself facing the lofty duty . . . of keeping channels open for the future."

128. Diary of Colonel General Otto Dessloch, entries for August 19 and 20, 1944, N 292/34, p. 19.

129. Teletype message from Wehrmacht High Command/Wehrmacht Operations Staff, transmitted through Ia, OB West, to Army Group B on August 25, 1944, 1405 hours, RH 19 IX/7, p. 41.

130. "Tagebuch Dessloch" [Dessloch's Diary], entry for August 16, 1944, N 292/34, p. 18.

131. His resolute action on that issue was confirmed by various statements of testimony that were available to the author. Due to the rather problematical source situation (the available War Diaries of the Third Air Fleet began only on August 27, 1944), there were no other items of file evidence to the effect that Dessloch refused to obey Hitler's order, with the justification that he did not have the necessary operational aircraft. The above-mentioned items of evidence include the following: Certificate by Dr. Carl Ziegler (former member of Dessloch's Operations Staff) of October 26, 1986. This confirmation furthermore contains a pertinent statement by Colonel Paul-Franz Roehre, Dessloch's former aide, and the notarized, sworn statement by Mrs. Anni Dessloch, the general's widow, dated January 5, 1987.

132. "Tagebuch Dessloch," entry for August 18, 1944, N 292/34, p. 19.

133. War Diary, No. 79 (August 27–September 30, 1944) of Headquarters, Third Air Fleet, entry for August 27, 1944, RL 7/118, pp. K4232 ff.

134. Telephone conversation between Speidel and Chief of Staff, Third Air Fleet, dated August 26, 1944, 1245 hours, RH 19 IX/88, p. 153.

135. On August 25, Hitler ordered Jodl to prepare "several [V-1] sites to the east of the Somme River, aiming them at Paris." See also: Signed, by order, Jodl, Wehrmacht High Command/Wehrmacht Operations Staff, Operations Section, No. 773018/44, radio-teletype, dated August 25, 1944, 1820 hours, RH 19 IV/102, p. 8. But this intention was no longer carried out. On the other hand, the employment of the V-2 missiles began at 0840 hours on September 7, 1944, with a launch aimed at Paris. A total of ten V-2 missiles had been fired at Paris by October 3, 1944, when the fire against the French metropolis was "for the time being discontinued for political reasons. . . ." See also: Signed, by order, Jodl, Wehrmacht High Command/Wehrmacht Operations Staff/Operations Section (Army), Operations Section, No. 773619/44, dated October 3, 1944, RH 19 IV/102, pp. 53 and 100

ff. That number rose to nineteen by the end of the war. See: Hölsken, "V-Waffen," p. 163.

136. Individual Resistance nests held out in the city for several days; see Hesse, "Paris," MS-B-611, p. 22.

137. According to Jodl's testimony during the Nürnberg Trial, it would take the transportation space of four divisions and the "Emergency Support Train Bavaria" to save Paris from starvation.

138. Ruppenthal, *Logistical Support of the Armies,* I, p. 577.

139. From August 27 to September 2, 1944: 42.2 percent for American troops, 20.5 percent for British troops, 37.3 percent for Paris. See: Ruppenthal, *Logistical Support of the Armies,* I, p. 582, footnote 141.

140. See also, among others, Pogue, *The Supreme Command,* pp. 241 ff; Blumenson, *Breakout and Pursuit,* pp. 617 ff.

141. Michel, *Paris,* p. 301.

142. There are examples for the tensions between regular French soldiers and the French Forces of the Interior: In his letter to de Gaulle, Leclerc stated that the French Forces of the Interior included only "10 percent of very good and brave members who are really fighting men." See: Michel, *Paris,* p. 319. Regarding de Gaulle's attitude toward the French Forces of the Interior: He rebuked Leclerc because he allowed French Forces of the Interior Chief Rol-Tanguy also to sign the "Capitulation Document," and because the typed document thus contained a subsequent reference to the role played by the French Forces of the Interior. See: de Gaulle, "Memoiren," pp. 282 ff.

143. Blumenson, *Breakout and Pursuit,* p. 620.

144. The French 2nd Armored Division indeed did not return to the front line until September 8, 1944. See: Pogue, *The Supreme Command,* pp. 242 ff.

145. Blumenson, *Breakout and Pursuit,* p. 625, translated from: "Sylvan Diary," August 26, 1944.

146. The first instances of ill will emerged when Leclerc conducted the surrender negotiations with Choltitz in the absence of his superior Gerow and signed exclusively in the name of the Provisional French Government. See: Blumenson, *Breakout and Pursuit,* pp. 617 ff.

147. Eisenhower's letter to Marshall, dated August 31, 1944; cf., Blumenson, *Breakout and Pursuit,* p. 625.

148. According to Pogue, *The Supreme Command,* p. 242, Eisenhower felt inclined to visit Paris on August 27 to demonstrate, among other things, that the Americans did "participate" in the city's liberation.

149. Eisenhower, *The Crusade in Europe,* p. 361.

150. Blumenson, *Breakout and Pursuit,* p. 628.

8. Command Decisions and the Course of Operations Leading to the Climax of the Crisis

1. The quotes in this chapter, unless otherwise indicated, are taken from the situation estimate of OB West: Headquarters, Army Group B, Op-

erations Section, No. 6360/44, dated August 24, 1944, 2300 hours, quoted in: OB West, Operations Section, No. 762/44, dated August 25, 1944, RH 19 IV/54, p. 146 f.

2. Model assumed that there were fifty-three Allied divisions. By September 1, 1944, he figured that they might have been boosted to fifty-five to fifty-seven divisions in northern France.

3. Four corps headquarters (LXXXVI, LXXIV, LXXXI Army Corps, XLVII Panzer Corps) with the 711th and 346th Infantry Divisions, 3rd Parachute Division, 353rd, 271st, 331st, and 344th Infantry Divisions, Luftwaffe 17th Field Division, 49th Infantry Division, Luftwaffe 18th Field Division, 6th Parachute Division, and 275th Infantry Division.

4. In point of fact, there were only eleven divisions, as indicated in Model's directive of August 25, 1944 (Supreme Commander West, Operations Section, No. 7346/44, RH 19 IV/54, p. 172). In his situation estimate the night before—apart from misprints—there was one division listed (the 273rd) that did not at all exist in the west. Headquarters, Army Group, gradually lost track of the whereabouts of individual formations.

5. 352nd, 84th, 89th, 326th, 363rd, 276th, 277th, 708th, 272nd, 343rd Infantry Divisions, 5th Parachute Division.

6. War Diary, Army Group B, dated August 25, 1944, RH 19 IX/88, p. 132.

7. 276th, 277th, 326th, 363rd, 708th Infantry Divisions, Headquarters, Army Group B, Operations Section, No. 6684/44, dated August 27, 1944, RH 19 IX/4, p. 410 f.

8. Headquarters, LVIII Panzer Corps, Operations Section, No. 11/44, dated August 24, 1944, War Diary, LVIII Panzer Corps, Appendix, RH 24-58/9, p. 167.

9. *Hitlers Lagebesprechungen,* Conference on July 31, 1944, p. 595.

10. Conference between Model and Zimmermann, dated August 26, 1944, RH 19 IV/54, p. 196 f.

11. Warlimont, "Siegfriedline," MS-ETHINT 1, p. 47.

12. Telephone conversation between Blumentritt and Speidel, dated August 26, 1944, RH 19 IX/88, p. 151.

13. See Adolf Hitler, Wehrmacht Operations Staff, No. 772965/44, dated August 24, 1944, quoted in: OB West, Operations Section, No. 757/44, dated August 25, 1944, RH 19 IV/54, pp. 177 ff.

14. Letter, dated August 26, 1944, "Privatarchiv Model" [Model's private archives].

15. Middleton underestimated the German strength there considerably, giving a figure of sixteen thousand men. In point of fact, about thirty-seven thousand German soldiers were in the fortress; see Blumenson, *Breakout and Pursuit,* p. 634, and War Diary, OB West, dated August 29, 1944, RH 19 IV/54, p. 294.

16. According to Eisenhower, Bradley, and Patton, see Blumenson, *Breakout and Pursuit* pp. 633 ff.

17. Pogue, *The Supreme Command*, p. 217.

18. The Allies were regrouping their forces at a moment that was most critical for the Germans. Once again, the question of Army Group boundaries played a role. The Americans, who were attacking along the Seine River, were withdrawn "shortly before the goal" and were replaced by British and Canadian units; see ibid., p. 216 f. That helps explain the success of the German Panzer thrust on August 25, 1944, into the Elbeuf area. See Frank, "5. Panzerarmee," MS-B-729, p. 19 f.

19. Blumenson, *Breakout and Pursuit*, p. 582. This estimate would appear to be realistic because, on August 25, the Fifth Panzer Army reported a *combat* strength of about eighteen thousand personnel, RH 21-5/53, p. 76.

20. SHAEF G-2 Summaries, dated August 23, 24, and 26, 1944; cf., Pogue, *The Supreme Command*, p. 244 f.

21. Montgomery, dated August 26, 1944; cf. Blumenson, *Breakout and Pursuit*, p. 661.

22. The term "Broad Front" can be found in the SHAEF "Post-OVERLORD Planning" documents of May 1944; cf., Pogue, *The Supreme Command*, p. 249.

23. Ellis, *Victory in the West*, II, p. 93, and Ruppenthal, *Logistical Support of the Armies*, I, p. 485.

24. Pogue, *The Supreme Command*, p. 257.

25. Montgomery's letter to Chiefs of Staff, dated August 24, 1944, in: Ellis, *Victory in the West*, I, p. 463 f.

26. Montgomery's letter to Chiefs of Staff, dated August 18, 1944, in: Blumenson, *Breakout and Pursuit*, p. 658, and Ambrose, "Eisenhower," p. 43.

27. Pogue, *The Supreme Command*, p. 250.

28. See also and for the following material: Ambrose, *Eisenhower Papers*.

29. Ibid., p. 40.

30. Wilmot, *The Struggle for Europe*, p. 496.

31. Ehrman, *Grand Strategy*, V, p. 380.

32. Eisenhower's letter to Marshall, dated August 19, 1944; cf., Pogue, *The Supreme Command*, p. 264.

33. As of that date, Montgomery's command authority was confined to the 21st Army Group; cf., ibid., p. 253.

34. It is interesting to note Bennett's reference ("Ultra Normandy," p. 133 f) to the effect that ULTRA information had made this or the adherence to the supporting offensive in the south obvious, because it was learned that the Germans were afraid of a thrust into the "gap" between Army Group B and Army Task Group G. But there is no support for this thesis among the sources.

35. Eisenhower's letter to Marshall, dated August 24, 1944; cf., *Eisenhower Papers*, IV, p. 2092 f.

36. Blumenson, *Breakout and Pursuit*, p. 659.

37. Eisenhower's letters to Montgomery and Marshall, dated August 24, 1944; cf. *Eisenhower Papers*, IV, pp. 2090 ff.

38. His justification was typical for Eisenhower: Otherwise, one could not justify to Bradley that the U.S. First Army was to be employed to support Montgomery; see ibid. Accordingly, it was only logical that Montgomery would exploit *every* situation to employ the Airborne Army in order not to "lose" the formation of the point of main effort in his area.

39. British field marshal Sir Alan Brooke reproached Eisenhower for being not very steadfast in his decisions (Ambrose, "Eisenhower," p. 41). In the truest sense of the word, he simply did not "get along" with Montgomery, whose character was basically different and whom American generals considered to be "stubborn, fussy and terribly slow" (ibid., p. 39 f). At times, the two Allies doubted each other's military abilities (Ehrman, *Grand Strategy*, V, p. 380).

40. Pogue, *The Supreme Command*, p. 260.

41. Compared to the planning, the Allies had been bottled up in the Normandy bridgehead "too long" and, after the breakthrough, they had advanced "too fast"; cf., Ruppenthal, *Logistical Support of the Armies*, II, p. 4 f.

42. Ibid., I, pp. 547 ff.

43. At most, about 10 percent of the daily total requirements, ibid., p. 575 f.

44. At the end of August, 90–95 percent of the supplies were still being stored in supply dumps near the invasion beaches; see Blumenson, *Breakout and Pursuit*, p. 689.

45. About 82,000 tons were to be delivered there by September 1, 1944.

46. More than 12,300 tons were transported on that day. That figure was never reached again, although the Red Ball Express was running until November; see Ruppenthal, *Logistical Support of the Armies*, I, pp. 558 ff.

47. Ehrman, *Grand Strategy*, V, p. 379 f.

48. Ruppenthal, *Logistical Support of the Armies*, II, p. 349.

49. In retrospect, it appears relatively clear that this implied possession of the harbor and, above all, the control of the mouth of the Scheldt River, which was necessary to use the port in the first place. As it turned out later, the Allied command for the moment did otherwise. This is why special reference is made to Eisenhower's rather vague style.

50. At any rate, it was not mentioned among the objectives that the army groups were to reach; Montgomery's letter to the Chiefs of Staff, dated August 24, 1944. See Ellis, *Victory in the West*, I, p. 463 f.

51. Ibid., II, p. 3.

52. Ehrman, *Grand Strategy*, V, p. 381, and Pogue, *The Supreme Command*, p. 251 f.

53. Bradley's order, dated August 25, 1944. See Blumenson, *Breakout and Pursuit*, p. 659 f.

54. Eisenhower's letter to the Combined Chiefs of Staff, dated August 22, 1944. See *Eisenhower Papers*, IV, pp. 2087 ff.

55. OB West, Operations Section, No. 7346/44, dated August 25, 1944, RH 19 IV/54, p. 172.

56. War Diary, Headquarters, Fifth Panzer Army, dated August 25, 1944, RH 21-5/52, p. 34 f.

57. Frank, "5. Panzerarmee," MS-B-729, p. 26 f.

58. Morning Report, Army Group B, dated August 26, 1944, RH 19 IV/45, p. 170.

59. Luftwaffe 17th Field Division, 49th Infantry Division, Luftwaffe 18th Field Division, 6th Parachute Division, with remnants of other divisions.

60. Daily Report for August 27, 1944, OB West, Operations Section, No. 7441/44, RH 19 IV/54, pp. 228 ff.

61. War Diary, Army Group B, dated August 26, 1944, RH 19 IX/88, p. 149.

62. War Diary, Headquarters, Fifth Panzer Army, dated August 27, 1944, RH 21-5/52, p. 37 f.

63. Ibid., dated August 26, 1944, p. 36.

64. Frank, "5. Panzerarmee," MS-B-729, p. 7 f.

65. Ibid., p. 17 f, and War Diary, Headquarters, Fifth Panzer Army, dated August 26, 1944, RH 21-5/52, p. 36.

66. Lieutenant General Graf von Schwerin, "116. Pz. Div.," MS-ETHINT 18, p. 6 f.

67. Zimmermann, "OB West," MS-T-121, B VI, pp. 1784 ff.

68. War Diary, Army Group B, dated August 27, 1944, RH 19 IX/88, p. 164.

69. Ibid., p. 157.

70. The 711th, 346th, 331st Infantry Divisions.

71. They represented the remnants of five Panzer divisions that were employed west of the Seine River and that were still able to fight.

72. Ibid., pp. 163 and 172.

73. Ibid., p. 161 f.

74. Frank, "5. Panzerarmee," MS-B-729, p. 17 f.

75. Telephone conversation between Gause and Operations Officer, Army Group B, dated August 27, 1944, 1130 hours, RH 19 IX/88, p. 161 f.

76. Ibid.

77. War Diary, Army Group B, dated August 28, 1944, RH 19 IX/88, p. 177.

78. War Diary, Headquarters, Fifth Panzer Army, dated August 28, 1944, RH 21-5/52, p. 38 f.

79. Montgomery, *From Normandy to the Baltic,* pp. 182 ff.

80. Blumenson, *Breakout and Pursuit,* p. 673.

81. War Diary, Headquarters, Fifth Panzer Army, dated August 28, 1944, RH 21-5/52, p. 39.

82. War Diary, LXXXI Army Corps, dated August 28, 1944, RH 24-81/97, p. 158/1 f.

83. War Diary, Headquarters, Fifth Panzer Army, dated August 29, 1944, RH 21-5/52, p. 40.

84. War Diary, LXXXI Army Corps, dated August 28, 1944, RH 24-81/97, p. 158/1 f.

85. See Model, Headquarters, Army Group B, Operations Section, No. 6588/44, dated August 27, 1944, RH 19 IX/4, p. 408.

86. War Diary, Army Group B, dated August 28, 1944, RH 19 IX/88, p. 177.

87. Headquarters, Fifth Panzer Army, Operations Section, No. 1049/44, dated August 28, 1944, RH 21-5/53, Appendix 63, p. 90.

88. Frank, "5. Panzerarmee," MS-B-729, p. 19 f.

89. Zimmermann, "OB West," MS-T-121, B VI, pp. 1809 ff.

90. Zimmermann, "Operationen," MS-B-308, p. 142.

91. Frank, "5. Panzerarmee," MS-B-729, pp. 8 and 19 ff, as well as Staubwasser, "Feinbild" [Enemy Situation], MS-B-825, p. 96 f.

92. Zimmermann, "OB West," MS-T-121, B IV, pp. 1526 ff.

93. See Chevallerie, Headquarters, First Army, Operations Section, No. 3201/44, dated August 25, 1944, War Diary, LVIII Panzer Corps, Appendix 2, RH 24-58/11, p. 9.

94. Ibid.; War Diary, Army Group B, dated August 25, 1944, RH 19 IX/88, p. 134; and Zimmermann, "OB West," MS-T-121, B V, pp. 1809 ff.

95. Blumenson, *Breakout and Pursuit*, pp. 665 ff and 671 ff.

96. Daily Report for August 26, 1944, OB West, Operations Section, No. 7404/44, RH 19 IV/54, p. 206.

97. Ibid., p. 207.

98. Caspar, "48. Inf. Div.," MS-P-166, p. 12 f.

99. War Diary, Army Group B, dated August 26, 1944, RH 19 IX/88, p. 150.

100. Evening Report, Intelligence Section, dated August 26, 1944, Army Group B, Intelligence Section, No. 3360/44, RH 19 IX/26, Part 1, p. 37 f.

101. Conference between Model and Zimmermann, dated August 26, 1944, RH 19 IV/54, p. 196 f, and Evening Report, Army Group B, dated August 26, 1944, RH 19 IV/45, p. 172.

102. War Diary, Army Group B, dated August 27, 1944, RH 19 IX/88, p. 158, and OB West, Operations Section, No. 7385/44, dated August 26, 1944, RH 19 IV/54, p. 210.

103. War Diary, Army Group B, dated August 27, 1944, RH 19 IX/88, p. 158.

104. Ibid., Telephone conversation between Chevallerie and Speidel, dated August 27, 1944, 1100 hours, p. 160 f.

105. Caspar, "48. Inf. Div.," MS-P-166, p. 13.

106. War Diary, Army Group B, dated August 27, 1944, RH 19 IX/88, p. 170.

107. Ibid., p. 169 f.

108. Ibid., p. 173.

109. War Diary, Headquarters, Fifth Panzer Army, dated August 28, 1944, RH 21-5/52, p. 39.

110. Telephone conversations, dated August 28, 1944, 1315–1710 hours, War Diary, Army Group B, RH 19 IX/88, pp. 175–177.

111. Ibid.

112. Daily Report for August 28, 1944, OB West, Operations Section, No. 7450/44, RH 19 IV/54, pp. 252 ff.

113. Emmerich, "1. Armee," MS-B-728, p. 12; Krüger, "LVIII. PzK," MS-B-157, p. 4 f.

114. War Diary, OB West, dated August 28, 1944, RH 19 IV/45, p. 177, and War Diary, Army Group B, RH 19 IX/88, p. 182.

115. Ibid., p. 169.

116. Headquarters, Fifth Panzer Army, Operations Section, No. 1054/44, dated August 28, 1944, RH 21-5/53, Appendix 57, p. 84.

117. Model's order, dated August 28, 1944, 1250 hours, and telephone conversation between Model and Speidel, dated August 28, 1944, 1420 hours, RH 19 IX/88, p. 174 f.

118. See Model, Headquarters, Army Group B, Operations Section, No. 6704/44, dated August 29, 1944, RH 19 IX/8, pp. 131 ff.

119. Telephone conversation between Model and Chevallerie, dated August 28, 1944, 1830 hours and 1910 hours, RH 19 IX/88, p. 179.

120. Author's estimate. The Panzer battalions of the Panzer Grenadier divisions that were coming from Italy had not yet arrived in the west; ibid.

121. Telephone conversation between Blumentritt/Model and Jodl, dated August 28, 1944, 1920 hours, RH 19 IX/88, p. 180 f.

122. Ibid.

123. Ibid.

124. War Diary, Army Group B, dated August 29, 1944, 0910–1130 hours, RH 19 IX/88, p. 184 f.

125. Telephone conversation between Eberbach and Model, dated August 29, 1944, 2035 hours, and August 30, 1944, 0910 hours, RH 19 IX/88, pp. 189 f and 195.

126. War Diary, Fifth Panzer Army, dated August 29, 1944, 1000 hours, RH 21-5/52, p. 41.

127. Eberbach, "7. Armee," MS-B-841, pp. 9 ff.

128. Radio message, Wehrmacht High Command/Wehrmacht Operations Staff, dated August 28, 1944, 1500 hours, RH 19 IX/88, p. 186.

129. Zimmermann, "OB West," MS-T-121, B VI, p. 1820.

130. See Adolf Hitler, Wehrmacht High Command/Wehrmacht Operations Staff, No. 773095, dated August 29, 1944, quoted in: OB West, Operations Section, No. 772/44, RH 19 IX/7, p. 45 f.

131. See also telephone conversation between Zimmermann and Model, dated August 29, 1944, 2200 hours, RH 19 IX/88, p. 190 f.

132. Ibid.

133. See Adolf Hitler, Wehrmacht High Command/Wehrmacht Operations Staff, No. 773095, dated August 29, 1944, quoted in: OB West, Operations Section, No. 772/44, RH 19 IX/7, p. 45 f.

134. Telephone conversation between Zimmermann and Model/Speidel, dated August 29, 1944, 2200 hours, RH 19 IX/88, p. 190 f.

135. See Model, Headquarters, Army Group B, Operations Section, No. 6704/44, dated August 29, 1944, 2400 hours, with "Note by Chiefs of Staff," dated August 30, 1944, RH 19 IX/8, pp. 131 ff. Hitler's order was undoubtedly already known; see telephone conversation between Zimmermann and Model/Speidel, dated August 29, 2200 hours, RH 19 IX/88, p. 190 f. That Hitler's order was the cause of the situation estimate springs from the August 29 draft signed by Speidel that contains the subsequently deleted sentences: "Army Group would be delighted to follow through on any more extensive attack intentions, but these . . . regrettably are not doable" and "I believe that only the measures I have initiated are possible." Cf., RH 19 IX/4, p. 429 f.

136. Telephone conversation between Friedel (Wehrmacht Operations Staff) and Operations Officer, Headquarters, Army Group B, dated August 30, 1944, 1530 hours, and telephone conversation between Blumentritt and Model, 1620 hours, RH 19 IX/88, p. 198 f.

137. Noon Report, Army Group B, dated August 29, 1944, RH 19 IV/54, p. 269 f.

138. Daily Report for August 30, 1944, OB West, Operations Section, No. 7520/44, ibid., pp. 303 ff.

139. Ibid.

140. Zimmermann, "OB West," MS-T-121, B VI, pp. 1824 ff.

141. Status of rail movements as of August 31, 1944, RH 19 IV/54, p. 340.

142. Signed, Jodl, by order, Wehrmacht High Command/Wehrmacht Operations Staff, No. 773116/44, dated August 31, 1944, quoted from OB West, Operations Staff, No. 779/44, RH 19 IX/7, p. 47.

143. See Model, Headquarters, Army Group B, Operations Section, No. 6704/44, dated August 29, 1944, RH 19 IX/8, pp. 131 ff.

144. Ellis, *Victory in the West,* I, p. 449.

145. Lieutenant General Siegfried Macholz, "49. Inf. Div.," MS-B-743, p. 23 f.

146. War Diary, Headquarters, Fifth Panzer Army, dated August 30, 1944, RH 21-5/52, p. 43.

147. Eberbach, "7. Armee," MS-B-841, p. 9 f.

148. LXVII Army Corps (Fifteenth Army) with: 226th, 245th, and LXXXVI Army Corps (Fifth Panzer Army) with: 271st, 331st, 344th, 346th, 711th Infantry Divisions, and Luftwaffe 17th Field Division, Front Situation Maps, August 30/31, 1944, RH 19 IV/70, K [Maps] 6 and 7.

149. Ellis, *Victory in the West,* I, p. 469.

150. The adjutant and assistant adjutant, Lieutenant Colonel Horenburg and Captain Ratjen, as well as Major Winnen, the headquarters commandant, were captured. War Diary, Headquarters, Fifth Panzer Army, August 31, 1944, RH 21-5/52, p. 43 f.

151. Ibid.

152. Boundary of Fifteenth Army, which was in command to the north thereof: Arras–Flixecourt.

153. See Model, Headquarters, Army Group B, Operations Section, No. 6737/44, dated August 29, 1944, RH 19 IX/4, p. 427 f.

154. Telephone conversation between Zimmermann and Model, dated August 29, 1944, 1920 hours, RH 19 IX/88, p. 188.

155. Frank, "5. Pz. Armee," MS-B-729, p. 32.

156. See also Daily Report for August 31, 1944, OB West, Operations Section, No. 7571/44, RH 19 IV/54, pp. 336 ff.

157. Ibid.

158. Ibid.

159. Zimmermann, "Operationen," MS-B-308, p. 148.

160. Telephone conversation between Blumentritt at one end and Speidel and Model at the other end, dated August 31, 1944, 1845 hours, RH 19 IX/88, p. 219 f.

161. Blumentritt in: N 6/1, "Model," p. 241.

162. Gersdorff, "Untergang" [The End], p. 161.

163. See Model, Headquarters, Army Group B, Operations Section, No. 6704/44, dated August 29, 1944, RH 19 IX/8, pp. 131 ff.

164. See Blumentritt, OB West, Operations Section, No. 7568/44, dated August 31, 1944, RH 19 IV/54, p. 334 f.

165. Ibid.

166. Ibid.

167. Ibid.

168. These two terms—*Weststellung* and *Westwall*—although not identical, were frequently used synonymously by the German command in the west.

169. Telephone conversation between Blumentritt/Model and Jodl, dated August 28, 1944, 1920 hours, RH 19 IX/88, p. 180 f.

170. Ibid.

171. Hitler's "Order on the [*sic*] Improvement of the German Western Position" of August 24, 1944, had merely led to organizational preparations but had not yet resulted in any practical measures. "Order on [*sic*] Establishment of Defense Readiness in the West Wall," signed by Adolf Hitler, No. 773134/44, dated September 1, 1944, in: "Hitlers Weisungen" [Hitler's Directives], pp. 279 ff; "Order to Secure the German Western Position and the West Wall," signed by Keitel, Wehrmacht Operations Staff/Operations Section, No. 10654/44, September 1, 1944, in: ibid., pp. 282 ff.

172. *Hitlers Lagebesprechungen,* noon situation briefing, dated September 1, 1944, p. 647 f.

173. Ibid., conference on July 31, 1944, p. 596.

174. Warlimont, "Siegfriedline," MS-ETHINT 1, p. 47.

175. Quoted from Pommerin, "Überlegungen" [Considerations], pp. 8 ff.

176. Lieutenant General Walther Wollmann in: Zimmermann, "OB West," MS-T-121, Appendix Volume, Appendix 11a, p. 161.

177. Gross, "Westwall," p. 316 f.

178. Ibid., p. 33.

179. The weakest West Wall sector was located between Brüggen (north

of Geilenkirchen) and Rindern (near Kleve) with only two bunkers per kilometer; cf., Gross, "Westwall," pp. 89 ff.

180. Gersdorff, "Siegfriedline," MS-ETHINT 53, p. 1.

181. The following lines were to be improved or reinforced as the Western Position apart from the West Wall and its "extension all the way to the IJssel Sea": (a) Scheldt–Albert Canal, west of Aachen; (b) Mosel River line (Trier–Thionville–Metz)–St. Avold (Maginot line)–Saaralbe–Vosges Mountains (rim and ridge position)–Belfort; (c) Mosel River line (south of Metz)–Nancy–Epinal–St. Maurice.

182. "Order to Secure the German Western Position and the West Wall," signed by Keitel, Wehrmacht Operations Staff/Operations Section, No. 10654/44, dated September 1, 1944, in: "Hitlers Weisungen," pp. 282 ff.

183. "Führer Edict" on Cooperation between Party and Wehrmacht, dated July 13, 1944, RW 4/Vol. 703, p. 9 f, signed Keitel, Wehrmacht Operations Staff/Deputy Chief of Staff for Supply, No. 007715/44, dated July 18, 1944, ibid., pp. 11 ff.

184. Reich Minister of Interior, signed by order, Dr. Dellbrügge, II RV 1012/44-105, dated September 9, 1944, ibid., p. 51.

185. Chief, Army Armament and Commander of Replacement Army, I, No. 2830/44, dated August 31, 1944, ibid., pp. 42 ff.

186. Signed by Bormann, Circular letter to all duty stations of the NSDAP [National Socialist German Workers' Party], 124/44, dated May 31, 1944, War Diary, Wehrmacht High Command, Vol. IV/2, pp. 1565 ff.

187. This was done through the "Second Edict of the Führer on Command Authority in a Zone of Operations within the Reich," dated September 20, 1944, RW 4/Vol. 702, pp. 200 ff.

188. "Order to Secure the German Western Position and the West Wall," signed Keitel, Wehrmacht Operations Staff/Operations Section, No. 10654/44, dated September 1, 1944, in: "Hitler's Weisungen," pp. 282 ff.

189. Reich Commissar Dr. Seyss-Inquart was included in the setup for the Dutch sector of IJsselmeer–Njimwegen, along with Gauleiters Schlessmann (Essen), Florian (Düsseldorf), Grohé (Cologne-Aachen), Simon (Mosselland), Bürckel (Westmark), and Wagner (Baden-Alsace). Cf., "Order on [sic] Establishment of the West Wall's Defense Preparedness," signed by Adolf Hitler, No. 773134/44, dated September 1, 1944, in: "Hitlers Weisungen," pp. 279 ff.

190. War Diary, Wehrmacht High Command, Vol. IV/1, p. 380.

191. Signed Adolf Hitler, No. 772965/44, dated September 24, 1944, "Hitlers Weisungen," pp. 272 ff.

192. "Order to Secure the German Western Position and the West Wall," signed Keitel, Wehrmacht Operations Staff/Operations Section, No. 10654/44, dated September 1, 1944, ibid., pp. 282 ff.

193. Zimmermann, "OB West," MS-T-121, B VI, p. 1977.

194. "Meldungen aus dem Reich" [Reports from the Reich], Report dated October 28, 1944, pp. 6720 ff.

195. Ibid., Report of November 12, 1944, pp. 6726 ff.

196. Brandenberger, "7. Armee," MS-B-730, p. 59 f.

197. "Meldungen aus dem Reich," Report of November 12, 1944, pp. 6726 ff.

198. Ibid., Report of October 28, 1944, pp. 6720 ff.

199. Zimmermann, "OB West," MS-T-121, B VI, p. 1975.

200. "Order to Secure the German Western Position and the West Wall," signed by Keitel, Wehrmacht Operations Staff/Operations Section, No. 10654/44, dated September 1, 1944, in: "Hitlers Weisungen," pp. 282 ff.

201. The divisions were renamed Volksgrenadier [People's Grenadier] divisions on October 9, 1944.

202. In addition, the 3rd and 15th Panzer Grenadier Divisions were coming from Italy.

203. "Order to Secure the German Western Position and the West Wall," signed by Keitel, Wehrmacht Operations Staff/Operations Section, No. 10654/44, dated September 1, 1944, in: "Hitlers Weisungen," pp. 282 ff.

204. *Hitlers Lagebesprechungen,* noon situation briefing, dated September 1, 1944, p. 637.

205. "Tagebuch Botsch" [Botsch Diary] for August 25, 1944, RH 20-19/85, p. 21.

206. Headquarters, Nineteenth Army, Operations Section, No. 8786/44, dated August 24, 1944, RH 20-19/90, p. 20.

207. Ibid., p. 20.

208. Ibid.

209. Wietersheim, "11. Pz. Div.," MS-A-880, p. 15.

210. Daily Report for August 26, 1944, Headquarters, Army Task Group G, Operations Section, No. 2112/44, RH 19 XII/7, p. 316.

211. "Tagebuch Botsch" for August 26, 1944, RH 20-19/85, p. 22 f.

212. Ibid.

213. Ibid.

214. Wilt, *French Riviera Campaign of August 1944,* p. 140 f.

215. Evening Report for August 27, 1944, Headquarters, Army Task Group G, Operations Section, No. 2200/44, RH 19 XII/7, p. 329.

216. Botsch, "19. Armee," MS-B-518, p. 26.

217. "Tagebuch Botsch" for August 27, 1944, RH 20-19/85, p. 25.

218. Ibid., p. 24.

219. Ibid., for August 28, 1944, p. 28.

220. War Diary, Headquarters, Nineteenth Army, dated August 27, 1944, RH 20-19/90, p. 122.

221. War Diary, Army Task Group G, dated August 28, 1944, RH 19 XII/5, p. 164 f.

222. "Tagebuch Botsch" for August 28, 1944, RH 20-19/84, p. 28.

223. War Diary, Headquarters, Nineteenth Army, dated August 28/29, 1944, RH 20-19/91, pp. 10 and 24 ff.

224. Ibid., p. 27 f.

225. Report, 11th Panzer Division, dated August 29, 1944, RH 20-19/91, p. 72 f.

226. Wiese, "19. Armee," MS-B-787, p. 23.

227. War Diary, Headquarters, Nineteenth Army, dated August 31, 1944, RH 20-19/91, p. 111.

228. Botsch, "19. Armee," MS-B-696, p. 55.

229. "Tagebuch Botsch" for August 31, 1944, RH 20-19/85, p. 34.

230. Ibid., for August 25, 1944, p. 21.

231. War Diary, Army Task Group G, dated August 27, 1944, RH 19 XII/5, p. 160.

232. The pocket had no longer been completely closed since August 25, and the last route of retreat was covered "only" by artillery fire.

233. Daily Report, LXXXV Army Corps, dated September 2, 1944, RH 20-19/96, p. 50.

234. Headquarters, Army Task Group G, Operations Section, No. 2323/44, dated September 1, 1944, RH 19 XII/8, p. 31 f.

235. Baessler, the former commanding general of the 242nd Infantry Division (Toulon), died in Vienna in 1944.

236. Wilt, *French Riviera Campaign of August 1944*, p. 142.

237. Botsch, "Kommentar," MS-B-518, pp. 20 ff.

238. On August 26, he considered relieving Major General John E. Dahlquist (U.S. 36th Division) of command because of tactical errors. Cf., Wilt, *French Riviera Campaign of August 1944*, p. 140 f.

239. Blaskowitz, "Armeegruppe G," MS-B-800, p. 17.

240. Evening Report, Army Task Group G, dated August 31, 1944, RH 19 XII/7, p. 386 f.

241. Conference between Blaskowitz and Wiese, dated September 1, 1944, RH 20-19/96, p. 8 f.

242. Ibid.

243. See Blaskowitz, Headquarters, Army Task Group G, Operations Section, No. 2367/44, dated September 1, 1944, RH 19 XII/8, p. 14 f.

244. Ibid.

245. "Tagebuch Botsch" for September 1, 1944, RH 20-19/85, p. 36 f.

246. Conference between Blaskowitz and Wiese, dated September 1, 1944, RH 20-19/96, p. 8 f.

247. See Blaskowitz, Headquarters, Army Task Group G, Operations Section, No. 2324/44, dated September 1, 1944, RH 19 XII/8, p. 18.

248. War Diary, Army Task Group G, dated August 26, 1944, RH 19 XII/5, p. 158 f.

249. Activity Report, Army Personnel Office, dated July 29 and August 29, 1944, pp. 186 and 232.

250. Haeckel, "16. Inf. Div.," MS-B-245, p. 26.

251. See Blaskowitz, Headquarters, Army Task Group G, Operations Section, No. 1940/44, dated August 25, 1944, RH 19 XII/7, p. 291.

252. See Blaskowitz, Headquarters, Army Task Group G, Operations Section, No. 1961/44, dated August 26, 1944, ibid., p. 312.

253. Report of the Administrative Section of the Bordeaux Local Military Administrative Office, dated October 17, 1944, RW 35/1253, p. 71.

254. Along with the 15th Infantry Division, a bicycle unit under the command of Colonel Seiz with about five thousand men had been taken out of the former Southern March Group and had been sent on toward Dijon. Cf., Seiz, "159. Inf. Div.," MS-A-960, p. 4.

255. Report of the Administrative Section of the Bordeaux Local Military Administrative Office, dated October 17, 1944, RW 35/1253, pp. 71 ff.

256. Ibid.

257. Eyewitness statement, 1st Lieutenant Liese (16th Infantry Division) during the court-martial investigation of the "Elster Affair," OB West, Intelligence Section, No. 3045/44, dated October 7, 1944, RH 19 IV/141, p. 174 f.

258. Report of the Administrative Section of the Bordeaux Local Military Administrative Office, dated October 17, 1944, RW 35/1253, pp. 71 ff.

259. Elster had made his final decision in taking this step after he was assured that he would be captured by the Americans and not by the French Forces of the Interior. Cf., Nanteuil/Levy, "Elster," pp. 77 ff.

260. Nicault, "La Capitulation" [The Capitulation], pp. 91 ff.

261. Message from Army Group G, dated September 2, 1944, 0400 hours, RH 19 IV/46, p. 6.

262. War Diary, Ground Forces Group G, dated September 3, 1944, RH 19 XII/5, p. 191.

263. Headquarters, Nineteenth Army, Operations Section, No. 9156/44, dated September 5, 1944, RH 20-19/96, p. 191 f.

264. Author's calculations according to above-mentioned source. That number also included Elster's march group; Elster had left the operations staffs in the dark as to his intentions.

265. See Blaskowitz, Headquarters, Army Task Group G, Operations Section, No. 2386/44, dated September 2, 1944, RH 19 XII/8, pp. 34 ff.

266. Daily Report for September 3, 1944, OB West, Operations Section, No. 7642/44, RH 19 IV/55, pp. 78 ff.

267. The 159th Infantry Division was earmarked for the Remiremont area.

268. Until then, Lucht had directed the development of the Kitzinger Line between Langres and Pontarlier.

269. Battle Group Rauch, with two battalions and one artillery battery, War Diary, Army Task Group G, September 2, 1944, RH 19 XII/5, p. 190.

270. Daily Report for September 4, 1944, Headquarters, Army Task Group G, Operations Section, No. 2453/44, RH 19 XII/8, p. 72 f.

271. "Tagebuch Botsch" for September 3, 1944, RH 20-19/85, p. 40.

272. The bridges downstream along the Rhône River from St. Vallier, on the other hand, had been destroyed by the Allied air forces; cf., War Diary, Headquarters, Nineteenth Army, September 5, 1944, RH 20-19/96, p. 196.

273. Daily Report for September 3, 1944, OB West, Operations Section, No. 7642/44, RH 19 IV/55, pp. 78 ff.

274. Ibid., and Daily Report for September 4, 1944, Headquarters, Army Task Group G, Operations Section, No. 2353/44, RH 19 XII/8, p. 72 f.

275. According to the U.S. Army official history: "The 11th Panzer Division, with more enthusiasm than truth, reported to the Nineteenth Army that it had destroyed an entire American regiment. Actually, casualties of the 179th Infantry and supporting units numbered 3 men killed, 27 wounded, and 185 missing and probably captured. Materiel losses included 2 tank destroyers, 2 armored cars, 1 half-track, and 2 jeeps destroyed and about 20 other vehicles damaged. The most the German effort accomplished was to disrupt preparations by the 179th Infantry to participate in the 45th Division's attack on 2 September." Jeffrey J. Clarke and Robert Ross Smith, *Riviera to the Rhine*, Washington, D.C.: Center of Military History, 1993, p. 177.

276. Wilt, *French Riviera Campaign of August 1944*, p. 151.

277. Botsch, "Kommentar," MS-B-518, p. 35 f.

278. See Blaskowitz, Headquarters, Army Task Group G, Operations Section, No. 2386/44, dated September 2, 1944, Rh 19 XII/8, pp. 34 ff.

279. See also Daily Report for September 4, 1944, Headquarters, Army Task Group G, Operations Section, No. 2453/44, ibid., p. 72 f.

280. See Blaskowitz, Headquarters, Army Task Group G, Operations Section, No. 2386/44, dated September 2, 1944, ibid., pp. 34 ff.

281. One regiment each from Defense District V in the areas of Blamont–St. Dié–Belfort; see War Diary, Army Task Group G, dated September 2, 1944, RH 19 XII/5, p. 190.

282. Blaskowitz continued to consider Himmler only as "Reichsführer-SS"; in other words, he obviously did not accept him in his military assignment as "Chief of Army Armament and Commanding General of the Replacement Army"; see Blaskowitz, Headquarters, Army Task Group G, Operations Section, No. 2414/44, dated September 3, 1944, RH 19 XII/8, p. 50.

283. War Diary, Army Task Group G, dated September 3, 1944, RH 19 XII/5, p. 194 f.

284. See Blaskowitz, Headquarters, Army Task Group G, Operations Section, No. 2414/44, dated September 3, 1944, RH 19 XII/8, p. 50.

285. On December 2, 1944, Himmler, after all, was indeed appointed "Supreme Commander, Upper Rhine," and, finally, in January 1945, he was made Supreme Commander of Army Group Vistula.

286. War Diary, OB West, dated September 7, 1944, RH 19 IV/46, p. 38.

287. "Tagebuch Botsch" for September 3, 1944, RH 20-19/85, p. 40.

288. War Diary, OB West, dated September 5, 1944, RH 19 IV/46, p. 24.

289. Telephone conversation between Blumentritt and Speidel, dated September 1, 1944, 1730 hours, RH 19 IX/89, p. 8.

290. Intelligence Section Evening Report, dated September 1, 1944, Army Group B, Intelligence Section, No. 3439/44, RH 19 IX/26, Part 2, p. 248.

291. Telephone conversation between Feyerabend and Speidel, dated September 1, 1944, 2235 hours, RH 19 IX/89, p. 12.

292. Cole, "Lorraine," pp. 60 and 118.

293. OB West, Operations Section, 7590/44, dated September 2, 1944, RH 19 IV/55, p. 32.

294. OB West, Operations Section, No. 7595/44, dated September 2, 1944, ibid., p. 45.

295. War Diary, Army Group B, dated September 2, 1944, RH 19 IX/89, p. 28.

296. War Diary, OB West, dated September 1, 1944, RH 19 IV/46, p. 2 f.

297. Wehrmacht High Command/Wehrmacht Operations Staff, No. 773145/44, dated September 1, 1944, quoted in: OB West, Operations Section, No. 7611/44, dated September 2, RH 19 IV/55, p. 57.

298. See Adolf Hitler, Wehrmacht Operations Staff, Operations Order No. 773189/44, dated September 3, 1944, quoted in: OB West, Operations Section, No. 795/44, ibid., p. 63 f.

299. Telephone conversation between Feyerabend and Speidel, dated September 2, 1944, 0205 hours, RH 19 IX/89, p. 17 f.

300. Headquarters, LXXX Army Corps, originally was employed to build up the "Kitzinger Line," but after the American breakthrough, it was placed under the retreating First Army.

301. They were joined by the "von Fritschen Mobile Regiment" and Battle Group Brassert; cf., War Diary, LXXX Army Corps, September 1–5, 1944, RH 24-80/68, pp. 7 ff.

302. That headquarters had just arrived from the Channel coast (Headquarters, Fifteenth Army).

303. War Diary, OB West, dated September 2, 1944, RH 19 IV/46, p. 7.

304. Status of rail movements on September 4, 1944, OB West, Operations Section, No. 7666/44, RH 19 IV/55, p. 110.

305. Krause, "Metz," MS-B-042, pp. 2 ff.

306. Organization, Army Group B, dated September 5, 1944, RH 19 IV/55, p. 161.

307. Status of rail movements on September 4, 1944, OB West, Operations Section, No. 7666/44, RH 19 IV/55, p. 110.

308. Daily Report for September 4, 1944, OB West, Operations Section, No. 7675/44, ibid., pp. 106 ff.

309. Telephone conversation between Blumentritt and Speidel, dated September 4, 1944, 1940 hours, RH 19 IX/89, p. 58 f.

310. Headquarters, Seventh Army, relieved Dietrich's headquarters on September 4, 1944, 1900 hours, and took command.

311. Telephone conversation between Feyerabend and Speidel, dated September 4, 1944, 1910 hours, RH 19 IX/89, p. 57.

312. Telephone conversation between Chevallerie and Model, dated September 3, 1944, 0940 hours, ibid., p. 35.

313. War Diary, Army Group B, dated September 5, 1944, ibid., pp. 66 ff.

314. Organization, Army Group B, dated September 5, 1944, RH 19 IV/55, p. 161.

315. Headquarters, Army Group G, Operations Section, No. 7012/44, dated September 5, 1944, RH 19 IX/5, p. 509 f.

316. Daily Report for September 5, 1944, OB West, Operations Section, No. 7710/44, RH 19 IV/55, pp. 148 ff.

317. Ritgen, "Panzer-Lehr Division," p. 193.

318. See Model, Army Group B, Operations Section, No. 6913/44, dated September 3, 1944, RH 19 IX/5, p. 479.

319. Daily Report for September 5, 1944, OB West, Operations Section, No. 7710/44, RH 19 IV/55, pp. 148 ff.

320. Ibid.

321. War Diary, Army Group B, dated September 1, 1944, RH 19 IX/89, p. 8.

322. Obstfelder, who initially was to take command of the Seventh Army, was from time to time represented by Lieutenant General Hans-Kurt Höcker (Luftwaffe 17th Field Division).

323. Telephone conversation between Gersdorff and Tempelhoff, dated September 1, 1944, 1130 hours, RH 19 IX/89, p. 4 f.

324. War Diary, Army Group B, dated September 1, 1944, ibid., p. 9.

325. War Diary, OB West, dated September 2, 1944, RH 19 IV/46, p. 9.

326. Telephone conversation between Gause and Tempelhoff, dated September 1, 1944, 2330 hours, RH 19 IX/89, p. 13 f.

327. War Diary, OB West, dated September 2, 1944, RH 19 IV/46, p. 6.

328. Blumenson, *Breakout and Pursuit*, p. 679.

329. Bradley's order, dated August 31, 1944; cf., Blumenson, *Breakout and Pursuit*, p. 680.

330. War Diary, Headquarters, Fifth Panzer Army, dated September 3, 1944, RH 21-5/52, p. 45.

331. War Diary, 58th Panzer Corps, dated September 1, 1944, RH 24-58/10, p. 22.

332. Ibid.

333. LXXIV Army Corps with the following units: Luftwaffe 18th Field Division, 6th Parachute Division; LVIII Panzer Corps with the following units: 348th Infantry Division, 3rd Parachute Division; II SS Panzer Corps with the following divisions: 47th and 275th Infantry Divisions, 1st and 12th SS Divisions; 116th Panzer Division. See War Diary, Headquarters, Fifth Panzer Army, Appendix 72, dated September 1, 1944, RH 21-5/53, p. 99. But these are incomplete because the divisions were partly employed in a scattered form over a vast area. For example, the LXXIV Army Corps also had the artillery regiment of 49th Infantry Division; the LVIII Panzer Corps had Battle Group von Aulock. One battalion of the 348th Infantry Division, on the other hand, was fighting in the sector of the Fifteenth Army, while the Group Meyer of the 12th SS Panzer Division was fighting under the I SS Panzer Corps.

334. War Diary, LVIII Panzer Corps, dated September 1–2, 1944, RH 24-58/10. p. 22 f.

335. Krüger, "LVIII PzK," MS-B-157, p. 8 f.

336. Ibid.

337. War Diary, LVIII Panzer Corps, dated September 1, 1944, RH 24-58/10, p. 22 f.

338. General of Infantry Erich Straube, as the senior general, assumed overall leadership of the provisionally formed Army Task Group Straube. This is why the units of the LXXIV Army Corps (Luftwaffe 18th Field Division, 6th Parachute Division) were also placed under Krüger; see War Diary, LVIII Panzer Corps, dated September 2, 1944, RH 24-58/10, p. 24.

339. War Diary, 5th Panzer Corps, dated September 2, 1944, RH 21-5/52, p. 45.

340. Wahle, "47. Inf. Div.," MS-B-176, p. 17.

341. Daily Report for September 2, 1944, OB West, Operations Section, No. 7623/44, RH 19 IV/55, pp. 52 ff.

342. War Diary, LVIII Panzer Corps, dated September 3, 1944, RH 24-58/10, p. 27.

343. Blumenson, *Breakout and Pursuit,* p. 682 f.

344. Wahle, "47. Inf. Div.," MS-B-176, pp. 21 ff.

345. Activity Report, Army Personnel Office, dated September 19, 1944, p. 262.

346. Blumenson, *Breakout and Pursuit,* p. 684.

347. War Diary, Army Group B, dated September 3, 1944, RH 19 IX/89, p. 37.

348. Ibid., dated September 4, 1944, p. 46.

349. Ibid., dated September 1, 1944, p. 9.

350. Ibid., dated September 4, 1944, p. 46.

351. Ibid., p. 53.

352. Schack took command of the LXXXI Army Corps from Kuntzen on September 4, 1944.

353. Brandenberger, "7. Armee," MS-B-730, p. 6.

354. Daily Report for September 2, 1944, OB West, Operations Section, No. 7623/44, RH 19 IV/55, pp. 52 ff.

355. OB West, Operations Section, No. 7591/44, dated September 2, 1944, ibid., p. 36 f.

356. War Diary, LXXXIX Army Corps, dated September 1, 1944, RH 24-89/10, p. 5/2. The date, however, is uncertain. The "after-action report" was not written up until September 20, 1944.

357. Report on morale by Admiral, Netherlands G 25312 F III for the period of September 3–21, 1944, RM 7/131, pp. 492 ff.

358. War Diary, LXXXIX Army Corps, dated September 1, 1944, RH 24-89/10, p. 5/2.

359. The author received a copy of this appeal from Model's son, Bundeswehr Brigadier General Hansgeorg Model.

360. Model's letter, dated September 4, 1944: "Now of all times must we hold the line . . . because that is how we can decide the issue. . . . These are turbulent times! Nevertheless, hold on!" "Privatarchiv Model."

361. Telephone conversation between Speidel and Warlimont, dated September 3, 1944, 2335 hours, RH 19 IX/89, p. 38 f.

362. Daily Report for September 3, 1944, Supreme Commander West, Operations Section, No. 7642/44, RH 19 IV/55, pp. 78 ff.

363. War Diary, Army Group B, dated September 3/4, 1944, RH 19 IX/89, pp. 39 and 53.

364. War Diary, Headquarters, Fifth Panzer Army, dated September 3, 1944, RH 21-5/52, p. 46.

365. War Diary, Army Group B, dated September 3, 1944, RH 19 IX/89, p. 34.

366. Ibid., dated September 4, 1944, p. 47.

367. War Diary, LXXXVIII Army Corps, dated September 1, 1944, RH 24-88/91, pp. 52 ff.

368. In addition to the 719th, the remnants of the 347th Infantry Division that were still in the area of the canal were ordered to move up. The main body of this division in the meantime had been transferred to Namur.

369. War Diary, LXXXVIII Army Corps, dated September 1, 1944, RH 24-88/91, pp. 52 ff.

370. War Diary, Army Group B, dated September 4, 1944, 1145 hours, RH 19 IX/89, p. 49.

371. Commanding General, 136th Special Purpose Division in Antwerp. Division headquarters only had two battalions of men with stomach ailments.

372. Telephone conversation between Stolberg and Tempelhoff, dated September 4, 1944, 1425 hours, RH 19 IX/89, p. 51.

373. Telephone conversation between Krebs and Stolberg, dated September 4, 1944, 1445 hours, and Krebs and Blumentritt, 1455 hours, RH 19 IX/89, p. 52 f.

374. Ruppenthal, *Logistical Support of the Armies*, II, p. 105.

375. Ellis, *Victory in the West*, II, p. 414. Pogue figured the strength of the Belgian Resistance at about thirty thousand men; cf., *The Supreme Command*, p. 329.

376. Wilmot, *The Struggle for Europe*, p. 517.

377. Daily Report for September 4, 1944, OB West, Operations Section, No. 7675/44, RH 19 IV/55, pp. 106 ff.

378. The 59th, 64th, 70th, 226th, 245th, and 712th Infantry Divisions. After the German front was split up, Headquarters, Fifteenth Army, also got the LXXXVI Army Corps with the 331st, 346th, and 711th Infantry Divisions and the Luftwaffe 17th Field Division.

379. Total numbers include the fortress detachments. Cf., Montgomery, *From Normandy to the Baltic*, p. 188.

380. OB, Operations Section, No. 7577/44, dated September 1, 1944, and /607/44, dated September 3, 1944, RH 19 IV/556, pp. 20 f and 85 f.

381. War Diary, Army Group B, dated September 1, 1944, RH 19 IX/89, p. 8.

382. See Keitel, Wehrmacht High Command/Wehrmacht Operations Staff, Organization Section, No. 0010691/44, dated September 2, 1944, RW 4/Vol. 494, p. 62.

383. Ibid.

384. OB West, Operations Section, No. 6883/44, dated August 20, 1944, RH 19 IV/53, p. 345 f.

385. See Keitel, Wehrmacht High Command/Wehrmacht Operations Staff/Organization Section, No. 001–691/44, dated September 2, 1944, RW 4/Vol. 494, p. 66 f.

386. Note on noon situation briefing, dated September 3, 1944, see Warlimont, ibid., p. 66 f.

387. See Keitel, Wehrmacht High Command/Wehrmacht Operations Staff/Organization Section, No. 0010719/44, dated September 2, 1944, ibid., p. 60.

388. Proposal by General of Infantry Hermann Reinecke, chief, National Socialist Operations Staff at Wehrmacht High Command, dated September 4, 1944; activity report by Army Personnel Office, p. 241.

389. As stated in Hitler's Edict on the Introduction of National Socialist Leadership Officers, dated December 22, 1943.

390. See Model, Headquarters, Army Group B, dated September 4, 1944, RH 19 IX/8, p. 134 f.

391. War Diary, Army Group B, dated September 4, 1944, RH 19 IX/89, p. 47.

392. Daily Report for September 4, 1944, OB West, Operations Section, No. 7675/44, RH 19 IV/55, pp. 106 ff.

393. War Diary, Army Group B, dated September 4, 1944, RH 19 IX/89, p. 48.

394. Brandenberger, "7. Armee," MS-B-730, pp. 13 ff.

395. Daily Report for September 5, 1944, OB West, Operations Section, No. 7710/44, RH 19 IV/55, pp. 148 ff.

396. War Diary, Army Group B, dated September 4, 1944, RH 19 IX/89, p. 59.

397. "Valkyrie Allert" in Defense District VI on September 3, 1944; cf., RH 19 IV/46, p. 13. The disbanded Replacement Army alert units had originally been earmarked to deal with domestic unrest but also played an important role in connection with the events of July 20, 1944.

398. Telephone conversation between Krebs (or Speidel) and Guderian, dated September 4, 1944, 1855 hours, RH 19 IX/89, p. 56 f.

399. Ibid.

400. The estimate of the situation had been completed already at noon. In other words, the Seventh Army headquarters had not yet relieved Dietrich's headquarters (which happened at 1900). That is why Model was still mentioning the Fifth Panzer Army.

401. See Model, Headquarters, Army Group B, No. 6944/44, dated September 4, 1944, RH 19 IX/8, p. 134 f.

9. The Basis for Continued Combat Operations

1. The German army was "no longer a cohesive force but a number of fugitive battle groups, short of equipment and arms," quoted in: MacDonald, *The Siegfried Line Campaign*, p. 14.

2. Patton's Order, to the U.S. Third Army, dated September 5, 1944, cf., Cole, *The Lorraine Campaign*, p. 55.

3. See War Diary, U.S. Seventh Army, September 2–3, 1944, as well as Wilt, *The French Riviera Campaign of August 1944*, p. 150 f. Lieutenant General Patch's U.S. Seventh Army was still under the commander-in-chief of the Mediterranean theater of war, British General Henry Maitland Wilson. Patch's army and the French army under General Jean de Lattre de Tassigny (French Army B, renamed First French Army as of September 15) were combined under 6th Army Group commanded by Lieutenant General Jacob L. Devers and placed under Eisenhower's SHAEF.

4. See Ellis, *Victory in the West*, II, pp. 7 ff.; Pogue, *The Supreme Command*, pp. 253 ff.; Blumenson, *Breakout and Pursuit*, pp. 687 ff.; Ambrose, "Eisenhower as a Commander," in *Eisenhower Papers*, V, pp. 39–48.

5. See also chapter 8, section 2 (a), "The Strategy Debate and Eisenhower's August 24 Decision."

6. "The enemy is routed and running on our entire front," Eisenhower to Marshall, September 2, 1944, cf., *Eisenhower Papers*, IV, p. 2111 f.

7. "Enemy resistance on the entire front shows signs of collapse," Eisenhower Directive, September 4, 1944, ibid., p. 2115 f.

8. In the meantime, the DRAGOON forces, which were not yet under his command (only as of September 15), were to advance via Besancon–Dijon auf Belfort–Epinal, ibid.

9. Pogue, *The Supreme Command*, pp. 258 ff.

10. The British Second Army was to push toward Arnhem–Wesel, while the U.S. First Army was to head for Cologne–Bonn. One corps of Hodges's U.S. First Army was to advance through the Ardennes toward Koblenz in order thus to close the gap toward the U.S. Third Army. Patton's U.S. Third Army was assigned the Mainz–Mannheim area; cf., Conferences of Allied Commanders, September 2/3, 1944, in Ellis, *Victory in the West*, II, p. 7 f, and MacDonald, *The Siegfried Line Campaign*, p. 36 f.

11. "I now deem it important to get Patton moving once again . . . to carry out the original conception for the final stages of this campaign," Eisenhower Memorandum, September 5, 1944, cf., *Eisenhower Papers*, IV, p. 2121 f.

12. Eisenhower had recognized the *repercussions* of the supply crisis. Of course, he saw a "potential danger" in that the Germans were able to exploit a slowdown of the Allied offensives for the purpose of reorganizing the defenses along the West Wall "or even along the Rhine." His "conclusion" went like this: "We must now as never before keep the enemy stretched *everywhere*." Eisenhower to Marshall, September 4, 1944, cf., *Eisenhower Papers*, IV, p. 2118 f.

13. Ruppenthal, *Logistical Support of the Armies*, II, p. 6.

14. Ruppenthal, "Logistics and the Broad Front Strategy," in: *Command Decisions*, p. 323.

15. Ruppenthal, *Logistical Support of the Armies*, I, p. 492.

16. Blumenson, *Breakout and Pursuit,* pp. 681 and 694 f.

17. MacDonald, *The Siegfried Line Campaign,* p. 10.

18. Rouen fell on August 30, Dieppe on September 1, and Fécamp and St. Valéry en Caux fell into Allied hands without any fight on September 2.

19. Warlimont's communication, dated August 26, 1944, War Diary, Wehrmacht High Command, IV/1, p. 468.

20. Ruhfus, "Einsatz," MS-B-556, and Schaefer, "244. Inf. Div.," MS-A-884.

21. Ruppenthal, *Logistical Support of the Armies,* II, pp. 121 ff.

22. War Diary, Headquarters, Nineteenth Army, dated August 25, 1944, RH 20-19/90, p. 56 f.

23. Ruppenthal, *Logistical Support of the Armies,* II, pp. 121 ff.

24. Ibid., p. 49.

25. Ibid., p. 104 f.

26. Among the objectives that Eisenhower established for the central 12th Army Group on September 4, the capture of Brest showed up even *before* the breakthrough of the Siegfried Line; cf., *Eisenhower Papers,* IV, p. 2115 f.

27. U.S. VIII Corps: three divisions, one task force, and eighteen artillery battalions with a total of fifty thousand men, cf., Blumenson, *Breakout and Pursuit,* pp. 633 ff.

28. Brest, which was completely destroyed, fell on September 18–19. The harbor, however, had become worthless for the Americans and was no longer used for logistics purposes; cf., ibid., pp. 653 ff.

29. Ruppenthal, *Logistical Support of the Armies,* I, p. 535.

30. On September 5, Patton's U.S. Third Army relinquished command of the U.S. VIII Corps to the newly organized U.S. Ninth Army, under Lieutenant General William H. Simpson.

31. Blumenson, *Breakout and Pursuit,* p. 656.

32. Ruppenthal, *Logistical Support of the Armies,* I, p. 536.

33. Blumenson, *Breakout and Pursuit,* p. 656.

34. No matter how fanatically the Brest garrison might defend its positions, it constituted no threat whatsoever because it would be utterly unthinkable to mount a major offensive to relieve the infantry units that were trapped far from German lines. Brest could hardly be of any use even as a reserve port because it was even farther away from the front than Cherbourg.

35. Ramsay's telegram, dated September 3, 1944, to SHAEF and the 21st Army Group, cf., Ellis, *Victory in the West,* II, p. 5.

36. ULTRA Message Nos. XL 9219 and 9248, dated September 5, 1944, Bennett, "Ultra Normandy," p. 142.

37. *Eisenhower Papers,* IV, p. 2120, September 5, 1944.

38. Ibid.

39. Ambrose, "Eisenhower as a Commander," in *Eisenhower Papers,* V, p. 43.

40. On September 1 the primarily British army group in the north was

designated the 21st Army Group, while the U.S. army group in the center was designated the 12th Army Group.

41. The last V-1 was fired from Pas du Calais on September 3.

42. Montgomery, *From Normandy to the Baltic*, p. 189.

43. Ehrman, *Grand Strategy*, V, p. 382.

44. MacDonald, "The Decisions to Launch Operation MARKET-GARDEN," in *Command Decisions*, p. 339.

45. "Whatever action Hitler may now take it will be too late to affect the issue in the West," cf., Ellis, *Victory in the West*, II, p. 19.

46. U.S. Third Army G-2 estimate, dated August 28, 1944, cf., Pogue, *The Supreme Command*, p. 245.

47. See chapter 8, section 2 (a), for the now purely military-operational grounds that made it look so obvious to Eisenhower.

48. "Staatmänner und Diplomaten, Aufzeichnung über die Unterredung Hitlers mit Botschafter de Brinon vom 1.9.1944" [Statesmen and Diplomats—Notes on Hitler's Conference with Ambassador de Brinon on September 1, 1944], p. 502.

49. Jodl, "Ardennenoffensive" [The Ardennes Offensive], MS-ETHINT 50, p. 5.

50. *Hitlers Lagebesprechungen,* noon situation briefing, dated September 1, 1944, pp. 636 ff.

51. Schramm, "Ardennenoffensive," MS-A-862, pp. 15 ff and 56.

52. See chapter 6, section 1.

53. Warlimont, "Kommentare," MS-P-215, IV, Part 2, p. 323.

54. See the introduction and chapter 2, section 2, concerning the reasons for the formation of the main effort in the west as discussed earlier.

55. Greiffenberg, "Ardennes-Questionnaire," MS-P-32i, Appendix 1, p. 3.

56. *Hitlers Lagebesprechungen,* Conference on August 31, 1944, p. 615.

57. Ibid., noon situation briefing, dated September 1, 1944, p. 646.

58. Ibid., p. 637.

59. Ibid., p. 642 f.

60. The decisions as to the personnel reshuffling were made between September 1 and 5; see Activity Report, Army Personnel Office, pp. 233 ff.

61. Rundstedt had been born on December 12, 1875, and was now sixty-eight years old.

62. For an evaluation of Rundstedt, see: Günther Blumentritt, *Von Rundstedt: The Soldier and the Man*, London, 1952; Andreas Hillgruber, "Generalfeldmarschall Gerd von Rundstedt," in: Hillgruber, "Grossmachtpolitik" [Big-Power Politics], pp. 316–332; Ose, "Entscheidung," pp. 37–40.

63. Activity Report, Army Personnel Office, entry for August 26, 1944, p. 227.

64. Schramm, "Ardennenoffensive," MS-A-862, p. 119.

65. Blumentritt remained at his post until September 9.

66. Schramm, "Ardennenoffensive," MS-A-862, p. 122.

67. The decisive factor in this, however, was that Speidel was implicated

in connection with the events of July 20, 1944; Activity Report, Army Personnel Office, entry for August 25, 1944, p. 226.

68. In the capacity of Chief of Staff, Ninth Army, between January 1942 and March 1943.

69. The three generals were in Rastenburg between August 31 and September 3.

70. Zimmermann, "OB West," MS-T-121, B VI, p. 2007 f, and Westphal in: Greiffenberg, "Ardennes-Questionnaire," MS-P-31i, Appendix 3, p. 1.

71. Westphal in: Greiffenberg, "Ardennes-Questionnaire," MS-P-32i, Appendix 3, p. 3.

72. Ibid.

73. See Adolf Hitler, Wehrmacht High Command/Wehrmacht Operations Staff/Operations Section, No. 773189/44, dated September 3, 1944, quoted in: OB West, Operations Section, No. 795/44, RH 19 IV/55, p. 63 f.

74. Ibid., emphasis in the original.

75. Ibid., emphasis in the original.

76. Ibid.

77. Ibid., emphasis in the original.

78. Ibid., emphasis in the original.

79. Panzer-Lehr Division, 11th Panzer Division, 21st Panzer Division, 3rd Panzer Grenadier Division, 15th Panzer Grenadier Division, 17th SS Panzer Grenadier Division, and the 106th, 107th, 108th, 111th, 112th, and 113th Panzer Brigades.

80. See, also: "Tätigkeitsbericht Heerespersonalamt" [Activity Report, Army Personnel Office], pp. 233 ff.

81. Alman, "Eichenlaub" [Oak Leaves], p. 116 f.

82. The fact that Dietrich was simply in over his head became clear, especially during the last several days; see also, Personal letter from General of Panzer Troops Walter Krüger to Dietrich, dated September 10, 1944, War Diary, LVIII Panzer Corps, Appendices, RH 24-58/11, p. 214 f.

83. 7th Panzer Division, Grossdeutschland Panzer Grenadier Division.

84. Schramm, "Ardennenoffensive," MS-A-862, p. 128.

85. 1st, 2nd, 9th, 12th SS Panzer Divisions, 2nd, 9th, 21st, 116th Panzer Divisions, Panzer-Lehr Division, and 3rd and 15th Panzer Grenadier Divisions; cf., OB West, Operations Section, No. 7588/44, dated September 2, 1944, RH 19 IV/55, p. 31.

86. See Krebs, Headquarters, Army Group B, Operations Section, No. 6973/44, dated September 5, 1944, RH 19 IX/5, p. 497.

87. General Patton had described the 2nd Panzer Division—which von Lüttwitz had commanded earlier—as the best German Panzer division in the west. See also Cole, *The Lorraine Campaign*, p. 49.

88. That may also have been a reason for informing the commanding generals in the west rather late about the Ardennes plan.

89. See Blaskowitz, Headquarters, Army Task Group G, Operations Section, No. 2418/44, dated September 3, 1944, RH 19 XII/8, p. 48.

90. Telephone conversation between Jodl and Model, dated September 2, 1944, 1330 hours, RH 19 IX/89, p. 24 f.

91. See Model, Headquarters, Army Group B, Operations Section, No. 6912/44, dated September 3, 1944, RH 19 IX/5, p. 477.

92. Telephone conversation between Krebs and Guderian, dated September 4, 1944, 1855 hours, RH 19 IX/89, p. 56 f.

93. Colonel General Heinz Guderian, "Ost und Westfront" [Eastern and Western Front], MS-T-42, p. 35 f.

94. Although on September 6 he agreed with Jodl that a large-scale offensive in the west could be considered only as of November 1 (cf., Warlimont, "Hauptquartier," p. 506 f.), he was nevertheless determined to exploit any earlier developing—presumed—opportunity.

95. Warlimont, "Hauptquartier," p. 506.

96. Schramm, "Ardennenoffensive," MS-A-862, p. 22.

97. "Because of the breakthrough of enemy tank units in the direction toward Antwerp, holding the fortresses of Boulogne and Dunkirk, the Calais defense perimeter, the Island of Walcheren . . . , the bridgehead around Antwerp and the Albert Canal position . . . all are of decisive significance in terms of future combat operations"; "Führer Order," Wehrmacht High Command, Wehrmacht Operations Staff, No. 773222/44, dated September 4, 1944, quoted in: OB West, Operations Section, No. 794/44, RH 19 IV/55, p. 135 f.

98. "Führer Order," Wehrmacht High Command/Wehrmacht Operations Staff/Operations Section (Army), No. 0010887/44, dated September 6, 1944, quoted from: OB West, Operations Section, No. 7739/44, ibid., p. 209.

99. Telephone conversation between Major Friedel (Wehrmacht High Command) and von Tempelhoff, dated September 5, 1944, 1030 hours, "Führer again clearly expressed formation of main effort on southern wing of First Army," RH 19 IX/89, p. 65 f.

100. Apart from the 719th Infantry Division that also had elements of the 347th Infantry Division under its command.

101. Wehrmacht High Command/Wehrmacht Operations Staff, No. 773222/44, dated September 4, 1944, quoted in: OB West, Operations Section, No. 794/44, RH 19 IV/55, p. 135 f.

102. Telephone conversation between Krebs and Blumentritt, dated September 5, 1944, 1115 hours, RH 19 IX/89, p. 66 f.

103. Telephone conversation between Warlimont and Krebs, dated September 5, 1944, 1230 hours, RH 19 IX/89, pp. 67 ff.

104. See Rundstedt, "Der Oberbefehlshaber West" [The Supreme Commander West], September 5, 1944, 1930 hours, RH IV/55, p. 144.

105. By comparison, it is interesting to note the sober wording of the letter in which Rundstedt informed Himmler about the change of command: "As of this day, I have again assumed command as OB West on orders from the führer. Close cooperation will and must now lead to the goal." See Rundstedt, September 5, 1944, 1945 hours, RH 19 IV/55, p. 146.

106. War Diary, OB West, dated September 5, 1944, 1800 hours, RH 19 IV/46, p. 27.

107. Zimmermann, "OB West," MS-T-121, B VI, p. 2010.

108. This does not include the units still holding the fortresses; "Combat Strength of Troops in the West as of September 6," War Diary, Wehrmacht High Command, IV/2, p. 377.

109. September 7, 1944, Situation Estimate, see Rundstedt, OB West, Operations Section, No. 805/44, RH 19 IV/55, pp. 218 ff.

110. Ibid.

111. Pogue, *The Supreme Command*, p. 248.

112. Ibid.

113. This number includes the losses of the Operation DRAGOON forces, cf., Pogue, *The Supreme Command*, p. 248, footnote 10, and Wilt, *French Riviera Campaign of August 1944*, p. 160.

114. Losses of the Field Army between June 1, 1944, and January 10, 1945, "The Army Doctor in the Army High Command," General Staff of the Army/Deputy Chief of Staff for Supplies, File No. 1335 c/d, quoted in: Jung, "Ardennenoffensive," Appendix 5.

115. Brest: 37,000; Channel Islands: 31,000; St. Nazaire: 28,000; Lorient: 27,000; La Rochelle: 11,000; Le Havre, Calais, and Dunkirk each: 10,000; Boulogne: 9,900; Gironde fortresses: 9,000; Cape Gris Nez: 1,600 (see also: Ellis, *Victory in the West*, II, p. 66; War Diary, Wehrmacht High Command, IV/2, p. 376; Reports on strengths and supplies in the fortresses to Wehrmacht High Command/Wehrmacht Operations Staff, RW 4/Vol. 632, pp. 67 ff and 81). In addition to the 185,000 men, there were another about 30,000 who had been earmarked for the Scheldt River fortresses at IJmuiden and Hoek van Holland. See also: Reports . . . to Wehrmacht High Command/Wehrmacht Operations Staff, RW 4/Vol. 632, p. 70; Ellis, "Victory," II, pp. 104 and 1195; Montgomery, *From Normandy to the Baltic*, p. 233. At that point in time, the defense of Cherbourg, St. Malo, Marseille, and Toulon had already cost the Germans around 64,000 men.

116. SHAEF G-2 Situation Estimate for the week of September 3–9, 1944, cf., Pogue, *The Supreme Command*, p. 283.

117. Ibid.

118. Reports on developments in public opinion formation, dated August 17, 1944, "Meldungen aus dem Reich" [Reports from the Reich], 17, pp. 6705 ff.

119. See J. Goebbels and M. Borman, "Order for the Implementation of Total War Effort," dated August 16, 1944; "Strength Report," Higher SS and Police Leader West, IfZ [Contemporary History Institute], MA 434.

120. For the basis of calculation, see Keitel, Chief, Wehrmacht High Command, Id, No. 7/44, dated November 11, 1944, Military replacements from "total war effort during the months of August to October," RW 4/Vol. 865, pp. 100 ff. Accordingly, 342,000 men were made available to the Replacement Army in August and September as a result of the "Goebbels Drive." To

this, one must add 108,000 soldiers, who were yielded by the Luftwaffe and navy, plus 79,000 "planned draftees" of the birth-year classes of 1926/1927.

121. The "standard yardstick" was considered to be around ninety thousand men per month. The level of the rate in August 1944 was also attained in September. Cf.: Wehrmacht High Command, Strength/Losses of the Wehrmacht, RW 4/Vol. 481, p. 22.

122. See Keitel, The Chief, Wehrmacht High Command, Id, No. 7/44, dated November 11, 1944, RW 4/Vol. 865, p. 100.

123. Manstein, "Verlorene Siege" [Lost Victories], p. 309.

124. In other words, in disciplinary court-martial terms and in terms of training; "Tätigkeitsbericht Heerespersonalamt" [Army Office Activity Report], dated September 14, 1944, p. 256.

125. "Address by Reichsführer-SS at the Conference of Gauleiters in Posen on August 3, 1944, in: "Ursachen und Folgen" [Causes and Consequences], 21, pp. 490–512, specifically, p. 510.

126. Jung, "Ardennenoffensive," p. 296.

127. Department P 7, Army Personnel Office, cf., "Tätigkeitsbericht HPA" [Army Personnel Office Activity Report], dated September 1, 1944, p. 233 f and dated October 8, 1944, p. 280.

128. Of course, their mobility was restricted, and there were almost no supply trains; cf., Tessin, "Verbände," 1, p. 88.

129. The strength of these newly organized formations varied: The 105th–108th Panzer Brigades had one Panzer battalion each, plus one Panzer Grenadier battalion with five companies; 111th and 112th Panzer Brigades had one Panzer battalion each, plus one Panzer Grenadier regiment with six companies. 113th Panzer Brigade, in addition to the Panzer battalion, had one Panzer Grenadier regiment with eight companies (cf., Tessin, "Verbände," 1, p. 166 f). The number of Panzers fluctuated between forty-seven and ninety per brigade. 105th–108th Panzer brigades had eleven P IV and thirty-six P V (Panther) fighting vehicles; 111th–113th Panzer brigades had forty-five P IV and P V each; General Inspekteur der Panzertruppen [Inspector-General of Panzer Forces], No. 2920/44, dated September 13, 1944, RH 10/90, p. 78.

130. Belonging to 29th–32nd waves (cf., Tessin, "Verbände," 1, pp. 88 ff, and Mueller-Hillebrand, "Heer" [Army], III, pp. 235 ff). Orders were issued to organize another six divisions of the 32nd wave as of the middle of September. The following comparison may indicate the enormous scope of the organization of new formations that was ordered in the summer of 1944: Between September 1943 and May 1944, "only" 37 army divisions were organized.

131. Guderian, "Erinnerungen" [Memoirs], p. 327.

132. The 1406th–1409th Fortress Infantry Battalions and the 26th–30th Fortress Machine Gun Battalions (OB West, Operations Section, No. 7227/44, dated August 23, 1944, RH 19 IV/54, p. 87). In addition to the total of thirty-three fortress infantry battalions organized as of the beginning of

August, there were 120 fortress machine gun battalions, forty-one fortress artillery battalions, as well as forty Luftwaffe fortress battalions (Author's calculation based on Tessin, "Verbände," pp. 1 ff).

133. See Adolf Hitler, Directive for Further Combat Operations, OB West, dated September 3, 1944, quoted in: OB West, Operations Section, No. 795/44, RH 19 IV/55, p. 63 f, and OB West, Operations Section, No. 766/44, dated August 27, 1944, RH 19 IV/54, p. 223 f.

10. From the Climax of the Crisis to the First Indications of a Stabilization of the Western Front

1. Daily Report for September 4, 1944, OB West, Operations Section, No. 7675/44, RH 19 IV/55, pp. 106 ff.

2. Zimmermann, "OB West," MS-T-121, B VI, p. 1993 f.

3. Ibid.

4. Wilmot, *Struggle for Europe*, p. 516.

5. Montgomery, *Normandy to the Baltic*, pp. 191 ff.

6. Wilmot, *Struggle for Europe*, p. 517.

7. Blumenson, *Breakout and Pursuit*, pp. 692 ff.

8. Ibid.

9. Telephone conversation between Krebs and Wühlisch, dated September 5, 1944, 1000 hours, RH 19 IX/89, p. 64.

10. Including remnants of the 84th, 85th, and 89th Infantry Divisions; War Diary, Army Group B, dated September 9, 1944, ibid., p. 142.

11. Telephone conversation between Gersdorff and Krebs, dated September 5, 1944, 1245 hours, RH IX/89, p. 69 f.

12. See Krebs, Headquarters, Army Group B, Operations Section, No. 7006/44, dated September 5, 1944, RH 19 IX/5, p. 507 f.

13. See also Daily Report for September 7, 1944, OB West, Operations Section, No. 7792/44, RH 19 IV/55, pp. 232 ff.

14. Ibid., and Status of Rail Movements, dated September 8, 1944, OB West, Operations Section, No. 7813/44, ibid., p. 260.

15. Author's estimate.

16. The Hermann Göring Replacement Regiment, 6th Parachute Regiment, five additional parachute regiments that were then combined in the Erdmann Parachute Division (later redesignated the 7th Parachute Division); cf., Tessin, "Verbände," 14, p. 69.

17. War Diary, Army Group B, dated September 6, 1944, RH 19 IX/89, p. 83 f.

18. Admiral, Netherlands, G.25312 F III for the period of September 3–21, 1944, RM/131, pp. 492 ff.

19. Of the thirty attacking tanks, eight were knocked out, as against six German losses; War Diary, Army Group B, dated September 7, 1944, RH 19 IX/89, p. 111.

20. Montgomery, *Normandy to the Baltic*, pp. 191 ff.

21. War Diary, Army Group B, dated September 8, 1944, RH 19 IX/89, pp. 120 ff.

22. Telephone conversation between Krebs and Operations Officer, Headquarters, First Parachute Army, dated September 7, 1944, 1905 hours, RH 19 IX/89, p. 108.

23. Wilmot, *The Struggle for Europe*, p. 517.

24. Montgomery, *Normandy to the Baltic*, p. 192.

25. In the meantime, the British 50th Infantry Division had formed a bridgehead at Geel.

26. Telephone conversation between Operations Officer, Headquarters, First Parachute Army, and Operations Officer, Army Group B, dated September 8, 1944, 1540 hours, RH 19 IX/89, p. 120.

27. Lieutenant General Wolfgang Erdmann, chief of staff, First Parachute Army, led this quickly organized division.

28. Noon Report, Army Group B, dated September 10, 1944, RH 19 IV/46, p. 57 f.

29. Telephone conversation between Student and Krebs, dated September 10, 1944, 1135 hours, RH 19 IX/89, p. 147.

30. Ibid.

31. Telephone conversation between Student and Tempelhoff, dated September 10, 1944, 2030 hours, ibid., p. 150 f.

32. Telephone conversation between Krebs and Operations Officer, Headquarters, First Parachute Army, dated September 11, 1944, 0015 hours, ibid., p. 157.

33. War Diary, Army Group B, dated September 11, 1944, RH 19 IV/46, p. 61.

34. Daily Report for September 10, 1944, OB West, Operations Section, No. 7916/44, RH 19 IV/55, pp. 322 ff.

35. War Diary, Army Group B, dated September 12, 1944, RH 19 IX/89, p. 175.

36. Montgomery, *Normandy to the Baltic*, pp. 191 ff.

37. Zangen, "15. Armee," MS-B-249, p. 25 f.

38. Ibid.

39. Telephone conversation between Warlimont and Krebs, dated September 5, 1944, 1230 hours, RH 19 IX/89, p. 67 f.

40. Report, Operations Officer, Headquarters, Fifteenth Army, dated September 5, 1944, 1650 hours, ibid., p. 71 f, and Zangen, "15. Armee," MS-B-249, p. 26 f.

41. In addition, there was the 5th Security Regiment that was transferred to Boulogne; cf., ibid.

42. Model's order, dated September 5, 1944, Headquarters, Army Group B, Operations Section, No. 6975/44, RH 19 IX/89, p. 80.

43. Telephone conversation between Warlimont and Krebs, dated September 5, 1944, 1230 hours, ibid., p. 67 f.

44. Telephone conversation between Krebs and Warlimont, dated September 5, 1944, 1840 hours, ibid., p. 74 f.

45. Telephone conversation between Krebs and Wühlisch, dated September 6, 1944, 2140 hours, ibid., p. 92 f.

46. Ibid.

47. After-action report, LXXXIX Army Corps, entry for September 7, 1944, 0630 hours, RH 24-89/10, p. 6/2.

48. Zangen, "15. Armee," MS-B-249, p. 35 f.

49. On September 9, Lieutenant General Has-Kurt Höcker (Luftwaffe 17th Field Division) was ordered to direct the crossing operations at Terneuzen; Schwalbe continued to supervise at Breskens.

50. Telephone conversation between Wühlisch and Krebs, dated September 8, 1944, 1755 hours, RH 19 IX/89, p. 121.

51. September 6, 1944, Intelligence Section Evening Report, Army Group, Intelligence Section, No. 3492/44, RH 19 IX/26, Part 2, p. 211.

52. The ports of Ostende and Blankenberghe were destroyed and were evacuated by the German troops; see War Diary, OB West, September 7, 1944, RH 19 IV/46, p. 39.

53. Noon Report, dated September 9, 1944, OB West, Operations Section, No. 7834/44, RH 19 IV/55, p. 278.

54. According to Hitler's order, dated September 8, Walcheren and the bridgehead around Breskens, the subsequent so-called fortresses "Scheldt-North" and "Scheldt-South," were to be defended by one division each (cf., see Krebs, Headquarters, Army Group B, Operations Section, No. 7100/44, dated September 8, 1944, RH 19 IX/5, p. 575). The 70th Infantry Division was to hold Walcheren, while the 64th Infantry Division was to hold Breskens (see telephone conversation between Model and Zangen, dated September 8, 1944, 2235 hours, RH 19 IX/89, p. 125 f).

55. War Diary, OB West, dated September 9, 1944, RH 19 IV/46, p. 51.

56. Ellis, *Victory in the West*, II, p. 14 f.

57. Ibid., and Montgomery, *Normandy to the Baltic*, p. 188.

58. Telephone conversation between Wühlisch and Tempelhoff, dated September 9, 1944, 1425 hours, RH 19 IX/89, p. 134.

59. Daily Report for September 9, 1944, OB West, Operations Section, No. 7850/44, RH 19 IV/55, pp. 288 ff.

60. Zangen, "15. Armee," MS-B-249, p. 36 f.

61. Daily Report for September 10, 1944, OB West, Operations Section, No. 7916/44, RH 19 IV/55, pp. 322 ff.

62. Daily Report for September 11, 1944, OB West, Operations Section, No. 7960/44, RH 19 IV/56, pp. 27 ff.

63. Ellis, *Victory in the West*, II, p. 14.

64. After the war, Wildermuth became Federal Minister of Housing Construction (1949 to 1952).

65. Montgomery, *Normandy to the Baltic*, p. 196.

66. Le Havre was used for major supply shipments only starting on October 9, 1944; cf., Ellis, *Victory in the West*, II, p. 15.

67. Telephone conversation between Hofmann and Krebs, dated September 12, 1944, 0915 hours, RH 19 IX/89, p. 176.

68. Ibid.

69. MacDonald, *The Siegfried Line Campaign,* p. 20.

70. Telephone conversation between Gersdorff and Krebs, dated September 5, 1944, 2245 hours, RH 19 IX/89, p. 78.

71. Brandenberger, "7. Armee," MS-B-730, p. 68 f.

72. In addition to the 347th, this included the 49th, 89th, 275th, and 353rd Infantry Divisions. The 352nd Infantry Division had also been employed in the Seventh Army sector for a short time; but it was transferred back to the Reich on September 7 for refitting; see War Diary, Army Group B, dated September 7, 1944, RH 19 IX/89, p. 111.

73. War Diary, Army Group B, dated September 5, 1944, RH 19 IX/89, p. 69 f.

74. Brandenberger, "7. Armee," MS-B-730, p. 70.

75. War Diary, OB West, dated September 6, 1944, RH 19 IV/46, p. 29.

76. Intelligence Section, Evening Report, dated September 6, 1944, Army Group B, Intelligence Section, No. 3492/44, RH 19 IX/26, Part 2, p. 211.

77. Brandenberger, "7. Armee," MS-B-730, p. 39.

78. Evening Report, Army Group B, dated September 6, 1944, RH 19 IV/46, p. 31.

79. See Blumentritt, OB West, Operations Section, No. 7720/44, dated September 6, 1944, 2045 hours, RH 19 IV/55, p. 176.

80. Cf., ibid., and Buechs, "Westwall," MS-ETHINT 37, p. 2; Jodl, "German Defenses," MS-ETHINT 52, p. 3.

81. The U.S. XIX Corps, in the meantime, closed up to the Albert Canal; cf., Blumenson, *Breakout and Pursuit,* pp. 692 ff.

82. See Rundstedt, OB West, Operations Section, No. 805/44, dated September 7, 1944, RH 19 IV/55, pp. 218 ff.

83. Ibid.

84. Of course, the so-called "fortress units" were sent west earlier than planned originally (see below); telephone conversation between Zimmermann and Tempelhoff, dated September 8, 1944, 1300 hours, RH 19 IX/89, p. 119.

85. See Adolf Hitler, Wehrmacht High Command/Wehrmacht Operations Staff/Deputy Chief of Staff for Supply, No. 0010783/44, dated September 7, 1944, quoted in: OB West, Operations Section, No. 7769/44, RH 19 IV/55, p. 231.

86. Telephone conversation between Model and Speer, dated September 9, 1944, 0125 hours, RH 19 IX/89, p. 131.

87. Daily Report for September 7, 1944, OB West, Operations Section, No. 7792/44, RH 19 IV/55, pp. 232 ff.

88. Schwerin, "116. Pz. Div.," MS-ETHINT 18, pp. 27 ff.

89. Telephone conversation between Gersdorff and Tempelhoff, dated September 6, 1944, 1410 hours, RH 19 IX/89, p. 89.

90. War Diary, Army Group B, dated September 8, 1944, RH 19 IX/89, pp. 115 ff.

91. See Rundstedt, OB West, Operations Section, No. 8088/44, dated September 8, 1944, 1600 hours, RH 19 IV/55, p. 250 f.

92. Telephone conversation between Zimmermann and Tempelhoff, dated September 8, 1944, 1300 hours, RH 19 IX/89, p. 119.

93. Ibid.

94. See Rundstedt, OB West, Operations Section, No. 7803/44, dated September 8, 1944, RH 19 IV/55, p. 253.

95. Brandenberger, "7, Armee," MS-B-730, p. 49 f.

96. See also Daily Report for September 9, 1944, OB West, Operations Section, No. 7850/44, RH 19 IV/55, pp. 288 ff.

97. Blumenson, *Breakout and Pursuit*, p. 693.

98. War Diary, LXXX Army Corps, dated September 10, 1944, RH 24-80/68, p. 48.

99. Ibid., pp. 54 ff.

100. On September 6 he had relieved Freiherr von Lüttwitz, who took command of the XLVII Panzer Corps.

101. Brandenberger, "7. Armee," MS-B-730, p. 52.

102. MacDonald, *The Siegfried Line Campaign*, p. 3.

103. War Diary, LXXX Army Corps, dated September 10, 1944, RH 24-80/68, p. 46.

104. Ibid., dated September 10, 1944, p. 47.

105. War Diary, LXXXI Army Corps, dated September 8, 1944, RH 24-81/97, p. 185/1.

106. Or his deputy, Schlessmann.

107. War Diary, Army Group B, dated September 9, 1944, RH 19 IX/89, p. 134.

108. Ibid.

109. Ibid.

110. Telephone conversation between Krebs and Gersdorff, dated September 8, 1944, 1800 hours, ibid., p. 121.

111. Brandenberger, "7. Armee," MS-B-730, p. 64.

112. Ibid., p. 59.

113. The LXXXI Army Corps with: 275th and 49th Infantry Divisions, 116th Panzer Division, Battle Group Müller (9th Panzer Division).

114. The LXXIV Army Corps with: 347th and 89th Infantry Divisions.

115. The I SS Panzer Corps with: 2nd SS and 2nd Panzer Divisions.

116. War Diary, Army Group B, dated September 11, 1944, RH 19 IX/89, pp. 165–171.

117. Daily Report for September 10, 1944, OB West, Operations Section, No. 7916/44, RH 19/55, pp. 322 ff.

118. See Adolf Hitler, Wehrmacht High Command/Wehrmacht Operations Staff, No. 773296, quoted in OB West, Operations Section, No. 7817/44, dated September 10, 1944, RH 19 IV/55, p. 301 f. The command takeover occurred at 0000 on September 11.

119. War Diary, Army Group B, dated September 10, 1944, RH 19 IV/46, p. 57.

120. Cf., chapter 8, section 3 (d).

121. See Rundstedt, OB West, Operations Section, No. 7842/44, dated September 10, 1944. As for the shortcomings in the fortifications, see: Westphal, OB West, Operations Section, No. 7843/44, dated September 10, 1944, RH 19 IV/55, pp. 307 and 308 f.

122. See Stöhr, 4th Directive of the Reich Defense Commissar for Position Construction in Gau [provincial party district] Westmark, Saarbrücken, November 11, 1944, quoted in: Contemporary History Institute, MA-137/1, p. 0157245 f.

123. See Stöhr, 6th Directive (see above), Saarbrücken, September 13, 1944, quoted from: Contemporary History Institute, MA-137/1, p. 0157242 f.

124. The divisions headquarters had supplied about thirty-seven hundred men, organized in three regional defense unit training battalions, War Diary, LXXXI Army Corps, RH 24-81/97, pp. 185/1 ff, Tessin, "Verbände," 10, p. 101 f.

125. A total of eighty-four hundred men, reinforced by five thousand stragglers in the Aachen area. Brandenberger, "7. Armee," MS-B-730, pp. 50 ff; Tessin, "Verbände," 11, p. 75 f.

126. The first-named divisions were under Defense District VI; the 172nd Division belonged to Defense District XII. Stationed behind the sector of Second Army (I SS Panzer Corps) were two regiments of that division with a strength of about three thousand men. The 3rd Regiment (Lott) was behind the LXXX Army Corps. Tessin, "Verbände," 8, p. 173 f, and War Diary, LXXX Army Corps, September 10, 1944, RH 24-80/68, p. 46 f.

127. Notes on the trip of Supreme Commander, Army Group B, September 11, 1944, RH 19 IX/5, p. 611 f.

128. See Model, Headquarters, Army Group B, Operations Section, No. 7277/44, dated September 11, 1944, 2215 hours, ibid., p. 613.

129. Zimmermann, "OB West," MS-T-121, B VI, p. 2062 f.

130. Telephone conversation between Krebs and Westphal, dated September 12, 1944, 1110 hours, RH 19 IX/89, p. 177 f.

131. This decision was made on September 11, 1944, cf., MacDonald, *The Siegfried Line Campaign*, p. 37 f.

132. Blumenson, *Breakout and Pursuit*, p. 701.

133. G-2 Estimate, U.S. V Corps, dated September 10, 1944, and G-2 Report No. 97 of U.S. VII Corps, according to: MacDonald, *The Siegfried Line Campaign*, p. 38.

134. Ibid., p. 37.

135. The title of the book by Dwight D. Eisenhower.

136. Cole, *The Lorraine Campaign*, p. 213.

137. OB West, Operations Section, No. 7992/44, dated September 12, 1944, RH 19 IV/56, p. 48 f.

138. Cole, *The Lorraine Campaign*, p. 124.

139. Knobelsdorff, "1. Armee," MS-B-222, p. 14.

140. Cole, *The Lorraine Campaign*, p. 197.

141. The 559th Grenadier Division, 462nd Division, 17th SS Panzer Grenadier Division, 3rd Panzer Grenadier Division, and 553rd Grenadier Division. The 15th Panzer Grenadier Division had already been gradually taken out of the front line for the planned offensive. The elements of the 19th Grenadier Division and of the 106th Panzer Brigade, likewise briefly employed in the area to the west of Thionville, were pushed to the northeast as a result of Patton's offensive.

142. War Diary, LXXX Army Corps, dated September 10, 1944, RH 24-80/68, pp. 54 ff.

143. Calculated according to: War Diary, LXXX Army Corps, dated September 10, 1944, ibid., pp. 54 ff, and Ritgen, "Panzer-Lehr Division," p. 196.

144. The "formations" of the LXXX Army Corps, the battle groups of the Panzer-Lehr Division and of the 5th Parachute Division, were received here by one regiment of the 172nd Replacement Army Division with four artillery batteries and were somehow beefed up with "straggler units"; see War Diary, LXXX Army Corps, dated September 10/11, 1944, RH 24-80/68, pp. 47 ff. The almost completely smashed 48th Infantry Division was placed under the LXXXII Army Corps on September 11 and was "refitted" behind the Mosel River. In addition to the 48th Infantry Division, this sector between Trier and Sierck, at that time, contained the 19th and 36th Grenadier Divisions, plus the 106th Panzer Brigade; see ibid., and Caspar, "48. Inf. Div.," MS-P-166, p. 17.

145. See Krebs, Headquarters, Army Group B, Operations Section, No. 6980, dated September 5, 1944, RH 19 IX/5, p. 496.

146. Cole, *The Lorraine Campaign*, p. 158 f.

147. Intelligence Section Evening Report, dated September 7, 1944, Army Group B, Intelligence Section, No. 3499/44, RH 19 IX/26, Part 2, p. 201 f.

148. Cf., Cole, *The Lorraine Campaign*, p. 159, and Daily Report for September 8, 1944, OB West, Operations Section, No. 7827/44, RH 19 IV/55, pp. 256 ff. The 106th Panzer Brigade lost more than twenty Panzers. On September 9, it only had nine operational fighting vehicles; fifteen were being repaired; see Daily Report for September 9, 1944, OB West, Operations Section, No. 7850/44, RH 19 IV/55, pp. 288 ff, and RH 19 XII/8, p. 224, dated September 14, 1944. The U.S. 7th Armored Division must also have suffered considerable losses: According to certainly exaggerated German accounts, the 106th Panzer Brigade, between September 6 and 11 alone, wiped out 110 tanks and thirty-three scout cars; see Intelligence Section Daily Report for September 12, 1944, OB West, Intelligence Section, No. 6211/44, RH 19 IV/137, p. 102 f.

149. Telephone conversation between Krebs and Zimmermann, dated September 7, 1944, 1350 hours, RH 19 IX/89, p. 104.

150. War Diary, Army Group B, dated September 7, 1944, 2345 hours, ibid., p. 109 f.

151. Cole, *The Lorraine Campaign*, p. 158.

152. Ibid., p. 157.

153. Krause, "Metz," MS-B-042, p. 10 f.

154. The training course students of the VI Officer Candidate School had been promoted to the rank of second lieutenant several days before. They were employed as officer companies in the front line; Activity Report, Army Personnel Office, dated September 9 and 18, 1944, pp. 246 and 260.

155. According to "Tätigkeitsbericht Heerespersonalamt," dated September 9, 1944, p. 246.

156. The XIII SS Army Corps took over the Thionville–Arry sur Moselle sector (south of Metz). The LXXXII Army Corps was employed in the sector of the front line adjoining to the north; cf., Daily Report for September 8, 1944, OB West, Operations Section, No. 7827/44, RH 19 IV/55, pp. 256 ff.

157. Ibid.

158. Cole, *The Lorraine Campaign*, p. 142.

159. Ibid., pp. 145 f and 154.

160. Daily Report for September 6, 1944, OB West, Operations Section, No. 7756/44, RH 19 IV/55, pp. 178 ff, as well as Cole, *The Lorraine Campaign*, p. 65, and Spiwoks, "XIII. SS-AK," p. 51 f.

161. Cole, *The Lorraine Campaign*, p. 69 f.

162. "Tätigkeitsbericht Heerespersonalamt," dated September 5, 1944, p. 242.

163. See Westphal, OB West, Operations Section, No. 7296/44, dated September 10, 1944, RH 19 IV/55, p. 331.

164. RW 4/Vol. 34, p. 59 f, and Warlimont, "Kommentare," MS-P-215, IV, Part 2, p. 348 f.

165. Major General Feyerabend was replaced by Colonel Willi Mantey.

166. Zimmermann, "OB West," MS-T-121, B VI, p. 2043.

167. Cole, *The Lorraine Campaign*, p. 156 f.

168. Ibid., p. 145.

169. OB West, Operations Section, No. 7917/44, dated September 11, 1944, RH 19 IV/56, pp. 6 ff.

170. Noon Report, dated September 11, 1944, OB West, Operations Section, No. 7931/44, ibid., pp. 17 ff.

171. Daily Report for September 11, 1944, OB West, Operations Section, No. 7940/44, ibid., pp. 27 ff.

172. Ibid., and Cole, *The Lorraine Campaign*, pp. 75 and 89.

173. Cole, *The Lorraine Campaign*, p. 142, and Spiwoks, "XIII. SS-AK," Report, 3rd Panzer Grenadier Division, p. 54.

174. Daily Report for September 13, 1944, OB West, Operations Section, No. 8081/44, RH 19 IV/56, pp. 91 ff.

175. Daily Report for September 12, 1944, OB West, Operations Section, No. 8035/44, ibid., pp. 67 ff.

176. Daily Report for September 13, 1944, OB West, Operations Section, No. 8081/44, ibid., pp. 91 ff.

177. See Rundstedt, OB West, Operations Section, No. 821/44, dated September 13, 1944, ibid. p. 81 f.

178. Intelligence Section Activity Report for the period of September 1–September 30, 1944, Headquarters, Army Group G [*sic*], Intelligence Section, No. 636/44, p. 2, RH 19 XII/31.

179. Cole, *The Lorraine Campaign*, p. 213.

11. The Situation Estimate Prepared by the Operations Staffs and the Failure of the Concept of a German "Counteroffensive from the Move"

1. "The hostile occupation . . . at the mouth of the Scheldt . . . will vitally influence the full development of our strategy . . . ," *Eisenhower Papers,* IV, pp. 2124 ff.

2. Pogue, "Supreme Command," p. 256.

3. Later on, the British 52nd Division (Airportable) was to be flown in.

4. MacDonald, *The Siegfried Line Campaign*, pp. 119 ff.

5. Of course, this fact, in contrast to what Wilmot assumes (*Struggle for Europe*, p. 519), probably did not play any *decisive* role. Eisenhower wrote to the Commanding General of the British Antiaircraft Command, General Sir Frederick Pile, on September 14, that he hoped soon to seize the area from which this "latest example of Hun terrorism" would be launched "sporadically." *Eisenhower Papers*, IV, p. 2142 f.

6. Eisenhower's letter to Marshall, dated September 14, 1944, ibid., pp. 2143 ff.

7. Cole, *The Lorraine Campaign*, p. 212 f.

8. On September 12, 1944 (D+97), the Allies had already reached a line that, according to the "Post-OVERLORD" plan, was to have been reached only in May 1945 (D+330); cf., Pogue, *The Supreme Command*, p. 257.

9. Ruppenthal, "Logistics and the Broad-Front Strategy (1944)," in *Command Decisions*, p. 327.

10. Ibid., p. 321.

11. Montgomery's letter to Eisenhower, dated September 11, 1944, Ellis, *Victory in the West*, II, p. 22.

12. Quoted, ibid., p. 23 f.

13. The following, unless otherwise noted, is also taken from Eisenhower's Directive FWD 14764, dated September 13, 1944, *Eisenhower Papers*, IV, pp. 2136 ff.

14. This supports a letter written by Montgomery to the Commanding General of the Canadian First Army, Lieutenant General Crerar, dated September 13, 1944. Accordingly, Crerar was to attack Boulogne, Dunkirk, and Calais and clear the enemy out of the Scheldt River mouth. The latter operation, according to Montgomery, is "probably the most important." Nevertheless, the ports were to be attacked "simultaneously." Cited from Moulton, "Antwerp," p. 67.

15. In the author's view, this was a rigid doctrine rather than a strategy at that point in time (September 13, 1944).

16. Ellis, *Victory in the West*, II, p. 352.

17. Eisenhower's memorandum for Chief of Staff, SHAEF, Lieutenant General Walter Bedell Smith, dated June 23, 1944, *Eisenhower Papers*, III, p. 1946 f.

18. Eisenhower's directive, dated September 13, 1944, ibid., IV, pp. 2136 ff.

19. Ellis, *Victory in the West*, II, p. 71.

20. MacDonald, *The Siegfried Line Campaign*, p. 121.

21. Eisenhower's letter to Marshall, dated September 14, 1944, *Eisenhower Papers*, IV, pp. 2143 ff.

22. Ibid., p. 2117.

23. Caspar, "Kriegslage" [Wartime Situation], p. 178.

24. Matloff, *Strategic Planning for Coalition Warfare 1943–1944*, pp. 508 ff.

25. This plan, among other things, called for Germany's extensive deindustrialization; the country was to be turned into an agrarian state. Shortly before Roosevelt put his initials under this plan, he left the British the more industrially oriented northwestern zone; Matloff, *Strategic Planning for Coalition Warfare 1943–1944*, p. 511, footnote 11.

26. Alfred Grosser, "Geschichte Deutschlands nach 1945" [History of Germany after 1945], Munich, 31975, p. 45 f.

27. For pertinent sources (regarding August 28 and September 18, 1944), see Steinert, "Hitlers Krieg" [Hitler's War], pp. 495 ff.

28. "Wöchentl. Tätigkeitsbericht der Propagandaämter vom 18.9.1944" [Weekly Activity Report of Propaganda Offices, dated September 18, 1944], ibid., p. 499 f.

29. Goebbels to Wilfred von Oven (his personal press aide), dated December 3, 1944, Oven, "Goebbels," p. 183 f.

30. Steinert, "Hitlers Krieg," p. 546.

31. Wilmot, "Kampf," p. 585.

32. Warlimont, "Hauptquartier," p. 506, and Schramm, "Ardennenoffensive," MS-A-862, p. 21 f.

33. War Diary, Wehrmacht High Command, IV/1, p. 367.

34. The fact that the offensive by the Fifth Panzer Army, which Hitler had ordered on September 3, temporarily moved out of his field of vision after the fall of Antwerp is also underscored by the fact that Headquarters, Fifth Panzer Army, at first was not ordered to the south but rather to Koblenz for refitting. See War Diary, Headquarters, Fifth Panzer Army, dated September 6, 1944, RH 21-5/52, p. 47; furthermore, Hitler allowed the First Army to conduct a local counterattack in the area southwest of Luxembourg with two formations originally earmarked for that offensive (106th Panzer Brigade, 15th Panzer Grenadier Division); see War Diary, Army Group B, dated September 5, 1944, RH 19 IX/89, p. 77.

35. Jodl, "Ardennenoffensive," MS-ETHINT 50, p. 5.

36. Schramm, "Ardennenoffensive," MS-A-862, p. 57.

37. War Diary, Army Task Group G, dated September 3, 1944, RH 19 XII/5, p. 193 f, and OB West, Operations Section, No. 810/44, dated September 11, 1944, RH 19 IV/56, p. 20 f.

38. See Keitel, Wehrmacht High Command/Wehrmacht Operations Staff/Operations Section, No. 773260, dated September 7, 1944, quoted in: OB West, Operations Section, No. 801/44, RH 19 IV/55, p. 207 f.

39. See Rundstedt, OB West, Operations Section, No. 7770/44, dated September 7, 1944, ibid., p. 211 f.

40. See Rundstedt, OB West, Operations Section, No. 805/44, dated September 7, 1944, RH 19 IV/55, pp. 218 ff.

41. See Rundstedt, OB West, Operations Section, No. 806/44, dated September 7, 1944, ibid., p. 225.

42. The 3rd and 15th Panzer Grenadier Divisions, 17th SS Panzer Grenadier Division, 11th and 21st Panzer Divisions, and the 106th, 107th, 108th, 111th, 112th, and 113th Panzer Brigades. See ibid. The Panzer-Lehr Division, which originally was also earmarked for this operation, was to be refitted first of all.

43. The 107th and 108th Panzer Brigades were to be moved up after September 15, 1944; see ibid.

44. See Rundstedt, OB West, Operations Section, No. 805/44, dated September 7, 1944, ibid., pp. 218 ff.

45. For comparison: According to Wehrmacht Operations Staff calculations as of the end of October 1944, the fuel requirement for the Ardennes Offensive was calculated at seventeen thousand cubic meters. It was believed that it would take four weeks to make that volume ready. Cf., War Diary, Wehrmacht High Command, IV/1, p. 434 f.

46. OB West, Operations Section, No. 7276/44, dated September 9, 1944, RH 19 IV/55, p. 298.

47. Ose, "Entscheidung," pp. 227 ff.

48. OB West, Operations Section, No. 813/44, dated September 10, 1944, RH 19 IV/55, p. 316 f.

49. See Jodl, Wehrmacht High Command/Wehrmacht Operations Staff, Operations Section, No. 773331 f, September 11, 1944, quoted in: OB West, Operations Section, No. 815/44, RH 19 IV/56, p. 22.

50. That was presumably Gauleiter Wagner.

51. Ibid.

52. RW 4/Vol. 34, p. 59 f.

53. The line ran as follows: Charmes (Mosel)–Neufchâteau–Chaumont–Châtillon sur Seine–Autun–Châlon sur Saône–Dôle (Doubs)–Swiss border.

54. "Tagebuch des Gen. Lt. Botsch" [Diary of Lieutenant General Botsch], RH 20-19/85, p. 42.

55. Ibid., for September 5, 1944, p. 47.

56. Daily Report for September 6, 1944, OB West, Operations Section, No. 7756/44, RH 19 IV/55, pp. 178 ff.

57. Täglichsbeck, "Südwestfrankreich" [Southwestern France], MS-A-886, p. 7.

58. Daily Report for September 4, 1944, Headquarters, Army Task Group G, Operations Section, No. 2453/44, RH 19 XII/8, p. 72 f.

59. RH 20-19/85 for September 6, 1944, p. 47.

60. After the 11th Panzer Division had been transferred "East."

61. Headquarters, Nineteenth Army, Operations Section, No. 9150/44, dated September 5, 1944, RH 20-19/96, p. 183.

62. RH 20-19/85 ("Tagebuch Botsch") for September 6, 1944, p. 50.

63. Conference between Blaskowitz and Wiese, dated September 1, 1944, RH 20-19/96, p. 9 f.

64. See Dehner, "Einsatz des Gen.Kdos. Dehner vom 1.-10.9" [Employment of Dehner Corps Headquarters between September 1 and 10], RH 20-19/98, pp. 134 ff.

65. RH20-19/85 for September 6, 1944, p. 50.

66. Ibid., for September 5, 1944, p. 45 f.

67. Ibid., p. 46.

68. Headquarters, Nineteenth Army, Operations Section, No. 9150/44, dated September 5, 1944, RH 20-19/96, p. 183 f, and War Diary, Army Task Group G, dated September 8, 1944, RH 19 XII/5, p. 222.

69. RH 20-19/85 for September 7, 1944, p. 50.

70. Both divisions had earlier been under the LXXXV Army Corps, which in the meantime had been ordered to Belfort; cf., Headquarters, Nineteenth Army, Operations Section, No. 9173/44, dated September 6, 1944, RH 20-19/97, p. 33.

71. General of Infantry Otto Lasch was to take over the two infantry divisions (716th and 189th) that had earlier been commanded by the Luftwaffe IV Field Corps here.

72. War Diary, Army Task Group G, dated September 7, 1944, RH 19 XII/5, p. 214 f.

73. RH 20-19/85 for September 7, 1944, p. 50.

74. Ibid., p. 51.

75. War Diary, Army Task Group G, dated September 7, 1944, RH 19 XII/5, p. 215, and Daily Report for September 7, 1944, Headquarters, Army Task Group G, Operations Section, No. 2635/44, RH 19 XII/8, p. 116.

76. The LXIV Army Corps with the 716th and 189th Infantry Divisions; Luftwaffe IV Field Corps with the 338th and 198th Infantry Divisions; Corps Dehner headquarters with the 159th Infantry Division; and the 11th Panzer Division.

77. War Diary, Army Task Group G, dated September 7, 1944, RH 19 XII/5, p. 214.

78. Telephone conversation between Wiese and Blaskowitz, dated September 8, 1944, 1827 hours, RH 20-19/97, p. 102.

79. See Dehner, dated September 12, 1944, RH 20-19/98, p. 155.

80. War Diary, Army Task Group G, dated September 15, 1944, RH 19 XII/5, p. 254.

81. Daily Report for September 8, 1944, OB West, Operations Section, No. 7827/44, RH 19 IV/55, pp. 256 ff.

82. RH 20-19/85 for September 7, 1944, p. 52 f.

83. Headquarters, Nineteenth Army, Operations Section, No. 9214/44, dated September 8, 1944, RH 20-19/97, p. 129.

84. See Blaskowitz, Headquarters, Army Task Group G, Operations Section, No. 77/44, dated September 11, 1944, RH 19 XII/9, pp. 34 ff.

85. War Diary, Army Task Group G, map dated September 14, 1944, RH 19 XII/5, p. 249.

86. RH 19 XII/8, Appendix for September 9, 1944, p. 149, and telephone conversation between Botsch and Operations Officer, 11th Panzer Division, dated September 12, 1944, RH 20-19/86, p. 32.

87. Daily Report for September 10, 1944, OB West, Operations Section, No. 7916/44, RH 19 IV/55, pp. 322 ff.

88. It consisted of the main body of the group under the command of Colonel Bauer, who had left Elster's formation in Poitiers and the 360th Cossack Regiment; cf. RH 20-19/97, p. 262.

89. Telephone conversation between Botsch and Gyldenfeldt, dated September 10, 1944, 0938 hours, ibid., p. 254.

90. Telephone conversation between Botsch and Gyldenfeldt, dated September 10, 1944, 1850 hours, ibid., p. 262.

91. Ibid.

92. In the evening of September 10/11, 1944, cf., Wilt, *The French Riviera Campaign of August 1944*, p. 154.

93. The units of Corps Dehner were placed under Petersen's Luftwaffe IV Field Corps on September 9. This meant that Luftwaffe IV Field Corps now had under command the 159th, 198th, and 338th Infantry Divisions; cf., War Diary, Army Task Group G, dated September 9, 1944, RH 19 XII/5, p. 224 f.

94. RH 20-19/85 for September 9, 1944, p. 56.

95. Telephone conversation between Blaskowitz and Wiese, dated September 9, 1944, 1230 hours, RH 20-19/97, p. 202.

96. Among others, Battle Group Degener with four battalions and about two thousand men.

97. Teletype message, LXXXV Army Corps, dated September 12, 1944, RH 20-19/86, p. 32 f.

98. Headquarters, Nineteenth Army, Operations Section, No. 9288/44, RH 20-19/98, p. 16 f.

99. RH 20-19/85 for September 9, 1944, p. 55.

100. Ibid., for September 10, 1944, p. 58.

101. Daily Report for September 10, 1944, Headquarters, Nineteenth Army, Operations Section, No. 9288/44, RH 20-19/98, p. 16 f.

102. Out of eighty-seven thousand men who started on the march. Major General Botho Elster capitulated with around twenty thousand men. On September 9, according to Botsch's data, of the remaining sixty-seven thousand men, only ten thousand men of the Bauer Group and the Cossack Regiment "were missing." Stragglers from the Bauer Group (see Report of the Administrative Group of the Bordeaux Regional Defense Headquar-

ters, dated October 17, 1944, RW 35/1253, pp. 71 ff) and the Cossack Regiment (fourteen hundred men, see Report, Operations Section, LXIV Army Corps, dated September 12, 1944, RH 20-19/98, p. 46) still reached the German lines after Dijon had already been given up.

103. See Blaskowitz, Headquarters, Army Task Group G, Operations Section, No. 77/44, dated September 11, 1944, RH 19 XII/9, pp. 34 ff.

104. War Diary, OB West, dated September 8, 1944, RH 19 IV/46, p. 48. Army Task Group G was renamed accordingly, effective as of September 11, 1944; see OB West, Operations Section, No. 7906/44, RH 19 IV/56, p. 40.

105. Wiese, "19, Armee," MS-B-787, p. 30.

106. RH 20-19/85 for September 9, 1944, p. 57.

107. Ibid., and Botsch, "19. Armee," MS-B-515, p. 63.

108. The U.S. XV Corps consisted of the U.S. 79th Infantry Division and the French 2nd Armored Division.

109. War Diary, Army Group G, dated November 11, 1944, RH 19 XII/5, p. 236.

110. See Rundstedt, OB West, Operations Section, No. 821/44, dated September 13, 1944, RH 19/56, p. 81 f.

111. Field Order No. 5, dated September 14, 1944. Accordingly, the French I and II Corps were now to be combined on the right wing before Belfort. The U.S. VI Corps was "reorganized" for the attack in the northeasterly direction (Strassburg); cf., Wilt, *French Riviera Campaign of August 1944*, p. 157.

112. Ibid., p. 156 f.

113. War Diary, OB West, dated September 10, 1944, RH 19 IV/46, p. 58.

114. See Rundstedt, OB West, Operations Section, No. 810/44, dated September 11, 1944, RH 19 IV/56, p. 20 f, and Inquiry, Army Group G, dated September 11, 1944, RH 19 IV/46, p. 64.

115. Status of rail movements as of September 11, 1944, OB West, Operations Section, No. 7954/44, RH 19 IV/56, p. 31.

116. Daily Report for September 11, 1944, OB West, Operations Section, No. 7960/44, ibid., pp. 27 ff.

117. Headquarters, Army Group G, Training Section, No. 824/44, dated September 14, 1944, RH 19 XII/8, p. 220.

118. See Rundstedt, OB West, Operations Section, No. 810/44, dated September 11, 1944, RH 19 IV/56, p. 20 f.

119. Wehrmacht High Command/Wehrmacht Operations Staff/Operations Section, No. 773348/44, dated September 12, 1944, quoted in: OB West, Operations Section, No. 814/44, ibid., p. 44.

120. See Rundstedt, OB West, Operations Section, No. 821/44, dated September 13, 1944, ibid., p. 81 f.

121. RH 20-19/85 ("Tagebuch Botsch") for September 12, 1944, p. 62.

122. Ibid.

123. The LXVI Army Corps had been under Headquarters, Nineteenth Army, since 0600 hours on September 12.

124. Telephone conversation between Wiese and Botsch, dated September 12, 1944, 1912 hours, RH 20-19/98, p. 44.

125. Telephone conversation between Botsch and Gyldenfeldt, dated September 12, 1944, 1930 hours, ibid., p. 44 f.

126. Telephone conversation between Colonel Siebert (Chief of Staff, LXVI Army Corps) and Operations Officer, Headquarters, Nineteenth Army, dated September 12, 1944, 2105 hours, ibid., p. 46.

127. Telephone conversation between Siebert and Botsch, dated September 12, 1944, 2230 hours, ibid., p. 47 f.

128. Ibid.

129. Wiese's conference at LXVI Army Corps, dated September 12, 1944, 1800–2000 hours, ibid., p. 60 f.

130. RH 20-19/85 for September 12, 1944, p. 63.

131. Ibid.

132. The War Diary, Headquarters, Nineteenth Army (RH 20-19/98, p. 86) also mentions General von Funck. It may be assumed that the officer keeping the War Diary failed to note the change of command between Funck and Lüttwitz in view of the hectic conditions during those days. According to the Activity Report of the Army Personnel Office, orders had already been issued on September 9 to transfer Funck to the Führer Reserve (see ibid., p. 247). See also Keilig, "Generale" [Generals], pp. 99 and 212.

133. Telephone conversation between Botsch and Lieutenant Colonel Kleinschmidt (XLVII Panzer Corps), dated September 13, 1944, 0200 hours, RH 20-19/98, p. 86.

134. Ibid.

135. Wiese's conference at LXVI Army Corps, dated September 12, 1944, RH 20-19/98, 1800–2000 hours, p. 60 f.

136. RH 20-19/85 for September 13, 1944, p. 66.

137. Fonde, "Panzerbrigade" [Panzer Brigade], pp. 177–201.

138. Ibid.

139. Telephone conversation between Gyldenfeldt and Botsch, dated September 13, 1944, RH 20-19/98, p. 106.

140. Ibid.

141. RH 20-19/85 for September 13, 1944, p. 67.

142. Ibid., p. 68.

143. Telephone conversation, XLVII Panzer Corps, dated September 15, 1944, 0030 hours, RH 20-19/99, p. 77.

144. Telephone conversation between Operations Officer, Army Group G, and Operations Officer, Headquarters, Fifth Panzer Army, dated September 14, 1944, 1315 hours, RH 19 XII/8, p. 220.

145. Fonde, "Panzerbrigade," p. 199. On September 15, it still had twenty-two operational Panzers (see also telephone conversation between Siebert and Botsch, dated September 15, 1944, 1310 hours, RH 20-19/99, p. 64 f). The French 2nd Armored Division lost about ten Sherman tanks (Fonde, "Panzerbrigade," pp. 177 ff).

146. In addition to division headquarters, only a total of thirty men were able to get out across the Mosel River by September 16; Daily Report for

September 16, 1944, OB West, Operations Section, No. 8274/44, RH 19 IV/56, pp. 191 ff.

147. RH 20-19/85 for September 14, 1944, p. 71.

148. War Diary, Army Group G, dated September 14, 1944, RH 19 XII/5, p. 246.

149. See Blaskowitz, Headquarters, Army Group G, Operations Section, No. 78/44, dated September 14, 1944, 1230 hours, RH 19 XII/9, p. 39 f.

150. See Westphal, OB West, Operations Section, No. 822/44, dated September 14, 1944, 1630 hours, RH 19 IV/56, pp. 117 ff.

151. Telephone conversation between Westphal and Gyldenfeldt, dated September 15, 1944, 0100 hours, RH 19 XII/5, p. 251.

152. Wehrmacht High Command/Wehrmacht Operations Staff/Operations Section, No. 773396/44, dated September 15, 1944, quoted in: OB West, Operations Section, No. 823/44, RH 19 IV/56, p. 138.

153. According to the testimony of General of Aviation Werner Kreipe, Hitler renounced that decision on September 16 around 1300 hours (cf., Greiffenberg, "Ardennes-Questionnaire," MS-P-32i, Appendix 6, pp. 1 ff. See also: Colonel Meyer-Detring, ibid., Appendix 2, p. 2).

154. Inspector-General of Panzer Forces, No. 2920/44; führer's decision regarding führer briefing of September 13, 1944, RH 10/90, p. 90 f. For this purpose, Headquarters, Sixth Panzer Army, was formed under the command of Colonel General of the Waffen-SS Dietrich (ibid.). The order to establish Headquarters, Sixth Panzer Army, quite characteristically went out on September 14 (cf., Schramm, "Ardennenoffensive," MS-A-862, p. 56).

12. The End of the Retreat Operations in the West and the Transition to Positional Warfare

1. See Rundstedt, OB West, Operations Section, No. 805/44, dated September 7, 1944, RH 19 IV/55, pp. 218 ff.

2. MacDonald, *The Siegfried Line Campaign*, pp. 66 ff.

3. Ibid.

4. G-2 situation estimates of the U.S. V and VII Corps as of September 10 or September 13, 1944, ibid., pp. 38 and 68.

5. Ibid., pp. 39 ff.

6. The city itself, of course, was in the sector of Headquarters, First Parachute Army.

7. With the 105th Panzer Brigade under command.

8. On September 12, the 116th Panzer Division had nineteen operational Panzers, while the 9th Panzer Division had three; see telephone conversation between Gersdorff and Tempelhoff at 2035 hours, RH 19 IX/89, p. 183 f. Major General Gerhard Müller's 9th Panzer Division was given nineteen model IV tank destroyers of the 394th Assault Gun Brigade on that same day; cf., Brandenberger, "7. Armee," MS-B-730, p. 74.

9. For example, to screen the Monschau–Ormont area, Headquarters, LXXIV Army Corps, had available only remnants of two infantry divisions

(the 89th and 347th), units of the Replacement Army (the 526th Division), and three Luftwaffe field battalions; see War Diary, Army Group B, September 12, 1944, p. 172, and September 14, 1944, p. 209.

10. Quoted from: OB West, Operations Section, No. 7853/44, dated September 11, 1944, RH 19 IV/56, p. 9 f.

11. Telephone conversation between Gersdorff and Krebs, dated September 13, 1944, 1610 hours, RH 19 IX/89, p. 192.

12. Between Alsdorf (fifteen kilometers northeast of Aachen) and Ormont (about twelve kilometers north of Prüm) the West Wall zone consisted of two lines of bunkers. Aachen was between the first line, the "Scharnhorst Line," and the second line, "Schill Line."

13. Schwerin, "116. Pz. Div.," MS-ETHINT 19, p. 36 f.

14. Ibid., pp. 41 ff.

15. Brandenberger, "7. Armee," MS-B-730, p. 83 f.

16. Daily Report for September 13, 1944, OB West, Operations Section, No. 8081/44, RH 19 IV/56, pp. 91 ff.

17. War Diary, LXXXI Army Corps, entry at 1205 hours (Message from 9th Panzer Division), RH 24-81/97, p. 212/1.

18. On September 13 alone, the U.S. 3rd Armored Division lost fourteen "Shermans"; MacDonald, *The Siegfried Line Campaign*, p. 74.

19. Report, 353rd Infantry Division, dated September 13, 1944, RH 24-81/97, p. 204/1.

20. Telephone conversation between Model and Krebs, dated September 13, 1944, 1300 hours, RH 19 IX/89, p. 205.

21. War Diary, OB West, dated September 14, 1944, RH 19 IV/46, p. 80 f.

22. War Diary, LXXXI Army Corps, entries for September 14, 1944, 2000 hours, and September 15, 1944, 2045 hours, RH 24-81/97, p. 215/1 and p. 224/1.

23. Telephone conversation between Gersdorff and Krebs, dated September 14, 1944, 2150 hours, RH 19 IX/89, p. 210.

24. Warlimont, "Hauptquartier," p. 510.

25. RW 4/Vol. 34 for September 14, p. 61.

26. Telephone conversation between Westphal and Krebs, dated September 15, 1944, 1630 hours, RH 19 IX/89, p. 219 f.

27. The organization of the "Volkssturm" [People's Emergency Levy] was ordered a few days later.

28. Wehrmacht High Command/Wehrmacht Operations Staff/Operations Section, No. 001273/44, dated September 16, 1944, quoted in: see Rundstedt, OB West, Operations Section, No. 8197/44, RH 19 IV/56, p. 187 f.

29. The visit to the front took place at the LXXX and LXXXII Army Corps in the forenoon of September 14, 1944. Cf., see Rundstedt, OB West, Operations Section, No. 8090/44, dated September 14, 1944, RH 19 IV/56, p. 121 f.

30. War Diary, LXXX Army Corps, RH 24-80/68, pp. 54 ff.

31. Telephone conversation between Gersdorff and Krebs, dated September 20, 1944, 0850 hours, RH 19 IX/90, p. 53 f.

32. Telephone conversation between Gersdorff and Tempelhoff, dated September 14, 1944, 0830 hours, RH 19 IX/89, p. 200.

33. Ibid.

34. MacDonald, *The Siegfried Line Campaign,* pp. 96 ff.

35. Noon Report, OB West for September 14, 1944, RH 19 IV/46, p. 79.

36. Evening Report, OB West for September 14, 1944, ibid., p. 81.

37. War Diary, LXXX Army Corps, RH 24-80/68, pp. 69 ff.

38. MacDonald, *The Siegfried Line Campaign,* p. 59 f.

39. Note for Chief of Staff, OB West, dated September 15, 1944, RH 19 IV/56, p. 150.

40. Daily Report for September 14, 1944, OB West, Operations Section, No. 8129/44, ibid., pp. 123 ff.

41. Daily Report for September 15, 1944, OB West, Operations Section, No. 8195/44, ibid., pp. 159 ff.

42. Cf., chapter 9, section 1.

43. Accordingly, Patton was to establish a big bridgehead on the east bank of the Mosel River as a source of constant threat to the Germans.

44. About thirty-five hundred tons each daily; cf., Cole, *The Lorraine Campaign,* p. 210.

45. On September 16, he assigned to his army the Mannheim–Frankfurt area as "Attack Objective"; ibid., p. 214.

46. Eisenhower's letter to Montgomery, dated September 15, 1944, *Eisenhower Papers,* IV, p. 2148 f.

47. Telephone conversation between Westphal and Krebs, dated September 15, 1944, 2345 hours, RH 19 IX/89, p. 223.

48. Telephone conversation between Colonel Wiese (LXXXI Army Corps) and Tempelhoff, dated September 16, 1944, 1305 hours, RH 19 IX/90, p. 4.

49. The 12th Infantry Division, however, was not complete until September 18; see Status of Rail Movements, OB West, Operations Section, No. 8326/44, dated September 18, 1944, RH 19 IV/56, p. 281.

50. Daily Report for September 16, 1944, OB West, Operations Section, No. 8274/44, pp. 191 ff.

51. MacDonald, *The Siegfried Line Campaign,* p. 89 f.

52. Ibid.

53. Report, dated September 18, 1944, ibid., p. 68.

54. Telephone conversation between Gersdorff and Krebs, dated September 20, 1944, 0850 hours, RH 19 IX/90, p. 53.

55. MacDonald, *The Siegfried Line Campaign,* p. 90.

56. Daily Report for September 20, 1944, OB West, Operations Section, No. 8395/44, RH 19 IV/56, pp. 330 ff.

57. Daily Reports for September 20/21, 1944, OB West, Operations Section, Nos. 8395 and 8450/44, ibid., pp. 330 ff, and RH 19 IV/57, pp. 29 ff.

58. Daily Report for September 18, 1944, OB West, Operations Section, No. 8332/44, RH 19 IV/56, pp. 274 ff.

59. MacDonald, *The Siegfried Line Campaign,* pp. 110 ff.

60. Tessin, "Verbände," 7, p. 219 f.

61. Daily Report for September 20, 1944, OB West, Operations Section, No. 8395/44, RH 19 IV/56, pp. 330 ff.

62. Telephone conversation between General Mattenklott (Defense District VI) and Tempelhoff, dated September 16, 1944, 2340 hours, RH 19 IX/90, p. 8 f.

63. Activity Report, Army Personnel Office, dated September 17, 1944, p. 259.

64. That at any rate can be gathered from Model's comments; see telephone conversation between Brandenberger and Model, dated September 18, 1944, 1910 hours, RH 19 IX/90, p. 32 f.

65. Ibid.

66. Schwerin, "116. Pz. Div.," MS-ETHINT 18, pp. 48 ff.

67. Telephone conversation between Brandenberger and Model, dated September 18, 1944, 1910 hours, RH 19 IX/90, p. 32 f. The author, however, was unable to discover any references to the fact that Model ordered Schwerin to be turned over to the People's Court. But that is what Schwerin maintained after the war; cf., MS-ETHINT 18, p. 51.

68. Telephone conversation between Brandenberger and Model, dated September 18, 1944, 1910 hours, RH 19 IX/90, p. 32 f.

69. Ibid.

70. Telephone conversation between Gersdorff and Krebs, dated September 19, 1944, 0910 hours, RH 19 IX/90, p. 41.

71. Activity Report, Army Personnel Office, October 2, 1944, p. 276.

72. Telephone conversation between Westphal and Krebs, dated September 15, 1944, 1815 hours, RH 19 IX/89, p. 222.

73. See Rundstedt, OB West, Operations Section, Nos. 8254 and 8256/44, dated September 17, 1944, RH 19 IV/56, pp. 210 and 214.

74. Daily Report for September 18, 1944, OB West, Operations Section, No. 8332/44, RH 19 IV/56, pp. 274 ff.

75. MacDonald, *The Siegfried Line Campaign*, p. 61 f.

76. The 108th Panzer Brigade had thirty-four Panzers, of which twenty-two were employed in action on September 19, 1944; cf., War Diary, LXXX Army Corps, dated September 19, 1944, pp. 81 ff.

77. MacDonald, *The Siegfried Line Campaign*, p. 65.

78. Daily Report for September 22, 1944, OB West, Operations Section, No. 8480/44, RH 19 IV/57, pp. 51 ff.

79. MacDonald, *The Siegfried Line Campaign*, p. 40.

80. Between September 13 and 18, the U.S. First Army received relatively little air support on account of rain and fog; see MacDonald, *The Siegfried Line Campaign*, p. 86.

81. See also War Diary, OB West, dated September 12, 1944 (Departure of 12th Infantry Division, September 13, 1944, 2400 hours), p. 67.

82. OB West, Operations Section, No. 8380/44, dated September 20, 1944, RH 19 IV/56, p. 336.

83. MacDonald, *The Siegfried Line Campaign*, p. 115.

84. In a conversation with Major General Manton Eddy, commanding general, U.S. XII Corps; cf., Cole, *The Lorraine Campaign*, p. 229.

85. See Rundstedt, OB West, Operations Section, No. 8234/44, dated September 16, 1944, RH 19 IV/56, p. 175 f.

86. Cole, *The Lorraine Campaign*, p. 174.

87. Ibid., p. 183.

88. The 103rd or 115th Panzer Battalion (establishment strength: forty-two assault guns each). On September 14, the 3rd Panzer Grenadier Division had thirty-nine assault guns operational, while the 15th Panzer Grenadier Division had seventeen; see Headquarters, Army Group G, Operations Section, No. 824/44, dated September 14, 1944, RH 19 XII/8, p. 224 f.

89. Morning Report, OB West, dated September 17, 1944, RH 19 IV/46, p. 95.

90. See also Daily Report for September 18, 1944, OB West, Operations Section, No. 8332/44, RH 19 IV/56, pp. 274 ff.

91. Headquarters, Army Group G, Operations Section, No. 2834, dated September 18, 1944, RH 19 XII/8, p. 275.

92. Lunéville was temporarily evacuated by the 15th Panzer Grenadier Division on September 17, 1944; cf., Daily Report for September 17, 1944, OB West, Operations Section, No. 8295/44, RH 19 IV/56, pp. 231 ff.

93. Cole, *The Lorraine Campaign*, p. 214 f.

94. See Rundstedt, OB West, Operations Section, No. 8308/44, dated September 18, 1944, RH 19 IV/56, p. 249.

95. Headquarters, Army Group G, Operations Section, No. 2830, RH 19 XII/8, p. 279.

96. Daily Report, Headquarters, Fifth Panzer Army, dated September 17, 1944, RH 21-5/55, p. 40. Accordingly, the Battle Group of 21st Panzer Division had thirty Panzers available, while the 111th Panzer Brigade had seventeen and the 113th Panzer Brigade was at forty-two. In addition, there were ten Panthers of the 111th Panzer Brigade and the PzKpfw IV battalion of the 113th Panzer Brigade that, however, had not yet arrived.

97. War Diary, Headquarters, Fifth Panzer Army, dated September 17, 1944, RH 21-5/54, p. 7.

98. Ibid., for September 18, 1944, p. 8.

99. Message, dated September 18, 1944, 1800 hours, ibid., p. 9.

100. War Diary, LVIII Panzer Corps, dated September 18, 1944, 1615 hours, RH 24-58/12, p. 12.

101. Morning Report, OB West, dated September 19, 1944, RH 19 IV/46, p. 111.

102. Manteuffel's verbal order, dated September 18, 1944, 2015 hours, RH 24-58/10, p. 13.

103. Overall, the strength of the attack group was about the same, with approximately 110 Panzers. Lüttwitz's XLVII Corps, of course, no longer participated, but, in return, Krüger—in addition to the twenty-five fighting

vehicles of the 111th Panzer Brigade—received additional reinforcement in the form of the PzKpfw IV battalion of the 113th Brigade that now also arrived on the battlefield; see telephone conversation between Colonel Dingler (Chief of Staff, LVIII Panzer Corps) and Kahlden, dated September 18, 1944, 1830 hours, RH 24-58/12, p. 13.

104. Manteuffel's situation briefing for Blaskowitz, dated September 19, 1944, 1430 hours, RH 21-5/54, p. 10.

105. Ibid., p. 11.

106. Cole, *The Lorraine Campaign*, pp. 221 ff.

107. Colonel Dingler's Report, dated September 19, 1944, 2120 hours, RH 21-5/54, p. 11 f.

108. Ibid., p. 11 f.

109. Telephone conversation between Kahlden and Gyldenfeldt in the morning of September 20, 1944, RH 21-5/54, p. 13.

110. Kahlden to LVIII Panzer Corps, dated September 19, 1944, 2140 hours, RH 24-58/12, p. 15.

111. See also Dingler's situation report to Kahlden, dated September 20, 1944, 2055 hours, RH 24-58/13, p. 19.

112. Cole, *The Lorraine Campaign*, pp. 226 ff.

113. Telephone conversation between Kahlden and Gyldenfeldt, dated September 20, 1944, RH 21-5/54, p. 13.

114. Final reports from the 111th and 113th Panzer Brigades in: Daily Report for September 22, 1944, OB West, Operations Section, No. 8480/44, RH 19 IV/57, pp. 51 ff.

115. Noon Report, OB West, dated September 20, 1944, RH 19 IV/46, p. 117.

116. Dividing lines: With the First Army: South from Nancy–Vic sur Seille–woods north of Dieuze; to the Nineteenth Army: Charmes–Rambervillers–Raon l'Etape; War Diary, Army Group G, dated September 21, 1944, RH 19 XII/5, p. 277 f.

117. See also: telephone conversation between Blaskowitz and Manteuffel, dated September 20, 1944, 2355 hours, RH 19 XII/5, p. 273.

118. Eddy Diary for September 20, 1944, quoted in: Cole, *The Lorraine Campaign*, p. 229.

119. Eisenhower's letters to Marshall, dated September 18, and to Montgomery, dated September 20, 1944, *Eisenhower Papers*, IV, pp. 2157 ff and 2164 ff.

120. Montgomery's letter M-222, dated September 21, 1944, ibid., p. 2186, and M-223, dated September 21, 1944, quoted in: Pogue, *The Supreme Command*, p. 293.

121. With reference thereto: see Blaskowitz, Headquarters, Army Group G, Operations Section, No. 80/44, dated September 15, 1944, RH 19 XII/9, p. 41 f.

122. Wilt, *French Riviera Campaign of August 1944*, p. 157.

123. Cole, *The Lorraine Campaign*, pp. 202 ff.

124. RH 20-19/85 for September 16, 1944, p. 74.

125. Ibid., for September 14, 1944, p. 71.

126. See Rundstedt, OB West, Operations Section, No. 8234/44, dated September 16, 1944, RH 19 IV/56, p. 175 f.

127. See Blaskowitz, Headquarters, Army Group G, Operations Section, 2801/44, dated September 16, 1944, RH 19 XII/8, p. 247.

128. Cf. Botsch, "19. Armee," MS-B-766, p. 5.

129. Headquarters, Nineteenth Army, Operations Section, No. 9458/44, dated September 17, 1944, RH 20-19/99, p. 196.

130. See Rundstedt, OB West, Operations Section, No. 828/44, dated September 19, 1944, RH 19 IV/56, pp. 287 ff.

131. "Forward Line of Nineteenth Army," according to Headquarters, Army Group G, Operations Section, No. 2834/44, dated September 18, 1944, RH 19 XII/8, p. 275.

132. Calculated according to the following: Headquarters, Nineteenth Army, Operations Section, No. 9559/44, dated September 20, 1944, RH 20-19/86, p. 46 f, and Reports, LXIV Army Corps, dated August 19 and 25, 1944, RH 19 IV/54, pp. 50 and 217. That number also includes Luftwaffe, navy, and SS personnel, military administration units, as well as members of other nationalities (Indians, Cossacks, and "Eastern troops," Italians, etc.).

133. Headquarters, Nineteenth Army, Operations Section, No. 9559/44, dated September 20, 1944, RH 20-19/86, p. 46 f. To explain this difference: the 16th Infantry Division, which likewise had still reached Dijon, was already broken up at that time. Out of around 7,500 men, only about 550 were able to fight their way through to their own lines (Daily Report, LXVI Army Corps, dated September 20, 1944, RH 20-19/100, p. 154 f). Another approximately 190,000 men, however, were already in staging camps or in their home defense districts (see Blaskowitz, Headquarters, Army Group G, Training Section, No. 887/44, RH 19 IV/56, pp. 301 ff). Besides, 7,300 navy personnel were also brought back; they are not contained in Nineteenth Army's "ration strength."

134. *Hitlers Lagebesprechungen*, noon situation briefing, dated September 1, 1944, p. 637.

135. See also chapter 8, section 4 (b). In his last reports as OB, Army Group G, Blaskowitz had to dispute the false insinuations ("stragglers") made by the gauleiters; see Blaskowitz, Headquarters, Army Group G, Training Section, No. 887/44, dated September 21, 1944, RH 19 XII/8, p. 328 f.

136. See Rundstedt, OB West, Operations Section, No. 828/44, dated September 19, 1944, RH 19 IV/56, pp. 287 ff.

137. See also telephone conversation between Blaskowitz and Botsch, dated September 20, 1944, 1110 hours, RH 20-19/100, p. 123.

138. See also telephone conversation between Gyldenfeldt and Schulz, dated September 19, 1944, 1940 hours, RH 20-19/100, p. 73.

139. Activity Report, Army Personnel Office, dated September 19, 1944, p. 261.

140. War Diary, Army Group G, dated September 21, 1944, RH 19 XII/5, p. 275.

141. Intelligence analysis, dated September 8, 1944, Army Group B, Intelligence Section, No. 3517/44, RH 19 IX/26, Part 2, p. 193.

142. *Emphasis in the original.*

143. Intelligence Section Evening Report, dated September 13, 1944, Army Group B, Intelligence Section, No. 3582/44, RH 19 IX/26, Part 2, p. 151.

144. Noon Report, OB West, dated September 13, 1944, RH 19 IV/46, p. 74.

145. Quoted in: Ellis, *Victory in the West,* II, p. 68.

146. Montgomery's Directive, dated September 14, 1944, quoted in: Ellis, *Victory in the West,* II, pp. 27 and 59.

147. Ibid.

148. A total of about three to six major units. The Canadian II Corps (Canadian 4th Division, Polish 1st Armored Division) and the British I Corps (49th Infantry Division). The British XII Corps (7th Armoured Division, 15th Infantry Division, 53rd Infantry Division) of the British Second Army was moved into the area west of Herentals by September 17 to secure the flank of MARKET-GARDEN; see Montgomery, *Normandy to the Baltic,* pp. 198 ff.

149. See Krebs, Headquarters, Army Group B, Operations Section, No. 7484/44, dated September 17, 1944, RH 19 IX/5, p. 702.

150. The 59th, 70th, 245th, 331st, 346th, 711th, and 712th Infantry Divisions. Of the Luftwaffe 17th Field Division, only remnants were left, and they were attached to other units, except for division headquarters, which, under Lieutenant General Hans-Kurt Höcker, directed the crossing at Terneuzen. The division was dissolved officially on September 28; see Tessin, "Verbände," 4, p. 60.

151. See Model, Headquarters, Army Group B, Operations Section, No. 7380/44, dated September 15, 1944, RH 19 IX/5, pp. 560 ff.

152. Zangen, "15. Armee," MS-B-249, p. 42.

153. Evening Report, OB West, dated September 15, 1944, RH 19 IV/46, p. 88.

154. Telephone conversation between Hofmann and Krebs, dated September 12, 1944, 0915 hours, RH 19 IX/89, p. 176.

155. Telephone conversation between Chief of Training, Headquarters, Fifteenth Army, and Tempelhoff, dated September 16, 1944, 1155 hours, RH 19 IX/90, p. 3.

156. Zangen, "15. Armee," MS-B-249, pp. 36 ff.

157. Telephone conversation between Krebs and Westphal, dated September 22, 1944, 1810 hours, RH 19 IX/90, p. 84.

158. Telephone conversation between Wühlisch and Krebs, dated September 18, 1944, 1145 hours, ibid., p. 28.

159. Report, Army Group B, dated September 17, 1944, RH 19 IV/46, p. 99.

160. Ellis, *Victory in the West,* II, p. 61 f.

161. This is indicated by the Daily Reports from OB West for September 13 to 17, 1944; RH 19 IV/56, pp. 91 ff, 123 ff, 159 ff, 171 ff, 231 ff.

162. The 346th, 711th, and 59th Infantry Divisions.

163. The 245th Infantry Division initially was earmarked for Südbeveland.

164. Model's order to Headquarters, Fifteenth Army, dated September 18, 1944, 0800 hours, RH 19 IX/90, p. 22.

165. Daily Report for September 19, 1944, OB West, Operations Section, No. 8359/44, RH 19 IV/56, pp. 301 ff.

166. Ibid., and Daily Report for September 20, 1944, OB West, Operations Section, No. 8395/44, RH 19 IV/56, pp. 330 ff.

167. Noon Report, OB West, dated September 22, 1944, RH 19 IV/46, p. 128.

168. Report, OB West, Operations Section (no number), dated September 23, 1944, RH 19 IV/57, p. 71.

169. According to the Daily Report for September 22, 1944 (OB West, Operations Section, No. 8480/44, RH 19 IV/57, pp. 51 ff), around 82,000 men were ferried across by September 21. Some, however, were still ferried across on September 22, so that the number given by the author is probably approximately correct. According to a report from Admiral, Netherlands (G.25312 F III, RM 7/131, pp. 492 ff), the number was as high as 85,000–90,000 men. MacDonald, *The Siegfried Line Campaign,* p. 219, gave the following ferrying statistics: 86,000 men, 600 artillery pieces, 6,000 vehicles, and 6,000 horses.

170. MacDonald, *The Siegfried Line Campaign,* p. 219.

171. The harbor could not be put into operation until October 12, 1944; cf., Ellis, *Victory in the West,* II, pp. 61 ff.

172. Cf., Daily Report for September 22, 1944, OB West, Operations Section, No. 8480/44, RH 19 IV/57, pp. 51 ff.

173. Zangen, "15. Armee," MS-B-730, p. 39.

174. Here, we might mention, for example, the very thorough studies by MacDonald (in: *The Siegfried Line Campaign,* pp. 119–206) and by Ellis (*Victory in the West,* II, pp. 28–58). Cornelius Ryan addressed a broader public in *A Bridge Too Far.*

175. Eisenhower's letter to Marshall, dated September 14, 1944, *Eisenhower Papers,* IV, pp. 2143 ff.

176. Later—according to plan on September 19—the Polish 1st Airborne Brigade and then the 52nd Lowland Division were to follow; MacDonald, *The Siegfried Line Campaign,* pp. 131 ff.

177. Ibid., p. 198.

178. MacDonald, "The Decisions to Launch Operation MARKET-GARDEN," in *Command Decisions,* p. 338.

179. Bennett, *Ultra in the West: The Normandy Campaign, 1944–45,* pp. 145 ff.

180. MacDonald, *The Siegfried Line Campaign,* p. 122.

181. Ellis, *Victory in the West,* II, p. 30.

182. Ibid., p. 52.

183. Ibid., p. 30.

184. MacDonald, *The Siegfried Line Campaign*, p. 133 f.

185. Ibid.

186. Ellis, *Victory in the West*, II, p. 52.

187. Long after the war, Montgomery maintained that this "advantage" mitigated in favor of MARKET-GARDEN; Montgomery, *Normandy to the Baltic*, p. 198.

188. See also Lewin, "Ultra," p. 420, and Bennett, *Ultra in the West: The Normandy Campaign, 1944–45*, p. 147. Both of these authors here referred to German radio messages that were decoded on September 9, 12, and 15.

189. Intelligence Section Evening Report, dated September 12, 1944, Army Group B, Intelligence Section, No. 3566/44, RH 19 IX/26, Part 2, p. 161.

190. Intelligence Section Evening Report, dated September 15, 1944, Army Group B, Intelligence Section, No. 3593/44, ibid., Part 2, pp. 129 ff.

191. War Diary, Army Group B, dated September 10, 1944, RH 19 IX/89, p. 144.

192. See also: War Diary, Army Group B, dated September 10, 1944, ibid., p. 153.

193. War Diary, Army Group B, dated September 10, 1944, ibid., p. 158.

194. In response to inquiry by OB West, answer: "Wehrmacht Senior Officer," dated September 17, 1944, 1500 hours, RH 19 IV/46, p. 97.

195. MacDonald, *The Siegfried Line Campaign*, p. 139.

196. Quoted from Colonel Freyberg (Aide, OB, Army Group B) in: N 6/1, "Model," p. 247.

197. Tempelhoff's Report, dated September 17, 1944, 1640 hours, RH 19 IV/46, p. 98.

198. Freyberg's letter to Rommel, dated September 24, 1944, RH 19 IX/1, pp. 111 ff.

199. Intelligence Section Evening Report, dated September 17, 1944, Army Group B, Intelligence Section, No. 3627/44, RH 19 IX/26, Part 2, p. 105 f.

200. Army Group B message, dated September 18, 1944, 1135 hours, RH 19 IV/46, p. 105.

201. In addition to the battle groups of the 9th and 10th SS Panzer Divisions, the first elements of the Fifteenth Army (the 59th Infantry Division) and the parachute units of the II Parachute Corps could be thus designated in the depth of the penetration area. Meindl's paratroopers were from the very beginning sent from Defense District VI to the provisional "Corps Feldt"; see also Model, Headquarters, Army Group B, Operations Section, No. 7503/44, dated September 17, 1944, RH 19 IX/5, p. 699.

202. Defense District X mobilized the 180th and 190th Divisions. The code names "Blücher" and "Gneisenau" were announced in Defense District VI; see War Diary, OB West, dated September 17, 1944, RH 19 IV/46,

pp. 99 ff. The soldiers in Defense District VI were commanded within the 406th Special Purpose Division (Corps Feldt) or—such as, for example, the Panzer replacement units—they were sent toward the front in the form of individual battalions; see, for example, OB West, Morning Report, dated September 20, 1944, RH 19 IV/46, p. 116.

203. For example, Battle Group Tettau organized by Wehrmacht Commander, Netherlands. Its five battalions consisted of men from the replacement and training units of the Waffen-SS, ship cadre units, and alert detachments of the Luftwaffe; see also Christiansen, Wehrmacht Commander, Netherlands, Operations Section, No. 4510/44, dated September 24, 1944, RH 19 IX/5, p. 801 f.

204. Army Group B message, dated September 18, 1944, 1135 hours, RH 19 IV/46, p. 105.

205. OB West Noon Report, dated September 18, 1944, ibid., p. 106.

206. Ibid.

207. Telephone conversation between Krebs and Wühlisch, dated September 18, 1944, 1600 hours, RH 19 IX/90, p. 31.

208. Telephone conversation between Wühlisch and Krebs, dated September 19, 1944, 1520 hours, ibid., p. 45.

209. Telephone conversation between Wühlisch and Krebs, dated September 20, 1944, 1835 hours, ibid., p. 61 f.

210. Telephone conversation between Westphal and Krebs, dated September 21, 1944, 1345 hours, ibid., p. 71.

211. Telephone conversation between Bittrich and Krebs, dated September 20, 1944, 2330 hours, ibid., p. 64.

212. Daily Report for September 21, 1944, OB West, Operations Section, No. 8450/44, RH 19 IV/57, pp. 29 ff.

213. OB West Noon Report, dated September 22, 1944, RH 19 IV/46, p. 128.

214. Evening Report, OB West, dated September 22, 1944, ibid., p. 129.

215. Headquarters, Fifteenth Army, took command of the western wing of the corridor that had resulted from MARKET-GARDEN on September 23; cf., Model, Headquarters, Army Group B, Operations Section, No. 7710/44, dated September 23, 1944, RH 19 IX/5, p. 824. Five of the seven major units that were under Zangen's command here were divisions that had retreated across the Scheldt River shortly before; see also OB West, Operations Section, No. 8375/44, dated September 29, 1944, RH 19 IV/57, p. 282 f.

216. In addition to the 59th Infantry Division, men of the 6th Parachute Infantry Regiment, later on the Chill Battle Group (85th Infantry Division), and the 712th Infantry Division participated in these attacks; see War Diary, LXXXVIII Army Corps, dated September 18, 1944, RH 24-88/91, p. 103; Noon Report, OB West, dated September 26, 1944, RH 19 IV/46, p. 150.

217. Morning Report, Army Group B, dated September 18, 1944, RH 19 IV/46, p. 104.

218. Later on, they were joined by the first elements from the 180th Replacement Army Division. The attacking forces were combined in the so-called "Walther Battle Group"; see Message, Army Group B, dated September 22, 1944, (no number), RH 19 IV/57, p. 42. In response to the code word "Alert Coast," Defense District X (Hamburg) within three days sent a total of eighteen thousand men (the 180th and 190th Divisions) to the Netherlands; cf., Tessin, "Verbände," 3, pp. 164 f, and 7, pp. 203 f and 251 f.

219. Headquarters, Army Group B, Operations Section, No. 7465/44, dated September 16, 1944, RH 19 IX/5, p. 687, and Daily Report for September 19, 1944, OB West, Operations Section, No. 8359/44, RH 19 IV/56, pp. 301 ff.

220. MacDonald, *The Siegfried Line Campaign,* p. 153.

221. Supply traffic was unhindered only on September 21, 1944; cf., Ellis, *Victory in the West,* II, pp. 39 ff.

222. Cf., ibid., p. 42.

223. MacDonald, *The Siegfried Line Campaign,* p. 196.

224. On account of the landings in the Nijmegen area, Model expected that the Allies would now change their direction and wheel southeast toward the Ruhr region across the Rhine River and the Meuse River; cf., telephone conversation between Student and Krebs, dated September 23, 1944, 2315 hours, RH 19 IX/90, p. 102 f. Rundstedt went along with this estimate; cf., Rundstedt, OB West, Operations Section, No. 835/44, dated September 24, 1944, RH 19 IV/57, pp. 107 ff.

225. The remainder of the Polish 1st Separate Airborne Brigade no longer landed at Driel but rather in the Grave area, where it reinforced the U.S. 82nd Airborne Division, under whose command it was placed. On the same day, Dempsey decided not to commit any additional airborne troops; see MacDonald, *The Siegfried Line Campaign,* p. 196.

226. On September 24, 1944, ibid., p. 197.

227. Ellis, *Victory in the West,* II, p. 44.

228. II SS Panzer Corps message, dated September 26, 1944, 1155 hours, RH 19 IX/90, p. 129.

229. See Christiansen, Wehrmacht Commander, Netherlands, Operations Section, No. 4510/44, dated September 24, 1944, RH 19 IX/5, p. 801 f.

230. See also Daily Report for September 24, 1944, OB West, Operations Section, No. 8547/44, RH 19 IV/57, pp. 122 ff.

231. See Model (no number), dated September 27, 1944, RH 19 IX/5, p. 882.

232. This figure pertains to the losses arising during the "Airborne Phase" and in connection with the thrust by the British Second Army; cf., MacDonald, *The Siegfried Line Campaign,* p. 199, and Ellis, *Victory in the West,* II, p. 55 f.

233. Daily Report for September 26, 1944, OB West, Operations Section, No. 8607/44, RH 19 IV/57, pp. 174 ff.

234. Apart from the fact that a main-effort offensive along the Scheldt

River mouth could have yielded more decisive results, the best window for an airborne landing operation in Holland had passed.

13. Conclusion

1. "The ultimate goal," said Rundstedt on September 21, 1944, must be "to be able to attack the enemy at a later date in one place and to beat him decisively. That is the only way the threat to German soil can be eliminated." See Rundstedt, OB West, Operations Section, No. 835/44, dated September 21, 1944, RH 19 IV/57, pp. 11 ff.

2. "The enemy has now succeeded in establishing a relatively stable and cohesive front," Eisenhower's letter to the Combined Chiefs of Staff, dated September 29, 1944, in: *Eisenhower Papers*, IV, pp. 2199 ff.

3. See General of Infantry Edgar Röhricht, N 6/1, "Model," p. 69.

4. Up to September 30, 1944, the losses of the field army in the west came to around 419,000 men. During the month of September, around 126,000 men were reported as wounded, missing, or killed in action in the west as compared to 121,000 men in the east; see "Der Heeresarzt im OKH" [The Army Doctor in the Armed Forces High Command], Army General Staff/Deputy Chief of Staff for Supply/File No. 1335 c/d, quoted in: Jung, "Ardennenoffensive," Appendix 5.

5. Jacobsen, "Krieg in Wiltanschauung und Praxis des Nationalsozialismus" [War in the Ideology and Practice of National Socialism], see: id., Karl Dietrich Bracher, Manfred Funke (editor), "Nationalsozialistische Dikatur" [National Socialist Dictatorship], pp. 427–439, specifically p. 431.

6. Eisenhower's letter to Marshall, dated September 21, 1944, in: *Eisenhower Papers*, IV, pp. 2167 ff.

7. The first convoy consisting of seventeen Liberty ships reached Antwerp on November 28, 1944; Ellis, *Victory in the West*, II, p. 127.

8. Montgomery's letter to Eisenhower, dated November 30, 1944, quoted in: Pogue, *The Supreme Command*, p. 312.

9. Hildebrand, "Das Dritte Reich," [The Third Reich], p. 105.

Bibliography

1. Unpublished Sources

a) Bundesarchiv-Militärarchiv (BA-MA), Freiburg im Breisgau

RW 4	*Bestand Oberkommando der Wehrmacht (OKW/WFSt)*
/v.33	KTB Jodl (offenbar Nachkriegsabschrift) 6.1.1943– 21.5.1945
/v.34	KTB Jodl (Fotokopie) 6.1.1943–21.5.1945
/v.37	Unterlagen Jodl (alle Fronten)
/v.481–/v.483	Bestand/Verluste Wehrmacht, Aug.–Okt. 1944
/v.485	Entwicklung und Verteilung von Waffen
/v.493	Feldjägerkommandos 1944/45
/v.494	Bildung der Auffangorganisation 1944
/v.632	Versorgungsführung im Westen (Festungen) 1944/45
/v.634	Personelle Räumung im Westen 1944/45
/v.636	Panzerlage West 1944/45
/v.702 u./v.703	Vorbereitungen für die Verteidigung des Reiches 1944/45
/v.828	Fanatisierung der Kampfführung im Westen (Führerbefehl)
/v.865	Durchführung des totalen Kriegseinsatzes 1944
RL 7	*Bestand Kommandobehörden der Luftwaffe*
/57–58	Kräfte der Luftflotte 3 und des III. Flakkorps Juli 1944
/118	KTB (Nr. 79) der Luftflotte 3 27.8.–30.9.1944
RH 10	*Bestand OKH/Generalinspekteur der Panzertruppen*
/90	Notizen für Vorträge des Gen.Insp.d.Pz.Tr./Chef des Stabes beim Führer 3.6.–29.12.1944
/141	Gliederung und Zustand 2. Pz.Div., Juli 1943–Febr. 1945
/148	Gliederung und Zustand 9. Pz.Div., Juli 1943–Mai 1945
/149	Gliederung und Zustand 11. Pz.Div., Aug.–Okt. 1944
/163	Gliederung und Zustand 116. Pz.Div., Aug.–Okt. 1944
/178	Gliederung und Zustand 3. Pz.Gren.Div., Aug.–Okt. 1944
/214	Gliederung und Zustand Pz.Brig. 107, Sept. 1944
/349	Panzer-/Sturmgeschützzuweisungen für die Truppe, Mai 1943–Okt. 1944
RH 19 IV	*Bestand OB West (HGr. D)*
/45	Ia-KTB 1.8.–31.8.1944
/52–54	– Anlagen 1.8.–31.8.1944

/46	Ia-KTB 1.9.–30.9.1944
/55–57	– Anlagen 1.9.–30.9.1944
/74	Ia-KTB 1.10.–31.10.1944
/77–79	– Anlagen 1.10.–31.10.1944
/68K–73K	– Lagekarten 11.8.–30.9.1944
/90K–92K	– Lagekarten 1.10.–31.10.1944
/87	– Wettermeldungen 1.10.–31.10.1944
/102–103	– V-Waffen Juli–Okt. 1944
/136	Ic-Tätigkeitsbericht 1.7.–31.12.1944
/137–138	– Anlagen 1.7.–31.12.1944
/139K	– Feindlagekarten 1.7.–30.12.1944
/140	– Feindlagebeurteilung Juli–Dez. 1944
/141	– Angelegenheiten Juli–Dez. 1944
/142	– Telephongespräche 1.7.–30.12.1944
/168	Nachrichtenführer-Tätigkeitsbericht 1.7.–30.9.1944
/169	– Anlagen 1.7.–30.9.1944
/170	Nachrichtenführer-Tätigkeitsbericht 1.10.–31.12.1944
/171	– Anlagen 1.10.–31.12.1944
/226	Tagesbefehle und dgl. 1944/45
RH 19 IX	*Bestand Heeresgruppe B*
/1	Oberbefehlshaber, Inspektionsfahrten etc. April–Sept. 1944
/4	Ia-Operationsbefehle 9.6.–31.8.1944
/5	Operationsbefehle 1.9.–30.9.1944
/6	Operationsbefehle 1.10.–15.10.1944
/7	Führerbefehle 17.6.–25.9.1944
/8	Wochenmeldungen (15.5.–21.8.) und Lagebeurteilungen 1.6.–11.10.1944
/9	Tagesmeldungen 6.6.–31.8.1944
/10	Tagesmeldungen 1.9.–15.10.1944
/12	Morgen-, Mittag-, Abendmeldungen 11.8.–30.9.1944
/13	Morgen-, Mittag-, Abendmeldungen 1.10.–16.10.1944
/47	NSFO-Unterlagen Sept. 1944–März 1945
/87	KTB 1.8.–15.8.1944
/88	KTB 16.8.–31.8.1944
/89	KTB 1.9.–15.9.1944
/90	KTB 16.9.–30.9.1944
/18	Ic-Feindlagebeurteilung 2.7.–15.9.1944
/19	Feindlagebeurteilung 16.9.–30.12.1944
/21–23	Einzelmeldungen 1.8.–31.10.1944
/26–27	Zusammenfassende Morgen- und Abendmeldungen 1.7.–31.12.1944
/29K–32K	Feindlagekarten 1.8.–31.10.1944

RH 19 XII	*Bestand Armeegruppe G (ab 11.9.: HGr. G)*
/5	Ia-KTB mit Karten 1.7.–30.9.1944
/7–8	Anlagen 1.8.–30.9.1944
/9	Chefsachen Juli–Sept. 1944
/10	Ia-KTB 1.10.–30.11.1944
/12–13	Anlagen 1.10.–31.10.1944
/18	Chefsachen Okt.–Dez. 1944
/19	Ferngespräche 21.10.–30.12.1944
/20K	Kartenanlagen Okt.–Dez. 1944
/31	Ic-Tätigkeitsbericht 1.7.–30.9.1944
/32	Abendmeldungen 1.10.–31.10.1944
/36	IIa-Tätigkeitsbericht mit Anlagen Okt.–Dez. 1944
/38	General der Pioniere – Tätigkeitsbericht Okt. 1944
/41	Nachrichtenführer – Tätigkeitsbericht Okt.–Dez. 1944
/43	Oberquartiermeister – Personalangelegenheiten Sept.–Okt. 1944
/47	Vorbereitung/Durchführung von ARLZ-Massnahmen Aug. 1944–Jan. 1945
RL 33	*Bestand 1. Fallschirmarmee*
/3	Höherer Art.Kdr., KTB Nr. 1 mit Anlagen 22.4.–15.10.1944
/109	Einsatz Fsj.Rgt. 6 17.–23.9.1944
/114–115	KTB Gen. z.b.V. beim Fs.AOK 1 mit Anlagen 9.9.–7.10.1944
RH 21-5	*Bestand 5. Panzerarmee*
/52	Ia-KTB 9.8.–9.9.1944
/53	Anlagen 9.8.–9.9.1944
/54	Ia-KTB 10.9.–22.10.1944
/55	Anlagen Sept.–Okt. 1944
/68	Nachkriegsbericht General von Manteuffels 6.9.–15.10.1944
RH 20-7	*Bestand 7. Armee*
/378	Tätigkeitsbericht des Bevollm. Trsp.Offz. 1.7.–31.12.1944
RM 7	*Seekriegsleitung (15. Armee, Scheldeübergang)*
/131	1. Seekriegsleitung KTB Nordsee-Norwegen 3.4.1944–10.1.1945
RH 20-19	*Bestand 19. Armee*
/85	Tagebuchnotizen des Genst Chefs (GenLt. Botsch) Aug.–Okt. 1944
/86	Anlagen (Telefongespräche, Befehle) Sept.–Okt. 1944
/88–119	Ia-KTB mit Anlagen 15.8.–31.10.1944
RH 24-58	*Bestand LVIII. Panzerkorps*
/8–9	Ia-KTB mit Anlagen Juli–Aug. 1944

/10	Zusammenfassender Gefechtsbericht 26.8.–4.9.1944
/11	Anlagen 25.8.–10.9.1944
/12–13	Ia-KTB mit Anlagen Sept.–Okt. 1944

RH 24-80	*Bestand LXXX. Armeekorps*
/68	Ia-KTB 22.8.–27.12.1944

RH 24-81	*Bestand LXXXI. Armeekorps*
/97–113	Ia-KTB mit Anlagen 2.8.–21.10.1944

RH 24-88	*Bestand LXXXVIII. Armeekorps*
/91–102	Ia-KTB mit Anlagen 1.7.–31.12.1944

RH 24-89	*Bestand LXXXIX. Armeekorps*
/10	Ia-Tätigkeitsbericht 28.8.–10.9.1944
/11	Korpsbefehle etc. Sept.–Nov. 1944

RW 24	*Bestand Rüstungsdienststellen in Frankreich*
/36	KTB des Rüst.- und Beschaffungsstabes Frankreich Juli–Okt. 1944

RW 35	*Bestand Militärbefehlshaber*
/1137	Bericht über die Ernährungslage von Paris 23.8.1944
/1252–1253	Erlebnis- und Schlussberichte einzelner Feldkommandanturen Aug. 1944–Jan. 1945

RH 36	*Bestand Kommandanturen-Militärverwaltung*
/50–51	Kommandantur Gross-Paris, Befehle und Berichte Aug. 1944

Msg 109	*Personengeschichte deutscher Generale 1918–1945*
/197	Generaloberst Johannes Blaskowitz
/382	General Dietrich v. Choltitz

N	*Nachlässe*
N 6/1	Unterlagen zum Lebenslauf des Generalfeldmarschall Model
N 292 /34–35	Tagebuch des Generaloberst Dessloch
N 413 /7	Tätigkeitsbericht des Stabes von Gen.d.Art. Theisen (AGr. G) 5.8.–26.8.1944

Pers 6	*Personalakten Generale*
/12	Generalfeldmarschall Model
/20	Generaloberst Blaskowitz

b) Institut für Zeitgeschichte (IfZg) München

MA 137/1   *NSDAP, Gau Westmark, Leiter Stellungsbau*
     138   NSDAP, Gau Köln-Aachen, Gaustabsamt Baden
     218   Ministerium für Rüstung und Kriegsproduktion
     434   Höherer SS- und Polizeiführer West

NOKW 141   Unterlagen zum Lebenslauf des Generaloberst Blaskowitz
und 2439

c) Verschiedenes

Interview des Verfassers mit Herrn Brig. Gen. H. Model vom 13.9.1986.
Dokumente aus dem Privatarchiv Model.
MGFA, Dok.zent.: Schematische Kriegsgliederung, Gen.St.d.H., Juli–Nov. 1944.
Unterlagen von Dr. Hubertus Dessloch.
ZDF-Protokoll zur Sendung "Kampf um Paris" vom 23.8.1984.

d) Foreign Military Studies (MGFA), Freiburg im Breisgau

Bahr, Joachim H., LXIV. AK, MS-A-866.
v. Berg, Kurt, Wehrkreis XII, MS-B-060.
Blaskowitz, Johannes, Lagebeurteilung von der Invasion, MS-B-421.
Ders., Armeegruppe G, MS-B-800.
Ders., German reaction to the Invasion, MS-A-868.
Botsch, Walter, 19. Armee, MS-B-515.
Ders., Kommentar zur 7. US-Army, MS-B-518.
Ders., 19. Armee, MS-B-696.
Ders., 19. Armee, MS-B-766.
Brandenberger, Erich, 7. Armee, MS-B-730.
Buechs, Herbert, Luftwaffe in Südfrankreich, MS-A-869.
Ders., Westwall, MS-ETHINT-37.
Caspar, Carl, 48. Inf. Div., MS-P-166.
Eberbach, Heinrich, 7. Armee, MS-B-841.
Emmerich, Albert, 1. Armee, MS-B-728.
Frank, Paul, 5. Panzerarmee, MS-B-729.
v. Gersdorff, Rudolf, 5. Panzerarmee, MS-B-726.
Ders., Siegfriedline, MS-ETHINT-53.
v. Greiffenberg, Hans (et al.), Ardennes-, Questionnaire, MS-P-32i.
Guderian, Heinz, Ost- und Westfront, MS-T-42.
v. Gyldenfeldt, Heinz, Armeegruppe G, MS-B-488.
Ders., Armeegruppe G, MS-B-552.
Haeckel, Ernst, 16. Inf. Div., MS-B-245.
Hesse, Kurt, Paris, MS-B-611.
Jodl, Alfred, Operationen nach Avranches, MS-A-927.
Ders., Ardennenoffensive, MS-ETHINT-50.
Ders., German Defenses, MS-ETHINT-52.

v. Kahlden, Wolf, 5. Panzerarmee, MS-B-472.

v. Knobelsdorff, Otto, 1. Armee, MS-B-222.

Kohl, Otto, 159. Inf. Div., MS-B-517.

Krause, Walter, Metz (Div. Nr. 462), MS-B-042.

Krüger, Walter, LVIII. Pz. Korps, MS-B-157.

Macholz, Sigfrid, 49. Inf. Div., MS-B-743.

v. Manteuffel, Hasso, 5. Panzerarmee, MS-B-757.

Mattenklott, Franz, Wehrkreis VI, MS-B-044.

Ottenbacher, Otto, Rückzugskämpfe (Südwestfrankreich), MS-B-538.

Ruhfus, Heinrich, Toulon, MS-B-556.

v. Rundstedt, Gerd, Bemerkungen zu MS-B-308, MS-B-633.

Schäfer, Hans, Marseille (244. Inf. Div.), MS-A-884.

Schramm, Percy E., Ardennenoffensive, MS-A-862.

Schulz, Fritz, 19. Armee, MS-B-514.

v. Schweppenburg, Leo, Panzergruppe West, MS-B-258.

v. Schwerin, Gerhard, 116. Pz. Div., MS-ETHINT-18.

Schuster, Kurt, LXIV. AK, MS-A-885.

Seiz, Gustav, 159. Inf. Div., MS-A-960.

Staubwasser, Anton, Feindbild HGr. B, MS-B-825.

Täglichsbeck, Hans, Rückmarsch Südwestfrankreich, MS-A-886.

Veiel, Rudolf, Wehrkreis V, MS-B-193.

Wahle, Carl, 47. Inf. Div., MS-B-176.

Walter, Eugen, V-Waffen, MS-B-689.

Warlimont, Walter, Siegfriedline, MS-ETHINT-1.

Ders., Kommentare zum Jodl-KTB, MS-P-215, Bd IV.

Wiese, Friedrich, 19. Armee, MS-B-787.

Ders., 19. Armee, MS-B-781.

v. Wietersheim, Wend, 11. Pz. Div., MS-A-880.

Wilutzky, Horst, Heeresgruppe G, MS-A-882.

v. Zangen, Gustav-Ad., 15. Armee, MS-B-249.

Ziegelmann, 352. Inf. Div., MS-B-741.

Zimmermann, Bodo (et al.), Geschichte des Ob. West, MS-T-121 Bde B III (Der Durchbruch von Avranches) bis B IX (Schlusswort).

Ders., Operation des Ob. West, MS-B-308, Bd IV.

2. Published Sources

Ausgewählte Dokumente zur Geschichte des Nationalsozialismus 1933–1945. Arbeitsblätter für politische und soziale Bildung, hrsg. von Hans-Adolf Jacobsen und Werner Jochmann, Bielefeld 1961.

Domarus, Max, Hitler. Reden und Proklamationen 1932–1945. Kommentiert von einem deutschen Zeitgenossen. Bd II: Untergang (1939–1945), Würzburg 1963.

Generalfeldmarschall Walter Model (1891–1945). Dokumentation eines Soldatenlebens, hrsg. von Hansgeorg Model und Dermot Bradley, Osnabrück 1991.

Halder, Franz, Kriegstagebuch. Tägliche Aufzeichnungen des Chefs des Generalstabes des Heeres, 1939–1942, bearb. von Hans-Adolf Jacobsen, hrsg. vom Arbeitskreis für Wehrforschung, 3 Bde, Stuttgart 1962–1964.

Hechler, Kenneth W., The Enemy Side of the Hill, Washington 1949, in: World War II German Military Studies Vol. I, Part I, Introduction and Guide, ed. by Donald S. Detwiler, New York 1979.

Heeresadjutant bei Hitler 1938–1943. Aufzeichnungen des Majors Engel, hrsg. von Hildegard v. Kotze, Stuttgart 1974.

Hitler, Adolf, Mein Kampf, München [12]1943.

Hitlers Lagebesprechungen. Die Protokollfragmente seiner militärischen Konferenzen 1942–1945, hrsg. von Helmut Heiber, Stuttgart 1962 (= Quellen und Darstellungen zur Zeitgeschichte, Bd 10).

Hitlers Weisungen für die Kriegführung 1939–1945. Dokumente des Oberkommandos der Wehrmacht, hrsg. von Walther Hubatsch, Frankfurt a.M. 1962.

Jacobsen, Hans-Adolf, 1939–1945, Der Zweite Weltkrieg in Chronik und Dokumenten, Darmstadt [6]1967.

Kriegstagebuch des Oberkommandos der Wehrmacht (Wehrmachtführungsstab) 1940–1945. Geführt von H. Greiner und P.E. Schramm. Im Auftrag des Arbeitskreises für Wehrforschung hrsg. von Percy Ernst Schramm. Bd IV: 1. Januar 1944–27. Mai 1945, Frankfurt a.M. 1961.

Lagevorträge des Oberbefehlshabers der Kriegsmarine vor Hitler 1939–1945. Im Auftrag des Arbeitskreises für Wehrforschung hrsg. von Gerhard Wagner, München 1972.

Meldungen aus dem Reich. Die geheimen Lageberichte des Sicherheitsdienstes der SS 1938–1945, hrsg. und eingel. von Heinz Boberach, 17 Bde, Herrsching 1984.

Der Prozess gegen die Hauptkriegsverbrecher vor dem Internationalen Militärgerichtshof (IMT), Nürnberg 14. November 1945–1. Oktober 1946, 42 Bde, Nürnberg 1947–1949, hier, Bde XV und XVI.

The Papers of Dwight David Eisenhower, ed. by Alfred E. Chandler (et. al.), Bde III–V, Baltimore, London 1970.

Staatsmänner und Diplomaten bei Hitler. Vertrauliche Aufzeichnungen über die Unterredungen mit Vertretern des Auslandes, hrsg. und eingel. von Andreas Hillgruber, Bd I: 1939–1941, Frankfurt a.M. 1967; Bd 2: 1942–1944, Frankfurt a.M. 1970.

Ursachen und Folgen. Vom deutschen Zusammenbruch 1918 und 1945 bis zur staatlichen Neuordnung Deutschlands in der Gegenwart. Eine Urkunden- und Dokumentensammlung zur Zeitgeschichte, hrsg. und bearb. von Herbert Michaelis und Ernst Schraepler, Bd 21: Das Dritte Reich. Der Sturm auf die Festung Europa. Emigration und Widerstand. Die Invasion der Anglo-Amerikaner. Der 20. Juli, und Bd 22: Das Dritte Reich. Der Angriff auf die deutschen Grenzen. Der Abfall der Bundesgenossen. Die Ardennenoffensive. Die Konferenz von Jalta. Der Einbruch der Gegner ins Reich, Berlin 1975.

3. Literature

Ambrose, Stephen E., Eisenhower as a Commander, in: The Papers of Dwight David Eisenhower: The War Years, V, pp. 39–45.

Anfänge westdeutscher Sicherheitspolitik 1945–1956. Bd 1: Von der Kapitulation bis zum Pleven-Plan. Von Roland G. Foerster, Christian Greiner, Georg Meyer, Hans-Jürgen Rautenberg und Norbert Wiggershaus, München, Wien 1982.

Aufstand des Gewissens. Der militärische Widerstand gegen Hitler und das NS-Regime 1933–1945. Im Auftrag des Bundesministeriums der Verteidigung zur Wanderausstellung hrsg. vom Militärgeschichtlichen Forschungsamt, Bonn, Herford ³1987 (erweiterte Neuauflage 1994).

Balck, Hermann, Ordnung im Chaos. Erinnerungen 1893–1948, Osnabrück 1980 (= Soldatenschicksale des 20. Jahrhunderts als Geschichtsquelle, Bd 2).

Beaufre, André, Die Revolutionierung des Kriegsbildes. Neue Formen der Gewaltanwendung, Stuttgart 1973.

Bennett, Ralph, Ultra in the West—The Normandy Compaign 1944/45, London ²1980.

Blumenson, Martin, Breakout and Pursuit, Washington 1961.

Ders., General Bradley's Decision at Argenton (1944), in: Command Decisions, S. 303–319.

Blumentritt, Günther, von Rundstedt—The soldier and the man, London 1952.

Bosl, K./Franz, G./Hofmann, H. H., Biographisches Wörterbuch zur deutschen Geschichte, München ²1974.

Bradley, Omar N., A Soldier's Story, New York 1951.

Das Bundesarchiv und seine Bestände. 3. ergänzte und neu bearbeitete Auflage von Gerhard Granier, Josef Henke und Klaus Oldenhage, Boppard a.Rh. 1977 (= Schriften des Bundesarchivs, Bd 10).

Cartier, Raymond, Der Zweite Weltkrieg, 2 Bde, Sonderausgabe, München o.J.

Caspar, Gustav-Adolf, Die Kriegslage vom Herbst 1943 bis zum Winter 1944/45 und das Entstehen der Vereinbarungen über die Grenzen der Besatzungszonen in Deutschland, in: MGM, 26 (1979), S. 173–183.

v. Choltitz, Dietrich, Brennt Paris?—Adolf Hitler, Mannheim, o.J.

Ders., Soldat unter Soldaten, Konstanz, Zürich, Wien 1951.

Cole, Hugh M., The Lorraine Campaign, Washington 1950.

Command Decisions, ed. by Kent Roberts Greenfield, Washington 1960.

Deutsch, Harold C., Verschwörung gegen den Krieg, München 1969.

Das deutsche Offizierkorps 1860–1960. In Verbindung mit dem Militärgeschichtlichen Forschungsamt hrsg. von Hanns Hubert Hofmann (†), Boppard 1980 (= Deutsche Führungsschichten in der Neuzeit, Bd 11).

Das Deutsche Reich und der Zweite Weltkrieg.

Bd 1: Ursachen und Voraussetzungen der deutschen Kriegspolitik, von

Wilhelm Deist, Manfred Messerschmidt, Hans-Erich Volkmann, Wolfram Wette, Stuttgart 1979.

Bd 2: Die Errichtung der Hegemonie auf dem europäischen Kontinent, von Klaus A. Maier, Horst Rohde, Bernd Stegemann, Hans Umbreit, Stuttgart 1979.

Bd 3: Der Mittelmeerraum und Südosteuropa. Von der "non belligeranza" Italiens bis zum Kriegseintritt der Vereinigten Staaten, von Gerhard Schreiber, Bernd Stegemann, Detlef Vogel, Stuttgart 1984.

Bd 4: Der Angriff auf die Sowjetunion, von Horst Boog, Jürgen Förster, Joachim Hoffmann, Ernst Klink, Rolf-Dieter Müller, Hans Umbreit, Stuttgart 1988.

Bd 6: Der globale Krieg. Die Ausweitung zum Weltkrieg und der Wechsel der Initiative 1941–1943, von Horst Boog, Werner Rahn, Reinhard Stumpf, Bernd Wegner, Stuttgart 1990.

v. Donat, Richard, Logistische Probleme beim Rückzug aus Südfrankreich (August/September 1944), in: Truppenpraxis, 7 (1963), S. 946–951, und 8 (1964), S. 27–31.

Ehrman, John, Grand Strategy, Vol. V und VI, London 1956.

Eisenhower, Dwight D., Kreuzzug in Europa, Amsterdam 1948.

Elble, Rolf, Die Schlacht an der Bzura 1939, Freiburg 1975 (= Einzelschriften zur Militärgeschichte, Bd 15).

Ellis, L. F., Victory in the West, Vol. I, Vol. II, London 1962 und 1968.

Erfurth, Waldemar, Geschichte des Deutschen Generalstabs 1918–1945, Göttingen 1957.

Fonde, J. J., L'Agonie d'une Panzerbrigade, in: RHA 1/1979, S. 177–201.

Forstreuter, Kurt, Gause, Fritz, Altpreussische Biographie, Bd 3, Marburg 1975.

Galland, Adolf, Die Ersten und die Letzten. Die Jagdflieger im Zweiten Weltkrieg, München 1953.

de Gaulle, Charles, Memoiren 1942–1946, Düsseldorf 1961.

Gebhardt, Bruno, Handbuch der deutschen Geschichte, Bd 4/2 (bearb. v. K. D. Erdmann), Stuttgart ⁹1976.

v. Gersdorff, Rudolf-Christoph, Soldat im Untergang. Frankfurt, Berlin, Wien 1977.

Görlitz, Walter, Model. Strategie der Defensive, Wiesbaden 1975.

Goetzel, Hermann, Die Erinnerungen des Generaloberst Kurt Student, Friedberg 1980.

Greenfield, Kent Roberts, Die acht Hauptentscheidungen der amerikanischen Strategie im Zweiten Weltkrieg, in: Probleme des Zweiten Weltkrieges, S. 271–276.

Groehler, Olaf, Die Auswirkungen der Niederlagen im Sommer 1944 auf die Kampfmoral der faschistischen Streitkräfte in Westeuropa, in: Mititärgeschichte, 15 (1976), S. 418–426.

Ders., Die Schlacht um Aachen, in: Mititärgeschichte, 18 (1979), S. 321–323.

v. Groote, Wolfgang, Militärgeschichte, in: MGM, 1 (1967), S. 5–19.

Gross, Manfred, Der Westwall zwischen Niederrhein und Schnee-Eifel, Köln 1982.

Der gross, Atlas zum 2. Weltkrieg, hrsg. von Peter Young, München 1974.

Guderian, Heinz, Erinnerungen eines Soldaten, Stuttgart ¹¹1979.

Hahlweg, Werner, Typologie des modernen Kleinkrieges, Wiesbaden 1967.

Hansen, Reimer, Aussenpolitik im Zusammenbruch des Dritten Reiches, in: Hitler, Deutschland und die Mächte, S. 115–134.

v. Hassell, Ulrich, Vom andern Deutschland. Aus den nachgelassenen Tagebüchern 1938–1944, Zürich 1946.

Haupt, Werner, Rückzug im Westen, Stuttgart 1976.

Hildebrand, Klaus, Das Dritte Reich, München ³1987 (= Oldenbourg. Grundriss der Geschichte, Bd 17).

Hillgruber, Andreas, Deutsche Grossmacht- und Weltpolitik im 19. und 20. Jahrhundert, Düsseldorf ²1979.

Ders., Die "Endlösung" und das deutsche Ostimperium als Kernstück des rassenideologischen Programms des Nationalsozialismus, in: ders., Deutsche Grossmacht- und Weltpolitik, S. 252–275.

Ders., Generalfeldmarschall v. Rundstedt, in: ders., Deutsche Grossmacht- und Weltpolitik, S. 316–332.

Ders., Hitler, König Carol und Marschall Antonescu, Wiesbaden 1954.

Ders., Militarismus am Ende der Weimarer Republik und im Dritten Reich, in: ders., Deutsche Grossmacht- und Weltpolitik, S. 134–148.

Ders., Das Problem der "Zweiten Front" in Europa 1941–44, in: ders., Deutsche Grossmacht- und Weltpolitik, S. 332–350.

Ders., Der Zweite Weltkrieg. Kriegsziele und Strategie der grossen Mächte, Berlin, Köln, Mainz 1982.

Hillgruber, Andreas, Hümmelchen, Gerhard, Chronik des Zweiten Weltkrieges. Kalendarium militärischer und politischer Ereignisse 1939–1945, Düsseldorf 1978.

Hinsley, Francis Harry with E. E. Thomas, C. F. G. Ransom, R. C. Knight, British Intelligence in the Second World War. Its Influence on Strategy and Operations, Vol 3 Part I, London 1984.

Hitler, Deutschland und die Mächte. Materialien zur Aussenpolitik des Dritten Reichs, hrsg. von Manfred Funke, Düsseldorf 1978.

Die höheren Dienststellen der deutschen Wehrmacht 1933–1945. Im Auftrag des Instituts für Zeitgeschichte zusammengestellt und erläutert von Fritz Frhr. v. Siegler, München 1952.

Hölsken, Dieter, Die V-Waffen, Stuttgart 1984.

Hoffmann, Peter, Widerstand, Staatsstreich, Attentat, Frankfurt, Berlin, Wien 1970.

Ders., Der militärische Widerstand in der zweiten Kriegshälfte 1942–1944/45, in: Der militärische Widerstand, S. 110–134.

Irving, David, Hitler und seine Feldherren, Frankfurt, Berlin, Wien 1975.

Ders., Krieg zwischen den Generälen, Hamburg 1983.

Jäckel, Eberhard, Frankreich in Hitlers Europa, Stuttgart 1966.

de Jong, Louis, Zwischen Kollaboration und Résistance, in: Probleme des Zweiten Weltkrieges, S. 245–265.

Jung, Hermann, Die Ardennenoffensive 1944/45, Göttingen 1971.

Keilig, Wolf, Das Deutsche Heer 1939–1945. Gliederung, Einsatz, Stellenbesetzungen, 3 Bde, Bad Nauheim 1956–1970.

Ders., Die Generale des Heeres, Friedberg 1983.

Klein, Friedrich, Militärgeschichte in der Bundesrepublik Deutschland, in: Militärgeschichte in Deutschland und Österreich, S. 183–214.

Knipping, Franz, Militärische Konzeptionen der Französischen Résistance im Zweiten Weltkrieg, in: Partisanen und Volkskrieg, S. 125–146.

Krausnick, Helmut, Hitler und die Morde in Polen, in VfZG, 11 (1963), S. 196–209.

Krausnick, Helmut/Wilhelm, Hans Heinrich, Die Truppe des Weltanschauungskrieges. Die Einsatzgruppen der Sicherheitspolizei und des SD 1938–1942, Stuttgart 1981 (= Quellen und Darstellungen zur Zeitgeschichte. Veröffentlichungen des Instituts für Zeitgeschichte Bd 22).

Leighton, Richard, OVERLORD versus the Mediterranean at the Cairo-Theran Conferences (1943), in: Command Decisions, S. 182–209.

Leighton, Richard M./Coakley, Robert W., Global Logistics and Strategy 1940–1943, Washington 1955.

Leppa, Konrad, Generalfeldmarschall Walter Model, Nürnberg 1961.

Lewin, Ronald, Entschied Ultra den Krieg? Alliierte Funkaufklärung im 2. Weltkrieg, Koblenz, Bonn 1981.

Liddell Hart, Basil H., Deutsche Generale des Zweiten Weltkrieges, Düsseldorf-Wien 1964.

Ders., Geschichte des Zweiten Weltkrieges, Wiesbaden ⁶1985.

Ders., Jetzt dürfen sie reden. Hitlers Generale berichten, Stuttgart 1950.

Ludewig, Joachim, Stationen eines Soldatenschicksals: Generalfeldmarschall Walter Model, in: Militärgeschichtliche Beiträge, 5 (1991), S. 69–75.

Luther, Hans, Der französische Widerstand gegen die deutsche Besatzungsmacht und seine Bekämpfung, Tübingen 1957.

MacDonald, Charles B., The Decision to Launch Operation MARKET-GARDEN (1944), in Command Decisions, S. 285–302.

Ders., The Siegfried Line Campaign, Washington 1963.

v. Manstein, Erich, Verlorene Siege, Bonn 1964.

Matloff, Maurice, The ANVIL Decision: Crossroads of Strategy (1944), in: Command Decisions, S. 285–302.

Ders., Strategic Planning for Coalition Wafare 1943–1944, Washington 1959.

Mennel, Rainer, Landung der Alliierten an der Küste der Provence und Durchbruch durch das Rhônetal bis zur Burgundischen Pforte 1944, in: Wehrforschung, 23 (1974), S. 110–117.

Ders., Militärgeographische Betrachtungen über die Kampfführung in der Normandie 1944, in: Wehrforschung, 21 (1972), S. 154–158.

Ders., Die Schlussphase des Zweiten Weltkrieges im Westen 1944/1945. Eine Studie zur politischen Geographie, Osnabrück 1981.

Messerschmidt, Manfred, Die Wehrmacht im NS-Staat. Zeit der Indoktrination, Hamburg 1969.

Meyer, Georg, Auswirkungen des 20. Juli 1944 auf das innere Gefüge der Wehrmacht bis Kriegsende und auf das soldatische Selbstverständnis im Vorfeld des westdeutschen Verteidigungsbeitrages bis 1950/51, in: Der militärische Widerstand, S. 153–186.

Ders., Zur Situation der deutschen militärischen Führungsschicht im Vorfeld des westdeutschen Verteidigungsbeitrages 1945–1950/1951, in: Anfänge westdeutscher Sicherheitspolitik, S. 577–735.

Michel, Henri, Histoire de la Résistance en France 1940–44, Paris ⁷1975.

Ders., Paris Résistant, Paris 1982.

Militärgeschichte in Deutschland und Österreich vom 18. Jahrhundert bis in die Gegenwart, Bonn, Herford 1985 (= Vorträge zur Militärgeschichte, Bd 6).

Der militärische Widerstand gegen Hitler und das NS-Regime 1933–1945, Bonn, Herford 1984 (= Vorträge zur Militärgeschichte, Bd 5).

Moll, Otto E., Die deutschen Generalfeldmarshcälle 1935–1945, Rastatt 1961.

Montgomery Bernard L., Von der Normandie zur Ostsee, Bern 1949.

Mordal, Jacques, Die letzten Bastionen, Oldenburg, Hamburg 1966.

Moulton, J. L., Battle for Antwerp, London 1978.

Müller, Klaus Jürgen, Das Heer und Hitler. Armee und nationalsozialistisches Regime 1933–1940, Stuttgart 1969 (= Beiträge zur Militär- und Kriegsgeschichte, Bd 10).

Ders., Zu Vorgeschichte und Inhalt der Rede Himmlers vor der höheren Generalität am 13. März 1940 in Koblenz, in: VfZG, 18 (1970), S. 95–120.

Mueller-Hillebrand, Burkhart, Das Heer 1933–1945. Die Entwicklung des oranisatorischen Aufbaus, Bd 3: Der Zweifrontenkrieg. Das Heer vom Beginn des Feldzuges gegen die Sowjetunion bis zum Kriegsende, Franfurt 1969.

de Nanteuil, H./Levy, G., La reddition de la colonne Elster, in: RHA 3/1974.

Nicault, Maurice, La Capitulation de la Colonne Elster, RHDGM, 99 (1975), S. 91–99.

Ose, Dieter, Entscheidung im Westen, Stuttgart 1981 (= Beiträge zur Militär- und Kriegsgeschichte, Bd 22).

v. Oven, Wilfried, Mit Goebbels bis zum Ende, Buenos Aires 1950.

Partisanen und Volkskrieg, hrsg. von Gerhard Schulz, Göttingen 1985.

Patton, George S., War as I knew it, New York 1947.

Pogue, Forrest C., The Supreme Command, Washington 1954.

Pohlman, Hartwig, Die Festung Gironde Nord (Royan) 1944, in: Feldgrau 7 (1959), H. 1 — Feldgrau, 8 (1960), H. 4.

Probleme des Zweiten Weltkrieges, hrsg. von Andreas Hillgruber, Köln, Berlin 1967.

Ritgen, Helmut, Die Geschichte der Panzer-Lehr Division im Westen 1944/45, Stuttgart 1979.

Robichon, Jacques, Invasion Provence, München 1965.

Ruppenthal, Roland, Logistical Support of the Armies, Vol I und II, Washington 1953 und 1959.

Ders., Logistics and the Broad-Front Strategy (1944), in: Command Decisions, S. 320–328.

Rohwer, Jürgen, Der Einfluss der alliierten Funkaufklärung auf den Verlauf des Zweiten Weltkrieges, in: VfZG, 27 (1979), S. 325–369.

Ruge, Friedrich, Rommel und die Invasion, Stuttgart 1959.

Salewski, Michael, Die deutsche Seekriegsleitung 1935–1945, 3 Bde, München 1970–1975.

Schreiber, Gerhard, Der Zweite Weltkrieg—Probleme und Ergebnisse der Forschung I und II, in : Neue Politische Literatur, 29 (1984), S 453–482, und 30 (1985), S. 421–439.

v. Senger und Etterlin, Frido, Strategische Kontroversen der Alliierten, in: Probleme des Zweiten Weltkrieges, S. 277–291.

Showalter, Dennis E., German Military History 1648–1982. A Critical Bibliography, New York, London, 1984.

Speer, Albert, Erinnerungen, Frankfurt, Berlin, Wien 1969.

Speidel, Hans, Invasion 1944. Ein Beitrag zu Rommels und des Reiches Schicksal, Stuttgart ³1950.

Spiwoks, Erich, Endkampf zwischen Mosel und Inn (XIII. SS-AK), Osnabrück 1976.

Stacey, Charles P., The Victory Campaign, Ottawa 1960.

Staiger, Joerg, Rückzug durchs Rhônetal. Abwehr- und Verzögerungskampf der 19. Armee im Herbst 1944 unter besonderer Berücksichtigung des Einsatzes der 11. Panzerdivision, Neckargemünd 1965 (= Die Wehrmacht im Kampf, Bd 39).

Steinert, Marlis G., Hitlers Krieg und die Deutschen. Stimmung und Haltung der deutschen Bevölkerung im Zweiten Weltkrieg, Genf, Düsseldorf, Wien 1970.

Streit, Christian, Keine Kameraden. Die Wehrmacht und die sowjetischen Kriegsgefangenen 1941–1945, Stuttgart 1978.

Stumpf, Reinhard, Die Wehrmacht-Elite. Rang- und Herkunftsstruktur der deutschen Generale und Admirale 1933–1945, Boppard 1982 (= Militärgeschichtliche Studien, Bd 29).

Sur la Résistance (Kolloqium Oktober 1974 in Paris), in: RHDGM, 99 (1975), S. 101–106.

Tätigkeitsbericht des Chefs des Heerespersonalamtes, hrsg. von Dermot Bradley und Richard Schulze-Kossens, Osnabrück 1984.

Teske, Hermann, Die silbernen Spiegel. Generalstabsdienst unter der Lupe, Heidelberg 1952.

Tessin, Georg, Verbände und Truppen der deutschen Wehrmacht und Waffen-SS in Zweiten Weltkrieg 1939–1945, Bde 1–15, Franfurt 1965–88.

Ueberschär, Gerd R., Ansätze und Hindernisse der Militäropposition gegen Hitler in den ersten beiden Kriegsjahren (1939–1941), in: Aufstand des Gewissens, S. 365–393.

Umbreit, Hans, Der Militärbefehlshaber in Frankreich 1940–1944, Boppard 1968 (= Militärgeschichtliche Studien, Bd 7).

Ders., La Stratégie défensive de L'Allemagne sur le front de L'Ouest en 1944, in: RHA 4/1974, S. 122–138.

Vogelsang, Thilo, Neue Dokumente zur Geschichte der Reichswehr 1930–1933, in: VfZG, 2 (1954), S. 397–436.

v. Vormann, Nikolaus, Der Feldzug 1939 in Polen, Weissenburg 1958.

Warlimont, Walter, Im Hauptquartier der Deutschen Wehrmacht 1939–1945. Grundlagen, Formen, Gestalten, Frankfurt 1964.

Wegmüller, Hans, Die Abwehr der Invasion. Die Konzeption des Oberbefehlshabers West 1940–1944, Freiburg 1979 (= Einzelschriften zur Militärgeschichte, Bd 22).

Die Wehrmachtberichte 1939–1945, hrsg. von Erich Murawski, München 1985.

Westphal, Siegfried, Erinnerungen, Mainz ²1975.

Ders., Heer in Fesseln. Aus den Papieren des Stabschefs von Rommel, Kesselring und Rundstedt, Bonn 1950.

Wilmot, Chester, Kampf um Europa, Frankfurt, Berlin 1954.

Wilt, Alan F., The Atlantic Wall. Hitler's Defenses in the West, Ames, Iowa 1975.

Ders., French Riviera Campaign of August 1944, Illinois 1981.

Der Zweite Weltkrieg. Analysen, Grundzüge, Forschungsbilanz. Im Auftrag des Militärgeschichtlichen Forschungsamtes hrsg. von Wolfgang Michalka, München ²1990.

Index